Study Guide

for use with

Statistical Techniques in Business & Economics

Thirteenth Edition

Douglas A. Lind
Coastal Carolina University
University of Toledo

William G. Marchal
University of Toledo

Samuel A. Wathen
Coastal Carolina University

Prepared by
Kathleen Whitcomb
University of South Carolina

McGraw-Hill Irwin

Boston   Burr Ridge, IL   Dubuque, IA   Madison, WI   New York   San Francisco   St. Louis
Bangkok   Bogotá   Caracas   Kuala Lumpur   Lisbon   London   Madrid   Mexico City
Milan   Montreal   New Delhi   Santiago   Seoul   Singapore   Sydney   Taipei   Toronto

McGraw-Hill
Irwin

Study Guide for use with
STATISTICAL TECHNIQUES IN BUSINESS & ECONOMICS
Douglas A. Lind, William G. Marchal, Samuel A. Wathen

Published by McGraw-Hill/Irwin, an imprint of The McGraw-Hill Companies, Inc., 1221 Avenue of the
Americas, New York, NY 10020. Copyright © 2008 by The McGraw-Hill Companies, Inc. All rights reserved.

2 3 4 5 6 7 8 9 0 QPD/QPD 0 9 8 7

ISBN 978-0-07-303033-3
MHID 0-07-303033-3

www.mhhe.com

PREFACE

This study guide is especially designed to accompany the Thirteenth Edition of *Statistical Techniques in Business and Economics* by Douglas A. Lind, William G. Marchal, and Samuel A. Wathen. It can also be used alone, or as a companion to most other introductory statistics texts. It provides a valuable source of reinforcement for the material in the text. The chapters in the text and the study guide are parallel in topics, notation, and the numbering of formulas. Students will attain the most benefit if they study the textbook first, and then read the corresponding chapter in the study guide. The major features of the study guide include:

- **Chapter Goals**. They are listed first and stress the main concepts covered and the tasks students should be able to perform after having studied the chapter. It is recommended that students refer to the goals before reading the chapter to get an overview of the material to be studied and again after completing the chapter to confirm mastery of the material.

- **Brief Introduction.** A brief Introduction follows the goals. In capsule form the material covered in previous chapters is tied with that covered in the current chapter, thus maintaining continuity throughout the book.

- **Definitions**. Key words are defined and used in their correct statistical context. | **Key Words** are in a text box for easy reference.

- **Formulas.** The formulas are placed in a formula box for easy reference. | **Formula box** is used to emphasize

- A **glossary** follows the chapter discussion. The glossary provides definitions of the key words used in the chapter and is a handy reference.

- **Chapter Problems.** Chapter problems, including solutions, come next. In this section the step-by-step method of solution is presented along with an interpretation of the results. The aim is to emphasize a particular statistical concept without complicating the problem with unnecessary numeric details.

- **Exercises.** Following the chapter problems is an exercise. The student completes the exercise and checks the answer in the Exercise Answer Section at the end of the guide. Thus the student can check his/her comprehension of the material as he/she progresses through the chapter.

- **Chapter Assignments.** Chapter assignments cover the entire chapter and are intended to be completed outside the classroom. Part I of the assignment consists of multiple-choice questions, Part II consists of problems, with space for students to show essential work and a box for the answers. The pages are perforated, so that assignments can be torn out and handed in to the instructor for grading.

ACKNOWLEDGEMENTS

I would like to acknowledge Walt Lange, the previous author of the study guide, for his extensive contributions to the current edition. I am also very grateful to the editing team of Christina Sanders and Dick Hercher for their assistance and patience. They provided immediate answers and solutions to any question or problem that I had while working on the study guide. And thank you Jacob, Daniel and Tina for being so helpful and understanding—you guys are great!

TABLE OF CONTENTS

CHAPTER 1
WHAT IS STATISTICS?

Chapter Goals

After completing this chapter, you will be able to:

1. Understand why we study statistics.

2. Explain what is meant by *descriptive statistics* and *inferential statistics*.

3. Distinguish between a *qualitative variable* and a *quantitative variable*.

4. Distinguish between a *discrete variable* and a *continuous variable*.

5. Distinguish among *nominal*, *ordinal*, *interval*, and *ratio* levels of measurement.

Introduction

No doubt you have noticed the large number of facts and figures, often referred to as *statistics*, that appear in the newspapers and magazines you read, websites you visit, television you watch (especially sporting events), and in grocery stores where you shop. A simple figure is called a *statistic* (singular). A few examples:

- Home and condominium sales declined 6.5% in Charleston, South Carolina in April, 2006 compared to sales in April, 2005. (*The Sun News*, May 24, 2006).

- Tuition and fees for resident undergraduate students at public four year institutions averaged $5,491 for 2005-06, a 7.1%increase over 2004-05. (http://www.aascu.org).

- Approximately 24 million medicare beneficiaries were enrolled in the new prescription drug program as of January, 2006. (http://www.cms.hhs.gov).

- Pensacola reported the lowest cost for self-service regular gasoline in Florida at $2.74 per gallon (*The Business Journal of Jacksonville*, May 26, 2006).

- The government reported that 138,000 jobs were added to the economy in April, 2006. (http://MSNBC..MSN.com).

- The Dow Jones Industrial Average was 11,094.04 on May 30, 2006. (MSNBC.MSN.com).

The Dow Jones average of 11094.04 is a statistic. A collection of such figures can be called statistics (plural). For example, some major stock indexes reported by MSNBC are shown on the right. (http://MSNBC..MSN.com).

Markets	
DJIA	11094.04
FTSE (London)	5652.00
DAX (Frankfurt)	5622.43
Nikkei (Tokyo)	15542.91
Hang Seng (Hong Kong)	15857.59

You may think of statistics simply as a collection of numerical information. However, *statistics* has a much broader meaning.

> *Statistics:* The science of collecting, organizing, presenting, analyzing, and interpreting data to assist in making more effective decisions.

Note in this definition of statistics that the initial step is the collection of pertinent information. This information may come from newspapers or magazines, various websites, a company's human relations director, the local, state, or federal government, universities, nonprofit organizations, the United Nations, and so on. A few actual publications of the federal government and others are:

- *Statistical Abstract of the United States*, published annually by the U.S. Department of Commerce.
- *Monthly Labor Review*, published monthly by the U.S. Department of Labor.
- *Survey of Current Business*, published monthly by the U.S. Department of Commerce.
- *Social Security Bulletin*, published annually by the U.S. Social Security Administration.
- *Crime in the United States*, published annually by the U.S. Federal Bureau of Investigation.
- *Vital Statistics of the United States*, published annually by the National Center for Health Statistics.
- *United Nations Statistical Databases*, available from the U.N. Statistics Division.

If the information is not available from company records or public sources, it may be necessary to conduct a *survey.* For example, the A.C. Nielsen Company surveys about 1200 homes on an ongoing basis to determine which TV programs are being watched, and Gallup surveys registered voters before an election to estimate the percent that will vote for a certain candidate. These firms also sample the population regarding food preference, what features in automobiles are desirable, and what appliances consumers will most likely purchase next year.

Fortune annually surveys 4,000 senior executives, outside directors, and securities analysts to evaluate the companies in their industry to find the ten most admired firms, and the least admired firms. Each executive is asked to rate a list of firms on eight attributes; namely, innovativeness, quality of management, quality of products and services, long-term investment value, financial soundness, employee talent, social responsibility to the community and the environment, and wise use of corporate assets. Each attribute is rated on a scale of zero (poor) to ten (excellent). The ten most admired companies are listed in the table.

Rank	Company
1	General Electric
2	Federal Express
3	Southwest Airlines
4	Proctor & Gamble
5	Starbucks
6	Johnson & Johnson
7	Berkshire Hathaway
8	Dell
9	Toyota Motor
10	Microsoft
Source: **Fortune**, March 6, 2006	

Why Study Statistics?

Statistics is required for many college programs for three reasons.

1. **Numerical information is everywhere.** If you look in various newspapers (*USA Today, Wall Street Journal*), magazines (*Time, Business Week, U.S. News and World Report, People*) you will be bombarded with numerical information. You need to be able to determine if the conclusions as reported are reasonable. Was the sample large enough? You must be able to read and interpret the charts or graphs.

2. **Statistical techniques are used to make decisions that affect our lives.** Insurance companies use statistics to determine the premiums you pay for automobile insurance, the Environmental Protection Agency uses various statistical tools to determine air and water quality in your area, and medical researchers use statistical designs of experiments to evaluate the effectiveness of new drug therapies.

3. **Knowledge of statistical methods will help you understand why decisions are made and give you a better understanding of how they affect you.** No matter what line of work you select, you will find yourself faced with decisions where an understanding of data anaylsis is helpful.

Types of Statistics - Descriptive and Inferential Statistics

The definition of statistics referred to collecting, organizing, and presenting numerical information. Data stored in a computer's memory or in a filing cabinet are of little value. Techniques are available that organize this information in a more meaningful form. Such aids are called *descriptive statistics*.

> *Descriptive statistics*: Methods of organizing, summarizing, and presenting data in an informative way.

We often present statistical information in a graphical form. A statistical tool designed to describe the movement of a series of numbers over a long period of time (such as production, imports, wages and stock market trends) is called a line chart. The line chart below, for example, depicts the upward movement of the Dow Jones average of 30 industrials year-end closing prices since 1989.

Notice how easy it is to describe the trend of stock prices: The price of the 30 industrials, as represented by the Dow, rose steadily from 1989 through 1994, and saw strong gains from 1995 until its peak of more than 11,000 in 1999. The Dow declined sharply during the next three years before it resuming an upward trend in 2003. Another descriptive measure is referred to as an average. Some examples are:

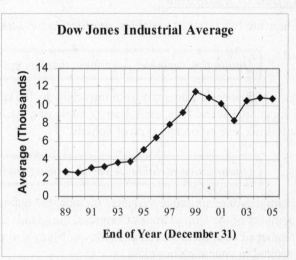

Dow Jones Industrial Average

- The 2006 Honda Odyssey minivan averages 19 miles per gallon in city driving and 25 miles per gallon in highway driving. *(http//www.forbesautos.com)*.

- The annual premium for an employer health plan covering a family of four averaged $10,800 in 2005. (http://www.nchs.org).

- The average monthly price for a cable television basic programming package was $39.96 in 2005. (National Cable and Telecommunications Association).

- The median (an average) selling price of a new construction single-family home in the greater Phoenix area was $240,610 during the second quarter of 2005. (http://Phoenix.about.com)

The Bureau of Labor Statistics describing the labor force in the United States reported that the average number of employed persons in April of 2006 was 143,688,000 and the average hourly earnings were $16.61. The average number of unemployed people was 7,123,000. Averages and other descriptive measures are presented in Chapter 3.

A second aspect of statistics is called *inferential statistics*.

> *Inferential statistics*: The methods used to estimate something about a *population*, based on a *sample*.
>
> *Population*: The entire set of all individuals or objects of interest or the measurements obtained from all individuals or objects of interest.

A population might consist of all the 8,541,221 people in North Carolina, or all 22,490,022 people in Texas. Or, the population might consist of all the teams in the Canadian Football League, the PE ratios for all chemical stocks, or the total assets of the 20 largest banks in the United States. A population, therefore, can be considered the total collection of people, prices, ages, square footage of homes being constructed in Flint, Michigan in 2006, and so on.

To infer something about a population, we usually take a *sample* from the population.

> *Sample*: A portion, or part, of the population of interest.

A sample might consist of 2,000 people out of the 22,490,022 people in Texas, 12 headlights selected from a production run of 1000 for a life test, or three scoops of grain selected at random to be tested for moisture content from a 15-ton truckload of grain. If we found that the three scoops of grain consisted of 9.50 percent moisture, we would infer that all the grain in the 15-ton load had 9.50 percent moisture. We start our discussion of inferential statistics in Chapter 8.

Types of Variables

There are two types of variables, *qualitative* and *quantitative*.

> *Qualitative variable*: A variable that has the characteristic of being nonnumeric.

A classification of students at your university by the state of birth, gender, or college affiliation (Business, Education, Liberal Arts, etc.) is an example of a qualitative variable. Other examples include: brand of soft drink, eye color, and type of vehicle.

> *Quantitative variable*: A variable being studied that can be reported numerically.

Examples of quantitative variables include: the balance in your checking account, the ages of the members of the United States Congress, the speeds of automobiles traveling along I-70 in Kansas, the number of customers served yesterday at Macy's in the Columbia Mall or the number of students enrolled in your statistics class.

There are two types of quantitative variables, *discrete* and *continuous*.

> *Discrete variable*: A quantitative variable that can only assume certain values and there are "gaps" between the values.

Examples of discrete variables are: the number of children in a family, the number of customers in a carpet store in an hour, or the number of commercials aired last hour on radio station WNOK. A family can have two or three children, but not 2.445, or WNOK can air five or six commercials, but not 5.75. Usually discrete variables result from counting.

> *Continuous variable:* A quantitative variable that can assume any value within a range.

Examples of continuous variables are: the amount of snow for the winter of 2005-2006 in Toronto, Ontario, the pressure in a tire, or a person's weight. Typically, continuous variables are the result of measuring something. We can measure the pressure in a tire, or the amount of snow in Toronto.

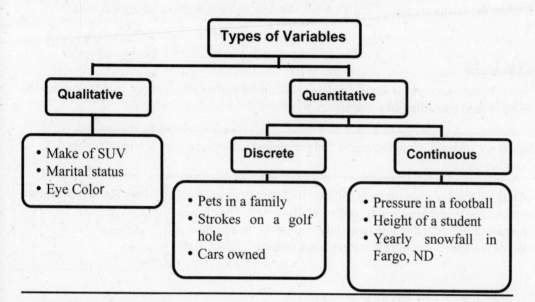

Levels of Measurement

Data may be classified into four levels of measurement. These levels are nominal, ordinal, interval, and ratio. The level of measurement of the data dictates the calculations that can be done to summarize and present the data.

Nominal Level Data

The nominal level of measurement is the lowest or most primitive level of measurement. When data can only be sorted into distinct categories or classes, we refer to it as being *nominal* level data .

> *Nominal level*: A level of measurement in which the data are sorted into classes with no particular order to the classes.

For example, the table at the right shows data for the number of doctorates awarded to U.S. citizens in engineering fields in 2004 (http://www.nsf.org). The data is nominal level because it can only be classified into distinct categories (chemical, civil, electrical, mechanical, or other) . The order in which they are listed is immaterial. Do not be distracted by the fact that the variable 'engineering field' is summarized by reporting the number of doctorates awarded in the right column—the variable itself is nonnumeric.

Sometimes the classes or categories of the nominal level variable are given a numerical code to process the data using computers.

Engineering Field	Number
Chemical	312
Civil	224
Electrical	498
Mechanical	299
Other	849
Total	**2182**

For example, we might assign chemical, civil, electrical, mechanical, and other engineering the codes 1, 2, 3, 4, and 5, respectively. However, this arbitrary assignment of numeric codes to nominal level data does not mean that we have transformed 'engineering field' into numeric data. For example, it makes no sense to say that 1 (chemical engineering) + 2 (civil engineering) = 3 (electrical engineering) !

To summarize, nominal level data has these properties:

- Data categories are represented by labels or names.
- Even when the labels are numerically coded, the data categories have no logical order.

Ordinal Level Data

The ordinal level of measurement is used for data that can be sorted into distinct categories and the categories can be ranked according to some criterion.

> *Ordinal level*: A level of measurement that presumes that one category is ranked higher than another category.

An example of ordinal level of measurement follows: undergraduate students in a basic statistics class were classified according to class rank. The classes are distinct. A student is counted in one (and only one) class. In addition, a ranking of students is implied meaning that juniors are ranked "higher" than sophomores.

Class Rank	Number
Freshman	13
Sophomore	17
Junior	9
Senior	5

To summarize, ordinal level data has these properties:

- Data classifications are represented by distinct labels or names that have relative values (e.g., extra large, large, medium, small, extra small ; gold, silver, bronze; hot, medium, mild).
- Because of the relative values, the data classified can be ranked.

Interval Level Data

The *interval level* of measurement is the next highest level.

> *Interval level:* Includes the ranking characteristics of the ordinal scale and, in addition, the difference between values is a constant size.

Temperature on the Fahrenheit scale is an example. Suppose the high temperature for the last three days was 85, 73, and 78 degrees Fahrenheit. We can easily put the readings in a rank order, but in addition we can study the difference between readings. Why is this so? One degree on the Fahrenheit temperature scale is a constant unit of measurement. Note in this example that the zero point is just another point on the scale. It does not represent the absence of temperature, just that it is cold! Test scores are another example of the interval scale of measurement.

In addition to the constant difference characteristic, interval scaled data have all the features of nominal and ordinal measurements. Temperatures are distinct, that is, the high temperature yesterday cannot be both 88 and 85 degrees. The "greater than" feature of ordinal data permits the ranking of daily high temperatures.

The properties of the interval scale are:

- Data classifications are ordered according to the amount of the characteristic they possess.
- Equal differences in the characteristic are represented by equal differences in the measurement.

Ratio Level Data

The *ratio level* of measurement is the highest level of measurement.

> ***Ratio level***: Has all the characteristics of the interval scale, but additionally there is a meaningful zero point and the ratio between two values is meaningful.

Weight, height, and money are examples of the ratio scale of measurement. If you have $20 and your friend has $10, then you have twice as much money as your friend. The zero point represents the absence of money. That is, the zero point is fixed and represents the absence of the characteristic being measured. If you have zero dollars, you have none of the characteristic being measured.

The properties of the ratio level are:
- Data classifications are ordered according to the amount of the characteristic they posses.
- Equal differences in the characteristic are represented by equal differences in the numbers assigned to the classifications.
- The zero point reflects the absence of the characteristic.

Levels of Measurement			
Nominal	**Ordinal**	**Interval**	**Ratio**
↓	↓	↓	↓
Data may only be classified	Data are ranked	Meaningful difference between values	Meaningful 0 point and ratio between values
↓	↓	↓	↓
• Hair color • Zip code • Make of truck	• Order of finish • Military rank	• Score on test • Temperature • Shoe size	• Income • Weight • Distance traveled

Glossary

Continuous variable: A quantitative variable that can assume any value within a range.

Descriptive statistics: Methods of organizing, summarizing, and presenting data in an informative way.

Discrete variable: A quantitative variable that can only assume certain values. There is a "gap" between the values.

Inferential statistics: The methods used to estimate something about a population, based on a sample.

Interval level: Includes the ranking characteristics of the ordinal scale and, in addition, the difference between values is a constant size.

Nominal level: A level of measurement in which the data are sorted into classes with no particular order to the classes.

Ordinal level: A level of measurement that presumes that one category is ranked higher than another category.

Population: The entire set of all individuals or objects of interest or the measurements obtained from all individuals or objects of interest.

Qualitative variable: A variable that has the characteristic of being nonnumeric.

Quantitative variable: A variable being studied that can be reported numerically.

Ratio level: Has all the characteristics of the interval scale, but additionally there is a meaningful zero point and the ratio of two values is meaningful.

Sample: A portion, or part, of the population of interest.

Statistics: The science of collecting, organizing, presenting, analyzing, and interpreting data to assist in making more effective decisions.

CHAPTER 1 ASSIGNMENT

WHAT IS STATISTICS?

Name _____   Section _____   Score _____

Part I   Classify the following sets of data as qualitative or quantitative.

_____ 1.   The religious affiliations of college students

_____ 2.   The height of each member of a basketball team

_____ 3.   Students' scores on the first statistics exam

_____ 4.   The color of new SUV's on a car lot

_____ 5.   The Olympic track and field world records, such as the time for the steeplechase.

Part II   Classify the following sets of data as continuous or discrete.

_____ 6.   The number of students enrolled in an accounting class

_____ 7.   The number of General Electric microwaves sold by Home Depot last month

_____ 8.   The acceleration time of an automobile

_____ 9.   The temperature of a refrigerator

_____ 10.   The number of people aboard a commercial airplane

Part III   Identify the measurement scale as nominal, ordinal, interval, or ratio for each of the following.

_____ 11.   the temperature readings in Washington, D.C.

_____ 12.   brand of laptop computer

_____ 13.   college major

_____ 14.   military rank

_____ 15.   number of vehicles produced

_____ 16.   time required to download a computer file

_____ 17.   order of finish in the 2006 Indianapolis 500 auto race

_____ 18. the color of the students' hair in your statistics class

_____ 19. Scholastic Aptitude Test (S.A.T.) scores for incoming freshmen

_____ 20. number of people at a board of directors meeting

Part IV Select the correct answer and write the appropriate letter in the space provided.

_____ 21. The collection of all possible individuals, objects, or measurements is called

   a. a sample.
   b. a ratio measurement.
   c. an inference.
   d. a population

_____ 22. Techniques used to organize, summarize, and present the data that have been collected are called

   a. populations.
   b. samples.
   c. descriptive statistics.
   d. inferential statistics.

_____ 23. Quantitative variables

   a always use the interval level of measurement.
   b always use the ratio level of measurement.
   c can not have "gaps" between values.
   d are either discrete or continuous

_____ 24. Techniques used to estimate something about a population, based on a sample, are called

   a. descriptive statistics.
   b. inferential statistics.
   c. populations.
   d. samples.

_____ 25. Which of the following is *not* true of the interval scale?

   a. the interval scale is used for ordered data
   b. equal differences in the characteristic lead to equal differences in the measurement
   c. the zero point on the interval scale represents the absence of the characteristic measured
   d. the interval scale is not used for numeric data

CHAPTER 2
DESCRIBING DATA: FREQUENCY TABLES, FREQUENCY DISTRIBUTIONS AND GRAPHIC PRESENTATION

Chapter Goals

After completing this chapter, you will be able to:

1. Organize qualitative data into a frequency table.

2. Present a frequency table as a bar chart or pie chart.

3. Organize quantitative data into a frequency distribution.

4. Present a frequency distribution for quantitative data using histograms, frequency polygons, and cumulative frequency polygons.

Introduction

This chapter begins our study of *descriptive statistics.* Recall from Chapter 1 that when using descriptive statistics we describe a set of data using methods that organize or summarize the data set. For example, descriptive statistics may be used to organize data to show the general shape of the data, where the data tends to concentrate, or to expose extreme or unusual data values.

The first procedure we present for organizing and summarizing a set of data is the *frequency table*.

> *Frequency Table*: A grouping of qualitative data into mutually exclusive categories showing the number of observations in each category.

Recall from Chapter 1 that qualitative data is nonnumeric and can only be classified into distinct categories. There is no particular order to the categories. Examples of qualitative variables include: brand of computer sold by Best Buy (Hewlett Packard, Gateway, Toshiba, Sony, Compaq or Averatec), month of birth (January,.....,December), or the major airlines that fly out of a particular airport (US Airways, Delta, United, and Continental).

To illustrate construction of a frequency table, suppose that the following data set reports the movie just seen for each person in a sample of 25 people exiting a local multiplex on June 12, 2006:

02, 04, 01, 01, 04, 03, 02, 05, 01, 02, 04, 02, 01, 04, 05, 02, 01, 01, 03, 02, 04, 05, 02, 01, 02

(01=Cars, 02=The Da Vinci Code, 03= Over the Hedge, 04=The Break-Up, 05= The Omen)

The frequency table for this data set is shown below.

The left column lists the *classes* for the qualitative variable 'movie just seen'. Note that the classes are mutually exclusive since only one movie was seen by each person on that visit to the multiplex. The right column shows the number of people observed for each class or the *class frequency*. For example, the class frequency for Cars is 7.

Movie	Number of People
Cars	7
The Da Vinci Code	8
Over The Hedge	2
The Break-Up	5
The Omen	3

Class frequencies can be converted to *relative class frequencies* in order to show the fraction of the total number of observations for each class. A frequency table is converted to a *relative frequency table* by dividing each class frequency by the total number of observations. For example, the relative frequency for the number of movie patrons in the sample who just saw Over the Hedge is .08, found by dividing 2 by 25. The relative frequency table for the movie data set is represented by the first and third columns in the following table:

Movie	Number of People	Relative Frequency
Cars	7	0.28
The Da Vinci Code	8	0.32
Over the Hedge	2	0.08
The Break-Up	5	0.20
The Omen	3	0.12

Note that the sum of the relative frequency column is always equal to 1.0, just as the sum of the frequency column is always equal to the total number of observations in the data set.

Graphic Presentation of Qualitative Data

A bar chart is the most often used graph for presenting qualitative data. Typically, the horizontal axis is used to display the different classes of the variable and the vertical axis shows the frequency or relative frequency for each class. The height of the bar represents the frequency (or relative frequency) for each class. The bars are of uniform width and there is a gap between adjacent bars.

> **Bar Chart.** A graph in which the classes are reported on the horizontal axis and the class frequencies on the vertical axis. The class frequencies are proportional to the heights of the bars.

The frequency bar chart for the movie data is shown below:

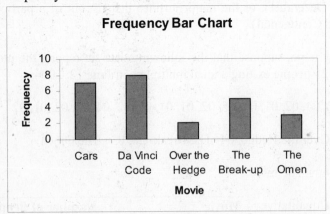

A relative frequency bar chart for the movie data is also shown. The difference between the two charts is the scale of the vertical axis. The vertical axis for the relative frequency bar chart represents the fraction of the total number of observations in each class.

Describing Data: Frequency Tables, Frequency Distributions, and Graphic Presentation

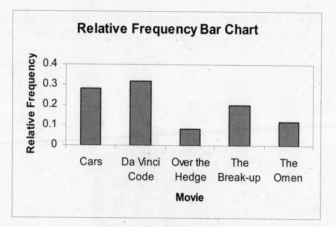

Relative Frequency Bar Chart

The **pie chart** is another common graph used to portray information for qualitative data.

Pie Chart. A chart that shows the proportion or percent that each class represents of the total.

As an example, suppose that Danny's Fun Center would like to determine the contribution to total revenue made by each of the center's activities last year. The information is given in the table.

Activity	Revenue (in $1,000s)	Percent of Revenue
Laser Tag	125	10
Miniature Golf	225	18
Raceway	250	20
Video Games	312.5	25
Food	275	22
Batting Cages	62.5	5
Total	1250	100

To plot the pie chart, after drawing a circle (pie) we put 0 on the top and go around the circle in increments of 5. To plot the percent of total revenue earned by laser tag, draw a line from 0 to the center of the circle and another line from the center to 10. Then, 10 + 18 = 28. This slice represents the percentage of the total earned by miniature golf. This process is continued for the remaining items. The pie reveals that food, video games, raceway and miniature golf account for most of the revenue. Video games are the biggest contributor, generating somewhat more revenue than food, raceway, and miniature golf. Laser tag and batting cages contribute much smaller portions of the revenue.

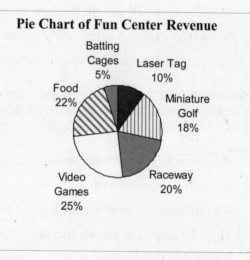

Pie Chart of Fun Center Revenue

Pie charts can also be used to display relative frequency data. For example, relative frequencies for the movie data, expressed as percentages, are shown in the pie chart below.

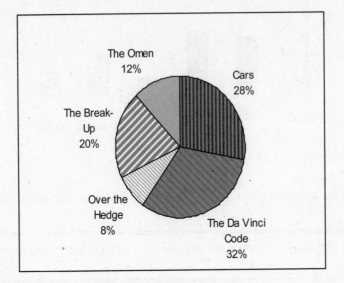

Frequency Distributions for Quantitative Data

A *frequency distribution* is a useful statistical tool for organizing a set of quantitative data in various ways. It can be used to show the shape of the data, where the data is concentrated, and to detect extreme values.

> **Frequency Distribution**: A grouping of data into mutually exclusive classes showing the number of observations in each.

The steps to follow in developing a frequency distribution are:

1. Decide on the number of classes.

2. Determine the class interval or width.

3. Set the individual class limits.

4. Tally the observations into the appropriate classes.

5. Count the number of tallies (items) in each class.

Length of Service (in years)					
4	3	2	10	6	6
5	8	4	8	4	
6	2	3	3	7	5

As an example, the lengths of service, in years, of a sample of seventeen employees are given above.

The seventeen observations are referred to as **raw data** or **ungrouped data.** To organize the lengths of service into a frequency distribution:

1. We decide to have five classes.

2. We used a class width of 2.

3. We used classes 1 up to 3, 3 up to 5, and so on.

4. **Tally** the lengths of service into the appropriate classes.

5. Count the number of tallies in each class as shown.

Frequency Distribution		
Lengths of service	**Tallies**	**Number of employees**
1 up to 3 years	//	2
3 up to 5 years	//////	6
5 up to 7 years	/////	5
7 up to 9 years	///	3
9 up to 11 yrs.	/	1
Total		17

Describing Data: Frequency Tables, Frequency Distributions, and Graphic Presentation

How many classes should there be? A common guideline is from 5 to 15. Having too few or too many classes gives little insight into the data. A rule for determining the number of classes is shown on the next page. The **class interval** is the size or width of the class. The class interval may be a value such as 3, 5, 10, 15, 20, 50, 100, 1,000, and so on. More formally, the class interval can be defined as follows:

> **Class Interval**: The difference between the limits of two consecutive classes.

The class interval can be approximated by text formula [2-1]

Class Interval

$$\text{Class Interval}(i) \geq \frac{\text{highest value} - \text{lowest value}}{\text{number of classes}} \text{ or } i \geq \frac{H - L}{k} \qquad [2-1]$$

Where:
i is the class interval.
H is the highest observed value.
L is the lowest observed value.
k is the number of classes.

If we apply the formula to our example, then $H = 10$, $L = 2$, and $k = 5$. We get a class interval of 2,

found by: $\quad i \geq \dfrac{10 - 2}{5} \geq \dfrac{8}{5} \geq 1.6$ which is rounded to 2.

Each class has a lower class limit and an upper class limit. The lower limit of the first class is usually slightly below the smallest value in the data set and, if possible, is a multiple of the class interval.

In the previous example, the smallest number of years of service is 2. We selected 1, which is slightly below 2, as the lower limit of the first class. The lower limit of the second class is 3 years, and so on.

The number of tallies or observations that occurs in each class is called the *class frequency*.

> **Class frequency**: The number of observations in each class.

In the example, the class frequency of the lowest class is 2. For the next higher class it is 6. The *class midpoint* divides a class into two equal parts.

> **Class Midpoint**: The point halfway between the lower limits of two consecutive classes.

The class midpoint is computed by adding the lower limit of consecutive classes and dividing the result by two.

In the example, the class midpoint of the 5 up to 7 class is 6 found by $(5 + 7)/2$. The class interval is the distance between the lower limit of two consecutive classes. It is 2, found by subtracting 1 (the lower limit of the first class) from 3 (the lower limit of the second class).

Suggestions on Constructing Frequency Distributions

When constructing frequency distributions, follow these guidelines:

1. *The class intervals used in the frequency distribution should be equal.* Unequal class intervals present problems in graphically portraying the distribution. However, in some situations unequal class intervals may be necessary in order to avoid a large number of empty classes.

2. Text formula [2-1] is based on the number of classes, and is useful for determining the class interval.

$$\text{Class Interval}(i) \geq \frac{\text{highest value} - \text{lowest value}}{\text{number of classes}} \text{ or } i \geq \frac{H-L}{k} \qquad [2-1]$$

3. *Your professional judgment can determine the number of classes.* Too many classes or too few classes might not reveal the basic shape of the distribution. A general rule is that it is best to use at least 5 and not more than 15 classes when constructing a frequency distribution.

4. *The "2 to the k rule" is also used to determine the number of classes.* To estimate the number of classes we select the smallest integer (whole number) such that $2^k \geq n$ where n is the total number of observations. Suppose a set of data has 60 observations. If we try $k = 5$, we get $2^5 = 32$, which is less than 60, so we try $2^6 = 64$, which is greater than 60. Thus the recommended number of classes is 6. The table is based on the *"2 to the k rule."*

2 to the *k* Rule for Number of Classes	
Total Number of Observations	**Recommended Number of Classes**
9 – 16	4
17 – 32	5
33 – 64	6
65 – 128	7
129 – 256	8
257 – 512	9
513 – 1,024	10

5. *The lower limit of the first class should be an even multiple of the class interval.* Suppose a sample of weight losses ranged from 25 pounds to 64 pounds. We want to organize the weight losses into a frequency distribution with an interval of 6 pounds. The lower limit of the first class would be 24, found by multiplying 4, the even multiple, by 6, the class interval. Obviously this suggestion was not followed in the above example for length of service. Keep in mind that these are only suggestions not rules.

6. *Avoid overlapping stated class limits.* Class limits such as 4-6 and 6-8 should not be used. Use 4 up to 6, then 6 up to 8. This way you can determine in which class to tally 6.

7. *Try to avoid open-ended classes.* Open-ended classes cause serious graphing problems and make it difficult to calculate various measures described in Chapter 3.

Relative Frequency Distribution

It is often helpful to know the fraction of the total number of observations that appear in each class or *relative class frequencies*.

> *Relative class frequency*: Shows the fraction of the total number of observations in each class.

The relative class frequency is found by dividing each of the class frequencies by the total number of observations.

Using the distribution of the lengths of service of the seventeen employees, the relative frequency for the 1 up to 3-year class is 0.1176 found by $2/17 = 0.1176 = 12\%$. Thus 12% of the employees had 1 up to 3 years of service. The relative frequencies for the remaining classes are shown.

Relative Frequency Distribution			
Length of service (in years)	Number of employees	Relative Frequency	Found by
1 up to 3 years	2	0.1176	2/17
3 up to 5 years	6	0.3529	6/17
5 up to 7 years	5	0.2941	5/17
7 up to 9 years	3	0.1765	3/17
9 up to 11 years	1	0.0588	1/17
Total	17	0.9999	

Graphic Presentation of a Frequency Distribution

To get reader attention a frequency distribution is often portrayed graphically as a histogram, a frequency polygon and the cumulative frequency polygon.

Histogram

The simplest type of a statistical chart is called a *histogram*.

> *Histogram:* A graph in which the classes are marked on the horizontal axis and the class frequencies on the vertical axis. The class frequencies are represented by the heights of the bars and the bars are drawn adjacent to each other.

For the length of service for the sample of seventeen employees a histogram would appear as shown on the right. Note that to plot the bar for the 5 up to 7 years (which has a midpoint of 6 years), we drew lines vertically from 5 and from 7 years to 5 employees on the *Y*-axis and then connected the end points by a straight line. The histogram provides an easily interpreted visual representation of a frequency distribution.

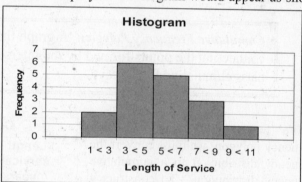

Frequency Polygon

A second type of chart used to portray a frequency distribution is the *frequency polygon*.

> *Frequency Polygon*: A graph that consists of line segments connecting the points formed by the intersection of the class midpoints and the class frequency.

For the frequency polygon, the assumption is that the observations in any class interval are represented by the class midpoint. A dot is placed at the class midpoint opposite the number of frequencies in that class. For the distribution of years of service, make the first plot by selecting 2 years on the *X*-axis (the midpoint) and then go vertically on the *Y*-axis to 2 and place a dot. This process is continued for all classes. Then connect the dots in order.

Normal practice is to anchor the frequency polygon to the *X*-axis. This is accomplished by extending the lines to the midpoint of the class below the lowest class (0) and to the midpoint of the class above the highest class (12).

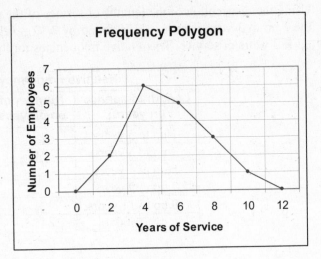

Cumulative Frequency Distributions

A *cumulative frequency distribution* reports the number and percent of observations that are less than a given value.

> **Cumulative Frequency Distribution**: A grouping of data into mutually exclusive classes showing the number of observations at or below the upper limit of each class.

A cumulative frequency distribution is graphically portrayed in a *cumulative frequency polygon*. A *cumulative frequency polygon* reports the number and percent of observations that are less than a given value.

> **Cumulative Frequency Polygon**: A graph that consists of line segments connecting the points formed by the intersection of the class endpoints and the class cumulative frequency.

Before we can draw a cumulative frequency polygon, we must convert the frequency distribution to a cumulative frequency distribution. To construct a cumulative frequency distribution, we add the frequencies from the lowest class to the frequency of the next highest class. We add this sum to the frequency of the next class, etc.

Cumulative Frequency Distribution			
Length of service (in years)	Class Frequency	Cumulative Frequency	Found by
1 up to 3 years	2	2	2
3 up to 5 years	6	8	2 + 6
5 up to 7 years	5	13	8 + 5
7 up to 9 years	3	16	13 + 3
9 up to 11 years	1	17	16 + 1

The cumulative frequencies are plotted on the vertical axis (Y-axis) and the lengths of service on the X-axis. It may be helpful to plot the cumulative frequencies on the left side of the vertical axis and the percent of the total on the right side as shown in the polygon above.

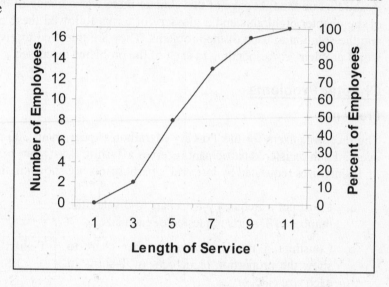

Glossary

Bar chart. A graph used for qualitative data in which the classes are reported on the horizontal axis and the class frequencies on the vertical axis.

Class interval: The size or width of the class.

Class frequency: The number of observations in each class.

Class midpoint: The point halfway between the lower limits of two consecutive classes.

Cumulative frequency distribution: A grouping of data into mutually exclusive classes showing the number of observations at or below the upper limit of each class.

Cumulative frequency polygon: A graph that consists of line segments connecting the points formed by the intersection of the class upper limit and the class cumulative frequency.

Frequency distribution: A grouping of quantitative data into classes showing the number of observations in each mutually exclusive class.

Frequency table: A grouping of qualitative data into mutually exclusive categoriess showing the number of observations in each category.

Frequency polygon: A graph that consists of line segments connecting the points formed by the intersection of the class midpoint and the class frequency.

Histogram: A graph in which the classes are marked on the horizontal axis and the class frequencies on the vertical axis. The class frequencies are represented by the heights of the bars and the bars are drawn adjacent to each other.

Pie Chart. A chart that shows the proportion or percent that each class represents of the total.

Relative class frequency: Shows what fraction each class is of the total number of observations.

Note to students:

Recall that on the first page of this chapter there was a listing of the chapter goals. A brief discussion of the chapter highlights and a glossary of terms followed these goals. Now come several problems and the solution to each of the problems. They are intended to give you a detailed solution to a real-world problem, corresponding to each of the problems discussed.

Chapter Problems

Problem 1

The race organizers for the Tri-City Marathon expect about 800 runners to participate in this year's event. Each registered participant receives a T-shirt. Last year, 680 runners entered. The distribution of T-shirt sizes requested by last year's participants are shown in the table.

a. Construct a frequency bar chart to display the number of T-shirts requested of each size.

b. Construct a relative frequency bar chart to show the proportion or percent of T-shirts in each size category.

c. Construct a pie chart to display the relative frequency of each T-shirt size.

T-shirt size	Frequency	Relative Frequency
XS	68	0.10=68/680
S	136	0.20=136/680
M	170	0.25=170/680
L	272	0.40=272/680
XL	34	0.05=34/680
Total	680	1.000

Solution 1

a. T-shirt sizes are scaled on the X-axis and frequencies are scaled on the vertical axis. The heights of the bars are proportional to the frequencies. Note that there is a gap between the bar for each category.

b. To construct a relative frequency bar chart scale T-shirt sizes on the horizontal axis and relative frequencies on the vertical axis. Make sure that there is a gap between the bars.

c. First draw a circle. Starting at the top of the pie mark off the pie in increments of 5 (0,5,10,…,100). Draw a vertical line from the center to the top of the pie. For the XS category draw a line from the center of the circle to 10 on the circumference. For the S category draw a vertical line to 30 on the circumference (10 + 20). Continue in this manner until the pie if filled with each category.

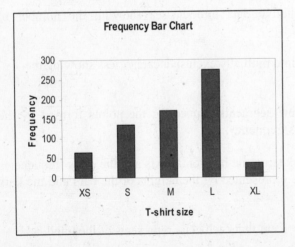

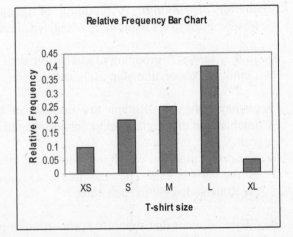

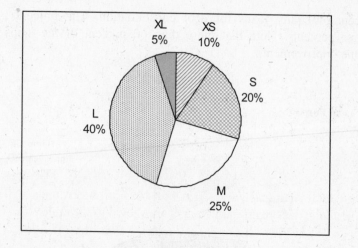

Exercise 2.1

This is the first in a series of exercises designed to check your comprehension of the material just presented. We suggest that you work all parts of the exercise. Then check your answers against those given in the answer section of this study guide.

The SaveMore Rental Car Agency at the Cincinnati airport would like to examine records from last summer in order to plan for the coming summer demand. The data for last year's demand, broken down by type of vehicle requested, is shown in the table below.

a. Construct a frequency and relative frequency bar chart for the data.
b. Construct a pie chart to display the relative frequency information.
c. This summer's demand is expected to be 20% higher than demand for last summer. Approximately how many luxury cars are expected to be rented this summer?

Vehicle Type	Frequency	Relative Frequency
Sub-compact	545	0.183
Compact	892	0.299
Full-size	740	0.248
Luxury	360	0.121
SUV	280	0.094
Van	168	0.056
Total	2985	1.001*

* Total is not equal to 1.000 due to rounding error.

Problem 2

The table to the right reports the purpose of home equity loans by the Home Bank and the percent each type of loan is relative to the total. Portray the home equity loan information in the form of a pie chart.

Loan Purpose	Percent Of Total	Cumulative Percent
Home improvement	32	32
Debt consolidation	30	62
Car purchase	11	73
Education	10	83
Other	9	92
Investments	8	100

Solution 2

The first step is to draw a circle. Next draw a line from 0 to the center of the circle and another from the center of the circle to 32%. Adding the 32% for home improvements and the 30% for debt consolidation gives 62%. A line is drawn from the center to 62%. The area between 32% and 62%

represents the percent of equity loans for debt consolidation. The process is continued for the remaining cumulative percents. Note that more than 60 percent of the loans are for either debt consolidation or home improvement.

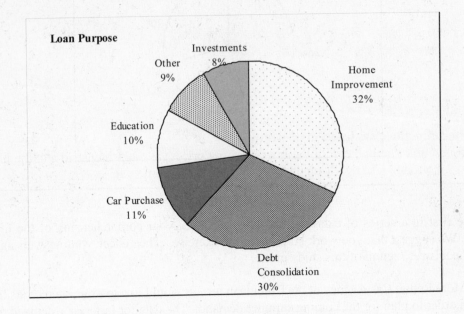

Exercise 2.2

Check your answers against those in the ANSWER section.

The data depicts new cars sold in the United States for the year, classified by manufacturer. Portray the "new cars sold" data in the form of a pie chart.

Manufacturer	Cars Sold Millions
General Motors	3100
Ford	1900
DaimlerChrysler	800
Toyota	800
Honda	800
Nissan	500
Other	1100
Total	9000

Problem 3

The marketing director at Gomminger Realty Company selected a sample of 30 homes for study. (Selling price is reported in thousands of dollars and is already ordered from low to high for convenience.) Organize these data into a frequency distribution and interpret your results.

125	167	179	207	229	270
135	169	180	211	240	273
140	170	182	213	242	282
151	172	190	215	252	295
163	175	193	226	257	315

Solution 3

Step 1: Decide the number of classes.

Determine the number of classes by using the *"2 to the k rule"*. To estimate the number of classes, select the smallest integer (whole number) such that $2^k \geq n$ where n is the total number of observations. Our set of data has 30 observations. If we try $k = 5$, we get $2^5 = 32$, which is more than 30. Thus the recommended number of classes is 5.

Selling Price ($1000)	Tallies	Number of Homes
$120 up to $160	////	4
$160 up to $200	₩₩ ₩₩ /	11
$200 up to $240	₩₩ /	6
$240 up to $280	₩₩ /	6
$280 up to $320	///	3
		30

Step 2: Determine the class interval or width.

Observe that the home with the lowest selling price was $125 thousand and the highest was $315 thousand. Use text formula [2-1] to determine the interval.

$$\text{Class Interval}(i) = \frac{\text{highest value} - \text{lowest value}}{\text{number of classes}} \text{ or } i \geq = \frac{H - L}{k} = \frac{315 - 125}{5} = \frac{190}{5} = 38$$

We round 38 up to 40, thus we let the class interval be $40 thousand.

Step 3: Set the individual class limit.

We decide to let $120 thousand be the lower limit of the first class. Thus, the first class will be $120 up to $160 thousand and the second class $160 up to $200 thousand, and so on.

Step 4: Tally the selling prices into each of the classes.

The first home sold for $125 thousand, so the price is tallied into the $120 thousand up to $160 thousand class. The procedure is continued, resulting in the frequency distribution shown above. Observe that the largest concentration of the data is in the $160 up to $200 thousand class.

Step 5: Count the number of items in each class.

As noted before, the class frequencies are the number of observations in each class. For the $120 up to $160 thousand class the class frequency is 4, and for the $160 up to $200 thousand class the class frequency is 11. This indicates that four homes sold in the $120 up to $160 thousand price range and eleven in the $160 up to $200 thousand range.

It is also clear that the interval between the lowest and highest selling price in each category is $40 thousand. How would we classify a home selling for $160 thousand? It would fall in the second class. Homes selling for $120,,000 up through $159,999.99 go in the first class, but a home selling for more than this amount goes in the next class. So the $160,000 selling price puts the home in the second class. The class midpoint is determined by going halfway between the lower limit of consecutive classes. Halfway between $120 and $160 is $140 thousand, the class midpoint.

Problem 4

Based on the information from Gomminger Realty in Problem 3,

a. Develop a relative frequency distribution.

b. What percent of the homes sold for a price from $200,000 up to $240,000?

Solution 4

a. Relative class frequencies show the fraction of the total number of observations in each class. These fractions are often expressed as percents. To convert a frequency distribution to a relative frequency distribution, each class frequency is divided by the total number of observations.

Using the distribution from Problem 3, the relative frequency for the $120 up to $160 class is 0.133, found by dividing 4 by 30. Thus, 13.3% of the homes sold from $120,000 up to $160,000.

All the relative frequencies are shown in the table.

Selling Price ($000)	Tallies	Number of Homes	Relative Frequency	Found by
$120 up to $160	////	4	0.1333 = 13.33%	4/30
$160 up to $200	### ### /	11	0.3667 = 36.67%	11/30
$200 up to $240	### /	6	0.2000 = 20.00%	6/30
$240 up to $280	### /	6	0.2000 = 20.00%	6/30
$280 up to $320	///	3	0.1000 = 10.00%	3/30
Total		30	1.0000 = 100.00%	
*Note that rounding caused the relative frequency to exceed 100%				

b. The relative frequency is .2000, which means 20.00% of the homes sold for a price from $200,000 up to $240,000.

Exercise 2.3

Check your answers against those in the ANSWER section.

The Jansen Motor Company has developed a new engine to further reduce gasoline consumption. The new engine was installed in 20 mid-sized cars and the number of miles per gallon recorded (to the nearest mile per gallon).

a. Use the "2 to the k rule" to determine the number of classes.
b. Determine the class interval.
c. Develop a frequency distribution.

29	32	20	30	39
27	28	21	36	20
27	18	32	37	29
30	23	25	19	30

Exercise 2.4

Check in the ANSWER section.

Use the Jansen Motor Company data in Exercise 2.3 to construct a relative frequency distribution.

Problem 5

Based on the information from Gomminger Realty in Problem 3, develop a histogram.

Solution 5

The class frequencies are scaled on the vertical axis (Y-axis) and the selling price on the horizontal (X-axis). A vertical line is drawn from the two class limits of a class to a height corresponding to the number of frequencies. The tops of the lines are then connected.

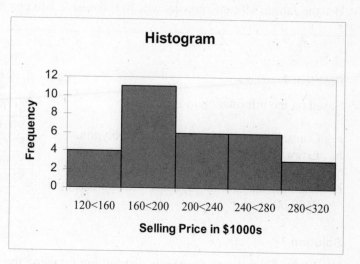

Exercise 2.5

Check your answers against those in the ANSWER section.

Use the Jansen Motor Company data in Exercise 2.3 to construct a histogram.

Problem 6

Using the information contained in Problems 3 and 4, construct a frequency polygon.

Solution 6

Class frequencies are scaled on the vertical axis (Y-axis) and class midpoints along the horizontal axis (X-axis). The first plot is at point 67.5 on the X-axis and 3 on the Y-axis. Next, the midpoints of the class below the first class and above the last class are added. This allows the graph to be anchored to the X-axis at zero frequencies.

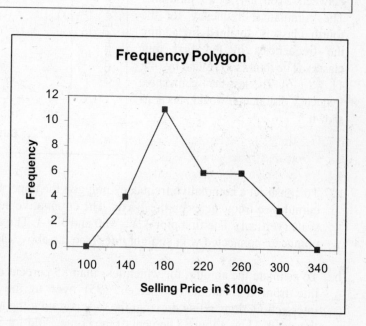

Check your answers against those in the ANSWER section.

Use the Jansen Motor Company data in Exercise 2.1 to construct a frequency polygon.

Problem 7

Based on the information in Problem 1

a. Construct a cumulative frequency polygon.
b. Estimate the price below which 85 percent of the homes were sold.
c. Estimate the number of homes sold for less than $190,000.

Class limits ($000)	Class Frequency	Cumulative Frequency
$120 up to $160	4	4
$160 up to $200	11	15
$200 up to $240	6	21
$240 up to $280	6	27
$280 up to $320	3	30

Solution 7

Construct a cumulative frequency distribution by using the class limits. The first step is to determine the number of observations "less than" the upper limit of each class. Four homes were sold for less than $160 and fifteen were sold for between $120 and $200 thousand. The fifteen is found by adding the four that sold for $120 to $160 thousand and the eleven that sold for between $160 and $200 thousand. The cumulative frequency for the fourth class is obtained by adding the frequencies of the first four classes. The total is 27, found by (4 + 11 + 6+ 6). The less-than cumulative frequency distribution would appear as shown.

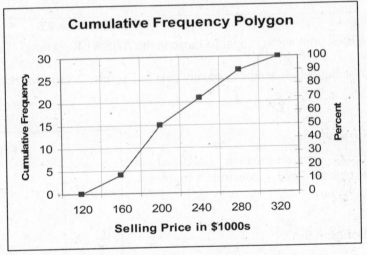

a. To construct a cumulative frequency polygon the upper limits are scaled on the X-axis and the cumulative frequencies on the Y-axis. The cumulative percents are placed along the right-hand scale (vertical). The first plot is $X = 160$ and $Y = 4$. The next plot is 200 and 15. As shown, the points are connected with straight lines (see the above chart).

b. To estimate the amount for which less than 85 percent of the homes were sold, draw a horizontal line from the cumulative percent (85) over to the cumulative frequency polygon. At the intersection, draw a line down to the X-axis giving the approximate selling price. It is about $270 thousand. Thus, about 85 percent of the homes sold for $270,000 or less.

c. To estimate the percent of the homes that sold for less than $215,000, first locate the value of $215 thousand on the X-axis. Next, draw a vertical line from the X-axis at 215 up to the graph. Draw a line horizontally to the cumulative percent axis and read the cumulative percent. It is about 60%. Hence, we conclude that about 60 percent of the homes were sold for less than $215,000.

Exercise 2.7

Check your answers against those in the ANSWER section.

Use the Jansen Motor Company data in Exercise 2.3.

a. Construct a cumulative frequency polygon.
b. Determine the percent of the automobiles getting less than 30 miles per gallon.
c. Estimate the miles per gallon such that ninety-five percent of automobiles obtain less than this mpg.

CHAPTER 2 ASSIGNMENT

DESCRIBING DATA: FREQUENCY TABLES, FREQUENCY DISTRIBUTIONS, AND GRAPHIC PRESENTATION

Name _____ Section _____ Score _____

Part I   Select the correct answer and write the appropriate letter in the space provided

_____ 1.   A grouping of data into classes giving the number of observations in each class is called a(an)
   a   bar chart.
   b.   frequency distribution.
   c.   pie chart.
   d.   cumulative frequency distribution.

_____ 2.   The distance between consecutive lower class limits is called the
   a.   class interval.
   b.   frequency distribution.
   c.   class midpoint.
   d.   class frequency.

_____ 3.   The class midpoint is
   a.   equal to the number of observations.
   b.   found by adding the lower class limits of two consecutive classes and dividing by 2.
   c.   equal to the class interval.
   d.   all of the above.

_____ 4.   The number of observations in a particular class is called the
   a.   class interval.
   b.   class frequency.
   c.   frequency distribution.
   d.   none of the above.

_____ 5.   A bar chart is used most often when
   a.   you want to show frequencies as compared to total observations.
   b.   you want to show frequencies by class intervals.
   c.   you want to display frequencies by category.
   d.   you want to organize data along certain time interval.

_____ 6.   In a *relative frequency* distribution
   a.   the class frequencies are divided by 100.
   b.   the data are related to each other rather than mutually exclusive.
   c.   the class frequency is divided by the total number of observations.
   d.   the frequencies are added together to give a relative set of numbers.

_____ 7.   Cumulative frequency polygons are constructed from line segments connecting
   a.   the upper class limits and corresponding cumulative frequencies.
   b.   the lower class limits and corresponding cumulative frequencies.
   c.   the interval midpoints and corresponding cumulative frequencies.
   d.   the upper class limits and corresponding frequencies.

Describing Data: Frequency Tables, Frequency Distributions, and Graphic Presentation

8. The suggested interval size of the class intervals for a histogram can be estimated by:
   a. consecutive lower class limits divided by 2.
   b. consecutive lower class limits divided by the total number of observations.
   c. using the formulas: $i \geq \dfrac{H - L}{k}$
   d. consecutive lower class limits divided by the number of frequencies in each class.

9. A pie chart requires at least what level of data?
   a. nominal
   b. ordinal
   c. interval
   d. ratio

10. A graphic representation of a frequency distribution constructed by connecting the class midpoints with lines is called a
    a. histogram.
    b. line chart.
    c. pie chart.
    d. frequency polygon.

Part II Show all of your work. Write the answer in the space provided.

11. The portfolio of a certain investor is described in the following table. Construct a pie chart that describes the percent contribution of each of the investment categories to the overall portfolio.

Category	Amount
Cash	$ 30,000
U.S. Stocks	$124,230
Non-U.S. Stocks	$ 38,434
Bonds	$150,000
Other	$ 72,544
Total	$415,208

12. Listed are the 2005-2006 cost of in-state undergraduate tuition and fees (in dollars) at the 34 AAU public universities (2005-2006 Tuition and Required Fees Report, University of Missouri, 2005). For this data construct:

    a. a frequency distribution (use a class interval of $1500 with $3000 as the lower limit of the first class).
    b. a relative frequency distribution.
    c. a cumulative frequency distribution..

11508	8082	6972	6284	5540
11436	7821	6770	6068	5413
9798	7457	6685	5634	5372
9221	7415	6512	5613	4613
8634	7370	6504	5612	4498
8622	7112	6458	5610	3094
8108	6997	6339	5575	

d. Construct a frequency histogram for the data.

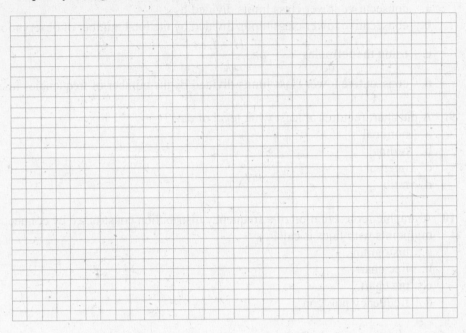

e. Construct a frequency polygon for the data.

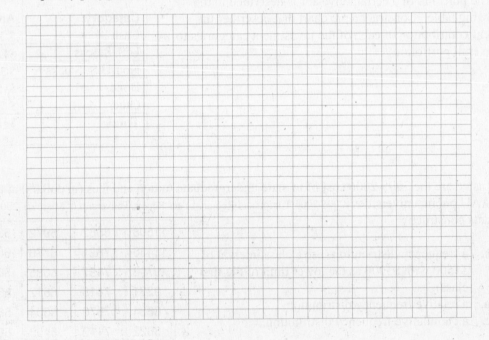

Describing Data: Frequency Tables, Frequency Distributions, and Graphic Presentation

f. Draw a cumulative frequency polygon

CHAPTER 3
DESCRIBING DATA: NUMERICAL MEASURES

Chapter Goals

After completing this chapter, you will be able to:

1. Calculate the arithmetic mean, weighted mean, median, mode, and geometric mean.

2. Explain the characteristics, uses, advantages, and disadvantages of each measure of location.

3. Identify the position of the mean, median, and mode for both symmetric and skewed distributions.

4. Compute and interpret the range, the mean deviation, variance, and the standard deviation.

5. Explain the characteristics, uses, advantages, and disadvantages of each measure of dispersion.

6. Understand Chebyshev's theorem and Empirical Rule as they relate to a set of observations.

Introduction

What is an average? It is a single number used to describe the central tendency of a set of data.

Examples of an average are:

1. The average length of the school year for students in public schools in the United States is 180 days.

2. The median household income for the United States was $44,389 in 2004, the most recent year for which this data is available (*http://www.census.gov*).

3. The median selling price for a single-family home in Boston in August, 2005 was $375,000 (*The Boston Globe*, October 26, 2005).

4. The mean wage for accountants was $24.56 per hour in 2004. (***The Census Bureau's Income Statistics Branch***, July, 2005).

5. Computer Software Engineers' pay averaged $38.44 per hour, while Library Technicians averaged $12.22 per hour. (***Bureau of Labor Statistics web site: http://stats.bls.gov, July, 2005***)

There are several types of averages. We will consider five: the arithmetic mean, weighted mean, the median, the mode, and the geometric mean.

Measures of Location

The purpose of a measure of location is to pinpoint the center of a set of observations.

> ***Measure of location***: A single value that summarizes a set of data. It locates the center of the values.

The arithmetic mean, or simply the mean, is the most widely used measure of location.

> ***Mean***: The sum of observations divided by the total number of observations.

The population mean is calculated as follows:

$$\text{Population mean} = \frac{\text{Sum of all values in the population}}{\text{Number of values in the population}}$$

In terms of symbols, the formula for the mean of a population is:

Population Mean $\qquad \mu = \dfrac{\Sigma X}{N} \qquad$ [3 – 1]

Where:

μ represents the population mean. It is the Greek letter "mu."
N is the number of items in the population.
X is any particular value.
Σ indicates the operation of adding all the values. It is the Greek letter "sigma."
ΣX is the sum of the X values.
[3-1]   indicates the formula number from the text.

Any measurable characteristic of a population is called a ***parameter***.

Parameter: A characteristic of a population.

The Sample Mean

As explained in Chapter 1, we frequently select a sample from the population to find out something about a specific characteristic of the population.

The mean of a sample and the mean of a population are computed in the same way, but the shorthand notation is different.

In terms of symbols, the formula for the mean of a sample is:

Sample Mean $\qquad \overline{X} = \dfrac{\Sigma X}{n} \qquad$ [3 – 2]

Where:

$\overline{X}$ is the sample mean; it is read as "X bar".
n is the number of values in the sample.
X is a particular value.
Σ indicates the operation of adding all the values.
ΣX is the sum of the X values.
[3-2]   is the formula number from the text.

The mean of a sample, or any other measure based on sample data, is called a ***statistic***.

Statistic: A characteristic of a sample.

"The mean weight of a sample of laptop computers is 6.5 pounds," is an example of a statistic.

In formulas [3-1] and [3-2] the mean is calculated by summing the observations and dividing by the total number of observations.

Suppose the Kellogg Company's quarterly earnings per share for the last five quarters are: $0.89, $0.77, $1.05, $0.79, and $0.95. If the earnings are a population, the mean is found by:

$$\mu = \frac{\Sigma X}{N} = \frac{(\$0.89 + \$0.77 + \$1.05 + \$0.79 + \$0.95)}{5}$$

$$= \frac{\$4.45}{5} = \$0.89$$

The mean quarterly earning per share is $0.89.

In some situations the mean may not be representative of the data.

As an example, the annual salaries of five vice presidents at AVX, LLC are $115,000, $135,000, $118,000, $126,000, and $350,000. The mean is:

$$\mu = \frac{\Sigma X}{N} = \frac{(\$115,000 + \$135,000 + \$118,000 + \$126,000 + \$350,000)}{5}$$

$$= \frac{\$884,000}{5} = \$168,800$$

Notice how the one extreme value ($350,000) pulled the mean upward. Four of the five vice presidents earned less than the mean, raising the question whether the arithmetic mean value of $168,800 is typical of the salary of the five vice presidents.

Properties of the Mean

As stated, the mean is a widely used measure of location. It has several important properties.

6. Every set of interval level and ratio level data has a mean.
7. All the data values are included in the calculation.
8. The mean in unique. That is, there is only one mean for a set of data.
9. The sum of the deviations of each value from the mean will always be zero, that is:

$$\boxed{\Sigma(X - \overline{X}) = 0}$$

Weighted Mean

The *weighted mean* is a special case of the arithmetic mean. It is often useful when there are several observations of the same value.

> *Weighted mean*: The value of each observation is multiplied by the number of times it occurs. The sum of these products is divided by the total number of observations to determine the weighted mean.

In general, the weighted mean of a set of values, designated $X_1, X_2, X_3, \ldots X_n$, with the corresponding weights $w_1, w_2, w_3, \ldots, w_n$ is computed by:

Weighted Mean	$\overline{X}_w = \dfrac{w_1 X_1 + w_2 X_2 + w_3 X_3 + \cdots + w_n X_n}{w_1 + w_2 + w_3 + \cdots + w_n}$	[3 – 3]

The weighted mean is particularly useful when various classes or groups contribute differently to the total. For example, the coronary care unit of a hospital consists of nurses–aides who are paid $14 per hour, nurses– assistants who earn $18 per hour, and registered nurses who earn $28 per hour.

To say the average hourly wage for the coronary unit is $20 per hour ($14 + $18 + $28) ÷ 3 would not be accurate unless there were the same number of people in each group.

Suppose the coronary care unit has ten employees: two aides who earn $14 per hour, 3 nurses–assistants who earn $18 per hour, and five registered nurses who earn $28 per hour. The weighted mean is:

$$\overline{X}_w = \frac{w_1 X_1 + w_2 X_2 + w_3 X_3 + \cdots + w_n X_n}{w_1 + w_2 + w_3 + \cdots + w_n}$$

$$= \frac{(2 \times \$14) + (3 \times \$18) + (5 \times \$28)}{2 + 3 + 5} = \frac{\$28 + \$54 + \$140}{10} = \frac{\$222}{10} = \$22.20$$

Thus the weighted mean is $22.20.

The Median

It was pointed out that the arithmetic mean is often not representative of data with extreme values. The *median* is a useful measure when we encounter data with an extreme value.

> *Median*: The midpoints of the values after all observations have been ordered from the smallest to the largest, or from largest to smallest.

Fifty percent of the observations are above the median and 50 percent are below the median. To determine the median, the values are ordered from low to high, or high to low, and the middle value selected. Hence, half the observations are above the median and half are below it. For the vice president incomes, the middle value is $44,000, the median.

$115,000 $118,000 $126,000 $135,000 $350,000

L

median

Obviously, it is a more representative value in this problem than the mean of $168,800.

Note that there were an odd number of vice president incomes (5). For an odd number of ungrouped values we just order them and select the middle value. To determine the median of an even number of ungrouped values, the first step is to arrange them from low to high as usual, and then determine the value half way between the two middle values.

As an example, the number of bronze castings produced in a day at Markey Bronze is 87, 62, 91, 58, 99, and 85. Ordering these from low to high:

$$58 \quad 62 \quad 85 \quad 87 \quad 91 \quad 99$$

The median number produced is halfway between the two middle values of 85 and 87. The median is 86. Thus we note that the median (86) may not be one of the values in a set of data.

Properties of the Median

The major properties of the median are:

10. It is not affected by extremely large or small values.
11. It can be computed for ordinal-level data or higher.
12. There is only one median value for each set of data.

The Mode

A third measure of location is the *mode*.

> *Mode*: The value of the observation that appears most frequently.

The mode is the value that occurs most often in a set of raw data. The dividends per share declared on five stocks were: $3, $2, $4, $5, and $4. Since $4 occurred twice, which was the most frequent, the mode is $4.

Properties of the Mode

13. The mode can be found for all levels of data (nominal, ordinal, interval, and ratio).
14. The mode is not affected by extremely high or low values.
15. A set of data can have more than one mode. If it has two modes, it is said to be bimodal.
16. A disadvantage is that a set of data may not have a mode because no value appears more than once.

The Relative Positions of the Mean, Median, and Mode

The mean, median, and mode of a set of data are usually not all equal. However, if they are identical, the distribution is a *symmetrical distribution*.

> *Symmetrical distribution*: A distribution that has the same shape on either side of the center.

The chart on the right shows the useful life of a sample of batteries used in a CD player. Note the symmetrical bell-shape of the distribution. In a symmetrical distribution the mean, median and mode are equal.

If the distribution is not symmetrical, it is skewed and the relationship between the mean, median, and mode changes. If the long tail is to the right, the distribution is said to be a *positively skewed distribution*.

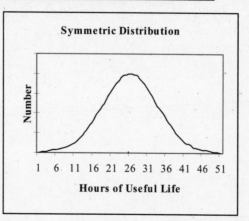

The chart on the right shows the years of service for a group of employees at an old manufacturing plant that was revitalized with a new product line and experienced a hiring surge about 13 years ago.

It is a positively skewed distribution. The mean is larger than the median, which is larger than the mode.

For a *negatively skewed distribution* the mean is the smallest of the three measures of central tendency (because it is being pulled down by the small observations). The mode is the highest of the three measures.

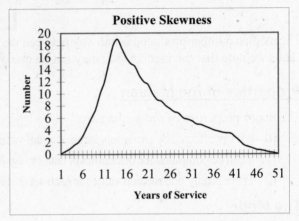

The chart on the right shows the years of service for a group of teachers in a school system that has an experienced staff and has not hired many staff in recent years. The mean is smaller than the median, which is smaller than the mode.

In skewed distributions the mode always appears at the apex or top (highest point) on the curve, and the mean is pulled in the direction of the tail. The median always appears between the mode and the mean, regardless of the direction of the tail.

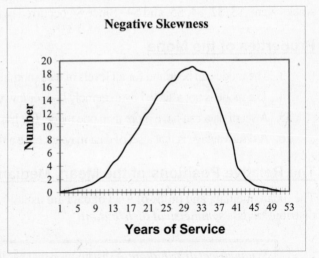

Chapter 3

Describing Data: Numerical Measures

The Geometric Mean

The geometric mean is used to determine the average change of percentages, ratios, indexes, or growth rates.

> **Geometric mean**: The nth root of the product of n values.

The formula for finding the geometric mean is:

Geometric Mean	$GM = \sqrt[n]{(X_1)(X_2)(X_3)\cdots(X_n)}$	[3 – 4]

Where:

$(X_1), (X_2), (X_3)$ etc.   are data values.

n is the number of values.

$\sqrt[n]{\ }$ is the nth root.

The geometric mean can be used for averaging percents. Suppose the return on investment for Parnell International for the past 4 years is 0.4%, 2.9%, 2.1%, and 12.3%. The GM increase over the period is 4.3 percent, found by:

$$GM = \sqrt[n]{(X_1)(X_2)(X_3)\cdots(X_n)}$$
$$= \sqrt[4]{1.004 \times 1.029 \times 1.021 \times 1.123}$$
$$= \sqrt[4]{1.18455} = 1.043$$

The geometric mean is fourth root of 1.18455, which is 1.043. The average return on the investment is found by subtracting one from the geometric mean. $(1.043 - 1.000) = 0.043 = 4.3\%$.

Another application of the geometric mean is to find average percent change over a period of time. Text formula [3-5] is used:

Average Percent Increase Over Time	$GM = \sqrt[n]{\dfrac{\text{Value at end of period}}{\text{Value at beginning of period}}} - 1$	[3 – 5]

Why Study Dispersion?

A direct comparison of two sets of data based only on two measures of location such as the mean and the median can be misleading since an average does not tell us anything about the spread of the data.

For example, the mean salary paid to baseball players for the New York Yankees is $7,095,078. However, the range is $25,349,577 with a low of $331,150 and a high of $25,680,727. The Boston Red Sox have a mean salary of $4,804,021. The range is $17,943,838 with a low of $335,400 and a high of $18,279,238. (*http://espn.go.com/mlb/clubhouses/salaries*). Suppose a statistics instructor has two classes, one in the morning and one in the evening; each with six students. In the morning class (AM) the students' ages are 18, 20, 21, 21, 23, and 23 years. In the evening class (PM) the ages are 17, 17, 18, 20, 25, and 29 years. Note that for both classes the mean age is 21 years but there is more variation or dispersion in the ages of the evening students.

A small value for a measure of dispersion indicates that the data are clustered closely, say, around the arithmetic mean. Thus the mean is considered representative of the data, that is, it is reliable. Conversely, a large measure of dispersion indicates that the mean is not reliable and is not representative of the data.

Measures of Dispersion

We will consider several measures of dispersion: the *range*, the *mean deviation*, the *variance*, and the *standard deviation*.

Range

The simplest measure of dispersion is the *range*.

> *Range*: The difference between the largest and smallest values in a data set.

The formula for range is:

Range	Range = Largest value – Smallest value	[3-6]

The statistics instructor referred to above has two classes with the ages indicated:

A.M. Class: 18, 20, 21, 21, 23, 23   **P.M. Class**: 17, 17, 18, 20, 25, 29

The range for the classes is:

A.M. Class: (23 – 18) = 5   **P.M. Class**: (29 – 17) = 12

Thus we can say that there is more spread in the ages of the students enrolled in the evening (P.M.) class compared with the morning (A.M.) class.

The characteristics of the range are:

17. Only two values are used in the calculation.
18. It is influenced by extreme values.
19. It is easy to compute and understand.
20. It can be distorted by an extreme value.

The range has two disadvantages. It can be distorted by a single extreme value. Suppose the same statistics instructor has a third class of five students. The ages of these students are given in the table.

Ages of Students				
20	20	21	22	60

The range of ages is 40 years, yet four of the five students' ages are within two years of each other. The 60-year old student has distorted the spread. Another disadvantage is that only two values, the largest and the smallest, are used in its calculation.

Mean Deviation

In contrast to the range, the *mean deviation* considers all the data.

> **Mean Deviation**: The arithmetic mean of the absolute values of the deviations from the arithmetic mean.

In terms of symbols, the formula for the mean deviation is:

Mean Deviation	$MD = \dfrac{\Sigma\left|X - \overline{X}\right|}{n}$	[3 – 7]

Where:

X is the value of each observation.
$\overline{X}$ is the arithmetic mean of the values.
n is the number of observations in the sample.
$\left|\ \right|$ indicates the absolute value.

We take the absolute value of the deviations from the mean because if we didn't, the positive and negative deviations from the mean exactly offset each other, and the mean deviation would always be zero. Such a measure (zero) would be a useless statistic.

The mean deviation is computed by first determining the difference between each observation and the mean. These differences are then averaged without regard to their signs. For the PM statistics class the mean deviation is 4.0 years, found by the table on the right:

$\left|X - \overline{X}\right|$		Absolute Deviation
$\left|17 - 21\right|$	$= \left|-4\right|$	= 4
$\left|17 - 21\right|$	$= \left|-4\right|$	= 4
$\left|18 - 21\right|$	$= \left|-3\right|$	= 3
$\left|20 - 21\right|$	$= \left|-3\right|$	= 1
$\left|25 - 21\right|$	$= \left|4\right|$	= 4
$\left|29 - 21\right|$	$= \left|8\right|$	= 8
$\Sigma\left|X - \overline{X}\right|$		= 24

Then

$$\overline{X} = \frac{\Sigma\left|X - \overline{X}\right|}{n} = \frac{24}{6} = 4$$

The parallel lines $\left|\ \right|$ indicate absolute value. To interpret, 4.0 years is the mean amount by which the ages differ from the arithmetic mean age of 21.0 years for the PM students.

Variance and Standard Deviation

The disadvantage of the mean deviation is that the absolute values are difficult to manipulate mathematically. Squaring the differences from each value and the mean eliminates the problem of absolute values. These squared differences are used both in the computation of the *variance* and the *standard deviation*.

> **Variance:** The arithmetic mean of the squared deviations from the mean.

The variance is non-negative and is zero only if all observations are the same.

> ***Standard Deviation:*** The square root of the variance.

Squaring units of measurement, such as dollars or years, makes the variance cumbersome to use since it yields units like "dollars squared" or "years squared." However, by calculating the standard deviation, which is the positive square root of the variance, we can return to the original units, such as years or dollars. Because the standard deviation is easier to interpret, it is more widely used than the mean deviation or the variance.

Population Variance

The formula for the population variance and the sample variance are slightly different. The formula for the population variance is:

$$\textbf{Population Variance} \quad \sigma^2 = \frac{\Sigma(X - \mu)^2}{N} \qquad [3-8]$$

Where:
σ^2 is the symbol for the population variance (σ is the Greek letter sigma). It is read as "sigma squared."
X is a value of an observation in the population.
μ is the arithmetic mean of the population.
N is the total number of observations in the population.

The major characteristics of the variance are:

1. All the observations are used in the calculations.

2. It is not as distorted by extreme observations as the range.

3. The units are somewhat difficult to work with. (They are the original units squared.)

Population Standard Deviation

The population standard deviation is the square root of the population variance. The formula for the population standard deviation is:

$$\textbf{Population Standard Deviation} \qquad \sigma = \sqrt{\frac{\Sigma(X - \mu)^2}{N}} \qquad [3-9]$$

Sample Variance

The conversion of the population variance formula to the sample variance formula is not as direct as the change made when we went from the population mean formula to the sample mean formula. Recall in that instance we replaced μ with $\overline{X}$ and N with n.

The conversion from population variance to sample variance requires a change in the denominator. Instead of substituting n, the number in the sample, for N, the number in the population, we replace N with $(n - 1)$. Thus the formula for the sample variance is:

$$\textbf{Sample Variance} \qquad s^2 = \frac{\Sigma(X - \overline{X})^2}{n - 1} \qquad\qquad [3-10]$$

Where:

s^2 is the symbol for the sample variance. It is read as "s squared."
X is the value of each observation in the sample.
$\overline{X}$ is the mean of the sample.
n is the total number of observations in the sample.

Changing the denominator to $(n - 1)$ seems insignificant, however the use of n tends to underestimate the population variance. The use of $(n - 1)$ in the denominator provides an appropriate correction factor.

Sample Standard Deviation

The sample standard deviation is used as an estimator of the population standard deviation. The sample standard deviation is the square root of the sample variance. The formula is:

$$\textbf{Standard Deviation} \qquad s = \sqrt{\frac{\Sigma(X - \overline{X})^2}{n - 1}} \qquad\qquad [3-11]$$

Interpretation and Uses of the Standard Deviation

The standard deviation is used to measure the spread of the data. A small standard deviation indicates that the data is clustered close to the mean, thus the mean is representative of the data. A large standard deviation indicates that the data are spread out from the mean and the mean is not as representative of the data.

Chebyshev's Theorem

We can use Chebyshev's theorem to determine the percent of the values that lie within a specified number of standard deviations of the mean.

> ***Chebyshev's theorem***: For any set of observations (sample or population), the proportion of the values that lie within k standard deviations of the mean is at least $1 - 1/k^2$, where k is any constant greater than 1.

The theorem holds for any set of observations regardless of the shape of the distribution.

The Empirical Rule

Chebyshev's theorem can be applied to any set of values: that is, the distribution of values can have any shape. If the distribution is approximately symmetrical and bell shaped, then the ***Empirical Rule,*** or ***Normal Rule*** as it is often called, is applied.

> ***Empirical Rule***: For a symmetrical, bell-shaped frequency distribution, approximately 68 percent of the observations will lie within plus and minus one standard deviation of the mean; about 95 percent of the observations will lie within plus and minus two standard deviations of the mean; and practically all (99.7 percent) will lie within plus and minus three standard deviations of the mean.

The rule states that:

21. The mean, plus and minus one standard deviation, will include about 68% of the observations.
22. The mean, plus and minus two standard deviations, will include about 95% of the observations.
23. The mean, plus and minus three standard deviations, will include about 99.7% of the observations.

The Mean and Standard Deviation of Grouped Data

The mean and the standard deviation are usually determined using the individual values. However, when given only a frequency distribution, we can estimate the mean and standard deviation. A mean or standard deviation from grouped data is an *estimate* of the corresponding actual values.

The Arithmetic Mean

To approximate the arithmetic mean of data organized into a frequency distribution, we begin by assuming the observations in each class are represented by the midpoint of the class. The mean of a sample of data organized in a frequency distribution is computed by:

$$\text{Arithmetic Mean of Grouped Data} \quad \bar{X} = \frac{\sum fM}{n} \qquad [3\text{-}12]$$

Where:

$\bar{X}$ is the designation for the sample mean.
M is the midpoint of each class.
f is the frequency in each class.
fM is the frequency in each class times the midpoint of the class.
$\sum fM$ is the sum of these products.
n is the total number of frequencies.

Standard Deviation

The formula for the sample standard deviation for grouped data is:

$$\text{Standard Deviation, Grouped Data} \quad s = \sqrt{\frac{\sum f(M - \bar{X})^2}{n-1}} \qquad [3\text{-}13]$$

Where:

s is the symbol for the sample standard deviation.
M is the midpoint of a class.
f is the class frequency.
n is the total number of observations in the sample.

Glossary

Arithmetic mean: The sum of observations divided by the total number of observations.

Chebyshev's theorem: For any set of observations (sample or population), the minimum proportion of the values that lie within k standard deviations of the mean is at least $1 - 1/k^2$, where k is any constant greater than 1.

Empirical Rule: For a symmetrical, bell-shaped frequency distribution, approximately 68 percent of the observations will lie within plus and minus one standard deviation of the mean; about 95 percent of the observations will lie within plus and minus two standard deviations of the mean; and practically all (99.7 percent) will lie within plus and minus three standard deviations of the mean.

Geometric mean: The nth root of the product of n values.

Mean Deviation: The mean of the absolute values of the deviations from the arithmetic mean.

Measure of location: A single value that summarizes a set of data. It locates the center of the values.

Median: The midpoints of the values after all observations have been ordered from the smallest to the largest, or from largest to smallest. Fifty percent of the observations are above the median and 50 percent are below the median.

Mode: The value of the observation that appears most frequently.

Negatively skewed distribution: The long tail is to the left or in the negative direction. The mean is smaller than the median or mode.

Parameter: A characteristic of a population.

Positively skewed distribution: The long tail is to the right; that is, in the positive direction. The mean is larger than the median or the mode.

Range: The difference between the largest and smallest values in a data set.

Standard Deviation: The square root of the variance.

Statistic: A characteristic of a sample.

Weighted mean: The value of each observation is multiplied by the number of times it occurs. The sum of these products is divided by the total number of observations to determine the weighted mean.

Symmetrical distribution: A distribution that has the same shape on either side of the median.

Variance: The arithmetic mean of the squared deviations from the mean.

Chapter Problems

Problem 1

A comparison shopper employed by a large grocery chain recorded these prices for a 340-gram jar of Kraft blackberry preserves at a sample of six supermarkets selected at random.

Supermarket	Price X
1	$1.56
2	1.60
3	1.51
4	1.67
5	1.56
6	1.58
Total	$9.48

a. Compute the arithmetic mean.

b. Compute the median.

c. Compute the mode.

Solution 1

a. Determine the mean price of this raw data by summing the prices for the six jars and dividing the total by six. Recall the formula for the mean of a sample was given previously. See Formula [3-2].

$$\bar{X} = \frac{\Sigma X}{n} = \frac{\$9.48}{6} = \$1.58$$

b. As noted above the *median* is defined as the middle value of a set of data, after the data is arranged from smallest to largest. The prices for the six jars of blackberry preserves have been ordered from a low of $1.26 up to $1.42. Because this is an even number of prices the median price is halfway between the third and the fourth price. The median is $1.32.

Prices Arranged from Low to High:

$1.51 $1.56 $1.56 $1.58 $1.60 $1.67

L   L

$$\text{Median} = \frac{\$1.56 + \$1.58}{2} = \$1.57$$

Suppose there are an odd number of blackberry preserve prices, such as shown in the table.

$1.56	$1.56	$1.58	$1.60	$1.67

The median is the middle value ($1.58). To find the median, the values must first be ordered from low to high.

c. The mode is the price that occurs most often. The price of $1.56 occurs twice in the original data and is the mode.

Exercise 3.1

Check your answers against those in the ANSWER section.

The number of semester credit hours for seven part-time college students is: 8, 5, 4, 10, 8, 3, and 4.

Compute the:

a. mean   b. median   c. mode

Problem 2

From 1992 to 2006 the number of cell phones sold per month by Wagoner Enterprises increased from 5 to 300 (in thousands). Compute the mean annual percent increase in the number of cell phones sold.

Solution 2

The geometric mean (*GM*) annual percent increase from one time period to another is determined using formula [3-5].

$$GM = \sqrt[n]{\frac{\text{Value at the end of the period}}{\text{Value at the start of the period}}} - 1 \qquad [3-5]$$

Note that there are 14 years between 1992 and 2006, so, $n = 14$.

$$GM = \sqrt[14]{\frac{300}{5}} - 1 = \sqrt[14]{60.0} - 1 = 1.33971 - 1.00000 = 0.33971$$

For those with a $\sqrt[x]{y}$ key on their calculator, the geometric mean can be solved quickly by:

$$GM = \sqrt[n]{\frac{300}{5}} - 1 = \sqrt[14]{60.0} - 1$$

Using $\sqrt[x]{y}$	Display
$300 \div 5 =$	60
Depress $\sqrt[x]{y}$	
Depress 14	1.33971
Depress $-1 =$	0.33971, or about 34%

The value 1 is subtracted, according to formula [3-5], so the rate of increase is 0.33971, or 33.971% per year. The sale of hospital beds increased at a rate of almost 34% per year.

Exercise 3.2

Check your answers against those in the ANSWER section.

In 1991, thirty acres of woods was valued at $475 per acre. In 2006 the acreage was valued at $2850 per acre.

What is the geometric mean annual percent increase in value?

Problem 3

A sample of the amounts spent in November for propane gas to heat homes of similar sizes in Duluth revealed these amounts (to the nearest dollar):

$241 $262 $226 $179 $156 $142 $158 $159 $153 $151 $225 $244

What is the range? Interpret your results.

Solution 3

Recall that the range is the difference between the largest value and the smallest value.

$$\text{Range} = \text{Largest Value} - \text{Smallest Value} = (\$262 - \$142) = \$120$$

This indicates that there is a difference of $120 between the largest and the smallest heating cost.

Problem 4

Using the heating cost data in Problem 3, compute the mean deviation.

Solution 4

The mean deviation is the mean of the absolute deviations from the arithmetic mean. For raw, or ungrouped data, it is computed by first determining the mean. Next, find the difference between each value and the arithmetic mean. Finally, total these differences and divide the total by the number of observations. We ignore the sign of each difference. Formula [3-2] for the sample mean and formula [3-7] for the mean deviation are shown below.

Sample Mean

$$\overline{X} = \frac{\Sigma X}{n} \quad [3-2]$$

Mean Deviation

$$MD = \frac{\Sigma \left| X - \overline{X} \right|}{n} \quad [3-7]$$

The table below shows the data values, each data value minus the mean, and the absolute value of the deviations from the mean.

In other words, the signs of the deviations from the mean are disregarded.

Payment X	$\left\| X - \overline{X} \right\|$		Absolute Deviations
$241	|$+48 |	=	$48
262	| +69 |	=	69
226	| +33 |	=	33
179	| −14 |	=	14
156	| −37 |	=	37
142	| −51 |	=	51
158	| −35 |	=	35
159	| −34 |	=	34
153	| −40 |	=	40
171	| −22 |	=	22
225	| +32 |	=	32
244	| +51 |	=	51
$2,316			$466

$$\overline{X} = \frac{\Sigma X}{n} = \frac{\$2,316}{12} = \$193.00$$

$$MD = \frac{\Sigma \left| X - \overline{X} \right|}{n} = \frac{\$466}{12} = \$38.83$$

The mean deviation indicates that the typical electric bill deviates $38.83 from the mean of $193.00.

Check your answers against those in the ANSWER section.

A sample of the amount of rent paid for one bedroom apartments of similar size near the University of Akron are:

$335 $515 $385 $635 $578 $500 $535 $462 $410 $373 $410 $430

a. What is the range? Interpret your results.   **b.** Compute the mean deviation.

Problem 5

The hourly wages for a sample of plumbers were grouped into the following frequency distribution. Since the wages have been grouped into classes, we refer to the following distribution as being *grouped* data. Compute the arithmetic mean.

Hourly Wages	Number f
$8 up to $10	3
$10 up to $12	6
$12 up to $14	12
$14 up to $16	10
$16 up to $18	7
$18 up to $20	2
	40

Solution 5

The arithmetic mean of this sample data, grouped into a frequency distribution involve using the following table and the formula [3-12].

To find the mean:

Step 1: Find the midpoint M of each class. It is assumed that the observations in each class are represented by the midpoint of the class.

For the first class it is:

$$M = \frac{8+10}{2} = \frac{18}{2} = 9$$

Wage Rate	Frequency f	Class Midpoint M	f M
$8 up to $10	3	$9.00	$27.00
$10 up to $12	6	11.00	66.00
$12 up to $14	12	13.00	156.00
$14 up to $16	10	15.00	150.00
$16 up to $18	7	17.00	119.00
$18 up to $20	2	19.00	38.00
Total	40		$556.00

Step 2: Multiply the frequency f by the midpoint M for each class.

For the first class it is: $f M = 3 \times 9 = 27$

Step 3: Find the sum of the fM column. $\Sigma f M = 556$

Step 4: Find the mean using formula [3-12]

$$\overline{X} = \frac{\Sigma f M}{n} = \frac{\$556.00}{40} = \$13.90$$

We computed two measures of location for the hourly wage data. Observe that the mean ($13.90) and the mode ($13.00) are different. Generally, this is the case.

Exercise 3.4

Check your answers against those in the Answer section. The annual exports of 50 medium-sized manufacturers were organized into a frequency distribution. (Exports are in $ millions). Compute the mean.

Exports	Frequency
$6 up to $9	2
$9 up to $12	8
$12 up to $15	20
$15 up to $18	14
$18 up to $21	6

Problem 6

At Sarasota College there are 10 instructors, 12 assistant professors, 20 associate professors, and 5 professors. Their average annual salaries are $54,000, $65,000, $78,000, and $88,000, respectively. What is the weighted mean salary?

Solution 6

The number of faculty for each rank is not equal. Therefore, it is not appropriate simply to add the average salaries of the four ranks and divide by 4. We have a better method for weighting the averages. In this problem the salaries for each rank are multiplied by the number of faculty in that rank, the products totaled, then divided by the number of faculty. The result is the weighted mean.

$$\overline{X} = \frac{w_1 X_1 + w_2 X_2 + w_3 X_3 + w_4 X_4}{w_1 + w_2 + w_{31} + w_4}$$

$$= \frac{10(\$54,000) + 12(\$65,000) + 20(\$78,000) + 5(\$88,000)}{10 + 12 + 20 + 5}$$

$$= \frac{\$3,320,000}{47}$$

$$= \$70,638$$

Exercise 3.5

Check your answers against those in the ANSWER section.

During the past month an electronics store sold 31 model EL733 calculators for $30 each, 42 model EL480 calculators for $10 each, 47 model FX115 calculators for $20 each, and 63 model BA35 calculators for $24 each.

What is the weighted mean price of the calculators?

Problem 7

Using the same heating cost data in Problem 3, compute the variance and the standard deviation.

Solution 7

The sample variance, designated s^2, is based on squared deviations from the mean. For ungrouped raw data, it is computed using formula [3-10].

$$s^2 = \frac{\Sigma(X - \overline{X})^2}{n - 1} \qquad [3-10]$$

To compute the variance:

Step 1: Compute the mean.

Step 2: Find the difference between each observation and the mean. Square the difference.

Step 3: Find the sum of all the squared differences.

Step 4: Divide the sum of the squared differences by the number of items in the sample minus one.

X	$\overline{X}$	$(X - \overline{X})$	$(X - \overline{X})^2$
$241	$193	$48	2,304
262	193	69	4,761
226	193	33	1,089
179	193	−14	196
156	193	−37	1,369
142	193	−51	2,601
158	193	−35	1,225
159	193	−34	1,156
153	193	−40	1,600
171	193	−22	484
225	193	32	1,024
244	193	51	2,601
$2,316		0	20,410

$$\overline{X} = \frac{\Sigma X}{n} = \frac{2,316}{12} = 193$$

$$s^2 = \frac{\Sigma(X - \overline{X})^2}{n-1} = \frac{20,410}{12-1} = 1,855.45$$

$$s = \sqrt{\frac{\Sigma(X - \overline{X})^2}{n-1}} = \sqrt{1,855.45} = 43.074 = 43.07$$

The standard deviation of the sample, designated by s, is the square root of the variance. The square root of 1,855.45 is $43.07. Note that the standard deviation is in the same unit as the original data, that is, dollars.

Exercise 3.6

Check your answers against those in the ANSWER section.

The manager of a fast-food restaurant selected several cash register receipts at random. The amounts spent by customers were $12, $15, $16, $10, and $27. Compute the:

a. range   **b.** the mean   **c.** the sample variance   **d.** the sample standard deviation

---

Problem 8

The office manager of the Mallard Glass Company is investigating the ages in months of the company's personal computers currently in use. The ages of 30 units selected at random were organized into a frequency distribution. Compute the range.

Age to the Nearest Month	Number of Personal Computers
20 up to 25	3
25 up to 30	5
30 up to 35	10
35 up to 40	7
40 up to 45	4
45 up to 50	1

Solution 8

The range is the difference between the lower class limit of the lowest class and the upper class limit of the highest class.

Range = Upper Class Limit − Lower Class Limit

Range = 50 − 20 = 30 months

Problem 9

Using the ages of the personal computer equipment in Problem 8, compute the mean, the variance, and the standard deviation for the grouped data.

Solution 9

Formula [3-12] is used to compute the mean for grouped data.

$$\text{Arithmetic Mean of Grouped Data} \quad \overline{X} = \frac{\Sigma f M}{n} \qquad [3\text{-}12]$$

Where:

$\overline{X}$ is the designation for the sample mean.
M is the midpoint of each class.
f is the frequency in each class.
fM is the frequency in each class times the midpoint of the class.
ΣfM is the sum of these products.
n is the total number of observations in the sample.

Formula [3-13] is used to compute the sample standard deviation for grouped data.

$$\text{Standard Deviation, Grouped Data} \quad s = \sqrt{\frac{\Sigma f (M - \overline{X})^2}{n-1}} \qquad [3\text{-}13]$$

Where:

s is the symbol for the sample standard deviation.
M is the midpoint of the class.
f is the class frequency.
n is the total number of observations in the sample.

Applying these formulas to the distribution of the ages of the personal computers in Problem 8, the mean is 33.67 the variance is 40.8345, and the standard deviation is 6.39 months.

The computations involve using the following table and the appropriate formulas.

Age to the Nearest Month	f	Midpoint M	fM	Midpoint – Mean	$(M-\overline{X})$	$(M-\overline{X})^2$	$f(M-\overline{X})^2$
20 up to 25	3	22.5	67.5	22.5 – 33.67 =	-11.17	124.77	374.31
25 up to 30	5	27.5	137.5	27.5 – 33.67 =	-6.17	38.07	190.35
30 up to 35	10	32.5	325.0	32.5 – 33.67 =	-1.17	1.37	13.70
35 up to 40	7	37.5	262.5	37.5 – 33.67 =	3.83	14.67	102.69
40 up to 45	4	42.5	170.0	42.5 – 33.67 =	8.83	77.97	311.88
45 up to 50	1	47.5	47.5	47.5 – 33.67 =	13.83	191.27	191.27
Σ	30		1010.0			0	1184.20

To find the mean:

Step 1: Find the midpoint M of each class. For the first class it is: $M = \dfrac{25 + 20}{2} = \dfrac{45}{2} = 22.5$

Step 2: Multiply the frequency f by the midpoint M for each class.

For the first class it is: $f M = 3 \times 22.5 = 67.5$

Step 3: Find the sum of the $f M$ column. $\Sigma f M = 1010.0$

Step 4: Find the mean using formula [3-12] $\overline{X} = \dfrac{\Sigma f M}{n} = \dfrac{1010}{30} = 33.666 = 33.67$

To find the standard deviation:

Step 1: Subtract the mean $\overline{X}$ from the midpoint M of each class. That is find $\left(M - \overline{X} \right)$.

For the first class it is: $\left(M - \overline{X} \right) = 22.5 - 33.67 = -11.17$

Step 2: Square the difference between the class midpoint and the mean. That is find: $\left(M - \overline{X} \right)^2$

For the first class it is: $\left(M - \overline{X} \right)^2 = (-11.17)^2 = 124.77$

Step 3: Multiply the squared difference between the class midpoint and the mean by the class frequency. That is find: $f \left(M - \overline{X} \right)^2$

For the first class it is: $f \left(M - \overline{X} \right)^2 = 3(124.77) = 374.31$

Step 4: Find the sum of the $f \left(M - \overline{X} \right)^2$ column. $\Sigma f (M - \overline{X})^2 = 1184.20$

Step 5: Find the standard deviation using formula [3-13]

$$s = \sqrt{\dfrac{\Sigma f (M - \overline{X})^2}{n - 1}} = \sqrt{\dfrac{1184.20}{30 - 1}} = \sqrt{\dfrac{1184.20}{29}} = \sqrt{40.8345} = 6.39019 = 6.39$$

Note that the variance is $s^2 = 40.8345$

Problem 10

A sample of the business faculty at state-supported institutions in Ohio revealed the mean income to be $72,000 for 9 months with a standard deviation of $4,000. Use Chebyshev's Theorem and the Empirical Rule to estimate the proportion of faculty who earn more than $64,000 but less than $80,000.

Solution 10

To find the proportion of faculty who earn between $46,000 and $58,000 we must first determine k; k is the number of standard deviations above or below the mean.

$$k = \frac{X - \bar{X}}{s} = \frac{\$64,000 - \$72,000}{\$4,000} = -2.00$$

$$k = \frac{X - \bar{X}}{s} = \frac{\$80,000 - \$72,000}{\$4,000} = 2.00$$

Applying Chebyshev's theorem: $1 - \dfrac{1}{k^2} = 1 - \dfrac{1}{2^2} = 0.75$

This means that at least 75 percent of the faculty earn between $64,000 and $80,000.

The Empirical rule states that about 68 percent of the observations fall within one standard deviation of the mean, 95 percent are within plus and minus two standard deviations of the mean, and virtually all (99.7%) will lie within three standard deviations from the mean. Hence, about 95 percent of the observations fall between $64,000 and $80,000, found by $\bar{X} \pm 2s = \$52,000 \pm 2(\$3,000)$. If we conclude that we have a bell shaped distribution, most of the observations fall within the interval.

CHAPTER 3 ASSIGNMENT

DESCRIBING DATA: NUMERICAL MEASURES

Name _____ Section _____ Score
_____

Part I   Select the correct answer and write the appropriate letter in the space provided.

_____ 1. The arithmetic mean is computed by
    a. finding the value that occurs most often.
    b. finding the middle observation and dividing by 2.
    c. summing the values and dividing by the number of values.
    d. selecting the value in the middle of the data set.

_____ 2. To compute the arithmetic mean at least the
    a. nominal level of measurement is required.
    b. ordinal level of measurement is required.
    c. interval level of measurement is required.
    d. ratio level of measurement is required.

_____ 3. The value that occurs most often in a set of data is called the
    a. mean.
    b. median.
    c. geometric mean.
    d. mode.

_____ 4. What level of measurement is required to determine the mode?
    a. at least nominal level
    b. at least ordinal
    c. at least interval level
    d. ratio

_____ 5. For a symmetric distribution
    a. the mean is larger than the median.
    b. the mode is the largest value.
    c. the mean is smaller than the median.
    d. the mean and median are equal.

_____ 6. Which of the following is *not* true about the arithmetic mean.
    a. all the values are used in its calculation
    b. half of the observations are always larger than the mean
    c. it is influenced by a large value
    d. it is found by summing all the values and dividing by the number of observations

_____ 7. In a *negatively* skewed distribution
   a. the mean is smaller than the median.
   b. the mean is larger than the median.
   c. the mean and median are equal.
   d. the median and the mode are equal.

_____ 8. What is the lowest level of measurement required for the median?
   a. nominal   b. ordinal
   c. interval   d. ratio

_____ 9. The Dow Jones Industrial Average increased from 6110 at the end of the first quarter in 1996 to 11,109 at the end of the first quarter in 2006. The annual rate of increase is best described by the
   a. geometric mean.   b. weighted mean.
   c. median.   d. mode.

_____ 10. What is the shape of a frequency distribution with an arithmetic mean of 12,000 pounds, a median of 12,000 pounds, and a mode of 12,000 pounds?
   a. flat   b. symmetric
   c. geometrically skewed   d. positively skewed

_____ 11. The mean deviation
   a. is the average of all the values.
   b. is the midpoint of the range.
   c. is the average of how far each value is from the median.
   d. is the average of how far each value is from the mean.

_____ 12. The sum of the deviations from the mean is always
   a. equal to the mean.
   b. equal to zero.
   c. always positive.
   d. equal to the median.

_____ 13. The square of the standard deviation is equal to
   a. the mean.
   b. the variance.
   c. the median.
   d. the mean deviation.

_____ 14. What is the shape of a frequency distribution with an arithmetic mean of 800 pounds, median of 758 pounds, and a mode of 750 pounds?
   a. negatively skewed   b. symmetric
   c. geometrically skewed   d. positively skewed

_____ 15. According to the Empirical Rule, about what percent of the observations are within 2 standard deviations of the mean?
   a. 50   b. 68
   c. 99.7   d. 95

Part II Find the answers to each of the following questions. Show essential calculations.

16. A study conducted by the Toledo police at the intersection of Byrne and Heatherdowns for the 7 to 9 AM drive time revealed the following number of vehicles proceeded through the intersection after the light changed. The information reported below is for a sample of seven days during a six month period

    | 6 | 12 | 7 | 12 | 8 | 4 | 5 |

    a. Compute the range.

a.

    b. Compute the sample mean.

b.

    c. What is the median?

c.

    d. What is the mode?

d.

    e. Describe the skewness.

e.

17. A shipment of packages to the Solomon Company included 10 packages weighing 7.4 pounds, 12 weighing 8.2 pounds and 6 weighing 8.7 pounds. What value would you use as a typical amount for the weight of a package?

17.

18. The mean daily attendance for eight large employers in Dade County is as follows:

95.7%, 95.3%, 95.5%, 95%, 94.7%, 93.7%, 93.8% 90.7%.

Find the average daily attendance for the county.

18.

19. From 1985 to 2006 the net sales for the J.M. Smucker Company increased from $157 million to $687 million. Compute the mean annual percent increase in net sales.

19.

20. The numbers of orders placed online with Jaysmart Electronics for the last 12 months were:
1136 1090 1273 1104 1180 1271 1211 887 1008 1300 1370 1263

a. Compute the range.

a.

b. Compute the mean deviation.

a.

c. Compute the standard deviation.

21. The mean number of gallons of gasoline pumped per customer at Ray's Marathon Station is 9.5 gallons with a standard deviation of 0.75 gallons. The median number of gallons pumped is 10.0 gallons. The arithmetic mean amount of time spent by a customer in the station is 6.5 minutes with a standard deviation of 2.0 minutes.

a. According to Chebyshev's Theorem, what proportion (percent) of the customers spend between 3.30 minutes and 9.70 minutes at the station?

a.

b. According to the Empirical Rule, what proportion of the customers pump between 8.00 gallons and 11.00 gallons?

b.

22. The Ohio Bureau of Employment gathered the following sample information on the number of hours unemployed workers spent looking for work last week.

Hours spent Searching	Number of Unemployed
0 up to 10	3
10 up to 20	7
20 up to 30	15
30 up to 40	10
40 up to 50	5
TOTAL	40

a. Determine the mean.

a.

b. Determine the variance and the standard deviation.

b.

CHAPTER 4
DESCRIBING DATA:
DISPLAYING AND EXPLORING DATA

Chapter Goals

When you have completed this chapter, you will be able to:

1. Develop and interpret a dot plot.

2. Develop and interpret a stem-and-leaf display.

3. Develop and interpret quartiles, deciles, and percentiles.

4. Construct and interpret box plots.

5. Compute and understand the coefficient of skewness.

6. Draw and interpret a scatter diagram.

7. Set up and interpret a contingency table.

Introduction

We continue our study of descriptive statistics with measures of dispersion, such as dot plots, stem and leaf displays, quartiles, percentiles, and box plots. Dot plots, a stem-and-leaf display, and box plots give additional insight into where the values are concentrated and dispersed and the general shape of the data. Finally we consider bivariate data where we observe two variables for each individual or observation selected.

Dot Plots

In Chapter 2 we grouped data in classes and constructed a histogram. When we organize the data into classes, we lose the exact value of the observations. *Dot plots* group data as little as possible, hence we do not lose the identity of the individual observations.

> *Dot Plot*: A graph for displaying a set of data. Each numerical value is represented by a dot placed above a horizontal number line.

To develop a dot plot we display a dot for each observation along a horizontal number line indicating the value of each piece of data. For multiple observations we pile the dots on top of each other.

The steps to follow in developing a dot plot graph are:

1. Sort the data from smallest to largest.

2. Draw and label a number line.

3. Place a dot ● for each observation.

Length of Service (in years)					
7	6	2	10	6	6
5	8	4	8	4	7
6	5	3	3	7	5

As an example, the lengths of service, in years, of a sample of eighteen employees are given.

Step 1: Sort the data from smallest to largest.

Step 2: Draw the number line and label it as shown.

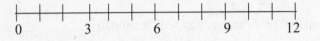

Step 3: Place a dot ● for each observation.

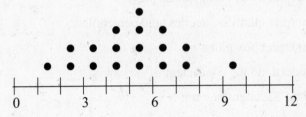

We note that the data range is from 2 to 10 years and that the data clusters around 6 years.

Stem-and-Leaf Displays

A stem-and-leaf display is a combination of sorting and graphing.

> ***Stem-and-Leaf Display***: A statistical technique for displaying a set of data. Each numerical value is divided into two parts: The leading digit(s) become the *stem*, and the trailing digits the *leaf*. The stems are located along the main vertical axis, and the leaf for each observation along the horizontal axis.

To develop a **stem-and-leaf chart** the first step is to locate the largest value and the smallest value. This will provide the range of the stem values. The **stem** is the leading digit or digits of the number, and the **leaf** is the trailing digit. For example, the number 15 has a stem value of 1 and a leaf value of 5. For another problem the number 231 has a stem value of 23 and a leaf value of 1.

Shown at the right are the amounts spent (in dollars) in the grocery store by a sample of 12 people.

$12	$28	$32	$24	$17	$6
$34	$18	$22	$42	$36	$26

The range of values is from $6 to $42. The first digit of each number is the stem and the second digit is the leaf. The first customer (upper left) spent $12. Hence, the stem value is 1 and the leaf value is 2. After each trailing digit is arranged from low to high, the completed display is shown at the right.

Leading Digit	Trailing Digit
0	6
1	278
2	2468
3	246
4	2

Other Measures of Dispersion

The standard deviation is the most widely used measure of dispersion. However there are several others, which include *Quartiles*, *Deciles*, and *Percentiles*.

Quartiles

Recall that the median divides data that has been placed in order from smallest to largest, such that half the values are below the median and half are above the median. If we divide the lower and upper set of values into two equal parts, we have quartiles. Quartiles divide a set of data into four equal parts.

> **First Quartile** The point below which one-fourth or 25% of the ranked data values lie. (It is designated Q_1)

> **Third Quartile** The point below which three-fourths or 75% of the ranked data values lie. (It is designated Q_3)

Logically the median is the **Second Quartile** (designated Q_2). The values corresponding to Q_1, Q_2 and Q_3 divide a set of data into four equal parts.

Deciles and Percentiles

Just as quartiles divide a distribution into 4 equal parts, deciles divide a distribution into ten equal parts; and percentiles divide a distribution into 100 equal parts.

For example: If you were told that your Scholastic Aptitude Test score was in the 9th decile, you could assume that 90 percent of those taking the test had a lower score than yours and that 10 percent had a higher score. A grade point average in the 55th percentile means that 55 percent of students have a lower GPA than yours and that 45 percent have a higher GPA.

The procedure for finding the quartile, decile, and a percentile for ungrouped data is to order the data from smallest to largest. Then use text formula [4-1].

> **Location of a Percentile** $\qquad L_p = (n+1)\dfrac{P}{100} \qquad [4-1]$

Where:
L_p refers to the location of the desired percentile.
n is the number of observations.
P is the desired percentile

Note that this is a generic formula for percentiles, deciles and quartiles.

For example, if you had a set of data with 49 observations in ordered array and wanted to locate the 78th percentile, then let $P = 78$ and $n = 49$ so $L_p = (n+1)\dfrac{P}{100} = (49+1)\dfrac{78}{100} = 39$. Thus you would locate the 39th observation.

If you wanted to locate the 6th decile, then let $P = 60$ and $L_p = (n+1)\dfrac{P}{100} = (49+1)\dfrac{60}{100} = 30$. Thus you would locate the 30th observation. Note that the 6th decile equals the 60 percentile.

Box Plots

A **box plot** is a graphical display that helps us picture how a set of data is distributed relative to the quartiles.

> **Box plot**: A graphical display based on five statistics: the minimum value, Q_1 (the first quartile), Q_2 the median, Q_3 (the third quartile) and the maximum value.

To construct a box plot we need five pieces of information. We need the minimum value, Q_1 (the first quartile), Q_2 the median, Q_3 (the third quartile) and the maximum value. The difference between Q_3 and Q_1 is called the **interquartile range**. The middle 50% of the data is contained within the interquartile range. The details for constructing and interpreting a box plot are found in Problem 4 of the Chapter Problems.

Skewness

Another characteristic of a set of data is the shape of the distribution. There are four shapes commonly observed: **symmetric**, **positively skewed**, **negatively skewed**, and **bimodal**. The measures of location and the measures of dispersion are both descriptive characteristics of a set of data.

A third characteristic of a distribution is its **skewness**. As noted before, a **symmetric** distribution has the same shape on either side of the median and it has no skewness. For a **positively skewed** distribution the long tail is to the right, the mean is larger than the median or the mode, and the mode appears at the highest point on the curve. For a **negatively skewed** distribution the mode is the largest value and is at the highest point of the curve, while the mean is the smallest. A bimodal distribution will have two or more peaks. The **coefficient of skewness** is used to describe how a distribution is skewed.

> **Coefficient of skewness:** A measure to describe the degree of skewness.

Text Formula [4–2] is for Pearson's Coefficient of Skewness.

$$\textbf{Pearson's Coefficient of Skewness} \qquad sk = \frac{3(\overline{X} - \text{Median})}{s} \qquad [4-2]$$

Where:

sk is the coefficient of skewness.
$\overline{X}$ is the mean.
s is the standard deviation.

Characteristics of the coefficient of skewness are:

- The coefficient of skewness, designated sk, measures the amount of skewness and may range from –3.0 to +3.0.

- A value near –3, such as –2.57, indicates considerable negative skewness.

- A value such as 1.63 indicates moderate positive skewness.

- A value of 0, which will occur when the mean and median are equal, indicates the distribution is symmetrical and that there is no skewness.

This information is summarized in the chart.

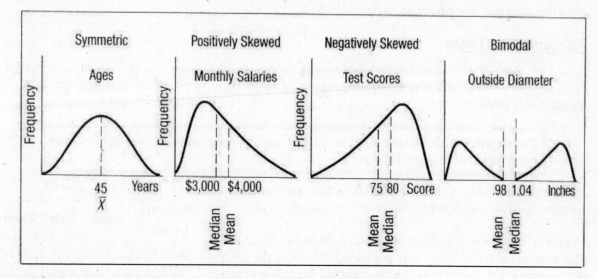

Describing the Relationship Between Two Variables

To summarize the distribution of a set of data, in Chapter 2 we used a histogram and in the first part of this chapter we used dot plots and stem-and-leaf displays. We studied a single variable sometimes called univariate data.

When we study the relationship between two variables we refer to the data as **bivariate**.

> **Bivariate data:** A collection of paired data values.

For example a realtor might want to study the relationship between the selling price of a home and the number of days the home is on the market.

One technique used to study the relationship between variables is a **scatter diagram**.

> **Scatter diagram:** A graph in which paired data values are plotted on an X,Y Axis.

The steps to follow in developing a scatter diagram are:

1. We need two variables.

2. We scale one variable (x) along the horizontal axis (X – Axis) of a graph and the corresponding variable (y) along the vertical axis (Y – Axis).

3. Place a dot ● for each (x, y) pair of observations.

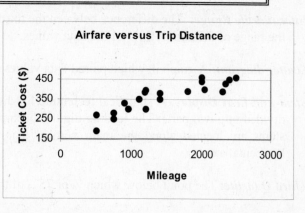

Usually one variable depends on another.

The scatter diagram shows the relationship between airfare and the total flight distance for a random sample of 20 airfares offered by a popular internet discount travel broker. It appears that as the flight distance increases, the cost of the airfare increases.

Contingency Table

When we study the relationship between two or more variables when one or both are nominal or ordinal scale, we tally the results into a two-way table. This two-way table is referred to as a *contingency table.*

> **Contingency table:** A table used to classify sample observations according to two or more identifiable characteristics.

A contingency table is a cross tabulation that simultaneously summarizes two variables of interest and their relationship.

A survey of 60 school children classified each as to gender and the number of times lunch was purchased at school during a four-week period. Each respondent is classified according to two criteria – the number of times lunch was purchased and gender.

Bought Lunch	Gender		
	Boys	Girls	Total
0 up to 10	10	5	15
10 up to 20	20	25	45
Total	30	30	60

Glossary

Bivariate data: A collection of paired data values.

Box Plot: A graphical display based on five statistics: the minimum value, Q_1 (the first quartile), Q_2 (the median), Q_3 (the third quartile) and the maximum value.

Contingency table: A table used to classify sample observations according to two or more identifiable characteristics.

Dot Plot: A graph for displaying a set of data. Each numerical value is represented by a dot placed above a horizontal number line.

First Quartile: The point below which ¼ or 25% of the ranked data values lie. (It is designated Q_1).

Interquartile Range: The difference between the third quartile, Q_3, and the first quartile, Q_1,. It is the range of the middle 50% of the data values.

Scatter diagram: A graph in which paired data values are plotted on an *X, Y Axis*

Stem-and-Leaf Display: A statistical technique for displaying a set of data. Each numerical value is divided into two parts: The leading digit(s) become the *stem*, and the trailing digits the *leaf*. The stems are located along the main vertical axis, and the leaf for each observation along the horizontal axis.

Third Quartile: The point below which ¾ or 75% of the ranked data values lie. (It is designated Q_3)

Chapter Problems

Problem 1

Computer City has compiled the following sales data regarding the number of computers sold each day for the past 18 days. Construct a dot plot for the data.

Solution 1

Step 1: Sort the data from smallest to largest.

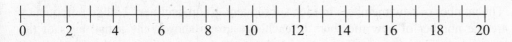

Number of computers sold					
8	12	5	12	16	9
11	18	9	11	12	10
11	15	3	10	10	12

Step 2: Draw the number line and label it as shown.

Step 3: Place a dot ● for each observation.

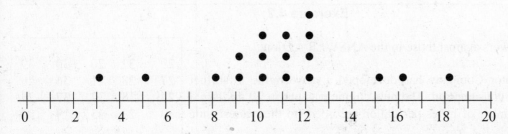

We note the data range is from 3 to 18 computers and the data clusters around 11 computers.

Exercise 4.1

Check your answers against those in the ANSWER section.

Listed below are the selling prices (in thousands of dollars) of a sample of 20 vehicles sold by salespeople employed by Ray Steele Auto Group in Albuquerque, New Mexico.

26	21	18	22	29
28	28	25	28	24
30	22	35	35	25
35	25	20	37	26

a. Sort the data from low to high. **b.** Draw a dot plot for the data.

Problem 2

The ages of 32 people who signed up for a one year membership at Gym last month are shown in the table at the right. Construct a stem-and-leaf chart for the ages of the new members.

28	37	23	33	35	21	←Low
46	30	36	28	42	39	
41	33	60	29	34	42	
32	51	55	28	49	61	←High
28	22	28	24	38	52	

Solution 2

As noted, an observation is broken down into a leading digit and a trailing digit. The leading digit is called the **stem** and the trailing digit the **leaf**. The youngest age of a new member is 21 years. This is represented by a stem unit of 2 and a leaf unit of 1. A new member who is 46 years old is represented by a stem unit of 4 and a leaf unit of 6. The youngest age is 21 and the oldest new member is 61. So the stem values range from 2 to 6 using an increment of 10 years. The usual practice is to order the leaf observations within from smallest to largest within each stem unit.

Stem	Leaf
2	1234688889
3	0233456789
4	12269
5	125
6	01

21	22	23	24	26	28	28	28	28	29	30	32	33	33	34
35	36	37	38	39	41	42	42	46	49	51	52	55	60	61

The display shows that there is a concentration of data in the 20 up to 30 years group and the 30 up to 40 years group. The number of new members in each subsequent group declines. Unlike a frequency table, not only are the number of new members in each age group shown, the actual ages of the members in each group are also shown. For example, there are three members in the 50 up to 60 years group and the three values are 51, 52, and 55.

Exercise 4.2

Check your answers against those in the ANSWER section.

The Jansen Motor Company has developed a new engine to further reduce gasoline consumption. The new engine was put in 20 mid-sized cars and the number of miles per gallon recorded (to the nearest mile per gallon).

29	32	20	30	39
27	28	21	36	20
27	18	32	37	29
30	23	25	19	30

Use the Jansen Motor Company data to construct a stem-and-leaf chart.

Problem 3

The selling prices (in thousands of dollars) for a sample of 15 recreational vehicles sold by GetAway RV's and Boats are shown in the table. Determine the following:

$20	$56	$65	$17	$26	$90	$13	$27
$16	$68	$86	$80	$50	$25	$92	

a. The first quartile. **b.** The third quartile. **c.** Determine the median.

Solution 3

Step 1: Organize the 15 observations into an ordered array from smallest to largest:

13	16	17	20	25	26	27	50	56	65	68	80	86	90	92

Step 2: Locate the first quartile, let $P = 25$ and $L_p = (n+1)\dfrac{P}{100} = (15+1)\dfrac{25}{100} = 4$

Describing Data: Displaying and Exploring Data

a. Step 3: Locate the 4th observation in the array which is 20. Thus $Q_1 = 20$ or $20,000.

Step 4: Locate the third quartile, let $P = 75$ and $L_p = (n+1)\dfrac{P}{100} = (15+1)\dfrac{75}{100} = 12$

b. Step 5: Locate the 12th observation in the array which is 80. Thus $Q_3 = 80$ or $80,000.

Step 6: Locate the median, let $P = 50$ and $L_p = (n+1)\dfrac{P}{100} = (15+1)\dfrac{50}{100} = 8$

c. Step 7: Locate the 8th observation in the array which is 50. Thus $Q_2 =$ the median $= 50$ or $50,000.

In the above example with 15 observations the location formula yielded a whole number result. Suppose we were to add one more observation (95) to the data list.

| 13 | 16 | 17 | 20 | 25 | 26 | 27 | 50 | 56 | 65 | 68 | 80 | 86 | 90 | 92 | 95 |

What is the third quartile now?

To locate the third quartile, let $P = 75$ and $n = 16$, so $L_p = (n+1)\dfrac{P}{100} = (16+1)\dfrac{75}{100} = 12.75$

Then locate the 12th and 13th observation in the array which are 80 and 86. The value of the third quartile is 0.75 of the distance between the 12th and 13th value. We must calculate $0.75(86 - 80) = 4.5$ Thus $Q_3 = (80 + 4.5) = 84.5$ or $84,500.

Problem 4

Use the selling price of the recreational vehicles data from Problem 3 to develop a box plot.

Solution 4

Step 1: Identify the five essential pieces of data:

Minimum value = 13, $Q_1 = 20$, $Q_2 = 50$ $Q_3 = 80$, Maximum value = 92

Step 2: Create an appropriate scale along the horizontal axis.

Step 3: Draw a box that starts at $Q_1 = 20$, and ends at $Q_3 = 80$. Inside the box we place a vertical line to represent the median 50. We then extend horizontal lines from the box to the minimum (12) and the maximum (92).

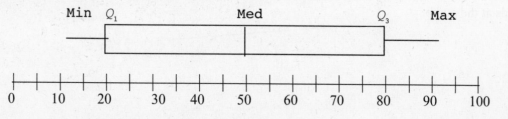

The box plot shows that the middle 50 percent of the RV's sold for between $20,000 and $80,00. Thus, the interquartile range is $80,000-$20,000 = $60,000. Also the distribution is somewhat positively skewed, since the line from Q_3 (80) to the maximum (92) is longer than the line from Q_1 (20) to the minimum (13).

In other words the 25% of the data larger than the third quartile is spread out more than the 25% of the data less than the first quartile.

Exercise 4.3

Check your answers against those in the ANSWER section.

Listed to the right are the selling prices (in thousands of dollars) for a sample of 19 lakeside lots in Pinnacle Peak, a vacation home community in the Blue Ridge mountains.

86	61	148	81
39	142	140	65
28	85	90	92
25	50	85	85
82	120	137	

Determine the following:
a. the first quartile   b. the third quartile
c. the median   d. Draw a box plot for the data.

Problem 5

The research director of a large oil company conducted a study of the buying habits of consumers with respect to the amount of gasoline purchased with credit cards at the pump. The arithmetic mean amount is 11.50 gallons, and the median amount is 11.95 gallons. The standard deviation of the sample is 4.5 gallons. Determine the coefficient of skewness. Comment on the shape of the distribution.

Solution 5

The coefficient of skewness measures the general shape of the distribution. A distribution that is symmetrical has no skewness and the coefficient of skewness is 0. Skewness ranges from −3 to +3. The direction of the long tail of the distribution points in the direction of the skewness. If the mean is larger than the median, the skewness is positive. If the median is larger than the mean, the skewness is negative.

The coefficient of skewness is found by formula [4-2]. For this problem:

$$sk = \frac{3(\overline{X} - \text{median})}{s}$$

$$= \frac{3(11.50 - 11.95)}{4.5}$$

$$= -0.30$$

This indicates that there is a slight negative skewness in the distribution of gasoline purchases with credit cards at the pump.

Problem 6

It is believed that the annual repair cost for the German sports car *Sprocket* is related to its age. A sample of 10 cars resulted in the scatter diagram shown at the right.

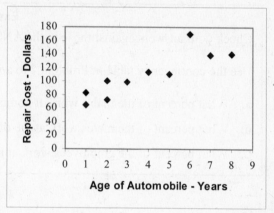

a.   How many cars were studied?

b.   Estimate the repair cost for a 7-year old car.

c.   How would you characterize the relationship between age and repair cost?

Solution 6

a.   Counting the points reveals that 10 cars were studied.

b.   The estimated repair cost for a 7-year old car is approximately $140.

c.   It appears that the older the car, the higher the repair cost.

Problem 7

A survey of the 40 employees of Systems Consultants LLC classified each as to gender and how many days a month they spent working at home or at the company office place.

Work	Gender		
Place	Male	Female	Total
Home	8	14	22
Office	12	6	18
Total	20	20	40

a.   What percent of the females work at home?

b.   What percent of the employees work at home?

c.   How would you characterize the relationship between working at home and gender?

Solution 7

a. Percent females working at home $= \dfrac{14}{20} = 0.70 = 70\%$

b. Percent employees working at home $= \dfrac{22}{40} = 0.55 = 55\%$

c. Obviously more females prefer to work at home

Exercise 4.6

Check your answers against those in the ANSWER section.

Use the contingency table in Problem 7 to answer the following:

a. What percent of the males work at home?

b. What percent of the males work at the office?

c. What percent of the employees work at the office?

Describing Data: Displaying and Exploring Data

CHAPTER 4 ASSIGNMENT

DESCRIBING DATA: DISPLAYING AND EXPLORING DATA

Name _____ Section _____ Score _____

Part I   Select the correct answer and write the appropriate letter in the space provided.

_____ **1.** A dot plot shows the range of values along the:
   a. vertical axis.   **b.** (x, y) diagonal axis.
   c. median axis.   **d.** horizontal axis.

_____ **2.** When displaying data with a dot plot, we:
   a. do not lose the identity of an individual data point
   b. are able to show the range of the values.
   c. are able to see the shape of the distribution.
   d. all of the above are correct.

_____ **3.** A scatter diagram is a graphic tool used to portray:
   a. the mean of the data values.   **b.** the range of the data values.
   c. the midpoint of data values.   **d.** the relationship between variables.

_____ **4.** In a stem and leaf display:
   a. the leaf is the leading digit or digits of the number.
   b. the stem is the leading digit or digits of the number.
   c. the stem or the leaf can be the leading digit or digits of the number.
   d. the stem is the trailing digit.

_____ **5.** Which one of the following measures of dispersion does *not* divide a set of observations into equal parts?
   a. quartiles   **b.** deciles
   c. percentiles   **d.** standard deviations

_____ **6.** The interquartile range is the difference between:
   a. the second and third quartile.   **b.** the second and fourth quartile.
   c. the first and third quartile.   **d.** the first and last quartile.

_____ **7.** A box plot is based on:
   a. the mean.   **b.** percentiles.
   c. deciles.   **d.** the first and third quartile, the median, the maximum and the minimum.

_____ **8.** A contingency table :
   a. can only be used when there are two levels of each variable.
   b. can be used to study the relationship between ordinal or nominal level variables.
   c. can only be used with interval or ratio level variables.
   d. is constructed from the quartiles of a data set..

_____ 9.The interquartile range is based on:
   a. the median.
   b. the mean deviation.
   c. the square of the mean deviation.
   d. the middle 50 percent of the observations.

_____ 10. The coefficient of skewness is a measure:
   a. of the relationship of the mode and median.
   b. based on the mean deviation.
   c. of the symmetry of a distribution.
   d. based on the middle 50 percent of the observations.

Part II   Show all of your work. Write the answer in the space provided.

11. The ages of a sample of 30 people living in assisted living facilities in Columbia, South Carolina are shown in the table.

Construct a dot plot for the data.

76	74	71	78	80	67
80	82	67	88	72	78
85	76	84	82	83	80
72	82	77	79	86	89
69	70	82	86	78	77

12. The following stem and leaf plot shows the scores on a recent test of Pre-Calculus students.

STEM	LEAF
5	6 8
6	1 2 2 4 8
7	0 4 6 6
8	0 4 4 6 6 6 6 6
9	0 2 6
10	0

a. How many students took the test?

a.

b. What were the highest and lowest scores?

b.

c. How many students scored 70 or higher?

c.

d. What percent of the students scored lower than 70?

d.

13. The revenues of the top eleven personal computer manufacturers are given (in hundred millions).

15	17	23	26	27	35
72	88	91	98	102	

a. Compute the first quartile.

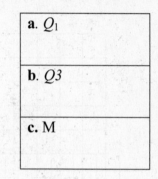

a. Q_1

b. $Q3$

c. M

b. The third quartile.

c. Determine the median.

d. Draw a box plot for the data.

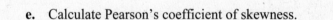

e. Calculate Pearson's coefficient of skewness.

e.

14. The following table gives the miles per gallon and the load capacity for 6 SUV's.

Miles per Gallons	Load Capacity
19	860
17	970
16	1035
16	1165
14	1180
13	1360

a. Develop a scatter diagram for the data.

b. How would you characterize the relationship between miles per gallon and load capacity?

_____

15. The Fulton County Farm Bureau held a health screening clinic for its members. The results for the blood pressure screening portion of the clinic are summarized in the table by age group and blood pressure.

Blood Pressure	Age			
	Under 25	25 to 50	Over 50	Total
Low	20	30	37	87
Medium	44	81	93	218
High	24	45	75	144
Total	88	156	205	449

a. What percent of the members have high blood pressure?

a.

b. What percent of the under age 25 members have low blood pressure?

b.

c. How would you characterize the relationship between medium blood pressure and being over age 50?

_____

CHAPTER 5
A SURVEY OF PROBABILITY CONCEPTS

Chapter Goals

When you have completed this chapter, you will be able to:

1. Define probability.

2. Describe the classical, empirical, and subjective approaches to probability.

3. Explain the terms *experiment*, *event*, *outcome*, *permutations,* and *combinations*.

4. Define the terms *conditional probability* and *joint probability*.

5. Calculate probabilities using the *rules of addition* and *rules of multiplication*.

6. Apply a tree diagram to organize and compute probabilities.

7. Calculate a probability using Bayes' theorem.

Introduction

The emphasis in Chapters 2, 3 and 4 is on *descriptive statistics*. In those chapters we described methods used to collect, organize, and present data, as well as measures of central location, dispersion, and skewness used to summarize data. A second facet of statistics deals with computing the chance that something will occur in the future. This facet of statistics is called *inferential statistics*.

An inference is a generalization about a population based on information obtained from a sample. Probability plays a key role in inferential statistics. It is used to measure the reasonableness that a particular sample could have come from a particular population.

What is Probability?

Probability allows us to measure effectively the risks in selecting one alternative over the others. In general, it is a number that describes the chance that something will happen.

> *Probability*: A value between zero and one, inclusive, describing the relative possibility (chance or likelihood) an event will occur.

Probability is expressed either as a percent or as a decimal. The likelihood that any particular event will happen may assume values between 0 and 1.0. A value close to 0 indicates the event is unlikely to occur, whereas a value close to 1.0 indicates that the event is quite likely to occur.

To illustrate, a value of 0.60 might express your degree of belief that tuition will be increased at your college, and 0.50 the likelihood that your first marriage will end in divorce.

In our study of probability we will make extensive use of several key words. They are: *experiment, outcome*, and *event*.

> *Experiment*: A process that leads to the occurrence of one and only one of several possible observations.

For example, you roll a die and observe the number of spots that appear face up. The experiment is the act of rolling the die. Your survey company is hired by Ford to poll consumers to determine if they plan to buy a new American-made car this year. You contact a sample of 5,000 consumers. The act of counting the consumers who indicated they would purchase an American-made car is the experiment.

> *Outcome*: A particular result of an experiment.

One outcome of the die-rolling experiment is the appearance of a 6. In the experiment of counting the number of consumers who plan to buy a new American-made car this year, one possibility is that 2,258 plan to buy a car. Another outcome is that 142 plan to buy one.

> *Event*: A collection of one or more outcomes of an experiment.

Thus, the *event* that the number appearing face up in the die-rolling experiment is an even number is the collection of the *outcomes* 2, 4, or 6. Similarly the event that more than half of those surveyed plan to buy a new American made car is the collection of the outcomes 2,501, 2,502, 2,503, and so on all the way up to 5,000.

Approaches To Probability

Two types or classifications of probability are discussed: the objective and subjective viewpoints. Objective probability is subdivided into *classical probability* and *empirical probability*.

Classical Probability

Classical probability is based on the assumption the outcomes of an experiment are equally likely.

> *Classical Probability*: A probability based on the assumption that outcomes of an experiment are *equally likely*.

To find the probability of a particular outcome we divide the number of favorable outcomes by the total number of possible outcomes as shown in text formula [5-1].

$$\text{Probability of an event} = \frac{\text{Number of favorable outcomes}}{\text{Total number of possible outcomes}} \qquad [5-1]$$

For example, you take a multiple-choice examination and have no idea which one of the choices is correct. In desperation you decide to guess the answer to each question. The four choices for each question are the outcomes. They are equally likely, but only one is correct. Thus the probability that you guess a particular answer correctly is 0.25 found by 1 ÷ 4.

If only one of several events can occur at one time, we refer to the events as *mutually exclusive*.

> **Mutually exclusive:** The occurrence of one event means that none of the other events can occur at the same time.

An employee selected at random is either a male or female but cannot be both. A computer chip cannot be defective and not defective at the same time.

If an experiment has a set of events that includes every possible outcome, then the set of events is called *collectively exhaustive.*

> **Collectively exhaustive:** At least one of the events must occur when an experiment is conducted.

For example: In a die-tossing experiment every outcome will be either an even number or an odd number. Thus the set is collectively exhaustive. If the set of events is collectively exhaustive and the events are mutually exclusive, the sum of the probabilities equals 1.

Empirical Concept

Empirical or *relative frequency* is the second type of objective probability. It is based on the number of times an event occurs as a proportion of a known number of trials.

> **Empirical probability:** The probability of an event happening is the fraction of the time similar events happened in the past.

To compute an empirical probability we use the following formula:

$$\text{Empirical Probability} = \frac{\text{Number of times the event occurs}}{\text{Total number of observations}}$$

For example, suppose the Civil Aeronautics Board maintained records on the number of times flights arrived late at the Newark International Airport. If 54 flights in a sample of 500 were late, then, according to the relative frequency formula, the probability a particular flight is late is found by:

$$\text{Probability of a late flight} = \frac{\text{number of late flights}}{\text{number of flights}} = \frac{54}{500} = 0.108$$

Based on past experience, the probability is 0.108 that a flight will be late.

The empirical approach is based on the *law of large numbers*. In brief, the law of large numbers says that more observations will provide a more accurate estimate of the probability.

> **Law of Large Numbers:** Over a large number of trials the empirical probability of an event will approach its true probability.

According to the law of large numbersers, we expect an empirical probability based on 500 observations to be closer to the true probability than an empirical probability based on 50 observations.

Subjective Probability

If there is little or no past experience or information on which to base a probability, a probability may be determined subjectively. Thus you evaluate the available opinions and other subjective information and then make a decision and arrive at a subjective probability.

> **Subjective concept of probability**: The likelihood (probability) of a particular event happening that is assigned by an individual based on whatever information is available.

Subjective probability is based on judgment, intuition, or "hunches." The likelihood that the horse, Sir Homer, will win the race at Ferry Downs today is based on the subjective view of the racetrack oddsmaker.

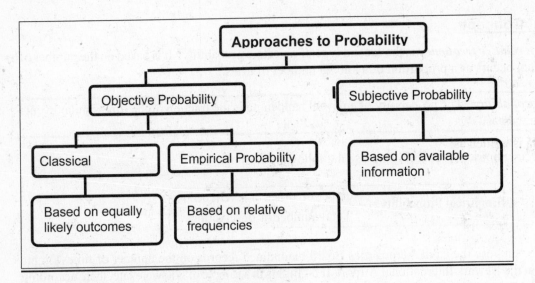

Some Rules for Assigning Probability

In the study of probability it is often necessary to combine the probabilities of events. This is accomplished through both *rules of addition* and *rules of multiplication*. There are two rules for addition, the *special rule of addition* and the *general rule of addition*.

Special Rule of Addition

To apply the special rule of addition, the events must be *mutually exclusive*. The special rule of addition states that the probability of the event A *or* the event B occurring is equal to the probability of event A plus the probability of event B. The rule is expressed by using text formula [5-2]:

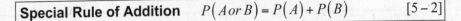

| **Special Rule of Addition** | $P(A \, or \, B) = P(A) + P(B)$ | [5 – 2] |

To apply the special rule of addition the events must be mutually exclusive. This means that when one event occurs none of the other events can occur at the same time.

Venn Diagram

Venn diagrams, developed by English logician J. Venn, are useful for portraying events and their relationship to one another. They are constructed by enclosing a space, usually in a form of a rectangle, which represents the possible events. Two mutually exclusive events such as A and B can then be portrayed as in the following diagram by enclosing regions that do not overlap (that is, that have no common area).

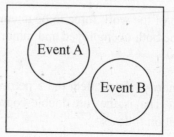

The Complement Rule

The probability of an event occurring, *P(A),* plus the probability the event *not* occurring, written P(~A), must logically equal one. This is expressed as:

$$P(A) + P(\sim A).$$

The ***complement rule*** is used to determine the probability of an event occurring by subtracting the probability of the event *not* occurring from one (1).

This formula is written as:

Complement Rule:	$P(A) = 1 - P(\sim A)$	$[5-3]$

In some situations it is more efficient to determine the probability of an event happening by determining the probability of it not happening and subtracting from 1.

General Rule of Addition

When we want to find the probability that two events will both happen, we use the concept known as *joint probability.*

> *Joint probability*: A probability that measures the likelihood two or more events will happen concurrently.

Note that if two events, A and B, are mutually exclusive, their joint probability equals zero. If two events are not mutually exclusive, their joint probability is greater than zero.

The general rule of addition is used for two events A and B not necessarily mutually exclusive. It is expressed using the text formula [5-4].

| **General Rule of Addition** | $P\left(A\ or\ B\right)=P\left(A\right)+P\left(B\right)-P\left(A\ and\ B\right)$ | [5 – 4] |

Where:

$P(A)$ is the probability of the event A.

$P(B)$ is the probability of the event B.

P(A and B)   is the probability that both events A and B occur.

For example, a study showed 15 percent of the work force to be unemployed, 20 percent of the work force to be minorities, and 5 percent to be both unemployed and minorities. What percent of the work force are either minorities or unemployed?

Note that if P (unemployed) and P (minority) are totaled, the 5 percent who are both minorities and unemployed are counted in both groups. That is, they are double-counted. They must be subtracted to avoid this double counting. The computation follows.

$$P\ (\text{unemployed or minority}) = P\ (\text{unemployed}) + P\ (\text{minority}) - P\ (\text{unemployed and minority})$$
$$= 0.15 + 0.20 - 0.05$$
$$= 0.30$$

These two events are not mutually exclusive and would appear as follows in a Venn diagram:

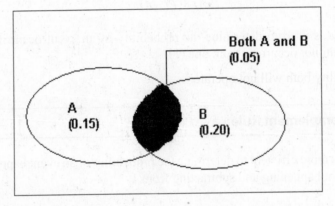

In the above example the likelihood of being both a minority and unemployed is a joint probability.

Using the Addition Rule

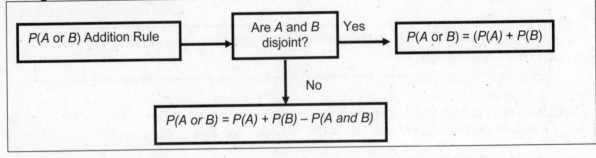

Rules of Multiplication

There were two rules of addition, the general rule and the special rule. We used the general rule when the events were not necessarily mutually exclusive and the special rule when the events were mutually exclusive. We have an analogous situation with the rules of multiplication.

Special Rule of Multiplication

We use the *special rule of multiplication* when the events A and B are *independent*. Two events are independent if the occurrence of one does not affect the probability of the other.

> ***Independence***: The occurrence of one event has no affect on the probability of the occurrence of another event.

A way to look at independence is to assume two events A and B occur at different times. For example, flipping a coin and getting tails is not affected by rolling a die and getting a two.

For two independent events A and B, the probability that A and B will both occur is found by multiplying the two probabilities. This is the *special rule of multiplication*.

The special rule of multiplication is used to combine events where the probability of the second event does not depend on the outcome of the first event.

It is written as shown in text formula [5-5].

Special Rule of Multiplication	$P(A \text{ and } B) = P(A) \times P(B)$	[5 – 5]

As an example, a nuclear power plant has two independent safety systems. The probability the first will not operate properly in an emergency $P(A)$ is 0.01, and the probability the second will not operate $P(B)$ in an emergency is 0.02. What is the probability that in an emergency both of the safety systems will not operate? The probability both will not operate is:

$$P(A \text{ and } B) = P(A) \times P(B)$$
$$= 0.01 \times 0.02$$
$$= 0.0002$$

The probability 0.0002 is called a joint probability, which is the simultaneous occurrence of two events. It measures the likelihood that two (or more) events will happen together (jointly).

The probability for three independent events, A, B, and C, the special rule of multiplication used to determine the probability of all three events will occur is:

$$P(A \text{ and } B \text{ and } C) = P(A) \times P(B) \times P(C)$$

If two events are not independent, they are referred to as *dependent*. That is, the probability of an event may depend on whether another event has occurred. Event dependence leads to another probability concept called *conditional probability*.

> ***Conditional probability***: The probability of a particular event occurring, given that another event has occurred.

Probability measures uncertainty, but the degree of uncertainty changes as new information becomes available. Symbolically, the probability of event A given that event B has occurred is written $P(A|B)$.

The vertical line " | " does not mean divide; it is read "given that" as in the probability of A "given that" B already occurred.

The concept of conditional probability provides us with another way to understand independence. If two events A and B are independent, then $P(A|B) = P(A)$ and also $P(B|A) = P(B)$.

General Rule of Multiplication

The *general rule of multiplication* is used to combine events that are not independent. That is, they are dependent on each other. For two events, the probability of the second event is affected by the outcome of the first event. Under these conditions, the probability of both A and B occurring is given in formula [5-6].

| General Rule of Multiplication | $P(A \text{ and } B) = P(A) \times P(B|A)$ | [5-6] |

Where $P(B|A)$ is the probability of B occurring given that A has already occurred.

For example, among a group of twelve prisoners, four had been convicted of murder. If two of the twelve are selected for a special rehabilitation program, what is the probability that both of those selected are convicted murderers?

Let A_1 be the first selection (a convicted murderer) and A_2 the second selection (also a convicted murderer). Then $P(A_1) = 4/12$. After the first selection, there are 11 prisoners, 3 of whom are convicted of murder, hence $P(A_2|A_1) = 3/11$. The probability of both A_1 and A_2 happening is:

$$P(A_1 \text{ and } A_2) = P(A_1) \times P(A_2 | A_1)$$
$$= \frac{4}{12} \times \frac{3}{11}$$
$$= 0.0909$$

Using the Multiplication Rule

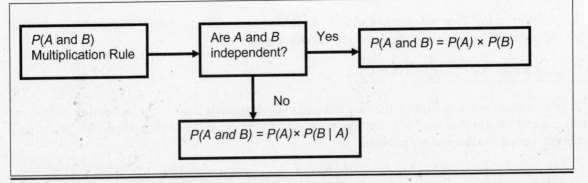

Recall from Chapter 4, that if we tally the results of a survey into a two-way table, the results of this tally can be used to determine various possibilities. This two-way table is referred to as a *contingency table.*

> *Contingency table:* A table used to classify sample observations according to two or more identifiable characteristics.

A contingency table is a cross tabulation that simultaneously summarizes two variables of interest and their relationship.

At the right is an example.

A survey of 200 school children classified each as to gender and the number of times Pepsi-Cola was purchased each month at school. Each respondent is classified according to two criteria-the number of times Pepsi was purchased and gender.

Bought Pepsi	Gender		
	Boys	Girls	Total
0	5	10	15
1	15	25	40
2 or more	80	65	145
Total	100	100	200

Tree Diagrams

The *tree diagram* is a graph that is helpful in organizing the calculations that involve several stages. Each segment in the tree is one stage of the problem. The branches are weighted probabilities. The concept is shown in Problem 6.

Bayes' Theorem

Bayes' Theorem is used to revise the probability of a particular event happening based on the fact that some other event had already happened.

For example, we have three machines each producing the same items. Machine A produces 10 percent defective and Machines B and C each 5 percent defective. Suppose each machine produces one-third of the total production. Since Machine A produces one-third of all the parts, we naturally expect that prior to any experiment the probability of a defective being produced by Machine A is 0.33. Logically, the 0.33 is called a *prior probability.*

> *Prior probability*: The initial probability based on the present level of information.

A part is selected at random. It was found to be defective. The question is: what is the probability that it was produced by Machine A? As noted above, Machine A produces twice as many defective parts as Machines B and C. (A produces 10%, B and C produce 5% each). Since we discovered that the part selected was defective, the probability it was manufactured by Machine A is now greater than 0.33. Bayes' Theorem will give us this revised probability. The text formula is [5-7].

$$P(A_1 | B) = \frac{P(A_1) \times P(B | A_1)}{P(A_1) \times P(B | A_1) + P(A_2) \times P(B | A_2) + \dots + P(A_n) \times P(B | A_n)} \qquad [5-7]$$

The probabilities to be inserted in the formula are:

$P(A_1)$ = Probability the part was produced by Machine A = 0.33
$P(A_2)$ = Probability the part was produced by Machine B = 0.33
$P(A_n)$ = Probability the part was produced by Machine C = 0.33
$P(B*A_1)$ = Probability of a defect being produced by Machine A = 0.10
$P(B*A_2)$ = Probability of a defect being produced by Machine B = 0.05
$P(B*A_n)$ = Probability of a defect being produced by Machine C = 0.05

$$P(A_1|B) = \frac{0.33(0.10)}{0.33(0.10) + 0.33(0.05) + 0.33(0.05)} = \frac{0.033}{0.033 + 0.0165 + 0.0165} = \frac{0.033}{0.066} = 0.50$$

Hence, the probability that the defective part was manufactured by Machine A is increased from 0.33 to 0.50. We revised upward the probability that the part was produced by Machine A, because we obtained the additional information that the part selected was defective. This revised probability is called a *posterior probability*.

> *Posterior probability*: A revised probability based on additional information.

Principles of Counting

If the number of possible outcomes in an experiment is small, it is relatively easy to count the possible outcomes. However, sometimes the number of possible outcomes is large, and listing all the possibilities would be time consuming, tedious, and error prone. Three formulas are very useful for determining the number of possible outcomes in an experiment. They are: the *multiplication formula*, the *permutation formula*, and the *combination formula*.

The Multiplication Formula

The general rule of multiplication is used to combine events that are dependent on each other.

> *Multiplication formula*: If there are *m* ways of doing one thing, and *n* ways of doing another thing, there are *m* × *n* ways of doing both.

In terms of a formula:

> **Multiplication Formula**   Total number of arrangements $= (m)(n)$ [5 – 8]

The Permutation Formula

The permutation is an arrangement of objects or things wherein order is important. That is, each time the objects or things are placed in a different order, a new permutation results.

> *Permutation*: Any arrangements of *r* objects selected from a single group of *n* possible objects.

The formula for the number of permutations is:

> **Permutation Formula** $_nP_r = \dfrac{n!}{(n-r)!}$ [5 – 9]

Where:
P   is the number of permutations, or ways the objects can be arranged.
n   is the total number of objects.
r   is the number of objects selected.
Note: the *n*! is a notation called "*n* factorial."
For example, 4! means 4 times 3 times 2 times 1 = $4 \times 3 \times 2 \times 1 = 24$

The Combination Formula

One particular arrangement of the objects without regard to order is called a *combination*.

> **Combination**: The number of ways to choose r objects from a group of n possible objects without regard to order.

The formula for the number of combinations is:

> **Combination Formula** $\qquad {}_nC_r = \dfrac{n!}{r!(n-r)!}$ $\qquad$ [5–10]

Where:
C is the number of different combinations.
n is the total number of objects.
r is the number of objects to be used at one time.

Glossary

Classical Probability: A probability based on the assumption that the outcomes for an experiment are equally likely.

Collectively exhaustive: At least one of the events must occur when an experiment is conducted.

Combination: The number of ways to choose r objects from a group of n possible objects without regard to order.

Complement rule: A way to determine the probability of an event occurring by subtracting the probability of an event **not** occurring from 1.

Conditional probability: The probability of a particular event occurring, given that another event occurred.

Contingency table: A table used to classify sample observations according to two or more identifiable characteristics.

Event: A collection of one or more outcomes of an experiment.

Experiment: A process that leads to the occurrence of one and only one of several possible observations.

Independence: The occurrence of one event has no affect on the probability of the occurrence of another event.

Joint probability: A probability that measures the likelihood two or more events will happen concurrently.

Law of large numbers: Over a large number of trials the empirical probability of an event will approach its true probability.

Multiplication formula: If there are m ways of doing one thing, and n ways of doing another thing, there are $m \times n$ ways of doing both.

Mutually exclusive: The occurrence of one event means that none of the other events can occur at the same time.

Outcome: A particular result of an experiment.

Permutation: Any arrangements of *r* objects selected from a single group of *n* possible objects.

Posterior probability: A revised probability based on additional information.

Prior probability: The initial probability based on the present level of information.

Probability: A value between zero and one, inclusive, describing the relative possibility (chance or likelihood) an event will occur.

Subjective concept of probability: The likelihood (probability) of a particular event happening that is assigned by an individual based on whatever information is available.

Chapter Problems

Problem 1

Dunn Pontiac has compiled the following sales data regarding the number of cars sold over the past 60 selling days. Answer the following questions for the sales data shown.

Dunn Pontiac Sales Data	
Number of Cars Sold	Number of Days
0	5
1	5
2	10
3	20
4	15
5 or more	5
Total	60

   a. What is the probability that two cars are sold during a particular day?

   b. What is the probability of selling 3 or more cars during a particular day?

   c. What is the probability of selling at least one car during a particular day?

Solution 1

This problem is an example of the relative frequency type of probability, because the probability of an event happening is based on the number of times the particular event happened in the past relative to the total number of observations.

   a. The probability that exactly two cars are sold is:

$$P(2 \text{ cars}) = \frac{\text{Number of days two cars were sold}}{\text{Total number of days}} = \frac{10}{60} = 0.17$$

   b. The probability of selling three or more cars is found by using a special rule of addition given in formula [5-2]. Let *X* represent the number of cars sold. (≥ is read "greater than or equal to." The notation > would be just greater than.) Then:

$$P(X \geq 3) = P(3) + P(4) + P(5 \text{ or more}) = \frac{20}{60} + \frac{15}{60} + \frac{5}{60} = \frac{40}{60} = 0.67$$

Interpreting, three cars or more are sold 67 percent of the days.

c. The probability of selling at least one car is determined by adding the probabilities of selling one, two, three, four, and five or more cars. Again let X be the number of cars sold, then

$$P(X \geq 1) = P(1) + P(2) + P(3) + P(4) + P(5 \text{ or more})$$

$$= \frac{5}{60} + \frac{10}{60} + \frac{20}{60} + \frac{15}{60} + \frac{5}{60} = \frac{55}{60} = 0.9166 = 0.92$$

The same result can also be found by using the complement rule. Obtain the probability of the occurrence of a particular event by computing the probability it did not occur and then subtracting that value from 1.0. In this example, the probability of not selling any cars is $\frac{5}{60} = 0.083 = .08$, then $(1 - 0.08) = 0.92$.

Exercise 5.1
Check your answers against those in the ANSWER section.

A study was made to investigate the number of times adult males over 30 visit a physician each year. The results for a sample of 300 were:

a. What is the probability of selecting someone who visits a physician twice a year?

b. What is the probability of selecting someone who visits a physician?

Number of Visits	Number of Adult Males
0	30
1	60
2	90
3 or more	120
Total	300

Problem 2

A local community has two newspapers. The **Morning Times** is read by 45 percent of the households. The **USA Today** is read by 60 percent of the households. Twenty percent of the households read both papers. What is the probability that a particular household in the city reads at least one paper?

Solution 2

If we combine the probabilities (0.45, 0.60, and 0.20), they exceed 1.00. The group that reads both papers, of course, is being counted twice and must be subtracted to arrive at the answer. Let T represent the **Morning Times**, and U represent **USA Today**, and use the general rule of addition, formula [5-4]:

$$P(T \text{ or } U) = P(T) + P(U) - P(T \text{ and } U)$$

$$= 0.45 + 0.60 - 0.20$$

$$= 0.85$$

Thus, 85 percent of the households in the community read at least one paper.

Problem 3

The probability that a driver whose vehicle is stopped for a traffic violation is wearing a seatbelt is 0.70. Suppose that three vehicles have just been stopped for traffic violations. What is the probability that all three drivers are wearing seatbelts? What is the probability that at least one is wearing his seatbelt?

Solution 3

These events are independent since the probability that one driver is wearing a seatbelt does not depend on whether the other drivers are wearing their seatbelts. The special rule of multiplication, formula [5-5], is used to find the joint probability. D_1 represents the first driver, D_2 the second driver, and D_3 the third driver.

$$P(\text{all 3 wear seatbelt}) = P(D_1) \times P(D_2) \times P(D_3)$$
$$= (0.70)(0.70)(0.70)$$
$$= 0.343$$

Hence the probability that all three are wearing seatbelts is 0.343.

The probability that at least one driver wears a seatbelt is found by combining the complement rule and the multiplication rule. To explain: The probability of the first driver not wearing a seatbelt is 0.30, found by $P(\sim D_1) = 1 - 0.70$. The probability for D_2 and D_3 is also 0.30. The multiplication rule is used to obtain the probability that all three are not wearing seatbelts. Let X be the number of drivers wearing seatbelts.

$$P(X > 0) = 1 - P(0) =$$
$$= 1 - P(\sim D) \times P(\sim D) \times P(\sim D)$$
$$= 1 - 0.30 \times 0.30 \times 0.30$$
$$= 1 - 0.027 = 0.973$$

Thus, the likelihood that at least one of the drivers is wearing his seatbelt is 0.973.

Problem 4

Yesterday, the Bunte Auto Repair Shop received a shipment of four carburetors. One is known to be defective. If two are selected at random and tested:

a. What is the probability that neither one is defective?

b. What is the probability that the defective carburetor is located by testing two carburetors?

Solution 4

a. The selections of the two carburetors are not independent events because the selection of the first affects the second outcome. Use formula [5-6]. Let G_1 represent the first "good" carburetor and G_2 the second "good" one.

$$P(G_1 \text{ and } G_2) = P(G_1) \times P(G_2|G_1)$$

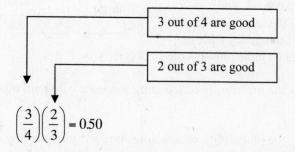

3 out of 4 are good

2 out of 3 are good

$$\left(\frac{3}{4}\right)\left(\frac{2}{3}\right) = 0.50$$

Hence, the probability that neither of the two selected carburetors is defective is 0.50.

b. The probability that the defective carburetor is found requires the general rule of multiplication and the general rule of addition.

In this case the defect may be detected either in the first test or in the second one. The general rule of multiplication is used. Let D_1 represent a defect on the first test and D_2 on the second test. The probability is:

$$P(\text{find the defect}) = P(G_1) \times P(D_2 \mid G_1) + P(D_1) \times P(G_2 \mid D_1)$$

$$= \left(\frac{3}{4}\right)\left(\frac{1}{3}\right) + \left(\frac{1}{4}\right)\left(\frac{3}{3}\right) = \frac{1}{4} + \frac{1}{4} = \frac{1}{2} = 0.50$$

To explain further, the probability that the first carburetor tested is good is $P(D_1) = \frac{3}{4}$. If the first one selected is good, then to meet the requirements of the problem the second one sampled must be defective. This conditional probability is $P(D_2|G_1) = 1/3$. The joint probability of these two events is 3/12 or $\frac{1}{4}$. The defective part could be found on the first test $P(D_1)$. Since there is one defect among the four carburetors, the probability that it will be found on the first test is $\frac{1}{4}$. If the defect is found on the first test, then the three remaining parts are good. Hence the conditional probability of selecting a good carburetor on the second trial is $1.0\ P(G_2|D_1)$. The joint probability of a defective part being followed by a good part is $\frac{1}{4}$, found by $P(D_1)$ x $P(G_2|D_1) = (1/4)(3/3) = \frac{1}{4}$. The sum of these two outcomes is 0.50.

Exercise 5.4

Check your answers against those in the ANSWER section.

Ten students are being interviewed for a class office. Six of them are female and four are male. Their names are all placed in a box and two students are selected for the interviews.

a. What is the probability that both of those selected are female?

b. What is the probability that at least one is male?

Problem 5

A large department store is analyzing the per-customer amount of purchase and the method of payment. For a sample of 140 customers, the following contingency table or cross-classified table presents the findings.

Payment Method	Amount of Purchase			Total
	B_1: Less than $20	B_2:$20 up to $50	B_3: $50 or more	
A_1: Cash	15	10	5	30
A_2: Check	10	30	20	60
A_3:Charge	10	20	20	50
Total	35	60	45	140

a. What is the probability of selecting someone who paid by cash or made a purchase of less than $20?

b. What is the probability of selecting someone who paid by check and made a purchase of more than $50?

Solution 5

a. If we combine the events "Less than $20" ($B_1$) and "Cash payment" ($A_1$), then those who paid cash for a purchase of less than $20 are counted twice. That is, these two events are not mutually exclusive. Therefore, the general rule of addition formula [5-4] is used.

$$P(A_1 \text{ or } B_1) = P(A_1) + P(B_1) - P(A_1 \text{ and } B_1)$$

$$= \frac{30}{140} + \frac{35}{140} - \frac{15}{140} = \frac{50}{140} = 0.36$$

The probability of selecting a customer who made a cash payment or purchased an item for less than $20 is 0.36.

b. Conditional probability is used to find the probability of selecting someone who paid by check (A_2) and who made a purchase of over $50 (B_3)

There are two qualifications: "paid by check" and "made a purchase of over $50." Referring to the table, 20 out of 140 customers meet both qualifications, therefore, $20 \div 140 = 0.14$.

This probability could also be computed in a three-step process.

1. The probability of selecting those who paid by check (A_2) is $60 \div 140 = 0.43$.

2. Of the 60 persons who paid by check, 20 made a purchase of over $50. Therefore $P(B_3|A_2) = 20 \div 60 = 0.33$

3. These two events are then combined using the general rule of multiplication, formula [5-6].

$$P(A_2 \text{ and } B_3) = P(A_2) \times P(B_3|A_2)$$
$$= (0.43)(0.33) = 0.14$$

Exercise 5.5			
Check your answers against those in the ANSWER section. Five hundred adults over 50 years of age were classified according to whether they smoked or not, and if they smoked, were they a moderate or heavy smoker. Also, each one was asked whether he or she had ever had a heart attack. The results are given.		Heart Attack	
	Yes	No	Total
Do not smoke	30	220	250
Moderate smoker	60	65	125
Heavy smoker	90	35	125
Totals	180	320	500

a. What is the probability of selecting a person who either has had a heart attack, or who is a heavy smoker?

b. What is the probability of selecting a heavy smoker who did not have a heart attack?

Problem 6

The probability that a person has "BLEEBS," a rare disease that occurs in young baseball players is 0.02. If a person has BLEEBS, the probability that the individual is diagnosed as having it is 0.80. On the other hand, if an individual does not have BLEEBS, the probability of being diagnosed as having it is 0.05. Given that a person is diagnosed as having BLEEBS, what is the probability that the person really does not have it?

Solution 6

This problem is solved using Bayes' Theorem. The various parts of the problem are as follows:

$P(B)$ is the probability of having BLEEBS. It is 0.02.

$P(NB)$ is the probability of not having BLEEBS. It is 0.98.

$P(D|B)$ is the probability of being diagnosed as having BLEEBS, given that the person has the disease. It is 0.80.

$P(D|NB)$ is the probability of being diagnosed as having BLEEBS, given that the person does not have the disease. It is 0.05.

$P(NB|D)$ is the revised probability of not having BLEEBS, given that the diagnosis is that of having BLEEBS.

A useful device for displaying conditional and joint probabilities is called a tree diagram. The tree diagram will be used to solve the above problem. The initial relationships are as follows.

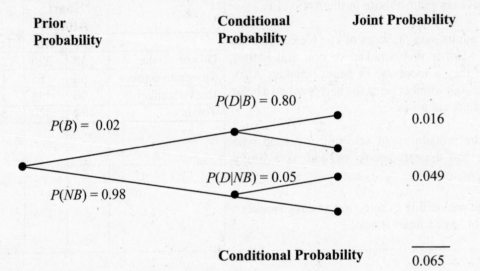

| Prior Probability | Conditional Probability | Joint Probability |

The computational form of Bayes' Theorem formula [5-7] is repeated.

$$P(NB|D) = \frac{P(NB)\,P(D|NB)}{P(B)\,P(D|B) + P(NB)\,P(D|NB)}$$

$$= \frac{(0.98)(0.05)}{(0.02)(0.80) + (0.98)(0.05)} = \frac{0.049}{0.016 + 0.049} = \frac{0.049}{0.065} = 0.7538 = 0.754$$

Interpreting, this means that even though a person is diagnosed as having BLEEBS, the probability of not actually having it is 0.754.

To explain this problem further, everyone falls into one of the two categories—they have BLEEBS or they don't. Only two percent of the population actually have the condition [$P(B) = 0.02$] and 98 percent do not [$P(NB) = 0.98$], but some people are diagnosed as having BLEEBS, when they actually do not [$P(D|NB) = 0.05$]. These are actually false positive readings.

The denominator of Bayes' Theorem computes the fraction of the population that are diagnosed as having BLEEBS. That fraction is obtained by combining the two joint probabilities as follows:

$$P(D) = P(B) \times P(D|B) + P(NB) \times P(D|NB) = \quad (0.02)(0.80) + (0.98)(0.05)$$
$$= \quad 0.065$$

The 0.065 is the fraction of the population that will be diagnosed as having BLEEBS. However, some of those diagnosed actually have the condition [$P(B) \times P(D|B) = (0.02)(0.80) = 0.016$] and some while diagnosed as having BLEEBS actually do not [$P(NB) \times P(D|NB) = (0.98)(0.05) = 0.049$]. We are interested in the fraction that are diagnosed as having the condition but really don't [$(0.049 \div 0.065) = 0.754$]. This result may seem rather startling, because more than 75 percent of the time the test results are actually incorrect. This indicates that the test for BLEEBS is not very discriminating.

Exercise 5.6
Check your answers against those in the ANSWER section.

A test on probability is to be given next week. Suppose 75 percent of the students study for the test and 25 percent do not. If a student studies for the exam, the probability that he or she will pass is 0.90. If the student does not study, the probability that he or she will pass is 20 percent. Given that the student passed the test, what is the probability he or she studied?

Problem 7

A deli bar offers a special sandwich for which there is a choice of five different cheeses, four different meat selections, and three different rolls. How many different sandwich combinations are possible?

Solution 7

Using the multiplication formula [5-8], there are five cheeses (c), four meats (m), and three rolls (r). The total number of possible sandwiches is 60 found by:

$$cmr = (5)(4)(3) = 60$$

Exercise 5.7
Check your answers against those in the ANSWER section.

The Swansons are planning to fly to Hawaii from Toronto with a stopover in Los Angeles. There are five flights they can take between Toronto and Los Angeles and ten flights between Los Angeles and Hawaii. How many different flights are possible between Toronto and Hawaii?

Problem 8

Three scholarships are available for needy students. Their values are: $2,000, $2,400, and $3,000. Twelve students have applied and no student may receive more than one scholarship. Assuming all twelve students are in need of funds, how many different ways could the scholarships be awarded?

Solution 8

This is an example of a permutation because a different assignment of the scholarships means another arrangement. Jones could be awarded the $2,000 scholarship, Sinski the $2,400 scholarship, and Peters the $3,000 scholarship. Or, Sinski could be awarded the $2,000, Seiple the $2,400 one, and Orts the $3,000 scholarship, and so on. Using formula [5-9]:

$$_nP_r = \frac{n!}{(n-r)!} = \frac{12!}{(12-3)!} = \frac{12 \times 11 \times 10 \times 9!}{9!} = 12 \times 11 \times 10 = 1,320$$

Where:

n is the total number of applicants

r is number of scholarships.

Note that the 9! in the numerator and the 9! in the denominator cancel each other.

Exercise 5.8

Check your answers against those in the ANSWER section.

Swanton Welding is setting up the shop for a new production run. Nine welding machines are available but only three spaces are available in the production area of the shop. In how many different ways can the nine welding machines be arranged in the three available spaces?

Problem 9

The basketball coach of Dalton University is quite concerned about their 40 straight losses. The frustrated coach decided to select the starting lineup for the DU-UCLA game by drawing five names from the 12 available players at random. (Assume that a player can play any position.) How many different starting lineups are possible?

Solution 9

This is an example of a combination because the order in which the players are selected is not important. Jocko, Camden, Urfer, Smith, and Marchal are the same starting lineup as Smith, Camden, Marchal, Jocko, and Urfer, and so on. Using formula [5-10]:

$$_nC_r = \frac{n!}{r!(n-r)!} = \frac{12!}{5!(12-5)!} = \frac{12 \times 11 \times 10 \times 9 \times 8 \times 7!}{5 \times 4 \times 3 \times 2 \times 1 \times 7!} = \frac{95,040}{120} = 792$$

Where:

n is the total number of available players.

r is the number in the starting lineup.

Exercise 5.9

Check your answers against those in the ANSWER section.

A major corporation has branch offices in eight major cities in the United States and Canada. The company president wants to visit five of these offices. How many different trip combinations are possible?

CHAPTER 5 ASSIGNMENT

A SURVEY OF PROBABILITY CONCEPTS

Name _____   Section _____   Score _____

Part I   Select the correct answer and write the appropriate letter in the space provided.

_____ 1.   Which of the following statements regarding probability is always correct?
   a.   A probability can range from 0 to 1.
   b.   A probability close to 0 means the event is not likely to happen.
   c.   A probability close to 1 means the event is likely to happen.
   d.   all of the above are correct.

_____ 2.   According to the classical definition of probability
   a.   All the events are equally likely.
   b.   The probability is based on hunches.
   c.   Divide the number of successes by the number of failures.
   d.   One outcome is exactly twice the other.

_____ 3.   The observation of some activity or the act of taking some measurement is called
   a.   an outcome.   **b.**   an experiment.
   c.   a probability.   **d.**   an event.

_____ 4.   The particular result of an experiment is called
   a.   an experiment.   **b.**   an event.
   c.   a probability.   **d.**   an outcome.

_____ 5.   An event is the collection of one or more
   a.   outcomes.   **b.**   combinations.
   c.   probabilities.   **d.**   experiments.

_____ 6.   If A and B are mutually exclusive events then $P(A \text{ or } B)$ equals
   a. $P(A) + P(B) - P(A \text{ and } B)$ **b.** $P(A) \times P(B)$
   c. $P(A) + P(B)$ **d.** $P(A|B) + P(B|A)$

_____ 7.   If A and B are independent events, then $P(A \text{ and } B))$ equals
   a. $P(A) + P(B|A)$.   **b.** $P(A) \times P(B)$.
   c. $P(A) + P(B)$.   **d.** $P(A|B) + P(B|A)$.

_____ 8.   Which formula represents the probability of the complement of event A?
   a. $1 + P(A)$ **b.** $1 - P(A)$
   c. $P(A)$ **d.** $P(A) - 1$

_____ 9.   The simultaneous occurrence of two events is called
   a.   prior probability   **b.**   subjective probability
   c.   conditional probability   **d.**   joint probability

10. If the probability of an event is 0.3, that means
   a. the event has a 70% chance of not occurring.
   b. the complement of the event has a 30% chance of occurring.
   c. the event has a 30% chance of not occurring.
   d. the complement of the event has a 70% chance of not occurring.

Part II Answer each question below. Be sure to show all of your work.

11. A recent study of young executives showed that 30 percent run, 20 percent bike and 12 percent do both. What is the percent of young executives who run or bike?

11.

12. A survey of publishing jobs indicates that 92 percent are completed on time. Assume that three jobs are selected for study.
   a. What is the probability they are all completed on time?

a.

   b. What is the probability that at least one was not completed on time?

b.

13. Today's local newspaper lists 20 stocks "of local interest." Of these stocks, ten increased, five decreased and five remained unchanged yesterday. If we decide to buy two of the stocks, what is the likelihood that both increased yesterday?

13.

14. Six employees of a marketing firm had effectiveness ratings as follows: 0.72, 0.46, 0.59, 0.64, 0.81 and 0.76. Find the probability of selecting an employee with the indicated effectiveness rating.
    a. Greater than 0.75.

    a. ☐

    b. Less than 0.75 but greater than 0.5.

    b. ☐

    c. Greater than the mean.

    c. ☐

    d. Not less than 0.9.

    d. ☐

15. A freight train is going to carry four tankers, six coal cars, and ten lumber cars. How many different arrangements of cars are possible?

    15. ☐

16. The United Way Campaign of Greater Toledo had fifteen applications for funding this year. If eight of these applications can be funded, how many different lists of successful applications are there?

    16. ☐

17. A market analyst is hired to provide information on the type of customers who shop at a particular store. A random survey is taken of 100 shoppers at this store. Of these 100, 73 are women. The shoppers are grouped in three age categories, under 30, 30 up to 50 and 50 and over. The data is summarized in the table.

	Women	Men	Total
Under 30	30	8	38
30 to 50	25	14	39
50 & over	18	5	23
Totals	73	27	100

Let W be the event that a randomly selected shopper is a woman.
Let A be the event that a randomly selected shopper is under 30.

a. Find the probability of $\sim W$.

a.

b. Find the probability of A.

b.

c. Find the probability of A and W.

c.

d. Find the probability of A or $\sim W$.

d.

e. Find the probability of A given W.

e.

18. Perry's Garden Center sells three brands of riding mowers—Ranger, Turfmaster, and Colt. Fifty percent of the riding mowers they sell are Rangers, thirty five percent Turfmasters, and fifteen percent Colts. Each brand of mower comes with a one-year parts and labor warranty. Based on their records, Perry knows that the chance of a warranty claim is five percent for the Ranger, 15% for the Turfmaster, and 25% for the Colt. If Perry's service manager tells him that a riding mower has just been brought in for a repair covered by the warranty,

   a. What is the chance that the riding mower is a Colt?

a.

   b. What is the chance that the riding mower is a Turfmaster?

b.

   b. What is the chance that the riding mower is a Ranger?

c.

CHAPTER 6
DISCRETE PROBABILITY DISTRIBUTIONS

Chapter Goals

After completing this chapter, you will be able to:

1. Define the terms *probability distribution* and *random variable*.

2. Distinguish between discrete and continuous probability distributions.

3. Calculate the mean, variance, and standard deviation of a discrete probability distribution.

4. Describe the characteristics of and compute probabilities using the binomial probability distribution.

5. Describe the characteristics of and compute probabilities using the hypergeometric probability distribution.

6. Describe the characteristics of and compute probabilities using the Poisson probability distribution.

Introduction

In the previous chapter we discussed the basic concepts of probability and described how the rules of addition and multiplication were used to compute probabilities. In this chapter we expand the study of probability to include the concept of a ***probability distribution***.

What is a Probability Distribution?

A ***probability distribution*** shows the possible outcomes of an experiment and the probability of each of these outcomes.

> ***Probability distribution***: A listing of all the outcomes of an experiment and the probability associated with each outcome.

How can we generate a probability distribution? As an example, the possible outcomes on the roll of a single die are shown at right.

Each face should appear on about one-sixth of the rolls. The table shows the possible outcomes and corresponding probabilities for this experiment. It is a discrete distribution because only certain outcomes are possible and the distribution is a result of counting the various outcomes.

Number of Spots on Die	Probability		
	Fraction		Decimal
1	1/6	=	0.1667
2	1/6	=	0.1667
3	1/6	=	0.1667
4	1/6	=	0.1667
5	1/6	=	0.1667
6	1/6	=	0.1667
Total	6/6	=	1.0002

The following are important characteristics of a discrete probability distribution:

1. The probability of a particular outcome is between 0 and 1 inclusive.

2. The outcomes are mutually exclusive events.

3. The list is exhaustive. So the sum of the probabilities of the various events is equal to 1.

This discrete probability distribution, presented above as a table, may also be portrayed in graphic form as shown on the right.

By convention the probability is shown on the Y-axis (the vertical axis) and the outcomes on the X-axis (the horizontal axis). This probability distribution is often referred to as a uniform distribution.

A probability distribution can also be expressed in equation form.

For example:

$P(x) = 1/6$, where x can assume the values 1, 2, 3, 4, 5, or 6.

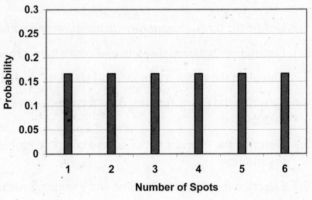

Random Variable

In any experiment of chance, the outcomes occur randomly. A ***random variable*** is a value determined by the outcome of an experiment.

> ***Random Variable***: A quantity resulting from an experiment that, by chance, can assume different values.

A random variable may have two forms: discrete or continuous. A ***discrete random variable*** may assume only distinct values and is usually the result of counting.

> ***Discrete random variable***: A variable that can assume only certain clearly separated values.

For example, the number of highway deaths in Arkansas on Memorial Day weekend may be 1, 2, 3,... Another example is the number of students earning a grade of B in your statistics class. In both instances the number of occurrences results from counting. Note that there can be 12 deaths or 15 B's but there cannot be 12.63 deaths or 15.27 B grades.

If we measure something, such as the diameter of a tree, the length of a field, or the time it takes to run the Boston Marathon, the variable is called a ***continuous random variable***.

> ***Continuous random variable***: A variable that can assume one of an infinitely large number of values within certain limitations.

In brief, if the problem involves counting something, the resulting distribution is usually a discrete probability distribution. If the distribution is the result of a measurement, then it is usually a continuous probability distribution.

What is the difference between a random variable and a probability distribution? A probability distribution lists all the possible outcomes as well as their corresponding probabilities. A random variable lists only the outcomes. We will examine the continuous random variable and the continuous probability distribution in the next chapter.

The Mean, Variance, and Standard Deviation of a Probability Distribution

In Chapter 3 we computed the mean and variance of a frequency distribution. The mean is a measure of location and the variance is a measure of the spread of the data. In a similar fashion the *mean* (μ) and the *variance* (σ^2) summarize a probability distribution.

The Mean

The *mean* μ, or expected value $E(x)$, is used to represent the central location of a probability distribution. It is also the long-run average value of the random variable. It is computed by the following formula:

| Mean of a Probability Distribution | $\mu = \Sigma\left[xP(x)\right]$ | [6–1] |

This formula directs you to multiply each outcome (x) by its probability $P(x)$; and then add the products.

Variance and Standard Deviation

While the mean is a typical value used to summarize a discrete probability distribution, it does not tell us anything about the spread in the distribution. The *variance* tells us about the spread or variation in the data. The variance is computed using the following formula:

| Variance of a Probability Distribution | $\sigma^2 = \Sigma\left[(x-\mu)^2 P(x)\right]$ | [6–2] |

The steps in computing the variance using formula [6-2] are:

1. Subtract the mean (μ) from each outcome (x) and square these differences.

2. Multiply each squared difference by its probability $P(x)$

3. Sum these products to arrive at the variance.

The *standard deviation* (σ) of a discrete probability distribution is found by calculating the positive square root of σ^2, thus $\sigma = \sqrt{\sigma^2}$.

Binomial Probability Distribution

One of the most widely used discrete probability distributions is the *binomial probability distribution*.

Characteristics of a binomial probability experiment:

1. An outcome of an experiment is classified into one of two mutually exclusive categories—a success or a failure.

2. The random variable is the number of successes in a fixed number of trials.

3. The probability of a success and failure stays the same for each trial.

4. The trials are independent, meaning that the outcome of one trial does not affect the outcome of any other trial.

Illustrations of each characteristic are:

1. Each outcome is classified into one of two mutually exclusive categories. An outcome is classified as either a "success" or a "failure." For example, 40 percent of the students at a particular university are enrolled in the College of Business. For a selected student there are only two possible outcomes—the student is enrolled in the College of Business (designated a success) or he/she is not enrolled in the College of Business (designated a failure).

2. The binomial distribution is the result of counting the number of successes in a fixed sample size. If we select 5 students, 0, 1, 2, 3, 4, or 5 could be enrolled in the College of Business. This rules out the possibility of 3.45 of the students being enrolled in the College of Business. That is, there cannot be fractional counts.

3. The probability of a success remains the same from trial to trial. In the example regarding the College of Business, the probability of a success remains at 40 percent for all five students selected.

4. Each sampled item is independent. This means that if the first student selected is enrolled in the College of Business, it has no effect on whether the second or the fourth one selected will be in the College of Business.

How a Binomial Probability Distribution is Computed

To construct a binomial probability distribution we need to know:

(1) The number of trials, designated n.
(2) The probability of success (π) on each trial.

The binomial probability distribution is constructed using the formula [6-3]:

Binomial Probability Distribution	$P(x) = {}_nC_x(\pi)^x(1-\pi)^{n-x}$	[6-3]

Where:

$_nC_x$ denotes a combination of n items selected x at a time

n is the number of trials

x is the random variable defined as the number of successes

π is the probability of success on each trial (Do not confuse it with the mathematical constant 3.416.)

The mean (μ) and variance (σ^2) of a binomial distribution can be computed by these formulas.

Mean of a binomial distribution	$\mu = n\pi$	[6-4]

Variance of a binomial distribution	$\sigma^2 = n\pi(1-\pi)$	[6-5]

Hypergeometric Probability Distribution

To qualify as a binomial distribution, the probability of a success must remain constant. In some situations this requirement can not be met. This usually happens when the size of the population is small and samples are drawn from the population and not replaced. This causes the probability of a success to change from one trial (or sample) to the next. This means the trials are not independent. As an example, suppose that we know that there are four diet sodas in a cooler containing 12 sodas. The chance of randomly selecting a diet soda from the cooler on the first try is 4/12. However, if a diet soda is selected on the first try and not put back into the cooler (i.e., not replaced), the probability of selecting a diet soda on the second try is 3/11. The probability of selecting a diet soda changed from the first to the second trial—the trials are not independent the change in the probability of the event "diet soda is selected" can only be computed if the size of the population is known. This assumes that the population is *finite*, that is, that the number of individuals, objects or measurements in the population is relatively small and known.

> *Finite population*: A population consisting of a known and relatively small number of individuals, objects, or measurements.

An outcome generating process that has all the characteristics of a binomial experiment except that the trials are not independent is called a *hypergeometric probability experiment*.

Characteristics of a hypergeometric probability experiment:

1. An outcome of each trial is characterized into one of two mutually exclusive categories—a success or a failure.

2. The random variable is the number of successes in a fixed number of trials.

3. The trials are *not independent*.

4. We assume that we sample from a finite population without replacement. So, the probability of a success *changes* from one trial of the experiment to the next.

For example, in a beverage cooler with 4 diet sodas and 8 regular sodas, what is the probability of randomly selecting two sodas that are both diet in just two tries? As describes above, the probability of a diet soda on the first try is 4/12. If a diet soda is selected on the first try and not returned to the cooler, the probability of a diet soda on the second trial is 3/11. So, the probability of selecting two diet sodas in just two attempts is $(4/12) \times (3/11) = 0.0909$. Note that in order to compute this probability it was necessary to know the size of the population.

This probability may also be calculated using the hypergeometric distribution, which is described by the formula:

Hypergeometric Distribution	$P(x) = \dfrac{\left(_{S}C_{x}\right)\left(_{N-S}C_{n-x}\right)}{\left(_{N}C_{n}\right)}$	[6 – 6]

Where:
N is the size of the population.
S is the number of successes in the population.
n is the size of the sample or the number of trials.
x is the number of successes in the sample.
C is the symbol for a combination.

In the example $N = 12$, $S = 4$, $n = 2$, and $x = 2$. Therefore,

$$P(2) = \frac{\left(_4C_2\right)\left(_{12-4}C_{2-2}\right)}{\left(_{12}C_2\right)}$$

$$= \frac{\left(\dfrac{4!}{2!2!}\right)\left(\dfrac{8!}{0!8!}\right)}{\left(\dfrac{12!}{2!10!}\right)} = \frac{\left(\dfrac{3 \cdot 2}{1}\right)\left(\dfrac{1}{1}\right)}{\left(\dfrac{12 \cdot 11}{2}\right)} = \frac{1}{11} = 0.0909$$

Hence, the probability of selecting two sodas from a cooler consisting of 4 diet sodas and eight regular sodas and getting diet sodas on both selections is 0.0909. This is the same probability we computed earlier.

Poisson Probability Distribution

Another discrete probability distribution is the *Poisson probability distribution*. It describes the number of times some event occurs during a specified interval. The intervals may be time, area, distance, or volume.

Characteristics of a Poisson probability experiment:

1. The random variable is the number of times some event occurs during a defined interval.

2. The probability of the event is proportional to the size of the interval.

3. The intervals do not overlap and are independent.

The formula for computing the probability of a success is:

| Poisson Distribution | $P(x) = \dfrac{\mu^x e^{-\mu}}{x!}$ | [6 − 7] |

Where:
$P(x)$ is the probability for a specified value of x.
x is the number of occurrences (successes).
μ is the arithmetic mean number of occurrences (successes) in a particular interval.
e is the mathematical constant 2.71828. (base of the Napierian logarithm system)

The Poisson probability distribution has many applications. For example, it can be used as a model to describe the number of new cars sold by a car salesperson in a week, the number of automobile accidents at a particular intersection in a month, or the number of incidents of a disease in a given area.

To demonstrate, suppose that the mean number of new cars sold by a particular car salesperson in a week is 7. Then the probability that this salesperson will sell exactly five new cars next week is:

$$P(5) = \frac{7^5 \times e^{-7}}{5!} \frac{16807 \times .000912}{120} = 0.1277 \ .$$

The Poisson probability distribution can also be used to approximate probabilities for a binomial probability distribution when the probability of a success on a single trial is very small and n is large. Note that the mean number of successes, μ, can be determined in binomial situations by $n\pi$, where n is the total number of trials and π is the probability of success.

Mean of a Poisson Distribution	$\mu = n\pi$	[6-8]

As an example where the Poisson distribution is applicable, suppose electric utility statements are based on the actual reading of the electric meter. In 1 out of 100 cases the meter is incorrectly read ($\pi = 0.01$). Suppose the number of errors that appear in the processing of 500 customer statements approximates the Poisson distribution ($n = 500$). In this case the mean number of incorrect statements is 5, found by $\mu = n\pi = 500 \ (0.01)$.

Using formula [6-3], finding the probability of exactly two errors appearing in 500 customer statements is rather tedious. Instead we use formula [6-7] with $\mu = 5$ and $x = 2$.

$$P(2) = \frac{5^2 \times e^{-5}}{2!} = \frac{25 \times .1353}{2} = 0.0842.$$

Or, we can merely refer to the Poisson distribution in Appendix B.5. Locate by $\mu = (5.0)$ at the top of a set of columns. Then find the x of 2 in the left column and read across to the column headed by 5.0. The probability of exactly 2 statement errors is 0.0842.

GLOSSARY

Binomial probability distribution: Describes the number of successes, x, in n independent trials of a statistical experiment. The probability of a success on a single trial, π, is the same for each trial.

Continuous random variable: A variable that can assume one of an infinitely large number of values within certain limitations.

Discrete random variable: A random variable that can assume only certain clearly separated values.

Finite population: A population consisting of a small number of individuals, objects, or measurements.

Hypergeometric probability distribution . Describes the number of successes, x, in n trials of a statistical experiment. Each trial is conducted by selecting an item without replacement from a finite population of size N.

Poisson probability distribution: Describes the number of times some event occurs during a specified interval. Also used to approximate a binomial probability distribution when the probability of success, π , is small, and n, the number of trials, is relatively large.

Probability distribution: A listing of all the outcomes of an experiment and the probability associated with each outcome.

Random Variable: A random variable whose value is determined by the outcome of a random experiment.

CHAPTER PROBLEMS

Problem 1

Bill Russe, production manager at Ross Manufacturing, maintains detailed records on the number of times each machine breaks down and requires service during the week. Bill's records show that the Puret grinder has required repair service according to the following distribution. Compute the arithmetic mean and the variance of the number of breakdowns per week.

Number of Breakdowns Per Week	Weeks	Probability
0	20	0.333
1	20	0.333
2	10	0.167
3	10	0.167
Total	60	1.000

Solution 1

The arithmetic mean, or expected number of breakdowns per week for the probability distribution, is computed using formula [6-1].

Number of Breakdowns Per Week	Probability	
x	$P(x)$	$xP(x)$
0	0.333	0.000
1	0.333	0.333
2	0.167	0.334
3	0.167	0.501
Total		1.168

$$\mu = \Sigma\left[x P(x)\right] \qquad [6-1]$$

The arithmetic mean number of times the Puret machine breaks down per week is 1.168. The variance of the number of breakdowns is computed using formula [6-2].

$$\sigma^2 = \Sigma\left[(x-\mu)^2 P(x)\right] \qquad [6-2]$$

Number of Breakdowns Per Week	Probability			
x	$P(x)$	$(x-\mu)$	$(x-\mu)^2$	$(x-\mu)^2 P(x)$
0	0.333	$0 - 1.168 = -1.168$	1.364	$(1.364)(0.333) = 0.454212$
1	0.333	$1 - 1.168 = -0.168$	0.028	$(0.028)(0.333) = 0.009324$
2	0.167	$2 - 1.168 = +0.832$	0.692	$(0.692)(0.167) = 0.115564$
3	0.167	$3 - 1.168 = +1.832$	3.356	$(3.356)(0.167) = 0.560452$
				Total 1.139552

The variance of the number of breakdowns per week is about 1.140. The standard deviation of the number of breakdowns per week is 1.07, found by $\sqrt{1.139552} = 1.0674 = 1.07$.

Problem 2

An insurance representative has appointments with four prospective clients tomorrow. From past experience she knows that the probability of making a sale on any appointment is 1 in 5 or 0.20. Use the rules of probability to determine the likelihood that she will sell a policy to 3 of the 4 prospective clients.

Solution 2

First note that the situation described meets the requirements of the binomial probability distribution. The conditions are:

1. There are a fixed number of trials—the representative visits four customers.

2. There are only two possible outcomes for each trial—she sells a policy or she does not sell a policy.

3. The probability of a success remains constant from trial to trial—for each appointment the probability of selling a policy (a success) is 0.20.

4. The trials are independent—if she sells a policy to the second appointment this does not alter the likelihood of selling to the third or the fourth appointment.

If S represents the outcome of a sale and NS the outcome of no sale, one possibility is that no sale is made on the first appointment but sales are made at the last 3.

(NS, S, S, S)

These events are independent; therefore the probability of their joint occurrence is the product of the individual probabilities. Therefore, the likelihood of no sale followed by three sales is $(0.8)(0.2)(0.2)(0.2) = 0.0064$. However, the requirements of the problem do not stipulate the location of NS. It could be the result of any one of the four appointments. The following summarizes the possible outcomes.

Location of *NS*	Order of Occurrence	Probability of Occurrence
1	*NS, S, S, S*	$(0.8)(0.2)(0.2)(0.2) = 0.0064$
2	*S, NS, S, S*	$(0.2)(0.8)(0.2)(0.2) = 0.0064$
3	*S, S, NS, S*	$(0.2)(0.2)(0.8)(0.2) = 0.0064$
4	*S, S, S, NS*	$(0.2)(0.2)(0.2)(0.8) = 0.0064$
Total		0.0256

The probability of exactly three sales in the four appointments is the sum of the 4 possibilities. Hence, the probability of selling insurance to 3 out of 4 appointments is 0.0256.

Problem 3

Now let's use formula [6-3] for the binomial distribution to compute the probability that the sales representative in Problem 2 will sell a policy to exactly 3 out of the 4 prospective clients.

Solution 3

To repeat, formula [6-3] for the binomial probability distribution is:

$$P(x) = {}_nC_x(\pi)^x(1-\pi)^{n-x} \qquad [6-3]$$

Where:

$_nC_x$ denotes a combination of n items selected x at a time

x is the number of successes, 3 in the example.

n is the number of trials, 4 in the example.

π is the probability of a success, 0.20.

$(1-\pi)$ is the probability of a failure, 0.80 found by (1 − 0.20).

The formula is applied to find the probability of selling an insurance policy to exactly 3 out of 4 potential customers.

$$P(x) = {}_nC_x(\pi)^x(1-\pi)^{n-x} = \frac{n!}{x!(n-x)!}(\pi)^x(1-\pi)^{n-x}$$

$$= \frac{4!}{3!(4-3)!}(0.20)^3(0.80)^{4-3} = 0.0256$$

Thus the probability is 0.0256 that the representative will be able to sell policies to exactly 3 out of the 4 clients visited. This is the same probability as computed earlier. Clearly, formula [6-3] leads more directly to a solution and better accommodates the situation where the number of trials is large.

Exercise 6.2

Check your answers against those in the ANSWER section.

It is known that 60 percent of all registered voters in the 42nd Congressional District are Republicans. Three registered voters are selected at random from the district. Compute the probability that exactly 2 of the 3 selected are Republicans, using:

a. The rules of probability   b. The binomial formula.

Problem 4

In Problems 2 and 3 the probability of 3 sales resulting from 4 appointments was computed using both the rules of addition and multiplication and the binomial formula. A more convenient way of arriving at the probabilities for 0, 1, 2, 3, or 4 sales out of 4 appointments is to refer to a binomial table. Use the binomial table to determine the probabilities for all possible outcomes.

Solution 4

Refer to Appendix B.9, the binomial table. Find the table where n, the number of trials, is 4. Next, find the row where $x = 0$, and move horizontally to the column headed $\pi = 0.20$. The probability of 0 sales is 0.410. The list for all possible outcome number of successes is shown at the right.

Binomial Probability Distribution	
$n = 4$	$\pi = 0.20$
Number of Successes (x)	Probability
0	0.410
1	0.410
2	0.154
3	0.026
4	0.002
	*1.002

*Slight discrepancy due to rounding

Problem 5

Use the information regarding the insurance representative, where $n = 4$ and $\pi = 0.20$, to compute the probability that the representative sells more than two policies. Also determine the mean and variance of the number of policyholders.

Solution 5

The binomial table (Appendix B.9) can be used to determine the probability. First, note that the solution must include the probability that exactly 3 policies are sold and exactly 4 policies are sold, but not 2. From Appendix B.9, $P(3) = 0.026$ and $P(4) = 0.002$. The rule of addition is then used to combine these mutually exclusive events.

$$P(\text{more than } 2) = P(3) + P(4)$$
$$= 0.026 + 0.002$$
$$= 0.028$$

Thus the probability that a representative sells more than 2 policies is 0.028.

Suppose the question asked is: "What is the probability of selling three or more policies in four trials?" Since there are no outcomes between "greater than 2" and "less than 3", the answer is exactly the same (0.028).

To determine the mean of a binomial we use text formula [6-4].

$$\mu = n\pi = 4(0.20) = 0.80$$

Thus if the sales representative has several days with 4 appointments, typically he/she will sell 0.80 policies per day.

To determine the variance of a binomial we use text formula [6-5].

$$\sigma^2 = n\pi(1-\pi) = 4(0.20)(0.80) = 0.64$$

So the standard deviation is $\sqrt{0.64} = 0.80$.

Exercise 6.3

Check your answers against those in the ANSWER section.

Labor negotiators estimate that 30 percent of all major contract negotiations result in a strike. During the next year, 12 major contracts must be negotiated. Determine the following probabilities using Appendix B.9:
a. no major strikes   b. at least 5   c. between 2 and 4 inclusive (that is 2, 3, or 4).

Exercise 6.4

Check your answers in the ANSWER section.

Refer to Exercise 6.3. Determine the mean and variance of the number of strikes next year.

Problem 6

Alden & Associates write weekend trip insurance at a very nominal charge. Records show that the probability a motorist will have an accident during the weekend and will file a claim is quite small (0.0005). Suppose Alden wrote 400 policies for the forthcoming weekend. Compute the probability that exactly two claims will be filed. Depict this distribution in the form of a chart.

Solution 6

The Poisson distribution is appropriate for this problem because the probability of filing a claim is small ($\pi = 0.0005$), and the number of trials n is large (400).

The Poisson distribution is described by formula [6-7]:

$$P(x) = \frac{\mu^x e^{-\mu}}{x!} \qquad [6-7]$$

Where:
x is the number of successes (claims filed). In this example $x = 2$
μ is the expected or mean number of claims to be filed $\mu = n\pi = (400)(0.0005) = 0.2$
e is a mathematical constant equal to 2.71828.

The probability that exactly two claims are filed is 0.0164, found by

$$P(2) = \frac{\mu^x e^{-\mu}}{x!} = \frac{(0.2)^2 (2.718)^{-0.2}}{2!} = \frac{(0.04)(0.81874)}{(2)(1)} = 0.0164$$

This indicates that the probability is small (about 0.0164) that exactly 2 claims will be filed. The calculations to determine the probability 0.0164 were shown above. As noted previously, a convenient way to determine Poisson probabilities is to refer to Appendix B.5. To use this table, first find the column where $\mu = 0.20$, then go down that column to the row where $X = 2$ and read the value at the intersection. It is 0.0164.

The probabilities computed using formula [6-8] and those in Appendix B.5 are the same. The complete Poisson distribution is shown at the right and a graph for the case where $\mu = 0.20$ is

Poisson Probability Distribution $\mu = 0.2$	
Number of Claims	Probability
0	0.8187
1	0.1637
2	0.0164
3	0.0011
4	0.0001
	1.0000

shown below. Note the shape of the graph. It is positively skewed, and as the number of claims increases, the probability of a claim decreases.

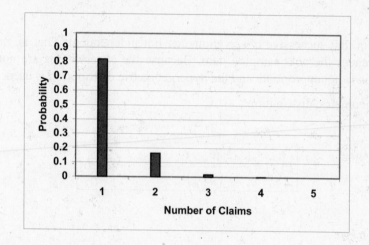

The Poisson probability distribution can be used to compute the probability of x occurrences of some event for a specified interval of time, area, volume, etc. In this case x is the number of "no shows" and the interval over which an event can occur is a single flight.

Exercise 6.5

Check your answers against those in the ANSWER section.
The probability of a typographical error on any page is 0.002. If a textbook contains 1,000 pages, compute the probability there are:

a.   No typos on a page   **b.**   At least 2 typos on a page.

Problem 7

On average 4 people per flight do not show up for the 7:30 a.m. Chicago to Denver flight on SkyBlue airlines. What is the probability that exactly 7 people do not show up for the next flight?

Solution 7

The Poisson probability distribution can be used to compute the probability of x occurrences of some event in a given interval of time, volume, distance, or area of opportunity. The probability of 7 "no shows" is computed using formula [6-7]:

$$P(x) = \frac{\mu^x e^{-\mu}}{x!}$$

$$P(x) = \frac{4^7 e^{-4}}{7!} = \frac{(16384)(0.01832)}{5040} = 0.0595$$

Exercise 6.6

Customers arrive at Speedy Oil Change at the rate of 10 per hour. What is the probability that exactly eight customers arrive at Speedy's in the next hour?

Problem 8

The government of an underdeveloped country has 8 loans payable, 5 of which are overdue. If a representative of the International Monetary Fund randomly selects 3 loans, what is the probability that exactly 2 are overdue?

Solution 8

Note in this problem that successive observations are not independent. That is, the outcome of one sampled item influences the next sampled item. Because the observations are not independent, the binomial distribution is not appropriate and the hypergeometric distribution is used. To repeat formula [6-6] for the hypergeometric distribution:

$$P(x) = \frac{(_sC_x)(_{N-S}C_{n-x})}{(_NC_n)} \qquad [6-6]$$

Where:

N is the population size
S is the number of successes in the population
n is the number sampled
x is the number of successes in the sample.

The problem asks for the probability of exactly 2 loans overdue in a sample of 3, so $x = 2$ and $n = 3$. There are 8 loans in the population, 5 of which are overdue, so $N = 8$ and $S = 5$.

The probability is computed as follows:

$$P(x) = \frac{(_sC_x)(_{N-S}C_{n-x})}{(_NC_n)} = \frac{(_5C_2)(_{8-5}C_{3-2})}{(_8C_3)} = \frac{\left(\dfrac{5!}{2!3!}\right)\left(\dfrac{3!}{1!2!}\right)}{\left(\dfrac{8!}{3!5!}\right)} = \frac{(10)(3)}{56} = 0.536$$

Interpreting: The probability that exactly 2 of the 3 sampled loans are overdue is 0.536.

Exercise 6.7

Check your answers against those in the ANSWER section.

A retailer of personal computers just received a shipment of 30 units of a new model. The store has a quality agreement with the manufacturer which states that four of the machines are to be selected for a thorough performance check. If more than one fails a performance test, the shipment is returned. Suppose the retailer did not know that 5 of the 30 incoming personal computers are defective. Compute the probability that exactly two computers of the four selected at random are defective.

CHAPTER 6 ASSIGNMENT

DISCRETE PROBABILITY DISTRIBUTIONS

Name _____ Section _____ Score _____

Part I   Select the correct answer and write the appropriate letter in the space provided.

_____ 1. A listing of all possible outcomes of an experiment and the corresponding probability is
called:
  a.   a random variable.   **b.**   a probability distribution.
  c.   the normal rule.   **d.**   the complement rule.

_____ 2. A probability distribution that can assume only certain values within a range is called
  a.   a Poisson probability distribution.   **b.**   a continuous probability distribution.
  c.   a random variable.   **d.**   a discrete probability distribution

_____ 3. Which of the following is **not** a requirement of the binomial distribution?
  a.   the trials must be independent
  b.   the probability of a success changes from one trial to the next
  c.   the sample size must be fixed
  d.   only two outcomes are possible

_____ 4. The mean of a discrete probability distribution is also called the
  a.   variance.   **b.**   expected value.
  c.   standard deviation.   **d.**   median.

_____ 5. Which of the following statements is true about a Poisson probability distribution?
  a.   The outcome of one trial affects the outcome of another trial.
  b.   The sample size is small.
  c.   Probability changes after each trial.
  d.   Can sometimes be used to approximate a binomial probability distribution.

_____ 6. Which distribution would be most appropriate if one wanted to find the probability of
selecting three Republicans from a sample of 15 politicians?
  a.   binomial   **b.**   continuous
  c.   hypergeometric   **d.**   Poisson

_____ 7. A discrete distribution is usually the result of
  a.   a measurement.   **b.**   a count.
  c.   a small sample.   **d.**   a small probability.

_____ 8. Which of the following is **not** a requirement for a discrete probability distribution?
  a.   The trials are independent.
  b.   The probability of each outcome is between 0 and 1.00.
  c.   The outcomes are mutually exclusive.
  d.   The sum of the probabilities is equal to 1.00.

9. To construct a binomial probability distribution, we need to know
  a. the mean and standard deviation.　　**b.** only the mean.
  c. the size of the sample.　　**d.** the number of trials and probability of success.

10. The difference between the binomial distribution and the hypergeometric distribution is
  a. the binomial requires a large sample.
  b. the mean and the variance are equal for the binomial.
  c. the probability of a success is not the same for all trials in the hypergeometric.
  d. the trials are not independent for the binomial.

Part II

Using the appropriate distribution answer the following questions. Show all your work. Write your answer in the answer box provided.

11. The number of connections on the Internet during any two-minute period is given by the distribution on the right.

Number of times	Proportion
0	0.1
1	0.2
2	0.1
3	0.4
4	0.2

a. Determine the mean number of times a connection is made during a two-minute period.

a.

b. Determine the standard deviation of the number of connections made during a two-minute period.

b.

12. According to a recent survey, 75% of all customers will return to the same grocery store. Suppose eight customers are selected at random, what is the probability that:

a. exactly five of the customers will return?

a. [ ]

b. all eight will return?

b. [ ]

c. at least seven will return?

c. [ ]

d. at least one will return?

d. [ ]

e. How many customers would be expected to return to the same store?

e. [ ]

13. Eighty percent of trees planted by a woodlands conservation group survive. What is the probability that:

    a. 10 of the 12 trees just planted will survive?

a.

    b. at least 10 of the trees just planted will survive?

b.

14. Customers use an automatic teller machine at an average rate of 15 per hour. What is the probability that exactly 12 will use the machine in the next hour?

14.

15. On average two new checking accounts are opened per day at the Farmer's Bank. What is the likelihood that for a particular day:

a. no new accounts are opened?

a.

b. at least one new account is opened?

b.

16. A management team is comprised of six sales managers and four floor employees. A subcommittee of four is being formed to handle labor negotiations. What is the probability that two sales managers and two floor employees are selected?

16.

17. In a statistics class with 15 males and 13 females, five students are selected to put problems on the board. What is the probability that:

    a. 3 females and 2 males are selected?

a.

    b. all five students selected are males?

b.

    c. all five students selected are females?

c.

    d. at least one male is selected?

d.

CHAPTER 7
CONTINUOUS PROBABILITY DISTRIBUTIONS

Chapter Goals

After completing this chapter, you will be able to:

1. Understand the difference between discrete and continuous distributions.

2. Compute the mean and standard deviation for a uniform distribution.

3. Compute probabilities using the uniform distribution.

4. List the characteristics of a normal probability distribution.

5. Define and calculate z values.

6. Determine the probability an observation is between two points on a normal probability distribution..

7. Determine the probability that an observation is above (or below) a point on a normal probability distribution.

8. Use the normal probability distribution to approximate the binomial distribution.

Introduction

The previous chapter dealt with discrete probability distributions. Recall for a discrete distribution the outcome can assume only a specific set of values. For example, the number of correct responses to ten true-false questions can only be the numbers 0, 1, 2, ..., 10.

This chapter continues our study of probability distributions by examining the *continuous probability distribution*. Recall that a continuous probability distribution can assume an infinite number of values within a given range. As an example, the weights for a sample of small engine blocks are: 54.3, 52.7, 53.1 and 53.9 pounds.

We consider two families of continuous probability distributions, the ***uniform probability distribution*** and the ***normal probability distribution***. Both of these distributions describe the likelihood of a continuous random variable that has an infinite number of possible values within a specified range.

An example of a uniform probability distribution is the flight time between Detroit and Chicago. Suppose the time to fly from Detroit to Chicago is uniformly distributed within a range of 55 minutes to 75 minutes. We can determine the probability that we can fly from Detroit to Chicago in less than 60 minutes. Flight time is measured on a continuous scale.

The normal probability distribution is described by its mean and standard deviation. Suppose the life of an automobile battery follows the normal probability distribution with a mean of 36 months and a standard deviation of 3 months. We can determine the probability that a battery will last between 36 and forty months. Life of a battery is measured on a continuous scale.

Characteristics of the Uniform Probability Distribution

The uniform probability distribution is the simplest distribution for a continuous random variable.

> ***Uniform probability distribution***: A continuous probability distribution with its values spread evenly over a range of values that are rectangular in shape and are defined by minimum and maximum values.

A uniform distribution is shown in Chart 7-1. The distribution's shape is rectangular and has a minimum value of "*a*" and a maximum value of "*b*". The height of the distribution is uniform for all values between "*a*" and "*b*". This implies that all the values in the range are equally likely.

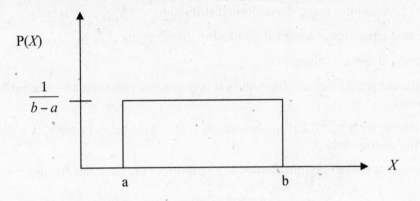

The mean of a uniform distribution is located in the middle of the interval between the minimum value of "*a*" and a maximum value of "*b*". It is calculated using Formula [7–1]:

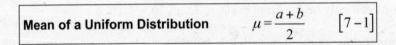

Mean of a Uniform Distribution	$\mu = \dfrac{a+b}{2}$	$[7-1]$

For example: Suppose that the time to fly from Detroit to Chicago is uniformly distributed within a range of 55 minutes minimum to 75 minutes maximum. The mean is found by using Formula [7–1]:

$$\mu = \frac{a+b}{2} = \frac{55+75}{2} = \frac{130}{2} = 65$$

Thus the mean flight time is 65 minutes.

The standard deviation describes the dispersion of a distribution. In a uniform distribution, the standard deviation is also related to the interval between the minimum value of "*a*" and a maximum value of "*b*". It is calculated using Formula [7–2]:

Standard Deviation of a Uniform Distribution	$\sigma = \sqrt{\dfrac{(b-a)^2}{12}}$	$[7-2]$

For the flight time from Detroit to Chicago example the standard deviation is calculated using Formula [7–2]

$$\sigma = \sqrt{\frac{(b-a)^2}{12}} = \sqrt{\frac{(75-55)^2}{12}} = \sqrt{\frac{(20)^2}{12}} = \sqrt{\frac{400}{12}} = \sqrt{33.3333} = 5.77 = 5.8$$

Thus the standard deviation for the flight is 5.8 minutes.

Another key element of the uniform distribution is the height: $P(x)$. The height is the same for all values of the random variable "x".The equation for the height of a uniform probability distribution is given in Formula [7–3]:

Uniform Distribution $P(x) = \dfrac{1}{(b-a)}$ if $a \le x \le b$ and 0 elsewhere $[7-3]$

In Chapter 6, we discussed the fact that probability distributions are useful when making probability statements concerning the values of a random variable. Also for continuous random variables, areas within the distribution represent probabilities. Recall that: $\sum P(x) = 1$ and $0 \le P(x) \le 1$ for all values of x.

The relationship between area and probabilities is applied to the uniform distribution and its rectangular shape using the area of a rectangle formula. Recall that:

$$\text{Area of a rectangle} = \text{Height} \times \text{Base}$$

For a uniform distribution the height is $P(x) = \dfrac{1}{(b-a)}$ and the length is $(b-a)$. If we calculate the area of the rectangle we have:

$$\text{Area of a rectangle} = \text{Base} \times \text{Height}$$
$$= \frac{1}{(b-a)} \times (b-a) = 1$$

Thus for any uniform distribution, the area under the curve is always 1.

For the flight time from Detroit to Chicago example the area is:

$$\text{Area of a rectangle} = \text{Height} \times \text{Base}$$
$$= \frac{1}{(b-a)} \times (b-a) = \frac{1}{(75-55)} \times (75-55) = \frac{20}{20} = 1$$

The Family of Normal Probability Distributions

The Greek letter μ (lower case), represents the mean of a normal probability distribution and the Greek letter σ represents the standard deviation.

Normal probability distribution: A continuous probability distribution uniquely determined by μ and σ.

The major characteristics of the normal probability distribution are:

1. The normal probability distribution is *"bell-shaped"* and the mean, median, and mode are all equal and are located in the center of the distribution. Exactly one-half of the area under the normal curve is above the center and one-half of the area is below the center.

2. The distribution is *symmetrical* about the mean. A vertical line drawn at the mean divides the distribution into two equal halves and these halves possess exactly the same shape.

3. It is *asymptotic*. That is, the tails of the curve approach the X-axis but never actually touch it.

4. A normal probability distribution is completely described by its mean and standard deviation. This indicates that if the mean and standard deviation are known, a normal probability distribution can be constructed and its curve drawn.

5. There is a "family" of normal probability distributions. This means there is a different normal probability distribution for each combination of μ and σ.

These characteristics are summarized in the graph.

The Standard Normal Probability Distribution

As noted in the previous discussion, there are many normal probability distributions — a different one for each pair of values for a mean and a standard deviation. This principle makes the normal probability distribution applicable to a wide range of real-world situations. However, since there are an infinite number of probability distributions, it would be awkward to construct tables of probabilities for so many different normal probability distributions. An efficient method for overcoming this difficulty is to *standardize* each normal probability distribution.

> ***Standard normal probability distribution***: A normal probability distribution with a mean of 0 and a standard deviation of 1.

An actual distribution is converted to a standard normal probability distribution using a *z* **value**.

> ***z value***: The signed distance between a selected value designated X, and the population mean, μ, divided by the population standard deviation, σ.

The formula for a specific standardized z value is text formula [7–5]:

$$\text{Standard Normal Value} \qquad z = \frac{X - \mu}{\sigma} \qquad [7-5]$$

Where:

X is the value of any particular observation or measurement.

μ is the mean of the distribution.

σ is the standard deviation of the distribution.

z is the standardized normal value, usually called the z value.

Applications of the Standard Normal Probability Distribution

To obtain the probability of a value falling in the interval between the variable of interest (X) and the mean (μ), we first compute the distance between the value (X) and the mean (μ). Then we express that difference in units of the standard deviation by dividing $(X - \mu)$ by the standard deviation. This process is called **standardizing.**

To illustrate the probability of a value being between a selected X value and the mean μ, suppose the mean useful life of a car battery is 36 months, with a standard deviation of 3 months. What is the probability that such a battery will last between 36 and 40 months?

The first step is to convert the 40 months to an equivalent standard normal value, using formula [7–5].

The computation is: $z = \dfrac{X - \mu}{\sigma} = \dfrac{40 - 36}{3} = \dfrac{4}{3} = 1.33$

Next refer to Appendix B.1, a table for the areas under the normal curve. A part of the table in Appendix B.1 is shown at the right.

To use the table, the z value of 1.33 is split into two parts, 1.3 and 0.03. To obtain the probability go down the left-hand column to 1.3, then move over to the column headed 0.03 and read the probability. It is 0.4082.

z	0.00	0.01	0.02	0.03	0.04	0.05
		!	!	!	!	
		!	!	!	!	
		!	!	!	!	
1.0						
1.1		0.3665	0.3686	0.3708	0.3729	
1.2		0.3869	0.3888	0.3907	0.3925	
1.3		0.4049	0.4066	0.4082	0.4099	
1.4		0.4207	0.4222	0.4236	0.4251	

The probability that a battery will last between 36 and 40 months is 0.4082. Other probabilities may be calculated, such as more than 46 months, and less than 33 months. Further details are given in Problems 1 through 5.

Empirical Rule

Before examining various applications of the standard normal probability distribution, three areas under the normal curve will be considered which will be used in the following chapters. They were also called the Empirical Rule in Chapter 3.

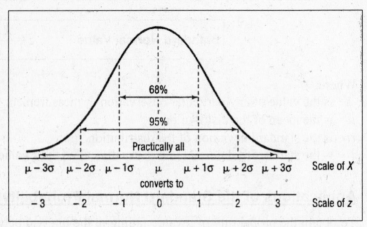

1. About 68 percent of the area under the normal curve is within plus one and minus one standard deviation of the mean. This can be written as $\mu \pm 1\sigma$.

2. About 95 percent of the area under the normal curve is within plus and minus two standard deviations of the mean, written $\mu \pm 2\sigma$

3. Practically all of the area under the normal curve is within three standard deviations of the mean, written $\mu \pm 3\sigma$.

The estimates given above are the same as those shown on the diagram.

The Normal Approximation to the Binomial

The binomial table (Appendix B.9) goes from a sample size of 1 to 15. What do we do when the sample size is greater than 15? A binomial probability can be estimated using the normal probability distribution.

> ***Normal approximation to the binomial***: A binomial probability can be estimated using the normal probability distribution.

To apply the normal approximation to the binomial, both $n\pi$ and $n(1-\pi)$ must be greater than 5. The sample size, or the number of trials, is designated by n, and π is the probability of a success. The mean and the standard deviation of the binomial are computed by:

$$\mu = n\pi$$
$$\sigma = \sqrt{n\pi(1-\pi)}$$

To illustrate, suppose 60 percent of the applications for an exclusive credit card are approved. In a sample of 200 applications, what is the probability that 130 or more applications are approved?

First verify that both $n\pi$ and $n(1-\pi)$ exceed 5.   For $n = 200$ and $\pi = 0.6$

$$n\pi = 200(0.60) = 120 \qquad n(1-\pi) = 200(1-0.6) = 200(0.4) = 80$$

Thus the normal approximation to the binomial may be used.

The mean and standard deviation are computed as follows:

$$\mu = n\pi = 200(0.60) = 120$$

$$\sigma = \sqrt{n\pi(1-\pi)} = \sqrt{200(0.60)(0.4)} = 6.93$$

This distribution is standardized by formula [7–5] and $\mu = 120$, $\sigma = 6.93$ and letting $X = 129.5$ (Not 130)

$$z = \frac{X-\mu}{\sigma} = \frac{129.5-120}{6.93} = 1.37$$

Why is 129.5 used instead of 130? It is used to "correct" for the fact that a continuous distribution (the normal) is used to approximate a discrete distribution (the binomial). On a continuous scale the value 130 would range from 129.5 to 130.5. On a discrete scale there would be a "gap" between 129 and 130 where there would not be any probability. The 0.50 is called the correction for continuity.

> *Continuity correction factor*: The value 0.5 subtracted or added, depending on the question, to a selected value when a discrete probability distribution is approximated by a continuous probability distribution.

The probability of a z value between 0 and 1.37 is 0.4147 (See Appendix B.1). Therefore the probability of a z value greater than 1.37 is 0.0853, found by 0.5000 - 0.4147. So, the probability that 130 or more applications will be approved is 0.0853.

Glossary

Continuity correction factor: The value 0.5 subtracted or added, depending on the question, to a selected value when a discrete probability distribution is approximated by a continuous probability distribution.

Normal approximation to the binomial: A binomial probability can be estimated using the normal probability distribution.

Normal probability distribution: A continuous probability distribution uniquely determined by Φ and σ.

Standard normal probability distribution: A normal probability distribution with a mean of 0 and a standard deviation of 1.

Uniform probability distribution: A continuous probability distribution with its values spread evenly over a range of values that are rectangular in shape and are defined by minimum and maximum values.

z value: The distance between a selected value and the population mean in units of the standard deviation.

Chapter Problems

Problem 1

A group of statistics students collected data at the Cedar Point amusement park and reported that the "wait time" to ride the "Top Thrill Dragster" roller coaster is uniformly distributed within a range of 40 minutes to 90 minutes.

a. Determine the height and draw this uniform distribution.

b. Show that the total area under the curve is 1.00.

c. Determine the mean and standard deviation.

d. What is the probability a particular student will wait between 50 and 60 minutes?

e. What is the probability a particular student will wait less than 60 minutes?

Solution 1

a. Determine the height using Formula [7 – 3]

$$P(x) = \frac{1}{(b-a)} = \frac{1}{(90-40)} = \frac{1}{50} = 0.02$$

Draw the uniform probability distribution.

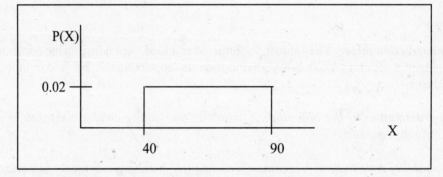

b. To show that the total area under the curve is 1.00, we use the area formula as follows:

Area of a rectangle = Height × Base

$$= \frac{1}{(b-a)} \times (b-a) = \frac{1}{(90-40)} \times (90-40) = \frac{50}{50} = 1$$

c. To determine the mean use Formula [7–1]. To determine the standard deviation use Formula [7–2].

$$\mu = \frac{a+b}{2} = \frac{90+40}{2} = \frac{130}{2} = 65$$

$$\sigma = \sqrt{\frac{(b-a)^2}{12}} = \sqrt{\frac{(90-40)^2}{12}} = \sqrt{\frac{(50)^2}{12}} = \sqrt{208.333} = 14.43$$

d. The probability a particular student will wait between 50 and 60 minutes is found by finding the area of the rectangle with a height of 0.02 and a base of 10.

$$P(50 < wait\ time < 60) = Height \times Base = \frac{1}{(90-40)} \times (60-50) = 0.02 \times 10 = 0.20$$

e. The probability a particular student will wait less than 60 minutes is found by finding the area of the rectangle with a height of 0.02 and a base of (60 – 40).

$$P(40 < wait\ time < 60) = Height \times Base = \frac{1}{(90-40)} \times (60-40) = 0.02 \times 20 = 0.40$$

This probability is illustrated by the following graph.

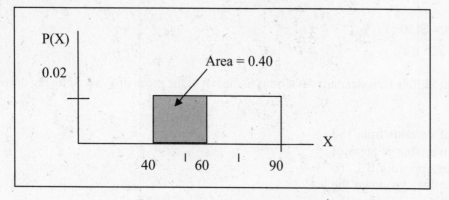

Exercise 7.1

Check your answers against those in the ANSWER section.

The time that the customers at the "self serve" check out stations at the Bi-More grocery store spend checking out follows a uniform distribution between 0 and 3 minutes.

a. Determine the height and draw this uniform distribution.

b. How long does the typical customer wait to check out?

c. Determine the standard deviation of the wait time.

d. What is the probability a particular customer will wait less than one minute?

e. What is the probability a particular customer will wait between 1.5 and 2 minutes?

Problem 2

The mean hourly rate charged by attorneys in Charleston, South Carolina is $150 with a standard deviation of $25. Compute the probability of selecting a lawyer who charges less than $120/hour. Assume that hourly rates charged by attorneys are normally distributed.

Solution 2

The first step is to find the z-score corresponding to $120 using formula [7-5].

$$z = \frac{X - \mu}{\sigma} \qquad [7-5]$$

Where:

X is any value of the random variable ($120 in this problem)

μ is the arithmetic mean of the normal probability distribution ($150)

σ is its standard deviation ($25).

Solving for z:

$$z = \frac{X - \mu}{\sigma} = \frac{\$120 - \$150}{\$25} = -1.20$$

This indicates that $120 is 1.20 standard deviations to the left of the mean of $150. Showing the problem graphically:

The probability of a z value from 150 to 120 is given in a table of areas of the normal curve, Appendix B.1. To obtain the probability, go down the left-hand column to 1.2 (since the normal probability distribution is symmetric, the area between 0 and +1.20 is identical to the area between 0 and -1.20). Next, move over to the column headed 0.00, and read the probability. It is 0.3849. The probability that a randomly selected lawyer in the Charleston area charges between $120 and $150 per hour is 0.3849.

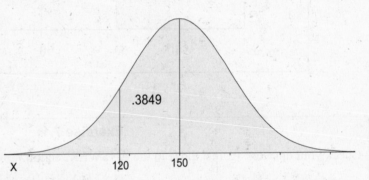

Problem 3

Refer to Problem 2. Compute the probability of a lawyer charging between $120 and $175 per month.

Solution 3

As shown in the following graph, the probability of a lawyer charging between $120 and $150 per month must be added to the probability of charging between $150 and $175 an hour to obtain the total probability.

$$z = \frac{X - \mu}{\sigma} = \frac{\$175 - \$150}{\$25} = \frac{25}{25} = 1.0$$

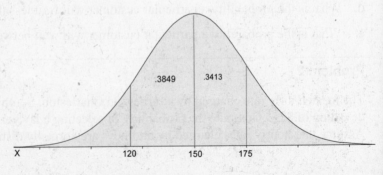

The probability of between $120 and $150 was computed in Problem 2. The probability of between $150 and $175 is found by first computing the z value of $175 using formula [7-5] as shown above. The probability is then found by moving down the left column of Appendix B.1 until a z value of 1.0 is found and then moving under the column headed 0.00. The area, or probability, is 0.3413. Adding the two probabilities together, we find that the probability of a lawyer charging between $120 and $175 is .7262.

Problem 4

Refer to Problem 2. What is the probability that a lawyer charges more than $210 per hour?

Solution 4

The area to be determined is shown at the right.

The z value for the area of the normal curve between $70 and $54 is −1.60, found by:

$$z = \frac{X - \mu}{\sigma} = \frac{\$210 - \$150}{\$25} = \frac{\$60}{\$25} = 2.40$$

Referring to Appendix B.1, and using a z of 2.40, the area of the normal curve between between μ ($150) and X ($210) is 0.4918. Since the total area to the left of $150 is 0.5000, the area greater than $210 is 0.5000-.4982 = 0.0082 .

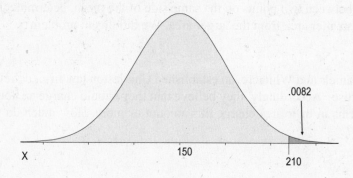

Problem 5

Again referring to Problem 1, find the probability that a lawyer charges between $180 and $$200 per hour.

Solution 5

The area to be determined is depicted in the diagram. The areas of the normal curve between $150 and $180, and $150 and $200 are determined using formula [7-5].

$$z = \frac{X - \mu}{\sigma} = \frac{\$180 - \$150}{\$25} = 1.20$$

$$z = \frac{X - \mu}{\sigma} = \frac{\$200 - \$150}{\$25} = 2.00$$

The probability corresponding to a z of 1.20 is 0.3849 (from Appendix B.1).

The probability corresponding to a z of 2.00 is 0.4773 (from Appendix B.1).

The probability of a lawyer charging between $180 and $200, therefore, is the difference between these two probabilities. Thus, (0.4773 – 0.3849) = 0.0924. That is, 9.24 percent of lawyers charge between $180 and $200 per hour.

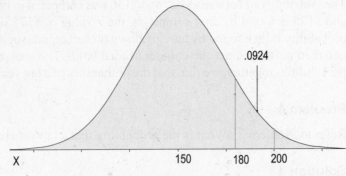

Brief Review

In brief there are four situations in which you may find the area under the standard normal probability distribution.

1. To find the area between 0 and z or $(-z)$ you look up the value directly in the table. We did this in problem 2.

2. To find the area between two points on different sides of the mean determine the two z values and add the corresponding areas. We did this in problem 3.

3. To find the area beyond z or $(-z)$ locate the probability of z in the table and subtract that value from 0.500. We did this in problem 4.

4. To find the area between two points on the same side of the mean, determine the two z values and subtract the smaller area from the larger area. We did this in problem 5.

Problem 6

Suppose that Jacobs, Daniels and Whitacre, an established Charleston law firm, believes that they offer exceptional legal expertise. Accordingly, they believe that they should charge an hourly rate such that only the top 10% of firms in their area charge this amount or more. How much do they believe they should charge per hour?

Solution 6

How much

The shaded area in the diagram on the right represents the upper 10 percent of law firms in terms of hourly compensation. An upper tail area of 0.1000 corresponds to an area of 0.4000 between the mean of the distribution and the upper value, found by 0.5000-0.1000. From the table of areas of the normal curve (Appendix B.1), the closest z value corresponding to the area 0.4000 is 1.28. The area for $z = 1.28$ is 0.3997 and for $z = 1.29$ it is 0.4015. We select the z value as 1.28 because it is the closest to 0.4000. This indicates that the unknown X value is 1.28 standard deviations above the mean.

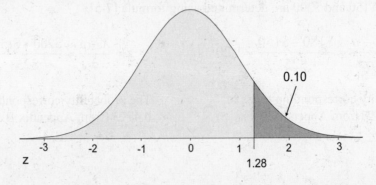

Substituting 1.28 in the equation [7-5] for z:

$$z = \frac{X - \mu}{\sigma} = 1.28 = \frac{X - \$150}{\$25}$$

$$X = \$182.00$$

Jacobs, Daniels and Whitacre should charge $182.00 per hour.

Exercise 7.2

Check your answers against those in the ANSWER section.

The length of time a domestic flight must wait between gate departure and takeoff taxi at Boston's Logan International Airport is approximately normally distributed with a mean of 20 minutes and a standard deviation of 5 minutes.

a.   What is the probability that a plane must wait between 18 and 24 minutes before taxiing for takeoff after leaving the gate?

b.   What is the probability a plane must wait between 22 and 30 minutes before taxiing for takeoff after leaving the gate?

c.   What is the probability a plane waits more than 12 minutes between gate departure and takeoff taxi?

d.   What is the length of time such that only 5% of planes wait this long or longer before gate departure and taxiing down the runway?

Problem 7

Super Fit Training and Diet Center determined that 15 percent of their clients drop out (stop coming to the center) prior to the expiration of their three month membership. What is the probability that for a sample of 80 clients, less than 10 drop out prior to expiration of their three month membership?

Solution 7

The answer could be determined by using the binomial distribution where π, the probability of a success, is 0.15, and where n, the number of trials, is 80. However, most binomial tables do not go beyond an n of 25 and the calculations by hand would be very tedious.

As noted previously, the probability can be accurately estimated by using the normal approximation to the binomial. The approximations are quite good when both $n\pi$ and $n(1-\pi)$ are greater than 5.

In this case, $n\pi = (80)(0.15) = 12$, and $n(1-\pi) = (80)(1-0.15) = 68$. Both are greater than 5. Recall the mean and variance of a binomial distribution are computed as follows:

$$\mu = n\pi = (80)(0.15) = 12$$

$$\sigma^2 = n\pi(1-\pi) = (80)(0.15)(0.85) = 10.2$$

The standard deviation is 3.19, found by $\sqrt{10.2}$. The area less than 9.5 is shown on the following diagram. Because we are estimating a discrete distribution using a continuous distribution, the continuity correction factor is needed. In this instance if we were actually using the binomial distribution we would add the probabilities of 0 customers not paying, one customer not paying, and so on, up to nine customers not paying the bill. With the discrete distribution there would be no probability of 8.6 customers not paying their bill.

When we estimate binomial probabilities using the normal probability distribution, the area for nine corresponds to the area from 8.5 up to 9.5 and the area for 10 corresponds to 9.5 up to 10.5. In this case, we want all the area below (to the left of) 9.5. This area is depicted schematically as shown below:

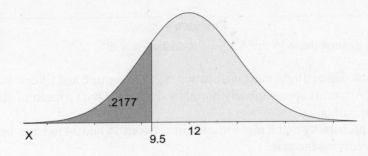

The z value associated with less than 9.5 customers is –0.78, found by

$$z = \frac{9.5 - 12.0}{3.19} = -0.78$$

The area to the left of –0.78 is 0.2177, found by (0.5000 – 0.2823). The probability that less than ten clients drop out prior to the expiration of their three month membership is 0.2177.

A note on the correction factor

We apply the correction factor in only four cases. They are:

1. For the probability *at least X* occurs, use the area above $(X - 0.5)$
2. For the probability that *more than X* occurs, use the area above $(X + 0.5)$
3. For the probability that *X or less* occurs, use the area below $(X + 0.5)$
4. For the probability that *less than X* occurs, use the area below $(X - 0.5)$

The following output from Excel shows the cumulative distribution for the case where $n = 80$ and $\pi = 0.15$. Look down the column labeled X to the row for 9 and read the probability. It is 0.2211. That is very close to our estimate of 0.2177.

x	P(x ≤ X)	x	P(x ≤ X)
0	2.26E-06	18	0.974132
1	3.41E-05	19	0.986849
2	0.000256	20	0.993695
3	0.001275	21	0.997146
4	0.004737	22	0.99878
5	0.014023	.	.
6	0.034506	.	.
7	0.072717	.	.
8	0.13425	77	1
9	0.221119	78	1
10	0.329961	79	1
11	0.45219	80	1
12	0.576217		
13	0.690703		
14	0.787391		
15	0.862466		
16	0.916289		
17	0.952046		

Exercise 7.3

Check your answers against those in the ANSWER section.

A new drug has been developed that is found to relieve nasal congestion in 90 percent of those with the condition. The new drug is administered to 300 patients with this condition. What is the probability that more than 265 patients will be relieved of the nasal congestion?

CHAPTER 7 ASSIGNMENT

CONTINUOUS PROBABILITY DISTRIBUTIONS

Name _____   Section _____   Score_____

Part I   Select the correct answer and write the appropriate letter in the space provided.

_____ 1.   In a uniform distribution
   a.   the mean and the median are always equal.
   b.   the mean and the standard deviation are always equal.
   c.   the mean is always larger than the median.
   d.   the mean is always smaller than the median.

_____ 2.   The normal probability distribution is
   a.   a bell-shaped distribution.   b.   a continuous distribution.
   c.   symmetric.   d.   all of the above.

_____ 3.   The standard normal probability distribution
   a.   is a special case of the normal probability distribution.
   b.   has a mean equal to 0 and a standard deviation equal to 1.
   c.   measures the distance from the mean in units of the standard deviation.
   d.   all of the above.

_____ 4.   A normal probability distribution is completely described by
   a.   its mean.   b.   its standard deviation.
   c.   its mean and standard deviation.   d.   none of the above.

_____ 5.   Any normal probability distribution can be converted to a standard normal probability distribution by
   a.   finding $\mu = n\pi$.   b.   determining that $n\pi$ is greater than 5.
   c.   finding $z = \dfrac{X - \mu}{\sigma}$ d.   finding $\sigma = \sqrt{n\pi(1-\pi)}$

_____ 6.   A normal probability distribution
   a.   has at least two peaks.   b.   is asymptotic.
   c.   increases as X increases.   d.   is discrete.

_____ 7.   The normal probability distribution can be used to approximate the binomial when
   a. $n\pi$ is at least 25.   b.   both $n\pi$ and $n(1 - \pi)$ are greater than 5.
   c. $n\pi(1 - \pi p)$ is larger than 5.   d.   only when the z-score is above 5.

_____ 8.   What percent of the area under the normal curve is within $\mu \pm 1\sigma$?
   a.   68%.   b.   34%.   c.   95%.   d.   none of the above.

_____ 9.   A z value
   a.   is the standard deviation for the standard normal probability distribution.
   b.   is a measure of how many standard deviations the mean is from the median.
   c.   is the difference of the mean and the probability of z.
   d.   is a measure of how many standard deviations a particular score is from the mean.

_____ **10.** The correction for continuity is used when
       a. the *z*-scores are integers.   **b.** the distribution is discrete.
       c. the *z*-scores are less than 0.5   **d.** the distribution is continuous.

Part II   Answer the following questions. Be sure to show your work.

11.   A statistics instructor collected data on the time it takes the students to complete a test. The test taking time is uniformly distributed within a range of 35 minutes to 55 minutes.

     a. Determine the height and draw this uniform distribution.

     b. How long does the typical test taking time?

> **b.**

     c. Determine the standard deviation of the test taking time.

> **c.**

     d. What is the probability a particular student will take less than 45 minutes?

> **d.**

     e. What is the probability a particular student will take between 45 and 50 minutes?

> **e.**

15. A clothing store asserts that 60% of its customers pay by credit. On a particular day, 35 customers purchased items at the store.

a. What is the mean and standard deviation of the binomial distribution?

a.

b. What is the probability that half (18 or more) of the customers paid by credit?

b.

c. What is the probability that 30 or more paid by credit?

c.

d. What is the probability that less than 12 paid by credit?

d.

e. What is the probability that 12 to 30 paid by credit?

e.

16. It is very difficult for small businesses to be successful. The Small Business Administration estimates that 20 percent will dissolve or go bankrupt within two years. A sample of 50 new businesses is selected.

a. What is the mean and standard deviation of this distribution?

a.

b. What is the probability that more than 16 in the sample will go bankrupt?

b.

c. What is the probability that exactly 14 will go bankrupt?

c.

d. What is the probability that between 7 and 9 businesses will go bankrupt?

d.

e. What is the probability that between 7 and 15 businesses will go bankrupt?

e.

Probability Sampling Methods

Four types of probability sampling are commonly used: *simple random sampling*, *systematic random sampling*, *stratified random sampling*, and *cluster sampling*. The most widely used type of sampling is a simple random sample.

> ***Simple random sample***: A sample selected so that each item or person in the population has the same chance of being included.

Several ways of selecting a simple random sample are:

1. The name or identifying number of each item in the population is recorded on a slip of paper and placed in a box. The slips of paper are shuffled and the required sample size is chosen from the box.

2. Each item is numbered and a *table of random numbers*, such as the one in Appendix B.6, is used to select the members of the sample.

3. There are many software programs, such as MINITAB and Excel, which have routines that will randomly select a given number of items from the population.

Another type of sampling is *a systematic random sample*.

> ***Systematic random sample***: A random starting point is selected and then every k^{th} member of the population is selected.

In a systematic random sample the items or individuals of the population are arranged in some way — alphabetically, in a file drawer by date received, or by some other method. A random starting point is selected, and then every k^{th} member of the population is selected for the sample. In a systematic random sample, you might take all the items in the population and number them 1, 2, 3,.... Next, a random starting point is selected, let's say 39. Every k^{th} item thereafter, such as every 100th, is selected for the sample. This means that 39, 139, 239, 339, and so on would be a part of the sample.

Another type of probability sample is referred to as *stratified random sampling*.

> ***Stratified random sample***: A population is divided into subgroups, called strata, and a sample is randomly selected from each stratum.

For example, if our study involved Army personnel, we might decide to stratify the population (all Army personnel) into generals, other officers, and enlisted personnel. The number selected from each of the three strata could be proportional to the total number in the population for the corresponding strata. Each member of the population can belong to only one of the strata. That is, a military person cannot be a general and a private at the same time.

Another common type of sampling is *cluster sampling*.

> ***Cluster sampling***: A population is divided into clusters using naturally occurring geographic or other boundaries. Clusters are then randomly selected and a sample is collected by randomly selecting from each cluster.

16. It is very difficult for small businesses to be successful. The Small Business Administration estimates that 20 percent will dissolve or go bankrupt within two years. A sample of 50 new businesses is selected.

    a. What is the mean and standard deviation of this distribution?

    b. What is the probability that more than 16 in the sample will go bankrupt?

    b.

    c. What is the probability that exactly 14 will go bankrupt?

    c.

    d. What is the probability that between 7 and 9 businesses will go bankrupt?

    d.

    e. What is the probability that between 7 and 15 businesses will go bankrupt?

    e.

CHAPTER 8
SAMPLING METHODS AND THE
CENTRAL LIMIT THEOREM

Chapter Goals

After completing this chapter, you will be able to:

1. Explain why a sample is often the only feasible way to learn something about a population.

2. Describe methods to select a sample.

3. Define and construct a sampling distribution of the sample mean.

4. Understand and explain the *central limit theorem*.

5. Use the *central limit theorem* to find probabilities of selecting possible sample means from a specified population.

Introduction

This chapter is the beginning of our study of sampling. Sampling is necessary because we want to make statements about a population but we do not want to (or cannot) examine all the items in that population. Recall from Chapter 1 that a **population** refers to the entire group of objects or persons of interest. The population of interest might be all the persons in the city receiving welfare payments or all the computer chips produced during the last hour. A **sample** is a portion, a part, or a subset of the population. Fifty welfare recipients out of 4,000 receiving payments might constitute the sample, or 20 computer chips might be sampled out of 1,500 produced last hour.

Reasons for Sampling

Why is it necessary to sample? Why can't we just inspect all the items? There are several reasons.

1. *To contact the whole population would often be very time consuming.* To ask every eligible voter if they plan to vote for the current senator in the forthcoming election would take months. The election would probably be over before the survey was completed.

2. *The cost of studying all the items in the population is often prohibitive.* Some television program ratings are established by analyzing the viewing habits of about 1,200 viewers. The cost of studying all the homes having television would be exorbitant.

3. *The physical impossibility of checking all the items in the population.* The South Dakota Game Commission, for example, cannot check all the deer, grouse, and other wild game because they are always moving.

4. *The destructive nature of certain tests.* The manufacturer of fuses cannot test all of them because in the testing the fuse is destroyed and none would be available for sale.

5. *The adequacy of sample results.* If the sample results of the viewing habits of 1,200 homes revealed that only 1.1 percent of the homes watched "60 Minutes" no doubt the program would be replaced by another show. Checking the viewing habits of all the homes regarding "60 Minutes" probably would not change the percent significantly.

Probability Sampling Methods

Four types of probability sampling are commonly used: *simple random sampling, systematic random sampling, stratified random sampling,* and *cluster sampling.* The most widely used type of sampling is a simple random sample.

> ***Simple random sample***: A sample selected so that each item or person in the population has the same chance of being included.

Several ways of selecting a simple random sample are:

1. The name or identifying number of each item in the population is recorded on a slip of paper and placed in a box. The slips of paper are shuffled and the required sample size is chosen from the box.

2. Each item is numbered and a *table of random numbers*, such as the one in Appendix B.6, is used to select the members of the sample.

3. There are many software programs, such as MINITAB and Excel, which have routines that will randomly select a given number of items from the population.

Another type of sampling is *a systematic random sample.*

> ***Systematic random sample***: A random starting point is selected and then every k^{th} member of the population is selected.

In a systematic random sample the items or individuals of the population are arranged in some way — alphabetically, in a file drawer by date received, or by some other method. A random starting point is selected, and then every k^{th} member of the population is selected for the sample. In a systematic random sample, you might take all the items in the population and number them 1, 2, 3,.... Next, a random starting point is selected, let's say 39. Every k^{th} item thereafter, such as every 100th, is selected for the sample. This means that 39, 139, 239, 339, and so on would be a part of the sample.

Another type of probability sample is referred to as *stratified random sampling.*

> ***Stratified random sample***: A population is divided into subgroups, called strata, and a sample is randomly selected from each stratum.

For example, if our study involved Army personnel, we might decide to stratify the population (all Army personnel) into generals, other officers, and enlisted personnel. The number selected from each of the three strata could be proportional to the total number in the population for the corresponding strata. Each member of the population can belong to only one of the strata. That is, a military person cannot be a general and a private at the same time.

Another common type of sampling is *cluster sampling.*

> ***Cluster sampling***: A population is divided into clusters using naturally occurring geographic or other boundaries. Clusters are then randomly selected and a sample is collected by randomly selecting from each cluster.

Cluster sampling is often used to reduce the cost of sampling when the population is scattered over a large geographic area. Suppose the objective is to study household waste collection in a large city.

Step 1: Divide the city into smaller units (perhaps precincts).

Step 2: The precincts are numbered and several selected randomly.

Step 3: Households within each of these precincts are randomly selected and interviewed.

Sampling "Error"

It is not logical to expect that the results obtained from a sample will coincide exactly with those from a population. For example, it is unlikely that the mean welfare payment for a sample of 50 recipients is exactly the same as the mean for all 4,000 welfare recipients. We expect a difference between a sample statistic and its corresponding population parameter. The difference is called *sampling error*.

> *Sampling error*: The difference between a sample statistic and its corresponding population parameter.

Because these errors happen by chance, they are referred to as chance variations.

Sampling Distribution of the Sample Mean

Suppose all possible samples of size *n* are selected from a specified population, and the mean of each of these samples is computed. The distribution of these sample means is called the *sampling distribution of the sample mean.*

> *Sampling distribution of the sample mean*: A probability distribution of all possible sample means of a given sample size.

The sampling distribution of the mean is a probability distribution and has the following major characteristics:

1. The mean of all the sample means will be exactly equal to the population mean.

2. If the population from which the samples are drawn is normal, the distribution of sample means is also normally distributed.

3. If the population from which the samples are drawn is not normal, the sampling distribution is approximately normal, provided the samples are "sufficiently" large (usually accepted to include at least 30 observations).

The Central Limit Theorem

The *central limit theorem* states that, for large random samples, the shape of the sampling distribution of the sample means is close to a normal probability distribution. The approximation is more accurate for large samples than for small samples. We can make logical and reasonable statements about the distribution of the sample means with little or no information about the shape of the original distribution from which we took the sample.

This phenomenon is called the *central limit theorem*.

> **Central limit theorem**: If all samples of a specified size are selected from any population, the sampling distribution of the sample means is approximately a normal distribution. This approximation improves with larger samples.

Standard Error of the Mean

The Central Limit Theorem does not address the dispersion of the sampling distribution of sample means nor does it address the comparison of the sampling distribution of sample means to the mean of the population. It can be shown that the mean of the sampling distribution is the population mean, and if the standard deviation in the population is σ, the standard deviation of the means is $\frac{\sigma}{\sqrt{n}}$, where n is the number of observations in each sample. We refer to $\frac{\sigma}{\sqrt{n}}$ as the **standard error of the mean.** It is actually the standard deviation of the sampling distribution of the sample mean:

> **Standard Error of the Mean**: The standard deviation of the sampling distribution of the sample mean.

The standard error is a measure of the variability of the sampling distribution of the means. It is computed using text formula [8-1]

Standard Error of the Mean	$\sigma_{\bar{x}} = \dfrac{\sigma}{\sqrt{n}}$	[8 – 1]

Where:

$\sigma_{\bar{x}}$ is the standard error of the mean

σ is the population standard deviation

n is the sample size

The size of the standard error is affected by the standard deviation. As the standard deviation increases so does the standard error. The standard error is also affected by the sample size. As the sample size increases the standard error decreases, which indicates that there is less variability in the distribution of the sample means. Obviously we conclude that as we increase the sample size the standard error decreases.

It is important to note the following:

1. The mean of the distribution of sample means will be *exactly* equal to the population mean if we are able to select all possible samples of a particular size from a given population. That is $\mu = \mu_{\bar{x}}$. Even if we do not select all samples, we can expect the mean of the distribution of the sample mean to be close to the population mean.

2. There will be less dispersion in the sampling distribution of the distribution of sample mean than in the population. If the standard deviation of the population is σ, the standard deviation of the distribution of sample means is $\frac{\sigma}{\sqrt{n}}$. Note that when we increase the size of the sample the standard error of the mean decreases.

Using the Sampling Distribution of the Sample Mean

The majority of statistical business decisions are made on the basis of sampling. Generally we have a population and wish to know something about that population, such as the mean. We take a sample from that population and wish to conclude whether the sampling error, that is the difference between the population parameter and the sample statistic, is due to chance.

We can compute the probability that a sample mean will fall within a certain range. The sampling distribution of the sample mean will follow the normal probability distribution under two conditions:

1. When the samples are taken from populations known to follow the normal distribution. In this case the size of the sample is not a factor.

2. When the shape of the population distribution is not known or the shape is known to be nonnormal, but the sample contains at least 30 observations.

Recall that we used the z-value found with Formula [7-1] to convert any normal distribution to the standard normal distribution. We can use the standard normal table to find the probability of selecting a value of an observation that falls within a specified range. The formula is:

$$\textbf{Standard Normal Value} \qquad z = \frac{X - \mu}{\sigma} \qquad [7-1]$$

In this formula X is the value of the random variable, μ is the population mean, and σ is the population standard deviation.

Since most business decisions are based on a sample, we are interested in the distribution of the sample mean $\overline{X}$ not the value of X, the value of one observation. Formula [7-1] is altered to reflect this need. We change X to $\overline{X}$. Then we change the population standard deviation to the standard error of the mean: $\frac{\sigma}{\sqrt{n}}$.

Thus we have Formula [8-2] that is used to find the z value for a normal population with a known population mean and standard deviation:

$$\textbf{Finding the } z \textbf{ Value of } \overline{X} \textbf{ When the Population} \atop \textbf{Standard Deviation is Known} \qquad z = \frac{\overline{X} - \mu}{\sigma / \sqrt{n}} \qquad [8-2]$$

Glossary

Central limit theorem: If all samples of a specified size are selected from any population, the sampling distribution of the sample means is approximately a normal distribution. This approximation improves with larger samples.

Cluster sampling: A population is divided into clusters using naturally occurring geographic or other boundaries. Clusters are then randomly selected and a sample is collected by randomly selecting from each cluster.

Sampling distribution of the sample mean: A probability distribution of all possible sample means of a given sample size.

Sampling error: The difference between a sample statistic and its corresponding population parameter.

Simple random sample: A sample selected so that each item or person in the population has the same chance of being included.

Standard Error of the Sample Mean: The standard deviation of the sampling distribution of the sample means.

Stratified random sample: A population is divided into groups, called strata, and a sample is randomly selected from each stratum.

Systematic random sample: A random starting point is selected and then every k^{th} member of the population is selected.

Chapter Problems

Problem 1

Listed below are the advertisers in the "Coupon Section" of the Fort Walton Beach/Destin Florida phone directory. Also noted is whether the *type* of advertiser is a service advertiser (**S**), personal care advertiser (**P**), auto related advertiser (**A**), or recreation oriented advertiser (**R**). Some of the advertisers are to be randomly selected and asked various questions regarding the coupons.

00	A to Z Lock & Safe	S	10	Meineke Discount Mufflers	A
01	Action on the Blackwater River	R	11	Merry Maids	S
02	Atlas Exterminating	S	12	Midas Auto Service Experts	A
03	Blackwater Canoe Rental	R	13	Payless Mechanical, Inc.	S
04	Cain's AC & Refrigeration	S	14	Private Mini Storage	S
05	Clean and Fresh Carpet	S	15	Profast Auto Service Centers	A
06	Dale's Carpet Cleaning	S	16	Shalimar Point Golf Club	R
07	Executive Car Wash	A	17	Studio 21 Hair Designs	P
08	Florida Steam Carpet	S	18	Trees Unlimited	S
09	Fred Astaire Dance Studio	R	19	Tropical Images Salon	P

a. Randomly select a sample of five advertisers.
b. Randomly select a second sample of five advertisers.
c. Randomly select a sample that consists of every fourth advertiser.
d. Select a sample of four advertisers so that one of each type of advertiser is included.

Solution 1

a. Use Appendix B.6 – Table of Random Numbers – and pick a starting point. The current time is 11:50 so we will start with the eleventh row down and the fifth column in from the left. The number is 07960.

- If we start with the first two digits, then the first two-digit number equal to or less than 19 is **07**.

- Working down the column the next two-digit number equal to or less than 19 is **05**.

- We skip 38, 88, 95, and pick **14**.

- We continue down the column and skip 76, 92, 46, and pick **03**.

- We skip 21, 89 and pick **06**.

- We have chosen advertisers number **07, 05, 14, 03**, and **06**. The random sample of advertisers is shown at the right.

0 3	Blackwater Canoe Rental
0 5	Clean and Fresh Carpet
0 6	Dale's Carpet Cleaning
0 7	Executive Car Wash
1 4	Private Mini Storage

b. Use Appendix B.6 – Table of Random Numbers – and pick a starting point. The current time is again 11:50 so we will start with the eleventh row down and the fifth column in from the left. The number is 07960. This time we will use the last two digits in the column.

- If we start with the last two digits then we need to skip 60, 43, 33, and the first two-digit number equal to or less than 19 is **08**.

- Working down the column we skip 85, 36, 39, 34, 91, 85, 64, 45, 79, 22, 85, 64, and pick **14**.

- We continue down the column we skip 80, 99, 94, 87 and the next two digit number equal to or less than 19 is **12**.

- We skip 33, 61, 83, 22, and pick **06**.

- We continue down the column and skip 29, 32, 75, 86, 72, 46, 70, and pick **17**.

- We have chosen advertisers number **08, 14, 12, 06**, and **17**. The random sample of advertisers is shown at the right.

0 6	Dale's Carpet Cleaning
0 8	Florida Steam Carpet
1 2	Midas Auto Service Experts
1 4	Private Mini Storage
1 7	Studio 21 Hair Designs

It is interesting to note that advertiser 06 and 14 were picked for both samples.

c. In order to pick every fourth advertiser we need an initial starting point. We need to determine if we will start with advertiser 00, 01, 02 or 03. We use the random number table and simply close our eyes and place our finger on the table. We picked the array that is in the sixteenth (16) row and the third (3) column headed by the numbers 37722.

- We move down the first column until we come to a single digit number less than or equal to 03. Thus we skip 37, 43, and 92 and pick **01**.

- We will pick our sample starting with **01** and pick every fourth advertiser, which would be **05, 09, 13**, and **17**. The random sample of advertisers is shown at the right.

0 1	Action on the Blackwater River
0 5	Clean and Fresh Carpet
0 9	Fred Astaire Dance Studio
1 3	Payless Mechanical, Inc.
1 7	Studio 21 Hair Designs

d. The process is similar to what we did in parts **a** and **b**, with the exception that we have to pay attention to the type of service performed by each advertiser. Use Appendix B.6 – Table of Random Numbers – and pick a starting point. The current time is 17:10 so we will start with the seventeenth row down and the tenth column in from the left. The number is 72949.

- This time we will use the second and third digits in the column. If we start with the second and third digits then we need to skip 29, 41, 56, 92, 78, and the first two-digit number less than or equal to 19 is **12**. We note that this is an auto care advertiser (**A**).

- Working down the column, skip 69, 25, 48, and pick **17**. This is a personal care advertiser (**P**).

- We continue down the column and skip 62. The next two-digit number equal to or less than 19 is **07**. We note that this is an auto service advertiser (**A**) and skip it since we already have such an advertiser.

- We skip 30, 61, 27, and pick **18**. We note that this is a service firm advertiser (**S**).

- We skip 40, 59, 81, 25, and pick **15**. We skip this one since it is also auto related (**A**).

- The next number is **12** which is also auto related (**A**).

- We skip 59, 95, 76, 38, 22, 88, 20, 44, 25, and pick **16**. We note that this is a recreation advertiser(**R**). Thus we have selected an advertiser from each of the types. The random sample of advertisers is:

1 2	Midas Auto Service Experts (A)
1 7	Studio 21 Hair Designs (P)
1 8	Trees Unlimited (S)
1 6	Shalimar Point Golf Club (R)

Exercise 8.1

Check your answers against those in the ANSWER section.

Refer to Problem One and the advertisers in the "Coupon Section" of the Fort Walton Beach/Destin Florida phone directory. Use Appendix B.6 – Table of Random Numbers.

a. Pick a sample of five advertisers. Start with row six and column six. The number is 84822. Use the first two numbers starting with 84.

b. Randomly select a second sample of five advertisers starting at the bottom right corner of the table. The number is 70603. Use the far right two digits starting with 03.

c. Randomly select a sample that consists of every fourth advertiser starting with 03.

Problem 2

Suppose that a population consists of the six families living in Brentwood Circle. You are studying the number of children in the six families. The population information is shown at the right.

List the possible samples of size 2 that could be selected from this population and compute the mean of each sample. Organize these sample means into a probability distribution.

Family	Number of Children
Clark	1
Walston	2
Dodd	3
Marshall	5
Saner	3
White	4

Solution 2

There are 15 different samples. The formula for the number of combinations is used to determine the total number of samples. Combination formula [5–10] is used.

$$_nC_r = \frac{n!}{r!(n-r)!}$$

There are six members of the population and the sample size is two.

$$_6C_2 = \frac{6!}{2!4!} = 15$$

Thus there are 15 different samples.

Sample Number	Families in the Sample	Total Number of Children in Sample	Mean Number of Children Per Family in Sample	
1	Clark, Walston	3	1.5	←3/2
2	Clark, Dodd	4	2.0	←4/2
3	Clark, Marshall	6	3.0	←6/2
4	Clark, Saner	4	2.0	←4/2
5	Clark, White	5	2.5	←5/2
6	Walston, Dodd	5	2.5	←5/2
7	Walston, Marshall	7	3.5	←7/2
8	Walston, Saner	5	2.5	←5/2
9	Walston, White	6	3.0	←6/2
10	Dodd, Marshall	8	4.0	←8/2
11	Dodd, Saner	6	3.0	←6/2
12	Dodd, White	7	3.5	←7/2
13	Marshall, Saner	8	4.0	←8/2
14	Marshall, White	9	4.5	←9/2
15	Saner, White	7	3.5	←7/2
		Total	45.0	

This information is organized into the following probability distribution called the sampling distribution of the means.

Problem 3

Using the Brentwood Circle data in Problem 2, compare the mean of the sampling distribution with the mean of the population. Compare the spread of the sample mean with that of the population.

Mean Number of Children	Frequency	Probability	
1.5	1	0.067	← 1/15
2.0	2	0.133	← 2/15
2.5	3	0.200	← 3/15
3.0	3	0.200	← 3/15
3.5	3	0.200	← 3/15
4.0	2	0.133	← 2/15
4.5	1	0.067	← 1/15
	15	1.000	

Solution 3

The mean of the sampling distribution and the mean of the population are the same. The population mean, written μ, is found by $\mu = [(1 + 2 + 3 + 5 + 3 + 4) \div 6] = 3.0$. The mean of the sampling distribution (written $\mu_{\bar{x}}$) because it is the mean of a group of sample means) is also 3.0, found by $45.0 \div 15$.

$\overline{X}$ Sample Means	f Frequency	$f \times \overline{X}$
1.5	1	1.5
2.0	2	4.0
2.5	3	7.5
3.0	3	9.0
3.5	3	10.5
4.0	2	8.0
4.5	1	4.5
	15	45.0

The calculations for the sample means are:

$$\mu_{\bar{x}} = \frac{\Sigma f \overline{X}}{\Sigma f} = \frac{45.0}{15} = 3.0$$

The population mean μ is exactly equal to the mean of the sampling distribution $\mu_{\bar{x}}$ (3.0). This is always true.

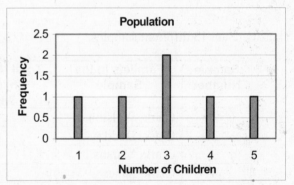

Note in the graphs at the right that there is less spread in the sampling distribution of the means (bottom chart) than in the population distribution (top chart). The sample means range from 1.5 to 4.5, whereas the population values ranged from 1 to 5.

Also note that the shape of the population is different than that of the sampling distribution. This phenomenon is described by the central limit theorem. Recall the central limit theorem states that regardless of the shape of the population the sampling distribution will tend toward normal as n increases.

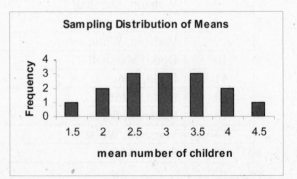

Exercise 8.2

Check your answers against those in the ANSWER section.

The real estate company of Kuhlman and Associates has five sales people. Listed below is the number of homes sold last month by each of the five associates. Bruce Kuhlman, the owner, wants to estimate the population mean number of homes sold based on samples of three.

Associate	Number of Homes Sold
A. Sue Klaus	6
B. John Bardo	2
C. Jean Cannon	5
D. A.J.Kemper	9
E. Carol Ford	3

a. If samples of size 3 are selected, how many different samples are possible?

b. List the various samples and compute the mean of each.

c. Develop a sampling distribution of the means.

d. Draw graphs to compare the variability of the sampling distribution of the mean with that of the population.

Problem 4

The foreman of the canning division of the Planters Peanuts Company observed that the amount of cashews in a 48-ounce can varies from can to can. Records indicate that the process follows the normal probability distribution with a mean of 48.5 ounces and a standard deviation of 0.25 ounces. The foreman randomly selects 25 cans from the canning line and determines that the mean amount of cashews per can is 48.6 ounces. Compute the probability that the sample of 25 cans would have a mean greater than or equal to 48.6 ounces.

Solution 4

We need to determine the likelihood that we could select a sample of 25 cans from a normal population with a mean of 48.5 ounces and a population standard deviation of 0.25 ounces and find the sample mean to be 48.6 ounces. We use formula [8-2] to find the value of z.

$$z = \frac{\bar{X} - \mu}{\sigma/\sqrt{n}} = \frac{48.6 - 48.5}{0.25/\sqrt{25}} = \frac{0.1}{0.05} = 2$$

In the equation the numerator $\bar{X} - \mu = 48.6 - 48.5 = 0.1$ is the sampling error.

The denominator $\sigma/\sqrt{n} = 0.25/\sqrt{25} = 0.05$ is the standard error of the distribution of sample means.

The z-value expresses the sampling error in standard units. We need to compute the probability of a z-value greater than 2.00. In Appendix B.1 we locate the probability corresponding to a z-value of 2.00. It is 0.4772. Thus the probability of a z-value greater than 2.00 is 0.0228, found by ($0.5000 - 0.4772$) = 0.0228.

Problem 5

RoadRunner Sports knows that the mean time it takes to process an order after it has been placed on its website is 23 minutes with a standard deviation of 8 minutes. If a random sample of 36 online orders is taken, what is the probability that the mean of the sample is less than 20 minutes ?

Solution 5

Since the sample is sufficiently large, the sampling distribution of the sample mean is approximately normal. The mean of the sampling distribution is $\mu_{\bar{x}}$ with standard deviation, $\sigma_{\bar{x}} = \sigma/\sqrt{n} = 8/\sqrt{36} = 8/6 = 1.333$. We use formula [8-2] to find the value of z.

$$z = \frac{\bar{X} - \mu}{\sigma/\sqrt{n}} = \frac{20 - 23}{8/\sqrt{36}} = -3/1.333 = -2.25$$

Referring to Appendix B.1, the z-value for -2.25 is 0.4878. The likelihood of finding a z-value less than -2.25 is found by $(0.5000 - 0.4878) = 0.0122$. There is about a one percent chance that we could select a sample of 36 online orders and find the mean processing time of the sample is 20 minutes or less, when the population mean is 23 minutes.

CHAPTER 8 ASSIGNMENT

SAMPLING METHODS AND THE CENTRAL LIMIT THEOREM

Name _____ Section _____ Score _____

Part I   Select the correct answer and write the appropriate letter in the space provided.

_____ 1.   The *population proportion* is an example of a
     a.   sample statistic.   **b.**   normal population.
     c.   sample mean.   **d.**   population parameter.

_____ 2.   In a *probability sample* each item in the population has
     a.   a chance of being selected.
     b.   the same chance of being selected.
     c.   a 50 percent chance of being selected.
     d.   no chance of being selected

_____ 3.   In a *simple random sample* each item in the population has
     a.   a chance of being selected.
     b.   the same chance of being selected.
     c.   a 50 percent chance of being selected.
     d.   no chance of being selected..

_____ 4.   The *sampling error* is
     a.   the difference between a sample statistic and a population parameter.
     b.   always positive.
     c.   the difference between the z value and the mean.
     d.   equal to the population value.

_____ 5.   The *sample mean* is an example of a
     a.   sample statistic.
     b.   normal population.
     c.   weighted mean.
     d.   population parameter.

_____ 6.   Suppose we have a negatively skewed population. According to the central limit
     theorem, the distribution of a sample mean of a particular size will
     a.   also be negatively skewed.
     b.   form a binomial distribution.
     c.   approach a normal distribution.
     d.   become positively skewed.

_____ 7.   The population is the five employees in a physician's office. The number of possible
     samples of 2 that could be selected from this population is
     a.   5   **b.**   10
     c.   15   **d.**   60

_____ 8.   The *sampling distribution of the sample mean* is the probability distribution of all

a. the sample statistics and their probability of occurrence..
b. the normal population parameters and their probability of occurrence..
c. the possible sample means of the same sizee.
d. sample means.

_____ 9. In *cluster sampling*
a. each item in the population has a chance of being selected more than once.
b. the population is divided into primary units, and then samples are drawn from these units.
c. each item in a primary unit has a 50 percent chance of being selected.
d. every k^{th} item has a chance of being selected.

_____ 10. In a *systematic sample* a random starting point is chosen, and
a. each item in the population has a chance of being selected more than once.
b. the population is divided into primary units, and then samples are drawn from these units.
c. each item in a population has a 50 percent chance of being selected.
d. every k^{th} item thereafter is selected for the sample.

Part II Answer the following questions. Be sure to show essential work.

11. Listed below are the rental agencies in the *Automobile Rental* section in the phone directory. Also noted is whether the rental agency is local (L), national (N), and whether the agency rents pickup trucks (T). Note that an agency could provide more than one service. Some of the agencies are to be randomly selected and asked various questions regarding the service they provide.

00	ADA Auto Rentals	L		10	General Motors Rental System	L,N,T
01	Alamo Rent a Car	L,N		11	Hertz Rent a Car	L,N,T
02	Avis Rent a Car	L,N		12	Lee's Sales and Service	L,T
03	Bill's Towing	L,T		13	National Car Rental	L,N
04	Budget Car and Truck Rental	L,N,T		14	Quality Imports	L
05	Charlie's Dodge	L,T		15	Rent a Wreck	L,T
06	EZ Rent a Car	L		16	Sears Car and Truck Rental	L,N,T
07	Enterprise	L,N		17	Thrifty Car Rental	L,N
08	Ford Rental System	L,N,T		18	Toyota Car Rental	L,N,T
09	Guardian Car Rentals	L,N		19	Wagoner Motor Sales	L,T

Use Appendix B.6 – Table of Random Numbers for the following problems:

a. Randomly select a sample of five rental agencies. Start with row two and column two. The number is 90935. Use the first two numbers starting with 90.

a.

b. Randomly select a second sample of five rental agencies starting at the bottom left corner of the table. The number is 11084. Use the far right two digits starting with 84.

b.

c. Randomly select a sample of six that consists of every third rental agency starting with 02.

c.

d. Select a sample of four rental agencies so that one of each type is included. Start at the top of column three. The number is 75997. Use the left two digits starting with 75.

d.

e. Randomly select a sample of five rental agencies that rent trucks. Start at the bottom of the third column of the table. The number is 78957. Use the far right two digits starting with 57.

e.

f. Randomly select a sample of two rental agencies that rent locally and nationally, but **do not** rent trucks. Start at the bottom of the fourth column of the table. The number is 77353. Use the second and third set of digits starting with 73.

f.

g. Use the table of random numbers to select your sample of five rental agencies. Specify in your answer where you started in the random number table and how you chose that starting point.

g.

12. Five bundles of pencils contain the quantities shown at the right.

a. How many different samples of 2 bundles each are there?

Bundle	Number of pencils
1	10
2	6
3	10
4	11
5	12

a.

b. List all possible samples of size 2 and compute the mean of each sample.

Sample Number	Bundle	Total Pencils	Mean Number of Pencils

c. Calculate the population mean and compare it to the mean of the sampling distribution.

c.

13. The quality assurance department for Pepsi Distributors, Inc. maintains meticulous records on the bottling line for two-liter Pepsi bottles. Records indicate that the process follows the normal probability distribution with a mean amount per bottle of 2.01 liters and a standard deviation of 0.025 liters. The foreman randomly selects 25 bottles from the bottling line and determines that the mean amount per bottle is 2.005 liters.

a. Compute the sampling error.

a.

b. Compute the standard error of the sampling distribution of sample means.

b.

c. Compute the probability that the sample of 25 bottles would have a mean of 2.005 liters or more.

c.

14. Suppose the foreman in Problem 13 selects a second sample of 16 bottles and determines that the mean is 1.994 liters. Compute the probability that the sample of 16 bottles would have a mean of 1.994 liters or more.

14.

15. Captain D's tuna is sold in cans that have a net weight of 8 ounces. The weights are normally distributed with a mean of 8.025 ounces and a standard deviation of 0.125 ounces. You take a sample of 36 cans. Compute the probability that the sample would have a mean:

a. greater than 8.03 ounces?

<table>
<tr><td>a.</td></tr>
</table>

b. less than 7.995 ounces?

<table>
<tr><td>b.</td></tr>
</table>

c. between 7.995 and 8.03 ounces?

<table>
<tr><td>c.</td></tr>
</table>

CHAPTER 9
ESTIMATION AND CONFIDENCE INTERVALS

Chapter Goals

After completing this chapter, you will be able to:

1. Define a point estimate.

2. Define level of confidence

3. Construct a confidence interval for the population mean when the population standard deviation is known.

4. Construct a confidence interval for a population mean when the population standard deviation is unknown.

5. Construct a confidence interval for a population proportion.

6. Determine the sample size for attribute and variable sampling.

Introduction

The previous chapter introduces sampling as a way to find information about a population. We noted that it is usually not possible or necessary to inspect the entire population. We gave the following as reasons for sampling:

1. To contact the whole population would often be very time consuming.

2. The cost of studying all the items in the population is often prohibitive.

3. The physical impossibility of checking all the items in the population.

4. The destructive nature of certain tests. The manufacturer of fuses cannot test all of them because in the testing the fuse is destroyed and none would be available for sale.

5. The adequacy of sample results.

We also made assumptions about the population, such as the mean, the standard deviation, or the shape of the distribution of the population. We note here that in most business situations such information is not known and the purpose of sampling may be to estimate some of these values.

This chapter considers several important aspects of sampling, such as point estimates and confidence intervals.

Point Estimates and Confidence Intervals

We begin our study of point estimates and confidence intervals by studying estimates of the population mean, μ. We will consider two cases:

- The population standard deviation (σ) is known.
- The population standard deviation is unknown. In this case, the sample standard deviation, s, is used in place of σ.

Population Standard Deviation Known σ

In many situations the population is large or it is difficult to identify all the members, so we need to rely on sample information. A single number used to estimate a population parameter is called a *point estimate*.

> *Point estimate*: The statistic, computed from sample information, which is used to estimate the population parameter.

- The sample mean, $\overline{X}$, is a point estimate of the population mean, μ.
- The sample proportion, p, is a point estimate of the population proportion, π.
- The sample standard deviation, s, is a point estimate of the population standard deviation, σ.

For example, a sample of 100 recent accounting graduates reveals a mean starting salary of $33,800. The $33,800 is a point estimate. The sample mean is a point estimate of the mean starting salary of all (population) accounting graduates.

We expect the point estimate to be close to the population parameter, but we would like to measure how close it really is. We need a measure that gives us a range of values into which our point estimate will fit. We use a confidence interval for this purpose.

Confidence Interval

The range of values, within which a population parameter is expected to lie, is usually referred to as the *confidence interval*.

> *Confidence Interval*: A range of values constructed from sample data so the parameter occurs within that range at a specified probability. This specified probability is called the *level of confidence*.

> *Level of confidence*: The measure of the confidence we have that an interval estimate will include the population parameter.

The *95 percent confidence interval* means that ninety-five percent of the sample means selected from a population will be within 1.96 standard deviations of the population mean μ.

The *99 percent confidence interval* means that ninety-nine percent of the sample means selected from a population will be within 2.58 standard deviations of the population mean μ.

The central limit theorem allows us to state or specify a range of values within which a population parameter, such as the population mean (μ), can be expected to occur.

How do we determine a confidence interval with a given confidence level, such as a 95 percent confidence interval? We briefly described how to find the z value for a given level of confidence.

The standard error of the mean, calculated using formula [8-1] is really the standard deviation of the distribution of sample means. The formula is repeated below:

$$\sigma_{\bar{x}} = \frac{\sigma}{\sqrt{n}}$$

Where:

$\sigma_{\bar{x}}$ is the symbol for the standard error of the mean.

σ is the population standard deviation.

n is the number of observations in the sample.

The confidence interval for the mean of a sample is when σ is known is computed by text formula [9-1].

Confidence Interval for the Population Mean with σ Known	$\overline{X} \pm z \dfrac{\sigma}{\sqrt{n}}$	[9 –1]

Where:
$\overline{X}$ is the sample mean.
z depends on the level of confidence.
σ is the population standard deviation.
n is the size of the sample.

Population Standard Deviation Unknown

In the previous section, we assumed that the population standard deviation was known. In most sampling situations the population standard deviation (σ) is not known. In these cases we can use s, the sample standard deviation, to estimate σ. But when we substitute s for σ, we can no longer use formula [9-1]. Because we do not know σ we cannot use the z distribution. When s replaces σ we use the t distribution in place of the z distribution.

The t distribution

The t distribution is based on the assumption that the population of interest is normal, or nearly normal.

1. It is, like the z distribution, a continuous distribution.

2. It is, like the z distribution, bell-shaped and symmetrical.

3. There is not one t distribution but rather a "family" of t distributions. All t distributions have a mean of 0, but their standard deviations differ according to the sample size n. There is a t distribution for a sample size of 20, another for a sample size of 22, and so on. The standard deviation for a t distribution with 5 observations is larger than for a t distribution with 20 observations.

4. The *t* distribution is more spread out and flatter at the center than is the standard normal distribution. As the sample size increases, however, the *t* distribution approaches the standard normal distribution, because the "error" in using *s* to estimate σ decreases with larger samples.

The chart on the right shows the relationship between the *t* distribution and the *z* distribution.

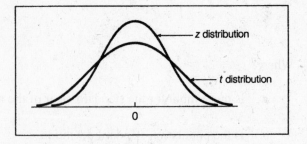

Note that the Student's *t* distribution has a greater spread than the *z* distribution, thus the value of *t* for a given level of confidence is larger in magnitude than the corresponding *z* values. Also note that for the same level of confidence the *t* distribution is more spread out than the *z* distribution.

To develop a confidence interval for the population mean with an unknown population standard deviation:

1. Assume the sampled population is either normal or approximately normal.

2. Estimate the population standard deviation σ with the sample standard deviation *s*.

3. Use the *t* distribution rather than the *z* distribution.

In order to develop a confidence interval for the population mean, using the *t* distribution, we adjust Formula [9-1] to create Formula [9-2]:

Confidence Interval for the Population Mean, σ unknown	$\bar{X} \pm t \dfrac{s}{\sqrt{n}}$	[9 – 2]

Where:
$\bar{X}$ is the sample mean.
t is the value associated with the given level of confidence.
s is the sample standard deviation.
n is the size of the sample.

We base the decision on whether to use the *t* or the *z* on whether or not we know σ, the population standard deviation. If we know the population standard deviation, then we use *z*. If we do not know σ, we use a t.

The chart below summarizes the decision-making process for determining when to use the *z* distribution or the *t* distribution.

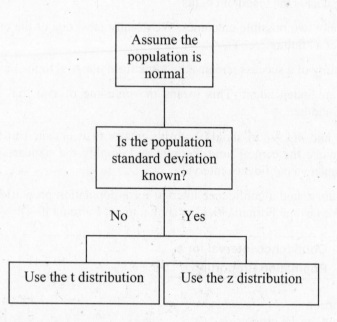

Confidence Interval for a Proportion

The previous material in this chapter dealt with the ratio scale of measurement. Variables might have been weights, lengths, distance, and income. We want to consider situations that involve the nominal scale of measurement. Recall that in the nominal scale of measurement, observations are classified into one or more mutually exclusive groups. For example, a survey may ask you if you watch "60 Minutes" on TV. Are you male or female? As a voter, are you Republican, Democrat, Independent, or other?

We are interested in knowing what ***proportion*** of a sample or population has a particular trait.

> ***Proportion***: The fraction, ratio, or percent indicating the part of the sample or the population having a particular trait of interest.

A sample proportion can be determined using text Formula [9-3]

$$\text{Sample Proportion} \qquad p = \frac{X}{n} \qquad [9\text{-}3]$$

Where:
p is the sample proportion
X is the number of successes in the sample.
n is the number of items sampled.

The population proportion is identified by π. Thus π refers to the percent of successes in the population. In Chapter 6, π is the proportion of successes in a binomial distribution.

To develop a confidence interval for a proportion we need to meet the following assumptions:

1. The binomial conditions, discussed in Chapter 6, have been met. Briefly, these conditions are:

    a. The sample data is the result of counts.

    b. There are only two possible outcomes. We usually label one of the outcomes a "success" and the other a "failure."

    c. The probability of a success remains the same from one trial to the next.

    d. The trials are independent. This means the outcome of one trial does not affect the outcome of another.

2. The values $n\pi$ and $n(1 - \pi)$ should both be greater than or equal to five. This condition allows us to invoke the central limit theorem and employ the standard normal distribution, that is z, to complete a confidence interval

Developing a point estimate and a confidence interval for a population proportion is similar to what we did for the mean. We change Formula [9-1] as shown to get Formula [9-4]:

$$\boxed{\textbf{Confidence Interval for a Population Proportion} \qquad p \pm z\,\sigma_p \qquad [9-4]}$$

Where:
p is the sample proportion
σ_p is the "standard error" of the proportion.

The "standard error" of the proportion measures the variability in the sampling distribution of the sample proportion. It is calculated using text Formula [9-5].

$$\boxed{\textbf{Standard Error of the Sample Proportion} \qquad \sigma_p = \sqrt{\dfrac{p(1-p)}{n}} \qquad [9-5]}$$

The confidence interval for a population proportion is found by text Formula [9-6]

$$\boxed{\textbf{Confidence Interval for a Population Proportion} \qquad p \pm z\sqrt{\dfrac{p(1-p)}{n}} \qquad [9-6]}$$

Where:
p is the sample proportion.
n is the sample size.
z is the z value for degree of confidence selected.

Finite-Population Correction Factor

If the sampling is done without replacement from a small population, the *finite population correction factor,* often shortened to, *FPC*, is used. Its purpose is to account for the fact that a parameter can be more accurately estimated from a small population when a large portion of that population's units is sampled. The correction factor is:

$$FPC = \sqrt{\frac{N-n}{N-1}} \; .$$

The standard error of the mean or the standard error of the proportion is multiplied by the correction factor.

Because the correction factor will always be less than 1.00, the effect is to reduce the standard error.

If N, the number of units in the population, is large relative to n, the sample size, the value of this correction factor is near 1.00.

For example, if $N = 10,000$ and a sample of 40 is selected, the value of the correction factor is 0.9980, found by $\sqrt{\frac{10,000-40}{10,000-1}} = 0.9980$.

However, if N is only 500, the correction factor is 0.9601, found by $\sqrt{\frac{500-40}{500-1}} = 0.9601$.

Logically, we can estimate a population parameter with a sample of 40 from a population of 500 more accurately than with a sample of 40 from a population of 10,000.

For a finite population, where the total number of objects is N and the size of the sample is n, we need to adjust the standard error in each of the confidence interval formulas. To find the confidence interval for the mean we adjust the standard error of the mean in formulas (9-1) and (9-2). To find the confidence interval for a proportion we need to adjust the standard error of the proportion in formula (9-3).

Choosing an Appropriate Sample Size

Sample size is always a concern when designing a statistical study. Too large a sample could be a waste of time and money collecting the data. Also, too small a sample may make the conclusions drawn from the data uncertain. The size of a sample required for a particular study is based on three factors.

1. The desired level of confidence. This is expressed in terms of z.

2. The maximum allowable error, E, the researcher will tolerate.

3. The variability in the population under study (as measured by σ).

The sample size for a confidence interval for the mean is computed using text Formula [9-7]:

$$\text{Sample Size for Estimating the Population Mean} \qquad n = \left(\frac{z\sigma}{E}\right)^2 \qquad [9-7]$$

Where:

n is the size of the sample.
z is the standard normal value corresponding to the desired level of confidence.
σ is the estimate of the population standard deviation.
E is the maximum allowable error.

A population with considerable variability (reflected by a large population standard deviation, σ) will require a larger sample than a population with a smaller standard deviation. E is the maximum allowable error that you, the researcher, are willing to accept. It is the amount that is added and subtracted from the sample mean to obtain the end points of the confidence limits.

The population standard deviation, σ, must often be estimated. The following three methods of estimation are suggested:

1. Use a comparable study where an estimate of dispersion in the population is available.

2. Use a range-based approach. If we know, or can estimate, the largest and smallest values in the population we can compute the range, R. The standard deviation can then be estimated as R/6 .

3. Conduct a pilot study. Take a small sample and estimate σ, by calculating s from the data obtained from the pilot study.

To determine the required sample size for a proportion, three items need to be specified:

1.   The desired level of confidence, usually 95 percent or 99 percent.

2.   The margin of error in the population proportion that is required.

3.   An estimate of the population proportion π.

Text formula [9-8] is used:

$$\text{Sample Size for the Population Proportion} \qquad n = p(1-p)\left(\frac{z}{E}\right)^2 \qquad [9-8]$$

Where:
p is the estimated proportion based on the pilot survey.
z is the z score associated with the degree of confidence selected.
E is the allowable error.

If no estimate of p is available, then let $p = 0.50$. The sample size will never be larger than that obtained when $p = 0.50$.

Glossary

Confidence Interval: A range of values constructed from sample data so the parameter occurs within that range at a specified probability. This specified probability is called the *level of confidence.*

Confidence limits: The end points of the confidence interval.

Level of confidence: The measure of the confidence we have that an interval estimate will include the population parameter.

Point estimate: The statistic, computed from sample information, which is used to estimate the population parameter.

Proportion: The fraction, ratio, or percent indicating the part of the sample or the population having a particular trait of interest.

Chapter Problems

Problem 1

Crossett Truck Rental has a large fleet of rental trucks. At times many of the trucks need substantial repairs. Mr. Crossett has requested a study of the repair costs. A random sample of 64 trucks is selected. The mean annual repair cost for the sample is $1,200. Estimate the mean annual repair cost for all rental trucks using a 95 percent confidence interval for the population mean. Assume that the population standard deviation, σ, is equal to $280.

Solution 1

The population parameter being estimated is the population mean — the mean annual repair cost of all Crossett rental trucks. This value is not known, but the best estimate we have of that value is the sample mean of $1,200. Hence, $1,200 is a point estimate of the unknown population parameter. A confidence interval is a range of values within which the population parameter is expected to occur. The 95 percent refers to the approximate percent of time that similarly constructed intervals would include the parameter being estimated.

The confidence interval for a mean is obtained by applying formula [9-1].

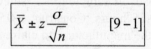

$$\bar{X} \pm z \frac{\sigma}{\sqrt{n}} \qquad [9-1]$$

How is the z value determined? In this problem the 95 percent level of confidence is used. This refers to the middle 95 percent of the values. The remaining 5 percent is divided equally between the two tails of curve. (See the following diagram.)

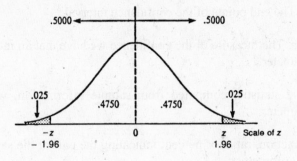

To find z, the standard normal distribution is used. Referring to Appendix B.1, the first step is to locate the value of 0.4750 in the body of the table, and then read the corresponding row and column values. The z value is 1.96.

Substitute the z value into the equation. The confidence interval is $1,131.40 to $1,268.60

$$\bar{X} \pm z\frac{\sigma}{\sqrt{n}} = \$1,200 \pm 1.96\frac{\$280}{\sqrt{64}}$$
$$= \$1,200 \pm \$68.6$$
$$= \$1,131.40 \quad to \quad \$1,268.60$$

This indicates that if 100 similar intervals were constructed, about 95 intervals would be expected to include the population mean.

Exercise 9.1

Check your answers against those in the ANSWER section.

The Internal Revenue Service is studying contributions to charity. The mean calculated from a random sample of 36 returns is $150. Assume that the population standard deviation is known and equal to $20. Construct a 98 percent confidence interval for the population mean.

Problem 2

A manufacturer of batteries for portable hand tools wishes to investigate the length of time a battery will last between charges at a fixed load. A sample of 12 batteries had a mean length of time of 4.3 hours with a standard deviation of 0.25 hours. Construct a 95 percent confidence interval for the population mean. Is it reasonable for the manufacturer to claim that the batteries will last 4.25 hours? How about 5 hours?

Solution 2

Use the t distribution because the population standard deviation is unknown.

We use Formula [9-2] to develop the confidence interval.

$$\overline{X} \pm t\frac{s}{\sqrt{n}} \qquad [9-2]$$

Where: $\overline{X} = 4.3$, $s = 0.25$, $n = 12$, and t is the value associated with the given level of confidence.

To find the value of t we use Appendix B.2.   Move across the row identified as "Confidence Interval" to the level of confidence—95 percent in this problem.

The column on the left, identified as "d.f.," is known as the Degrees of Freedom. The number of degrees of freedom is the number of observations in the sample minus the number of samples, written $(n-1)$. In this case it is $(12 - 1) = 11$.   The value of t is 2.201.   We substitute these values in Formula [9-2].

$$\overline{X} \pm t\frac{s}{\sqrt{n}} = 4.3 \pm 2.201\frac{0.25}{\sqrt{12}} = 4.3 \pm 0.159$$

The end points of the interval are: $4.3 - 0.159 = 4.141$ and $4.3 + 0.159 = 4.459$. Because 4.25 hours is in the interval between 4.141 hours and 4.459 hours, we conclude the population mean could be 4.25 hours. The manufacturer can be 95 percent confident that the mean life between charges is 4.25 hours, since this value is in the interval.

Because 5.00 hours is not in the interval, we conclude a value of 5 for the population mean is not reasonable.

Exercise 9.2

Check your answers against those in the ANSWER section.

SkyBlue Airways advertises that, on average, its New York to London flight is five hours and 30 minutes. A consumer advocacy group randomly selects ten New York to London flights on SkyBlue and finds that the sample mean is 5.67 hours with a sample standard deviation of 0.57 hour.
a.   What is the point estimate of the population mean?
c.   Construct a 95 percent confidence interval for the population mean.
d.   Explain why the t distribution is used as a part of the confidence interval.
e.   Is it reasonable for SkyBlue to claim a mean flight time of 5 hours and 30 minutes?

Problem 3

A market survey is conducted by your state legislator to determine the proportion of homeowners who would switch to a new "electrical energy supplier" if they had the opportunity afforded them by new state legislation. Of the 1,200 homeowners surveyed, 800 said they would switch.

a. Estimate the value of the population proportion.
b. Compute the standard error of the proportion
c. Develop a 99 percent confidence interval for the population proportion.
d. Interpret the results if the legislator states that 2/3 of the homeowners would switch.

Solution 3

a. Estimate the value of the population proportion. $p = \dfrac{X}{n} = \dfrac{800}{1200} = 0.667$

b. The standard error of the proportion is: $\sigma_p = \sqrt{\dfrac{p(1-p)}{n}} = \sqrt{\dfrac{0.667(1-0.667)}{1200}} = 0.0136$

c. The 99 percent confidence interval is found by:

$$p \pm z \sqrt{\dfrac{p(1-p)}{n}}$$

$$= 0.667 \pm 2.58 \sqrt{\dfrac{0.667(1-0.667)}{1200}}$$

$$= 0.667 \pm 2.58 \times 0.0136$$

$$= 0.667 \pm 0.035$$

$$= 0.632 \text{ and } 0.702$$

d. The value 0.667 is in the interval, thus the legislator is correct in stating that 2/3 of the homeowners would switch energy suppliers.

Problem 4

Gaston Home is a regional home builder. They would like to estimate the mean age of people who contract to build custom homes with them. Their records indicate that they have built 323 custom homes in the past year. They sample 28 of these customers and find that their mean age is 44.3 years with a standard deviation of 5.7 years. Construct a 95% confidence interval for the true mean age of customers for whom Gaston Home has built a custom home in the past year.

Solution 4

When the sample is more than 5 percent of the population, the finite population correction factor is used. In this case the sample size is 28 and the population size is 323. Thus, $n/N = 28/323 = 0.0867$ or 8.7 percent. The confidence interval is adjusted as follows.

$$\bar{X} \pm t_{\alpha/2,n-1} \dfrac{s}{\sqrt{n}} \left(\sqrt{\dfrac{N-n}{N-1}} \right) = 44.3 \pm 2.052 \dfrac{5.7}{\sqrt{28}} \left(\sqrt{\dfrac{323-28}{323-1}} \right)$$

$$= 44.3 \pm 2.052 (0.9572)$$

$$= 44.3 \pm 1.964$$

$$= 42.336 \quad to \quad 46.264$$

Notice that when the correction factor decreases the width of the confidence interval. This is logical because the number of items sampled is large relative to the population.

Exercise 9.3

Check your answers against those in the ANSWER section.

Refer to Exercise 9.1. Compute the 98 percent confidence interval if the population consists of 200 tax returns.

Problem 5

A human resource manager of a large company wants to determine the proportion of employees who would use an on-site daycare center if one were available. The human resource manager samples 200 of the employees and finds that 54 said that they would use an onsite daycare center. Construct a 98% confidence interval for the proportion of all employees who would use an onsite daycare center.

Solution 5

In the sample of 200 employees, 54 would use onsite daycare. The point estimate of the proportion of employees who would use onsite daycare is $X/n = 54/200 = 0.27$. The z value corresponding to a 98 percent level of confidence is 2.33 (from Appendix B.1). The formula for the confidence interval for the population proportion is text formula [9-6]:

$$p \pm z \sqrt{\frac{p(1-p)}{n}} = 0.27 \pm 2.33 \sqrt{\frac{(0.27)(1-0.27)}{200}} = 0.27 \pm (2.33)\sqrt{.000986} = 0.27 \pm 0.073$$

The confidence interval is 0.197 to 0.343. This means that about 98 percent of the similarly constructed intervals would include the population proportion.

Exercise 9.4

Check your answers against those in the ANSWER section.

A random sample of 100 light bulbs is selected. Sixty were found to burn for more than 1,000 hours. Develop a 90 percent confidence interval for the proportion of bulbs that will burn more than 1,000 hours.

Problem 6

Refer to the onsite daycare center data in Problem 5. Recall that 200 employees were sampled. Suppose there is a total of 2000 employees. Develop a 98 percent confidence interval for the proportion of employees who would use an onsite daycare center.

Solution 6

The finite population correction factor should be used because the sample is 10 percent of the population, found by $200 \div 2000$.

$$p \pm z \sqrt{\frac{p(1-p)}{n}} \left(\sqrt{\frac{N-n}{N-1}} \right) = 0.27 \pm 2.33 \sqrt{\frac{(0.27)(1-0.27)}{200}} \left(\sqrt{\frac{2000-200}{2000-1}} \right)$$

$$= 0.27 \pm 0.073(0.9489)$$

$$= 0.27 \pm 0.0693$$

Using the correction factor, the interval is reduced from 0.27 ± 0.073 to 0.27 ± 0.0693, or 0.2007 to 0.3393. Again, this is because the human resource manager has sampled a large proportion (10 percent) of its employees.

Problem 7

The manager of the Jiffy Supermarket wants to estimate the mean time a customer spends in the store. Use a 95 percent level of confidence. The standard deviation of the population based on a pilot survey is estimated to be 3.0 minutes. The manager requires the estimate to be within plus or minus 1.00 minute of the population value. What sample size is needed?

Solution 7

The size of the sample is dependent on three factors.

1. The allowable error (E).

2. The level of confidence (z).

3. The estimated variation in the population, usually measured by s, the sample standard deviation.

In this problem, the store manager has indicated that the estimate must be within 1.0 minute of the population parameter. The level of confidence is 0.95 and the population standard deviation is estimated to be 3.0 minutes. The formula [9-9] for determining the size of the sample is:

$$n = \left(\frac{zs}{E}\right)^2 \qquad [9-9]$$

Where:
z refers to the level of confidence.
s is the estimated population standard deviation.
E is the allowable error.

$$n = \left(\frac{(1.96)(3.0)}{1.0}\right)^2 = (5.88)^2 = 34.57 = 35$$

Hence, the manager should randomly select 35 customers and determine the amount of time they spend in the store.

Exercise 9.5

Check your answers against those in the ANSWER section.

A health maintenance organization (HMO) wants to estimate the mean length of a hospital stay. How large a sample of patient records is necessary if the HMO wants to be 99 percent confident of the estimate and wants the estimate to be within plus or minus 0.2 days? An earlier study showed the standard deviation of the length of stay to be 0.25 days.

Problem 8

The Ohio Unemployment Commission wants to estimate the proportion of the labor force that was unemployed during last year in a certain depressed region. The Commission wants to be 95 percent confident that their estimate is within 5 percentage points (written 0.05) of the population proportion. If the population proportion has been estimated to be 0.15, how large a sample is required?

Solution 8

Note that the estimate of the population proportion is 0.15. The allowable error (E) is 0.05. Using the 95 percent level of confidence, the z value is 1.96. Applying formula [9-10] to determine the sample size:

$$n = p(1-p)\left(\frac{z}{E}\right)^2 = 0.15(1-0.15)\left(\frac{1.96}{0.05}\right)^2 = 195.92 = 196$$

The required sample size is 196. When no estimate of population proportion is available, 0.50 is used. The size of the sample will never be larger than that obtained when $p = 0.50$. The calculations for the sample size when $p = 0.50$ are:

$$n = p(1-p)\left(\frac{z}{E}\right)^2 = 0.5(1-0.5)\left(\frac{1.96}{0.05}\right)^2 = 384.16 = 385$$

Note that the required sample size is considerably larger (385 versus 196) when p is set at 0.50.

Exercise 9.6

Check your answers against those in the ANSWER section.

A large bank believes that one-third of its checking customers have used at least one of the bank's other services during the past year. How large a sample is required to estimate the actual proportion within a range of plus and minus 0.04? Use the 98 percent level of confidence.

CHAPTER 9 ASSIGNMENT

ESTIMATION AND CONFIDENCE INTERVALS

Name _____ Section _____ Score _____

Part I   Select the correct answer and write the appropriate letter in the space provided.

_____   1.   A single number used to estimate a population parameter is
    a.   the confidence interval.   **b.**   the population parameter.
    c.   a point estimate.   **d.**   the mean of the population.

_____   2.   A range of values constructed from sample data so that the parameter occurs within that
          range at a specified probability is
    a.   a confidence interval.   **b.**   the population parameter.
    c.   a point estimate.   **d.**   the mean of the population

_____   3.   The size of the standard error is affected by the standard deviation of the sample and
    a.   a confidence interval.   **b.**   the population parameter.
    c.   the point estimate.   **d.**   the sample size

_____   4.   Suppose we select 100 samples from a population. For each sample we construct a 95
          percent confidence interval. We could expect about 95 percent of these confidence
          intervals to contain
    a.   a sample mean.   **b.**   the population mean.
    c.   a point estimate.   **d.**   the standard deviation of the population

_____   5.   The t distribution is a continuous distribution, with many similarities to
    a.   the confidence interval.   **b.**   the population parameter.
    c.   the standard normal distribution.   **d.**   the mean of the population

_____   6.   The t distribution is used when the population is normal and
    a.   the population standard deviation is unknown.
    b.   the population standard deviation is known.
    c.   the point estimate is known.
    d.   the mean of the population is unknown.

_____   7.   If the level of confidence is decreased from 95 percent to 90 percent, the width of the
          corresponding interval will
    a.   be increased.   **b.**   be decreased.
    c.   stay the same.   **d.**   not have an effect on the level of confidence

_____   8.   The finite population correction factor is used when
    a.   the sample is more than 5 percent of the population.
    b.   the sample is less than 5 percent of the population.
    c.   the sample is larger than the population.
    d.   the population cannot be estimated.

_____9. A 90 percent confidence interval for means indicates that 90 out of 100 similarly constructed intervals will include the
    a. sample mean.   **b.** sampling error.
    c. z value   **d.** population mean.

_____10. The fraction, ratio, or percent indicating the part of the sample or the population having a particular trait of interest is
    a. a confidence interval.   **b.** the population parameter.
    c. a point estimate.   **d.** the proportion.

Part II   Answer the following questions. Be sure to show essential work.

11. As part of a safety check, the Pennsylvania Highway Patrol randomly stopped 25 cars and checked their tire pressure. The sample mean was 32 pounds per square inch with a sample standard deviation of 2 pounds per square inch. Develop a 98 percent confidence interval for the population mean.

11.

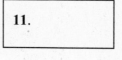

12. A human resource manager for Carver County is evaluating a recent effort to improve the health of the county's firefighters by providing an exercise room in each of the county's firehouses. Their records prior to installing the exercise rooms indicate that the mean weight of all county firefighters is 198 pounds with a standard deviation of 13 pounds. A random sample of 40 firefighters taken six months after the program was implemented revealed that the mean of the sample was 192 pounds. Construct a 96% confidence interval for the mean weight of all firefighters six months after the exercise rooms were installed. Assume that σ has not changed. Does it appear that the program is working?

12.

13. Suppose that Carver County only has 250 firefighters. Construct a 96 percent confidence interval for the mean weight of all firefighters six months after the exercise rooms were installed.

13.

14. A manufacturer of diamond drill bits for industrial production drilling and machining wishes to investigate the length of time a drill bit will last while drilling carbon steel. The production of the drill bits is very expensive, thus the number available for testing is small. A sample of 8 drill bits had a mean drilling time of 2.25 hours with a standard deviation of 0.5 hours. Is it reasonable for the manufacturer to claim that the drill bits will last 2.5 hours?

14.

15. Of a random sample of 90 firms with employee stock ownership plans, 50 indicated that the primary reason for setting up the plan was tax related. Develop a 90 percent confidence interval for the population proportion of all such firms with this as the primary motivation.

15.

16. A study of 305 computer chips found that 244 chips functioned properly. Develop a 99 percent confidence interval for the population proportion of properly functioning computer chips.

16.

17. A correctional institution would like to report the mean amount of money spent per day on operating the facilities. How many days should be considered if a 95 percent confidence is used and the estimate is to be within one hundred dollars? The standard deviation is $400.

17.

18. *The Corporate Lawyer*, a magazine for corporate lawyers, would like to report the mean amount earned by lawyers in their area of specialization. How large a sample is required if the 97 percent level of confidence is used and the estimate is to be within $2,500?   The standard deviation is $16,000.

18.

19. The Customer Relations Department at SkyBlue Airline wants to estimate the proportion of customers that carry only hand luggage. The estimate is to be within 0.03 of the true proportion with 95 percent level of confidence. No estimate of the population proportion is available. How large a sample is required?

19.

20. A survey is being conducted on a local mayoral election. If the poll is to have a 98 percent confidence level and must be within four percentage points, how many people should be surveyed?

20.

CHAPTER 10
ONE-SAMPLE TESTS OF HYPOTHESIS

Chapter Goals

After completing this chapter, you will be able to:

1. Define a hypothesis and hypothesis testing.

2. Describe the five-step hypothesis-testing procedure.

3. Distinguish between a one-tailed and a two-tailed test of hypothesis.

4. Conduct a test of hypothesis about a population mean.

5. Conduct a test of hypothesis about a population proportion.

6. Define *Type I* and *Type II* errors.

7. Compute the probability of a *Type II* error.

Introduction

In Chapter 8 we began our study of statistical inference by describing how we could select a random sample and then use the sample values to estimate the value of a population parameter. Recall that a sample is a part or subset of the population, while a parameter is a value calculated from the entire population. In Chapter 9 we estimated a population parameter from a sample statistic. In addition, we developed a range of values, called a confidence interval, within which we expected the population value to be located.

In this chapter, rather than developing a range of values within which we expect the population parameter to occur, we will conduct a test of hypothesis regarding the validity of a statement about a population parameter.

Two statements called hypotheses are made regarding the possible values of population parameters.

What is a Hypothesis?

A *hypothesis* is a statement about a population.

> *Hypothesis*: A statement about a population parameter developed for the purpose of testing.

In statistical analysis we make a claim, that is, state a hypothesis, and then follow up with tests to verify the assertion or to determine that it is untrue.

What is Hypothesis Testing?

The terms *hypothesis testing* and *testing a hypothesis* are used interchangeably. Hypothesis testing starts with a statement about a population parameter such as the mean.

> ***Hypothesis testing***: A procedure based on sample evidence and probability theory to determine whether the hypothesis is a reasonable statement.

For example, one statement about the performance of a new model car is that the mean miles per gallon is 30. The other statement is that the mean miles per gallon is not 30. Only one of these statements is correct.

Five-Step Procedure for Testing a Hypothesis

Statistical hypothesis testing is a five-step procedure. These steps are:

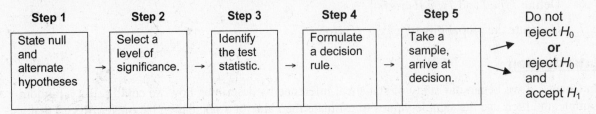

When we arrive at Step 5, we are ready to either accept or reject the null hypothesis. You should be aware that hypothesis testing as used by statisticians does not provide proof that something is true in the manner that a mathematician proves a statement. However, in cases where the null hypothesis is rejected, it does provide "proof beyond a reasonable doubt" that the null hypothesis is not true. The steps involved in hypothesis testing will now be described in more detail.

First we will concentrate on testing a hypothesis about a population mean. Then we will consider hypothesis testing for a population proportion. For a mean:

Step 1. State the null hypothesis (H_0) and the alternate hypothesis (H_1).

The first step is to state the hypothesis being tested. It is called the ***null hypothesis***, designated H_0, and read H sub zero. The capital letter H stands for hypothesis, and the subscript zero implies "no difference."

> ***Null hypothesis***: A statement about the value of a population parameter.

For example, a recent newspaper report made the claim that the mean length of a hospital stay was 3.3 days. You think that the true length of stay is some other length than 3.3 days.

The null hypothesis is written H_0: $\mu = 3.3$, where H_0 is an abbreviation of the null hypothesis. The null hypothesis will always contain the equal sign. It is the statement about the value of the population parameter, in this case the population mean. The null hypothesis is established for the purpose of testing. On the basis of the sample evidence, it is either rejected or not rejected.

If the null hypothesis is rejected then we accept the ***alternate hypothesis***.

> ***Alternate hypothesis***: A statement that is accepted if the sample data provide enough evidence that the null hypothesis is false.

The alternate hypothesis is written H_1. From the above example the alternate hypothesis is that the mean length of stay is not 3.3 days. It is written H_1: $\mu \neq 3.3$ ($\neq$ is read "not equal to"). H_1 is accepted only if H_0 is rejected. When the "$\neq$" sign appears in the alternate hypothesis, the test is called **a two-tailed test**.

There are two other formats for writing the null and alternate hypotheses. Suppose you think that the mean length of stay is greater than 3.3 days. The null and alternate hypotheses would be written as follows: ($\leq$ is read "equal to or less than").

$$H_0: \mu \leq 3.3$$
$$H_1: \mu > 3.3$$

Notice that in this case the null hypothesis indicates "no change or that μ is less than 3.3." The alternate hypothesis states that the mean length of stay is greater than 3.3 days. Acceptance of the alternate hypothesis would allow us to conclude that the mean length of stay is greater than 3.3 days.

What if you think that the mean length of stay is less than 3.3 days? The null and alternate hypotheses would be written as:

$$H_0: \mu \geq 3.3$$
$$H_1: \mu < 3.3$$

Acceptance of the alternate hypothesis in this instance would allow you to conclude the mean length of stay is less than 3.3 days. When a direction is expressed in the alternate hypothesis, such as $>$ or $<$, the test is referred to as being **one-tailed**.

Step 2. Select the Level of Significance.

After setting up the null hypothesis and alternate hypothesis, the next step is to state the ***level of significance***.

> ***Level of significance***: The probability of rejecting the null hypothesis when it is true.

The level of significance is designated α, the Greek letter alpha. The level of significance is sometimes called the level of risk. It will indicate when the sample mean is too far away from the hypothesized mean for the null hypothesis to be true. Usually the significance level is set at either 0.01 or 0.05, although other values may be chosen.

Testing a null hypothesis at the 0.05 significance level, for example, indicates that the probability of rejecting the null hypothesis, even though it is true, is 0.05. The 0.05 level is also stated as the 5% level. When a true null hypothesis is rejected, it is referred to as a ***Type I error***.

> ***Type I error***: Rejecting the null hypothesis, H_0, when it is true.

The decision whether to use the 0.01 or the 0.05 significance level, or some other value, depends on the consequences of making a Type I error. The significance level is chosen before the sample is selected.

If the null hypothesis is not true, but our sample results indicate that it is, we have a ***Type II error***.

> ***Type II error***: Accepting the null hypothesis when it actually is false.

For example, H_0 is that the mean hospital stay is 3.3 days. Our sample evidence fails to refute this hypothesis, but actually the population mean length of stay is 4.0 days. In this situation we have committed a Type II error by accepting a false H_0.

We refer to the probability of these two possible errors as *alpha* α and *beta* β. *Alpha* (α) is the probability of making a Type I error and *beta* (β) is the probability of making a Type II error. The table on the right summarizes the decisions the researcher could make and the possible consequences.

Null Hypothesis	Researcher	
	Accepts H_0	Rejects H_0
H_0 is true	Correct decision	Type I error
H_0 is false	Type II error	Correct decision

Step 3. Select the Test Statistic.

A ***test statistic*** is a quantity calculated from the sample information and is used as the basis for deciding whether or not to reject the null hypothesis.

> ***Test statistic***: A value, determined from sample information, used to determine whether to reject the null hypothesis.

Exactly which test statistic to employ is determined by factors such as whether the population standard deviation is known.

In hypothesis testing for the mean μ, when σ is known the test statistic z is computed by Formula [10-1]:

$$\text{Testing a Mean, } \sigma \text{ Known} \qquad z = \frac{\overline{X} - \mu}{\sigma / \sqrt{n}} \qquad [10-1]$$

Where:
z is the value of the test statistic.
$\overline{X}$ is the sample mean.
μ is the population mean.
σ is the population standard deviation.
n is the sample size.

Step 4. Formulate the Decision Rule.

A ***decision rule*** is based on H_0 and H_1, the level of significance, and the test statistic.

> ***Decision rule***: A statement of the conditions under which the null hypothesis is rejected and conditions under which it is not rejected.

The region or area of rejection indicates the location of the values that are so large or so small that the probability of their occurrence for a true null hypothesis is rather remote.

If we are applying a one-tailed test, there is one *critical value*. If we are applying a two-tailed test, there are two critical values.

> *Critical value*: The dividing point between the region where the null hypothesis is rejected and the region where it is not rejected.

Chart 10-1 shows the conditions under which the null hypothesis is rejected, using the 0.05 significance level, a one-tailed test, and the standard normal distribution.

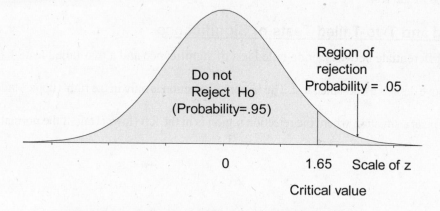

Do not
Reject Ho
(Probability=.95)

Region of
rejection
Probability = .05

0   1.65   Scale of z
Critical value

Chart 10-1 Sampling Distribution of the Statistic z,
Right-Tailed Test, 0.05 Level of Significance

The above diagram portrays the rejection region for a right-tailed test.

1. The area where the null hypothesis is not rejected is to the left of 1.65.

2. The area of rejection is to the right of 1.65.

3. A one-tailed test is being applied.

4. The 0.05 level of significance was chosen.

5. The sampling distribution of the test statistic z is normally distributed.

6. The value 1.65 separates the regions where the null hypothesis is rejected and where it is not rejected.

7. The value 1.65 is called the *critical value*.

When is the standard normal distribution used? It is appropriate when the population is normal and the population standard deviation is known.

If the computed value of z is greater than 1.65, the null hypothesis is rejected. If the computed value of z is less than or equal to 1.65, the null hypothesis is not rejected.

Step 5. Compute the value of the test statistic, make a decision, and interpret the results.

The final step in hypothesis testing after selecting the sample is to compute the value of the test statistic. This value is compared to the critical value, or values, and a decision is made whether to reject or not to reject the null hypothesis. Interpret the results.

A summary of the steps in hypothesis testing:

1. Establish the null hypothesis (H_0) and the alternate hypothesis (H_1).

2. Select the level of significance, that is α.

3. Select an appropriate test statistic.

4. Formulate the decision rule, based on steps 1, 2, and 3 above.

5. Make a decision regarding the null hypothesis based on the sample information. Interpret the results of the test.

One-Tailed and Two-Tailed Tests of Significance

We need to differentiate between a one-tailed test of significance and a two-tailed test of significance.

Chart 10-1 above depicts a one-tailed test. The region of rejection is only in the right (upper) tail of the curve.

Chart 10-2 depicts a situation where the rejection region is in the left (lower) tail of the normal distribution.

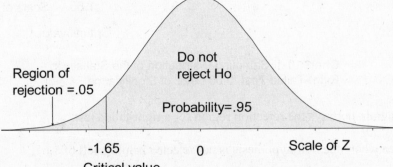

Chart 10-2 Sampling Distribution of the Statistic z, Left-Tailed Test, 0.05 Level of Significance

Chart 10-3 depicts a situation for a two-tailed test where the rejection region is divided equally into the two tails of the normal distribution.

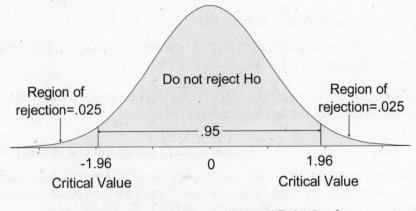

Chart 10-3 Regions of Nonrejection and Rejection for a Two-Tailed Test, 0.05 Level of Significance

Testing for a Population Mean with a Known Population Standard Deviation

Suppose we are concerned with a single population mean. We want to test if our sample mean could have been obtained from a population with a particular hypothesized mean. For example, we may be interested in testing whether the mean starting salary of recent marketing graduates is equal to $32,000 per year. It is assumed that:

1. The population is normally distributed.
2. The population standard deviation is known.

Under these conditions the test statistic is the standard normal distribution with the sample standard deviation s substituted for σ. Thus we use text formula [10-1].

$$z = \frac{\overline{X} - \mu}{\sigma / \sqrt{n}}$$

Where:

z is the value of the test statistic.
$\overline{X}$ is the sample mean.
μ is the population mean.
σ is the standard deviation of population.
n is the number in sample.

p-value in Hypothesis Testing

In the process of testing a hypothesis, we compared the test statistic to a critical value. We made a decision to either reject the null hypothesis or not to reject it. The question is often asked as to how confident we were in rejecting the null hypothesis.

A *p-value* is frequently compared to the significance level to evaluate the decision regarding the null hypothesis. It is a means of reporting the likelihood that H_0 is true.

> *p-value*: The probability of observing a sample value as extreme as, or more extreme than, the value observed, given that the null hypothesis is true.

- If the *p-value* is greater than the significance level, then H_0 is not rejected.
- If the *p-value* is less than the significance level, then H_0 is rejected.
- The *p*-value for a given test depends on three factors:
    1. whether the alternate hypothesis is one-tailed or two-tailed
    2. the particular test statistic that is used
    3. the computed value of the test statistic

For example, if $\alpha = 0.05$ and the *p*-value is 0.0025, H_0 is rejected. We report there is only a 0.0025 likelihood that H_0 is true.

Interpreting the weight of evidence against H_0.	If the p value is less than
	(a) 0.10, we have *some* evidence that H_0 is not true.
	(b) 0.05, we have *strong* evidence that H_0 is not true.
	(c) 0.01, we have *very strong* evidence that H_0 is not true.
	(d) 0.001, we have *extremely strong* evidence that H_0 is not true.

Testing for a Population Mean: Population Standard Deviation Unknown

In most cases the population standard deviation is unknown. Thus, σ must be based on prior studies or estimated by the sample standard deviation, s. In cases where we are using s in place of σ, Formula [10-1] is modified as follows:

$$\text{Testing a Mean, } \sigma \text{ Unknown} \qquad t = \frac{\bar{X} - \mu}{s/\sqrt{n}} \qquad [10\text{-}2]$$

with n-1 degrees of freedom, where:

t is the value of the test statistic.

$\bar{X}$ is the mean of the sample.

μ is the hypothesized population mean.

s is the standard deviation of the sample.

n is the number of observations in the sample.

This is similar to the situation that we encountered in Chapter 9 when constructing confidence intervals for μ. When sampling from a normal population and σ is unknown, we use a t distribution with n-1 degrees of freedom. In Chapter 9, we noted that the following major characteristics of the t distribution:

1. It is a continuous distribution.

2. It is bell shaped and symmetrical.

3. There is a "family" of t distributions. Each time the size of the sample changes, and thus the degrees of freedom change, a new t distribution is created.

4. As the number of degrees of freedom increases, the shape of the t distribution approaches that of the standard normal distribution.

5. The t distribution is more spread out (that is, "flatter") than the standard normal distribution.

Tests Concerning Proportions

In the previous chapter we discussed confidence intervals for proportions. We continue our study of hypothesis testing but expand the idea to a ***proportion***. What is a proportion?

Proportion: The fraction, ratio, or percent indicating the part of the population or sample having a particular trait of interest.

If we let p stand for the sample proportion then text formula [10-3] is:

$$\boxed{\textbf{Test of Hypothesis, One Proportion} \quad z = \frac{p - \pi}{\sigma_p} \qquad [10-3]}$$

Where:
z is the value of the test statistic
π is the population proportion.
p is the sample proportion.
σ_p is the standard error of the population proportion. It is computed by $\sqrt{\pi(1-\pi)/n}$ so the formula for z becomes text Formula [10–4]:

$$\boxed{\textbf{Test of Hypothesis, One Proportion} \quad z = \frac{p - \pi}{\sqrt{\dfrac{\pi(1-\pi)}{n}}} \qquad [10-4]}$$

Where:
z is the value of the test statistic
π is the population proportion.
p is the sample proportion.
n is the sample size.

For example, we want to estimate the proportion of all home sales made to first time buyers. A random sample of 200 recent transactions showed that 40 were first time buyers. Therefore, we estimate that 0.20, or 20 percent, of all sales are made to first time buyers, found by:

$$p = \frac{40}{200} = 0.20$$

To conduct a test of hypothesis for proportions, the same assumptions required for the binomial distribution must be met. Recall from Chapter 6 that those assumptions are:

1. Each outcome is classified into one of two categories such as, buyers were either first time home buyers or they were not.

2. The number of trials is fixed. In this case it is 200.

3. Each trial is independent, meaning that the outcome of one trial has no bearing on the outcome of any other. Whether the 20th sampled person was a first time buyer does not affect the outcome of any other trial.

4. The probability of a success is fixed. The probability is 0.20 for all 200 buyers in the sample.

Recall from Chapter 6 that the normal distribution is a good approximation of the binomial distribution when $n\pi$ and $n(1-\pi)$ are both greater than 5. In this instance n refers to the sample size and π to the probability of a success. The test statistic that is employed for testing hypotheses about proportions is the standard normal distribution.

Types of Tests of Hypothesis for a Proportion

There are three formats for testing a hypothesis about a proportion. For a one-tailed test there are two possibilities, depending on the intent of the researcher. For example, if we wanted to determine whether more than 25 percent of the sales of homes were sold to first time buyers, the hypotheses would be given as follows:

$$H_0: \pi \leq 0.25$$
$$H_1: \pi > 0.25$$

If we wanted to find out whether fewer than 25 percent of the homes were sold to first time buyers, the hypotheses would be given as:

$$H_0: \pi \geq 0.25$$
$$H_1: \pi < 0.25$$

For a two-tailed test the null and alternate hypotheses are:

$$H_0: \pi = 0.25$$
$$H_1: \pi \neq 0.25$$

Where $\neq$ means "not equal to." Rejection of H_0 and acceptance of H_1 allows us to conclude only that the population proportion is "different from" or "not equal to" the population value. It does not allow us to make any statement about the direction of the difference.

Type II Error

Recall that the level of significance, identified by the Greek letter alpha (α), is the probability that the null hypothesis is rejected when it is true. This is called a Type I error.

In a hypothesis testing situation there is also the possibility that a null hypothesis is not rejected when it is actually false. In other words we accept a false null hypothesis. This is called a Type II error. The probability of a Type II error is identified by the Greek letter beta (β)

The likelihood of a Type II error is found by text Formula [10–5]:

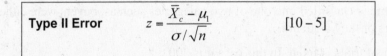

$$\text{Type II Error} \qquad z = \frac{\overline{X}_c - \mu_1}{\sigma / \sqrt{n}} \qquad [10-5]$$

Where:

$\overline{X}_c$ is the value of the sample mean corresponding to the critical value of the test statistic, z.

μ_1 is the alternate value of the population mean.

Glossary

Alternate hypothesis: A statement that is accepted if the sample data provide evidence that the null hypothesis is false.

Critical value: The dividing point between the region where the null hypothesis is rejected and the region where it is not rejected.

Decision rule: A statement of the conditions under which the null hypothesis is rejected and conditions under which it is not rejected.

Hypothesis: A statement about a population parameter developed for the purpose of testing.

Hypothesis testing: A procedure based on sample evidence and probability theory to determine whether the hypothesis is a reasonable statement.

Level of significance: The probability of rejecting the null hypothesis when it is true.

Null hypothesis: A statement about the value of a population parameter.

p-value: The probability of observing a sample value as extreme as, or more extreme than, the value observed, given that the null hypothesis is true.

Proportion: The fraction, ratio, or percent indicating the part of the population or sample having a particular trait of interest

Test statistic: A value, determined from sample information, used to determine whether to reject the null hypothesis.

Type I error: Rejecting the null hypothesis, H_0, when it is true.

Type II error: Accepting the null hypothesis, H_0, when it actually is false.

Chapter Problems

Problem 1

The manufacturer of the new subcompact Clipper claims in their TV advertisements thatit will average "40 or more miles per gallon on the open road". Some of the competitors believe this claim is too high. To investigate, an independent testing agency is hired to conduct highway mileage tests. A random sample of 64 Clippers showed their mean miles per gallon to be 38.9. If the population standard deviation, σ, is equal to 4.0 miles per gallon, test the manufacturer's claim that the Clipper averages 40 or more miles per gallon using a 0.01 significance level. Determine the p value. Interpret the result.

Solution 1

Step 1: *State the null and alternate hypotheses*:

The null hypothesis refers to the "no change" situation. That is, there has been no change in the Clipper's mileage; it is 40 or more mpg.

It is written: $H_0: \mu \geq 40$ and is read that the population mean is greater than or equal to 40.

The alternate hypothesis written: H_1: $\mu < 40$ and is read that the population mean is less than 40.

If the null hypothesis is rejected, then the alternate hypothesis is accepted. It would be concluded that the Clipper's mileage is less than 40 mpg.

Step 2: *Select the level of significance:*

The testing agency decided on the 0.01significance level. This is the probability that the null hypothesis will be rejected when in fact it is true.

Step 3: *Decide on a test statistic:*

In hypothesis testing for the mean (μ) when σ is known, the test statistic z is computed using text formula [10-1].

$$z = \frac{\overline{X} - \mu}{\sigma / \sqrt{n}}$$

Where:
$\overline{X}$ is the sample mean.
μ is the population mean.
σ is the population standard deviation.
n is the sample size.

Step 4: *Develop the decision rule:*

The decision rule is a statement of the conditions under which the null hypothesis is rejected. The decision rule is shown in the following diagram. If the computed value of z is to the left of –2.33, the null hypothesis is rejected. The –2.33 is the critical value. How is it determined?

Remember that the significance level stated in the problem is 0.01. This indicates that the area to the left of the critical value under the normal curve is 0.01. For the standard normal distribution the total area to the left of 0 is 0.5000. Therefore, the area between the critical value and 0 is 0.4900, found by 0.5000 – 0.0100. Now refer to Appendix B.1 and search the body of the table for a value close to 0.4900. The closest value is 0.4901. Read 2.3 in the left margin and 0.03 in the column containing 0.4901. Thus the z value corresponding to 0.4901 is 2.33.

Recall from Step 1 that the alternate hypothesis is H_1: $\mu < 40$. The inequality sign points in the negative direction. Thus the critical value is –2.33 and the rejection region is all in the lower left tail.

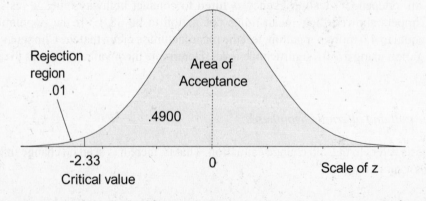

Step 5: *Compute the value of the test statistic, make a decision regarding the null hypothesis, and interpret the results*:

Repeating the formula for z:

$$z = \frac{\bar{X} - \mu}{\sigma / \sqrt{n}}$$

Recall that the manufacturer claims 40 mpg and the mean of the sample is 38.9 mpg and σ is 4.0. Solving for z:

$$z = \frac{38.9 - 40.0}{4.0 / \sqrt{64}} = \frac{-1.1}{0.5} = -2.20$$

The computed value of –2.20 is to the right of –2.33, so the null hypothesis is not rejected. We do not reject the claim of the manufacturer that the Clipper gets at least 40.0 miles per gallon. It is reasonable that the 1.1 miles per gallon between (40.0 and 38.9) could be due to chance.

We do observe, however, that –2.20 is fairly close to the critical value of –2.33. What is the likelihood of a z value to the left of –2.20? It is 0.0139, found by 0.5000 – 0.4861, where 0.4861 is the likelihood of a z value between 0 and 2.20. (The probabilities are found in Appendix B.1.)

The 0.0139 is referred to as the *p*-value. It is the probability of getting a value of the test statistic (z in this case) more extreme than that actually observed, if the null hypothesis is true. Had the significance level been set at 0.02 instead of ,0.0l, the null hypothesis would have been rejected. By reporting the *p*-value we give information on the strength of the decision regarding the null hypothesis.

Exercise 10.1

Check your answers against those in the ANSWER section.

Last year the records of Dairy Land Inc., a convenience store chain, showed the mean amount spent by a customer was $30. A sample of 40 transactions this month revealed the mean amount spent was $33. Assume that the population standard deviation, σ, is known and equal to $12. At the 0.05 significance level, can we conclude that the mean amount spent has increased? What is the *p*-value? Follow the five-step hypothesis testing procedure.

Problem 2

The mean construction time for a standard two-car garage by Arrowhead Construction Company is 3.5 days. The time for the construction process follows the normal distribution. The construction process is modified through the use of a "quick setting concrete" for the foundation and floor. This should allow the next phase of construction to start in a more timely manner. A sample of 12 garages had a mean construction time of 3.0 days with a standard deviation of 0.9 days. Does use of the quick setting concrete decrease the construction time?

Solution 2

Step 1: *State the null and alternate hypotheses*:

The null hypothesis is that there is no change in the construction time. That is, the construction time is at least 3.5 days. The alternate hypothesis is that the construction time is less than 3.5 days.

Symbolically, these statements are written as follows:

$$H_0: \mu \geq 3.5$$
$$H_1: \mu < 3.5$$

Step 2: *Select the level of significance:*

We decided on the 0.05 significance level. This is the probability that the null hypothesis will be rejected when in fact it is true.

Step 3: *Select the test statistic:*

The test static in this situation is the t distribution. The distribution of construction times follows the normal distribution, however we do not know the value of the population standard deviation. Also, we have a small sample.

We use text Formula [10-2]:

$$t = \frac{\overline{X} - \mu}{s / \sqrt{n}}$$

Where:
t is the value of the test statistic.
$\overline{X}$ is the sample mean. (3.0 days)
μ is the population mean. (3.5 days)
s is the standard deviation of the sample. (0.9 days)
n is the sample size. (12)

Thus: $t = \dfrac{\overline{X} - \mu}{s / \sqrt{n}} = \dfrac{3.0 - 3.5}{0.9 / \sqrt{12}} = \dfrac{-0.5}{0.2598} = -1.925$

Step 4: *Develop the decision rule:*

The decision rule is a statement of the conditions under which the null hypothesis is rejected. If the computed value of t is to the left of -1.796, the null hypothesis is rejected. The -1.796 is the critical value. How is it determined?

Remember that the significance level stated in the problem is 0.05. The critical values of t are given in Appendix B.2. The number of degrees of freedom is $(n - 1) = (12 - 1) = 11$. We have a one-tailed test, so we find the portion of the table labeled "one-tailed." Locate the column for the 0.05 significance level. Read down the column until it intersects the row with 11 degrees of freedom. The value is 1.796.

Since this is a one-tailed test and the rejection region is in the left tail, the critical value is negative.

The decision rule is to reject H_0 if the value of t is less than -1.796.

Step 5: *Make a decision regarding the null hypothesis and interpret the results*:

Because −1.925 lies to the left of the critical value −1.796, the null hypothesis is rejected at the 0.05 significance level. This indicates that the use of the "quick setting concrete" has reduced the mean construction time to less than 3.5 days.

Exercise 10.2

Check your answers against those in the ANSWER section.

The mean construction time for a standard two-car garage by Arrowhead Construction Company is 3.5 days. The time for the construction process follows the normal distribution. The construction process is modified through the use of "precut and assembled roof trusses" rather than onsite construction of roof rafters. This should shorten the construction time. A sample of 15 garages had a mean time of 3.40 days with a standard deviation of 0.8 days. Does use of the "precut and assembled roof trusses" decrease the construction time? Follow the five-step hypothesis testing procedure using the 0.05 significance level.

Problem 3

The Bunting Brass & Bronze Company has a computer controlled machine that is programmed to do precision cutting of a circular brass disc with a mean diameter of 6.125 inches. The shop foreman takes a random sample of 8 discs from the production line. The diameters are as follows:

> 6.115   6.127   6.129   6.113   6.124   6.121   6.131   6.124

The foreman suspects that the machine is out of adjustment. Use the hypothesis testing procedure to determine if the programmer needs to make adjustments.

Solution 3

Step 1: *State the null and alternate hypotheses*:

The null hypothesis is that the machine is not out of adjustment. That is, the mean diameter of the discs is 6.125 inches. The alternate hypothesis is that the mean diameter is not 6.125 inches. .

Symbolically, these statements are written as follows:

$$H_0 : \mu = 6.125$$
$$H_1 : \mu \neq 6.125$$

Step 2: *Select the level of significance:*

We decided on the 0.01 significance level. This is the probability that the null hypothesis will be rejected when in fact it is true.

Step 3: *Select the test statistic:*

The test statistic in this situation is the *t* distribution. The disc diameters follow the normal distribution, however we do not know the value of the population standard deviation. Also, we have a small sample.

Step 4: *Develop the decision rule:*

The decision rule is a statement of the conditions under which the null hypothesis is rejected. The alternate hypothesis does not state a direction, so this is a two-tailed test.

Remember that the significance level stated in the problem is 0.01. The critical values of t are given in Appendix B.2. The number of degrees of freedom is $(n-1) = (8-1) = 7$. We have a two-tailed test, so we find the portion of the table labeled "two-tailed." Locate the column for the 0.01 significance level. Read down the column until it intersects the row with 7 degrees of freedom. The value is 3.499.

The decision rule is: Reject the null hypothesis if the computed value of t is to the left of -3.449, or to the right of 3.449

Step 5: *Make a decision regarding the null hypothesis, and interpret the results:*

We use text Formula [10-2]:

$$t = \frac{\overline{X} - \mu}{s / \sqrt{n}}$$

Where:
t is the value of the test statistic.
$\overline{X}$ is the sample mean.
μ is the population mean. (6.125 inches)
s is the standard deviation of the sample.
n is the sample size. (8)

We first need to calculate the mean and standard deviation of the sample. The mean and standard deviation are computed as follows:

X	$X - \overline{X}$	$(X - \overline{X})^2$	X^2
6.115	−0.008	0.000064	37.393225
6.127	0.004	0.000016	37.540129
6.129	0.006	0.000036	37.564641
6.113	−0.010	0.000100	37.368769
6.124	0.001	0.000001	37.503376
6.121	−0.002	0.000004	37.466641
6.131	0.008	0.000064	37.589161
6.124	0.001	0.000001	37.503376
Σ 48.984	0.000	0.000286	299.929318

$$\overline{X} = \frac{\Sigma X}{n} = \frac{48.984}{8} = 6.123$$

$$s = \sqrt{\frac{\Sigma(X - \overline{X})^2}{n-1}} = \sqrt{\frac{0.000286}{8-1}}$$

$$= \sqrt{0.000040857} = 0.0063919 = 0.0064$$

The value of t is computed using Formula [10-2]:

$$t = \frac{\overline{X} - \mu}{s / \sqrt{n}} = \frac{6.123 - 6.125}{0.0064 / \sqrt{8}} = \frac{-0.002}{0.0022627} = -0.8839$$

The computed value of −0.8829 lies between the two critical values: −3.449 and 3.449. The null hypothesis is not rejected at the 0.01 significance level. The foreman's suspicion that the machine is out of adjustment cannot be substantiated with this sample.

Exercise 10.3

Check your answers against those in the ANSWER section.

A typical college student spends an average of 2.55 hours a day using a computer. A sample of 13 students at The University of Findlay revealed the following number of hours per day using the computer:

3.15	3.25	2.00	2.50	2.65	2.75	2.35	2.85	2.95	2.45	1.95	2.35	3.75

Can we conclude that the mean number of hours per day using the computer by students at The University of Findlay is the same as the typical student's usage? Use the hypothesis testing procedure and the 0.05 significance level.

Problem 4

The Dean of Students at Scandia Tech believes that 30 percent of the students are employed. You, as President of the Student Government, believe the proportion employed is less than 30 percent and decide to conduct a study. A random sample of 100 students revealed 25 were employed. At the 0.01 significance level, can the Dean's claim be refuted?

Solution 4

As usual, the first step is to state the null and alternate hypotheses. The null hypothesis is that there is no change in the percent employed. That is, the population proportion is at least 0.30. The alternate hypothesis is that the population proportion is less than 0.30. This is the statement we are trying to test empirically. Symbolically, these statements are written as follows:

$$H_0: \pi \geq 0.30$$
$$H_1: \pi < 0.30$$

The 0.01 significance level is to be used. The assumptions of the binomial distribution are met in the problem. That is

1. There are only two outcomes for each trial--the student is either employed or isn't employed.

2. The number of trials is fixed—100 students.

3. Each trial is independent, meaning the employment of one student selected does not affect another.

4. The probability that any randomly selected student is employed is 0.30.

The normal approximation to the binomial is used because both $n\pi$ and $n(1 - \pi)$ exceed 5. That is: $[n\pi = 100(0.30)] = 30$ and $n(1 - \pi) = 100(0.70) = 70$. The standard normal distribution, z is the test statistic. To formulate the decision rule, we need the critical value of z. Using the 0.01 significance level, the area is 0.4900, (0.5000 − 0.0100).

Search the body of Appendix B.1 for a value as close to 0.4900 as possible. It is 0.4901. The z value associated with 0.4901 is 2.33. The alternate hypothesis points in the negative direction, hence the rejection region is in the left tail and the critical value of z is −2.33.

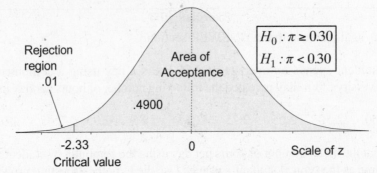

The decision rule is to reject the null hypothesis if the computed value of the test statistic lies in the rejection region to the left of −2.33.

Recall that the sample of 100 Scandia Tech students revealed that 25 were employed. The question is whether the sample proportion of 0.25, found by 25/100, is significantly less than 0.30.

$$z = \frac{p - \pi}{\sqrt{\dfrac{\pi(1-\pi)}{n}}} = \frac{0.25 - 0.30}{\sqrt{\dfrac{(0.30)(1-0.30)}{100}}} = -1.09$$

The computed value of z falls in the region between 0 and −2.33. H_0 is not rejected. There is a difference between the Dean's hypothesized proportion (0.30) and the sample proportion (0.25), but this difference of 0.05 is not sufficient to reject the null hypothesis. The 0.05 can be attributed to sampling (chance). The Dean's claim cannot be refuted.

The p-value is the probability of a z value to the left of −1.09. It is 0.1379, found by (0.5000 − 0.3621). The p-value is larger than the significance level of 0.01, which is consistent with our decision not to reject the null hypothesis.

Exercise 10.4

Check your answers against those in the ANSWER section.

The producer of a TV special expected about 40 percent of the viewing audience to watch a rerun of a 1965 Beatles Concert. A sample of 200 homes revealed 60 to be watching the concert. At the 0.10 significance level, does the evidence suggest that less than 40 percent were watching? Use the usual hypothesis testing format. What is the p-value?

Problem Five

Refer to Problem One. Suppose that the true mean mileage of the Clipper is 39.5 miles per gallon and the population standard deviation remains the same at $\sigma = 4$ miles per gallon. What is the probability that the hypothesis testing procedure will fail to detect this difference in the mean? That is, what is the probability of making a Type II error, β, if in fact the true mean, μ, is 39.5 miles per gallon?

Solution

Text formula [10-5] is used to determine the probability of a Type II error.

$$z = \frac{\bar{X}_c - \mu_1}{\sigma / \sqrt{n}} \qquad [10-5]$$

Where:
μ_1 refers to the alternate value of the population mean.
$\bar{X}_c$ is the value of the sample mean corresponding to the critical value of z.

First, find the critical value of the sample mean, $\bar{X}_c$ by substituting the critical value of z, -2.33, into text formula [10-1] and solving for $\bar{X}$:

$$-2.33 = \frac{\bar{X} - \mu}{\sigma / \sqrt{n}}$$

$$\bar{X}_c = \bar{X} = -2.33\left(4/\sqrt{64}\right) + 40.0$$

$$\bar{X}_c = 38.835 .$$

Next, substitute $\bar{X}_c = 38.835$ and $\mu_1 = 39.5$ into formula [10-5] and compute the z value.

$$z = \frac{\bar{X}_c - \mu_1}{\sigma / \sqrt{n}} =$$

$$\frac{38.835 - 39.5}{4/\sqrt{64}} = -1.33 .$$

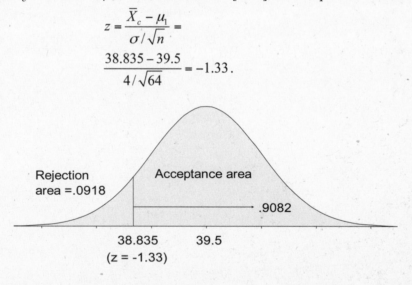

Rejection area = .0918

Acceptance area

.9082

38.835   39.5
(z = -1.33)

The rejection area is found by looking up a z value of 1.33 in Appendix B.1 and locating an area of 0.4082. Subtracting 0.4082 from 0.5000 we find that the tail area is .0918. We accept the null hypothesis when $\bar{X}_c$ is greater than or equal to 38.835. The probability of obtaining a sample mean, $\bar{X}$, of 38.835 or less when the population mean is 39.5 (the alternate value of the mean, μ_1) is 0.9082. Thus, the probability of a Type II error, β, when the true mean is 39.5 and we are testing at a significance level of 0.01 is 0.9082.

Exercise 10.5

Check your answers against those in the ANSWER section.

Refer to Exercise 10.1. Suppose that the mean amount spent has increased to $32. What is the probability that this increase will not be detected by the hypothesis testing procedure that we conducted in Exercise 10.1? That is, what is the probability of a Type II error, β?

ONE-SAMPLE TESTS OF HYPOTHESIS

Name _____ Section _____ Score _____

Part I   Select the correct answer and write the appropriate letter in the space provided.

_____ 1. The null hypothesis is a claim about
    a. the size of the sample.   **b.** the size of the population.
    c. the value of a sample statistic.   **d.** the value of a population parameter.

_____ 2. When the null hypothesis is rejected, we conclude that
    a. the alternate hypothesis is false also.   **b.** the alternate hypothesis is true.
    c. the sample size is too large.   **d.** we used the wrong test statistic.

_____ 3. A Type I error is committed when
    a. p value is larger than 1.0.   **b.** the significance level is greater than 0.05.
    c. we reject a true H_0.   **d.** we accept a false H_0.

_____ 4. The condition or conditions under which H_0 is rejected is
    a. called the decision rule.   **b.** the likelihood of a Type I error.
    c. called the test statistic.   **d.** called the p-value.

_____ 5. When the p-value is smaller than the significance level
    a. a Type I error is committed.   **b.** a Type II error is committed.
    c. the null hypothesis is rejected.   **d.** the critical value is correct.

_____ 6. A Type II error is
    a. rejecting H_1 when it is false.   **b.** accepting a false H_0.
    c. reject H_0 when it is true.   **d.** not rejecting a false H_1.

_____ 7. In a hypothesis test of a population proportion
    a. a t value is used for the test statistic   **b.** the parameter being tested is π
    c. p refers to p-value   **d.** the population that we sample from is normal

_____ 8. Under what conditions would a test be considered a one-tailed test.
    a. When H_0 contains $\neq$.   **b.** When there is more than one critical value.
    c. When H_1 contains =.   **d.** When H_1 includes a $<$ or $>$.

_____ 9. In a two-tailed test the rejection region is
    a. all in the upper tail of the standard normal distribution.
    b. all in the lower tail of the standard normal distribution.
    c. divided equally between the two tails.
    d. always equal to −1.96 or 1.96.

_____ **10.** To compare a sample proportion to a population proportion
  a. n must be less than 30.
  b. π must be less than 5.
  c. $n\pi$ and $n(1 - \pi)$ must both be greater than 5.
  d. σ must be given.

Part II Solve each problem below. Be sure to show essential calculations.

11. The following statements refer to the alternate hypothesis. In the space provided, in symbolic form using H_0, and H_1 , write the null and alternate hypothesis.

  a. The mean pulse of men over fifty years of age is different from 90 beats per minute.

  H_0: _____

  H_1: _____

  b. The mean salary of college presidents is less than $262,500.

  H_0: _____

  H_1: _____

  c. The mean IQ score of 20 year olds is more than 100.

  H_0: _____

  H_1: _____

  d. The mean annual income of sales associates is less than $35,000.

  H_0: _____

  H_1: _____

12. Identify the Type I and Type II error for each claim in question 11.

  a. _____
  _____

  b. _____
  _____

  c. _____
  _____

  d. _____
  _____

13. A recent article in a computer magazine suggested that the mean time to fully learn a new software program is 40 hours. A sample of 100 first-time users of a new statistics program revealed the mean time to learn it was 39 hours with the standard deviation of 8 hours. At the 0.05 significance level, can we conclude that users learn the package in less than a mean of 40 hours?

    a. State the null and alternate hypotheses.

        H_0: _____

        H_1: _____

    b. State the decision rule.

        _____

    c. Compute the value of the test statistic.

c.

    d. Compute the p-value.

d.

    e. What is your decision regarding the null hypothesis? Interpret the result.

        _____

        _____

14. A vinyl siding company claims that the mean time to install siding on a medium-size house is at most 20 hours with a standard deviation of 3.7 hours. A random sample of 40 houses sided in the last three years has a mean installation time of 20.8 hours. At the 0.05 significance level, can a claim be made that it takes longer on average than 20 hours to side a house?

    a. State the null and alternate hypotheses.

        H_0: _____

        H_1: _____

    b. State the decision rule.

        _____

    c. Compute the value of the test statistic.

c.

d. Formulate the decision rule.

_____

e. What is your decision regarding the null hypothesis? Interpret the result.

_____

_____

15. The mean cleanup and redecorating time for a one-bedroom student apartment at campus Housing is 16 hours. The time for the cleanup and redecorating process follows the normal distribution. The campus Housing administration instituted a "fee and fine system" that encourages students to clean their apartments when they vacate them. This should shorten the cleanup and redecorating time. A sample of 15 apartments had a mean cleanup and redecorating time of 14.5 hours with a standard deviation of 1.5 hours. Does use of the "fee and fine system" decrease the cleanup and redecorating time? Follow the five-step hypothesis testing procedure using the 0.05 significance level.

a. State the null and alternate hypotheses.

H_0: _____

H_1: _____

b. What is the level of significance?

b.

c. Compute the value of the test statistic.

c.

d. Formulate the decision rule.

_____

e. What is your decision regarding the null hypothesis? Interpret the result.

_____

_____

16. A typical college student drinks an average of 96 ounces per day of various beverages that contain caffeine. A sample of 12 students at Wallace College revealed the following amounts of beverages consumed containing caffeine:

| 108 | 96 | 84 | 84 | 120 | 96 | 108 | 132 | 72 | 120 | 72 | 96 |

Can we conclude that the average amount of beverages consumed containing caffeine at Ownes College is the same as the typical college student? Use the hypothesis testing procedure.

a. State the null and alternate hypotheses.

H_0: _____

H_1: _____

b. State the decision rule.

_____

Use the table to

c. & d.   Compute the mean and standard deviation.

c.

d.

X	$X - \bar{X}$	$\left(X - \bar{X} \right)^2$
108		
96		
84		
84		
120		
96		
108		
132		
72		
120		
72		
96		

e. Compute the value of the test statistic.

e.

f. Formulate the decision rule.

_____

_____

g. What is your decision regarding the null hypothesis? Interpret the result.

_____

_____

17. The central administration of Fairview College is resisting efforts to build a new student fitness center. In defending their opposition, they claim that 50% or fewer of the student body would use the facility on a regular basis if it were built. Fairview College's Office of Student Welfare believes that more than 50% of the student body would utilize an on-campus fitness facility if one were available. The Office of Student Welfare conducted a survey where 250 of their students were asked whether or not they would utilize an on-campus fitness facility two times a week or more if a new facility were built. One hundred and twenty-two students responded, "yes", that they would use the new facility at least twice per week. Conduct an appropriate test to determine if central administration's claim can be refuted. Use a .01 level of significance.

a. State the null and alternate hypotheses.

H_0: _____

H_1: _____

b. What is the level of significance?

b.

c. Compute the value of the test statistic.

c.

d. Formulate the decision rule.

_____

e. What is your decision regarding the null hypothesis? Interpret the result.

_____

CHAPTER 11
TWO-SAMPLE TESTS OF HYPOTHESIS

Chapter Goals

After completing this chapter, you will be able to:

1. Conduct a test of a hypothesis about the difference between two independent population means.

2. Conduct a test of a hypothesis about the difference between two population proportions.

3. Conduct a test of a hypothesis about the mean difference between paired or dependent observations.

4. Understand the difference between dependent and independent samples.

Introduction

In this chapter we continue our study of hypothesis testing. Recall that in Chapter 10 we considered hypothesis tests in which we compared the results of a single sample statistic to a population parameter. In this chapter, we expand the concept of hypothesis testing to two samples. We select random samples from two independent populations and conduct a hypothesis test to determine whether the population means are equal. We might want to test to see if there is a difference in the mean number of defects produced on the 7:00 AM to 3:00 PM shift and the 3:00 PM to 11:00 PM shift at the DaimlerChrysler Jeep Liberty plant in Toledo, Ohio. We also conduct a hypothesis tests to determine if two sample proportions come from populations which are equal. For example, we may want to determine if the proportion of Jumpin' Java customers who purchase frozen coffee drinks is the same for New England stores versus stores in the southeast.

Two-Sample Tests of Hypothesis: Independent Samples

As noted above, we expand the concept of hypothesis testing to two samples. When there are two populations, we can compare two sample means to determine if they came from populations with the same or equal means.

For example, a purchasing agent is considering two brands of tires for use on the company's fleet of cars. A sample of 60 Rossford tires indicates the mean useful life to be 65,000 miles. A sample of 50 Maumee tires reveals the useful life to be 68,000 miles. Could the difference between the two sample means be due to chance? The assumption is that for both populations (Rossford and Maumee) the standard deviations are known. The test statistic follows the standard normal distribution and its value is computed from text formula [11-2]:

Test Statistic for No Difference Between Two Sample Means	$z = \dfrac{\bar{X}_1 - \bar{X}_2}{\sqrt{\dfrac{\sigma_1^2}{n_1} + \dfrac{\sigma_2^2}{n_2}}}$	[11 – 2]

Where:

$\bar{X}_1$ and $\bar{X}_2$ refer to the two sample means.

σ_1^2 and σ_2^2 refer to the two sample variances.

n_1 and n_2,   refer to the two sample sizes.

The following are assumptions necessary for this two-sample test of means:

1. The two populations must be unrelated; that is, independent.

2. The standard deviations for both populations must be known.

Two-Sample Tests about Proportions

We are often interested in whether two sample proportions came from populations that are equal. For example, we want to compare the proportion of rural voters planning to vote for the incumbent governor with the proportion of urban voters. The test statistic is formula [11-3]:

Two-Sample Test of Proportions	$z = \dfrac{p_1 - p_2}{\sqrt{\dfrac{p_c(1 - p_c)}{n_1} + \dfrac{p_c(1 - p_c)}{n_2}}}$	$[11-3]$

Where:

p_1 is the proportion in the first sample possessing the trait.

p_2 is the proportion in the second sample possessing the trait.

n_1 is the number of observations in the first sample.

n_2 is the number of observations in the second sample.

p_c is the pooled proportion possessing the trait in the combined samples. It is called the pooled estimate of the population proportion and is found by formula [11-4]

Pooled Proportion	$p_c = \dfrac{X_1 + X_2}{n_1 + n_2}$	$[11-4]$

Where:

X_1 is the number possessing the trait in the first sample.

X_2 is the number possessing the trait in the second sample.

Comparing Population Means with Unknown Population Standard Deviations (the Pooled *t*-test)

We now consider the case in which the population standard deviations are unknown.

The following assumptions are required:

1. The sampled populations follow the normal distribution.

2. The two samples are from independent populations.

3. The standard deviations of the two populations are unknown but equal.

If these assumptions are met, the *t* distribution can be used for the test statistic for a test of hypothesis for the difference between two population means. The *t* statistic for the two sample cases is similar to that employed for the *z* statistic, with one additional calculation. The two sample variances must be "pooled" to form a single estimate of the unknown population variance.

This is accomplished by using text formula [11-5]:

$$\boxed{\textbf{Pooled Variance} \qquad s_p^2 = \frac{(n_1 - 1)s_1^2 + (n_2 - 1)s_2^2}{n_1 + n_2 - 2} \qquad [11-5]}$$

Where:

s_p^2 is the pooled estimate of the population variance.

s_1^2 is the variance of the first sample.

s_2^2 is the variance of the second sample.

n_1 is the number of observations in the first sample.

n_2 is the number of observations in the second sample.

The value of t is then computed using text formula [11-6].

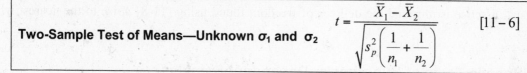

$$\boxed{\textbf{Two-Sample Test of Means—Unknown } \sigma_1 \text{ and } \sigma_2 \qquad t = \frac{\overline{X}_1 - \overline{X}_2}{\sqrt{s_p^2\left(\dfrac{1}{n_1} + \dfrac{1}{n_2}\right)}} \qquad [11-6]}$$

Where:

$\overline{X}_1$ is the mean of the first sample.

$\overline{X}_2$ is the mean of the second sample.

n_1 is the number of observations in the first sample.

n_2 is the number of observations in the second sample.

s_p^2 is the polled estimate of the population variance.

The number of degrees of freedom for a two-sample test is the total number of items sampled minus the number of samples. It is found by: $(n_1 + n_2 - 2)$.

Comparing Population Means with Unequal Standard Deviations

If the population standard deviations are unknown and it is not reasonable to assume that they are equal, we use a statistic similar to the one in formula [11-2]. However, the sample standard deviations, s_1 and s_2, are used in place of σ_1 and σ_2 as shown below in text formula [11-7]:

$$\boxed{\begin{array}{l}\textbf{Test Statistic for No Difference in Means,}\\ \textbf{Unequal Variances} \qquad\qquad t = \dfrac{\overline{X}_1 - \overline{X}_2}{\sqrt{\dfrac{s_1^2}{n_1} + \dfrac{s_2^2}{n_2}}} \qquad [11-7]\end{array}}$$

The degrees of freedom for the statistic in the formula are adjusted downward using a somewhat complicated approximation formula given in text formula [11-8]:

$$\text{Degrees of Freedom for Unequal Variance Test} \qquad df = \frac{\left[\left(s_1^2/n_1\right) + \left(s_2^2/n_2\right)\right]^2}{\dfrac{\left(s_1^2/n_1\right)^2}{n_1 - 1} + \dfrac{\left(s_2^2/n_2\right)^2}{n_2 - 1}} \qquad [11-8]$$

Where:

n_1 and n_2 are the respective sample sizes.

s_1 and s_2 are the respective sample standard deviations.

The usual practice is to round the degrees of freedom found using [11-8] *down* to the nearest whole number.

Two-Sample Tests of Hypothesis: Dependent Samples

Another hypothesis testing situation occurs when we are concerned with the difference in paired or related observations. These are situations in which the samples are not independent. Typically, it is a before-and-after situation, where we want to measure the difference.

To illustrate, suppose we administer a reading test to a sample of ten students. We have them take a course in speed reading and then we test them again. Thus the test focuses on the reading improvements of each of the ten students. The distribution of the population of differences is assumed to be approximately normal. The test statistic is t, and text formula [11-9] is used.

$$\text{Paired t test} \qquad t = \frac{\overline{d}}{s_d/\sqrt{n}} \qquad [11-9]$$

Where:
$\overline{d}$ is the mean of the difference between the paired or related observations.
s_d is the standard deviation of the differences between the paired or related observations.
n is the number of paired observations.

For a paired difference test there are $(n - 1)$ degrees of freedom.

The standard deviation of the differences s_d is computed using the familiar formula for the standard

deviation except that d is substituted for X. The text formula is: $s_d = \sqrt{\dfrac{\Sigma(d - \overline{d})^2}{n - 1}}$

Comparing Dependent and Independent Samples

When working with paired data, we need to distinguish between *dependent samples* and *independent samples*.

> *Dependent samples*: Two samples that are related to each other.

There are two types of dependent samples:

1. *Samples characterized by a measurement, an intervention of some type, and then another measurement.* This is often referred to as a "before" and "after" study. For example: A group of teenagers are enrolled in a weight reduction program. They are weighted, go through a diet and exercise program, and then they are weighed again. The two weights are paired weights and are considered to be dependent samples. The paired samples are dependent because the same individual is a member of both samples.

2. *Samples characterized by matching or pairing observations.* For example: The transportation manager wants to study the amount of "tire wear" on two brands of tire. One tire of each brand is placed on 15 company trucks and the wear is measured after 20,000 miles. The manager would have 30 observations with 15 pairs of data. The paired samples are dependent because the pairs came off the same truck.

When the samples chosen at random are in no way related to each other they are considered independent samples.

> *Independent samples*: Two samples that are unrelated to each other.

Independent samples are essentially samples taken from entirely different populations. Keep in mind, however that the populations need to share some similar characteristics. For example: The human resource director might want to test the "Microsoft Word" skills of two sets of graduates from two different secretarial business programs.

Glossary

Dependent samples: Two samples that are related to each other.

Independent samples: Two samples that are unrelated to each other.

Chapter Problems

Problem 1

Two manufacturers of sinus relief tablets, SINUS and ANTIDRIP, have made conflicting claims regarding the effectiveness of their tablets. A private testing organization was hired to evaluate the two tablets. The testing company tried SINUS on 100 sinus congestion sufferers and found the mean time to relief was 85.0 minutes. A sample of 81 sinus congestion sufferers used ANTIDRIP. The mean time to relief was 86.2 minutes. Assume that the population standard deviations of SINUS and ANTIDRIP are available from the manufacturer and are $\sigma_1 = 6.0$ minutes (SINUS) and $\sigma_2 = 6.8$ minutes (ANTIDRIP).

Does the evidence suggest a difference in the amount of time required to obtain relief? Use the 0.05 significance level and the five-step procedure. What is the p-value? Interpret it.

Solution 1

We use the five-step hypothesis testing procedure for the solution.

Step 1: State the null hypothesis and the alternate hypothesis.

Note that the testing company is attempting to determine only that there is a difference in the time required to affect relief. There is no attempt to show one tablet is "better than" or "worse than" the other. Thus, a two-tailed test is applied.

$$H_0: \mu_1 = \mu_2$$
$$H_1: \mu_1 \neq \mu_2$$

Where: μ_1 refers to the mean time to obtain relief using SINUS

μ_2 refers to the mean time to obtain relief using ANTIDRIP.

Step 2: Select a level of significance.

The 0.05 significance level is to be used. The alternate hypothesis does not state a direction, so this is a two-tailed test. The 0.05 significance level is divided equally into two tails of the standard normal distribution. Hence, the area in the left tail is 0.0250 and the area in the right tail is 0.0250.

Step 3: Identify the test statistic.

Because the population standard deviations are known the z distribution is used as the test statistic.

Step 4: Formulate a decision rule based on the selected test statistic and level of significance.

The critical values that separate the two rejection regions from the region of acceptance are −1.96 and +1.96. To explain: if the area in a rejection region is 0.0250, the acceptance area is 0.4750, found by 0.5000 − 0.0250. The z value corresponding to an area of 0.4750 is obtained by referring to the table of areas of the normal curve (Appendix B.1).

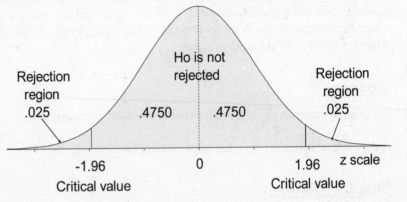

Search the body of the table for a value as close to 0.4750 as possible and read the corresponding row and column values. The area of 0.4750 is found in the row 1.9 and the column 0.06. Hence, the critical values are + 1.96 or −1.96.

This decision rule is shown on the diagram above.

Step 5: Make a decision to reject or not to reject the null hypothesis and interpret the results.

The computed value of z is -1.24, found by using formula [11-2]. Because the population standard deviations are not known, the sample standard deviations are substituted.

$$z = \frac{\bar{X}_1 - \bar{X}_2}{\sqrt{\dfrac{\sigma_1^2}{n_1} + \dfrac{\sigma_2^2}{n_2}}} = \frac{85.0 - 86.2}{\sqrt{\dfrac{(6.0)^2}{100} + \dfrac{(6.8)^2}{81}}} = -1.24$$

The computed value of z is between -1.96 and $+1.96$. Thus H_0 is not rejected. We conclude that there is no difference in the mean time it takes SINUS and ANTIDRIP to bring relief. The difference of 1.2 minutes (85.0 – 86.2) can be attributed to sampling error (chance).

To determine the p-value we need to find the area to the left of -1.24 and add to it the area to the right of 1.24. We are concerned with both tails because H_1 is two-tailed. The p-value is 0.2150, found by $2(0.5000 - 0.3925)$. Since the p-value of 0.2150 is greater than the level of significance of 0.05, do not reject H_0.

Exercise 11.1

Check your answers against those in the ANSWER section.

The county commissioners received a number of complaints from county residents that the Youngsville Fire Department takes longer to respond to emergency runs than the Claredon Fire Department. To check the validity of these complaints, a random sample of 60 emergency runs handled by the Youngsville Fire Department was selected. It was found that the mean response time was 6.9. A sample of 70 emergency runs handled by the Claredon Fire Department found the mean response time was 4.9 minutes. The population standard deviations for the Claredon and Youngsville Fire Department response times are 3.8 and 3.0 minutes, respectively. Does the data suggest that it takes longer for the Youngsville Department to respond? Use the 0.05 significance level.

Problem 2

Two different sites are being considered for a day-care center. One is on the south side of the city and the other is on the east side. The decision where to locate the day-care center depends in part on how many mothers work and have children under 5 years old.

A sample of 200 family units on the south

	South Side	East Side
Number of working mothers with children under 5	$X_1 = 88$	$X_2 = 57$
Number in sample	$n_1 = 200$	$n_2 = 150$
Proportion with children under 5 and mothers work	$p_1 = 0.44$	$p_2 = 0.38$

side revealed that 88 working mothers have children under 5 years. A sample of 150 family units on the east side revealed that 57 have children under 5 years and the mother worked. Summarizing the data above:

Can we conclude that in the population a larger proportion of mothers on the south side work and have children under 5 than on the east side? Or, can the difference be attributed to sampling variation (chance)? Use the 0.05 level of significance.

Solution 2

The problem is to examine whether a higher proportion of working mothers of young children live on the south side.

Step 1: State the null hypothesis and the alternate hypothesis.

The hypotheses are:

$$H_0 : \pi_1 \leq \pi_2$$
$$H_1 : \pi_1 > \pi_2$$

Where:

π_1 refers to the proportion of working mothers on the south side.

π_2 refers to the proportion of working mothers on the east side.

Step 2: Select a level of significance.

The 0.05 significance level is stated in the problem.

Step 3: Identify the test statistic.

The standard normal distribution is the test statistic to be used. The z value is computed using formula [11-3].

Step 4: Formulate a decision rule based on the selected test statistic and level of significance.

The alternate hypothesis indicates a direction, so this is a one-tailed test.

The critical value is 1.65 obtained from Appendix B.1. The area in the upper tail of the curve is 0.05, therefore the area between $z = 0$ and the critical value is 0.4500, found by (0.5000 − 0.0500). Search the body of the table for a value close to

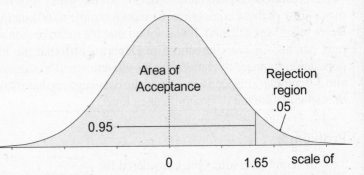

0.4500. Since 1.64 is equal to 0.4495 and 1.65 is equal to 0.4505, a value between 1.64 and 1.65 or (1.645) could be used as the critical value. We take the conservative approach and use 1.65. The null hypothesis is rejected if the calculated z value is greater than 1.65. This information is summarized in the diagram above.

Step 5: Make a decision to reject or not to reject the null hypothesis.

Formula [11-3] for z is repeated below.

$$z = \frac{p_1 - p_2}{\sqrt{\dfrac{p_c(1 - p_c)}{n_1} + \dfrac{p_c(1 - p_c)}{n_2}}}$$

where p_c is a pooled estimate of the population proportion and is computed using formula [11-4].

$$p_c = \frac{X_1 + X_2}{n_1 + n_2}$$

In this problem X_1, and X_2 refer to the number of "successes" in each sample (number of working mothers with children under 5 years), n_1 and n_2 refer to the number of housing units sampled in the south side and east side, respectively. The pooled estimate of the population proportion is 0.4143, found as follows:

$$p_c = \frac{X_1 + X_2}{n_1 + n_2} = \frac{88 + 57}{200 + 150} = 0.4143$$

Inserting the pooled estimate of 0.4143 in the formula and solving for z in formula [11-3] gives 1.13.

$$z = \frac{p_1 - p_2}{\sqrt{\dfrac{p_c(1 - p_c)}{n_1} + \dfrac{p_c(1 - p_c)}{n_2}}} = \frac{0.44 - 0.38}{\sqrt{\dfrac{(0.4143)(1 - 0.4143)}{200} + \dfrac{(0.4143)(1 - 0.4143)}{150}}} = 1.13$$

The computed value: $z = 1.13$, is less than the critical value of 1.65 so the null hypothesis is not rejected. The difference can be attributed to sampling error (chance). To put it another way, the proportion of mothers who work and have children under 5 on the south side is not significantly greater than the east side. The p-value is 0.1292, found by (0.5000 – 0.3708). So, the probability of finding a value of the test statistic this large or larger is 0.1292.

Exercise 11.2

Check your answers against those in the ANSWER section.
A recent study was designed to compare smoking habits of young women with those of young men. A random sample of 150 women revealed that 45 smoked. A random sample of 100 men indicated that 25 smoked. At the 0.05 significance level does the evidence show that a higher proportion of women smoke? Compute the p-value.

Problem 3

A study of recent graduates from your school reveals that for a sample of ten accounting majors the mean salary was $30,000 per year with a sample standard deviation of $2,000. A sample of eight general business majors reveals a mean salary of $29,000 per year with a standard deviation of $1,500. At the 0.05 significance level can we conclude accounting majors earn more?

Solution 3

The null hypothesis is that accounting majors earn the same or less than general business majors. The alternate hypothesis is that accounting majors earn more. They are written as follows:

$$H_0: \mu_1 \leq \mu_2$$
$$H_1: \mu_1 > \mu_2$$

Where:

μ_1 refers to accounting majors (graduates).
μ_2 refers to general business majors (graduates).

The required assumptions are:

1. The samples are independent.
2. The two populations follow the normal distribution.
3. The population standard deviations are equal.

The t distribution is the test statistic. There are 16 degrees of freedom, found by $(n_1 + n_2 - 2) = (10 + 8 - 2) = 16$. The alternate hypothesis is a one-tailed test with the rejection region in the upper tail. From Appendix B.2, the critical value is 1.746. Hence, H_0 is rejected if the computed value of the test statistic exceeds 1.746.

The first step is to pool the variances, using formula [11-5].

$$s_p^2 = \frac{(n_1 - 1)(s_1^2) + (n_2 - 1)(s_2^2)}{n_1 + n_2 - 2} = \frac{(10 - 1)(2{,}000)^2 + (8 - 1)(1{,}500)^2}{10 + 8 - 2} = 3{,}234{,}375$$

Next, the value of t is computed, using formula [11-6].

$$t = \frac{\bar{X}_1 - \bar{X}_2}{\sqrt{s_p^2\left(\frac{1}{n_1} + \frac{1}{n_2}\right)}} = \frac{\$30{,}000 - \$29{,}000}{\sqrt{(3{,}234{,}375)\left(\frac{1}{10} + \frac{1}{8}\right)}} = \frac{1{,}000}{\sqrt{3{,}234{,}375(0.225)}} = \frac{1{,}000}{853.073} = 1.17$$

Because the computed value of t (1.17) is less than the critical value of 1.746, H_0 is not rejected. The sample evidence does not suggest a difference in the mean salaries of the two groups.

We determine the p-value by using Appendix B.2. Move down the left column to the 16 degrees of freedom row. Move across the row until you locate a value larger than 1.17—the computed value of t. The value is in the first column. It is 1.337. Note that this column has 0.10 as a heading. Since this is a one-tailed test, we conclude that the p-value is greater than 0.10.

Exercise 11.3		
Check your answers against those in the ANSWER section.	**Downtown Store**	**Mall Store**
Average purchase amount	$36.00	$40.00
Sample standard deviation	$10.00	$12.00
Sample size	10	10

A large department store hired a researcher to compare the average purchase amounts for the downtown store with that of its mall store. The information shown was obtained. At the 0.01 significance level can it be concluded that the mean amount spent at the mall store is larger? Estimate the p-value.

Problem 4

The Yancey County 10 Kilometer Road Race is an annual event attracting hundreds of runners. Nearby Micahville hosts a 10 kilometer road race on the same weekend. Sponsors of the Yancey County race advertise that their race course results in significantly faster race times than the Micahville event. A sample of 25 race times from the Yancey County 10 K race showed a mean race time of 48 minutes and 36 seconds with a standard deviation of 5 minutes and 30 seconds. A sample of 22 race times from the Micahville 10 K race had a mean of 48 minutes and 54 seconds with a standard deviation of 5 minutes and 12 seconds. At the .01 level of significance, is there enough evidence to conclude that the Yancey

County race course is faster, on average, than the Micahville race course? Assume that the two population standard deviations are not the same.

Solution 4

Step 1: State the null hypothesis and the alternate hypothesis.

The Yancey County sponsors claim that their race course is, on average, faster than the Micahville course. Letting μ_1 refer to the mean race time for Yancey County and μ_2 refer to the mean race time of Micahville, the alternate hypothesis is that $\mu_1 < \mu_2$. The setup for the null and alternate hypotheses is:

$$H_0: \mu_1 \geq \mu_2$$
$$H_1: \mu_1 < \mu_2$$

Step 2: Select a level of significance.

The 0.01 significance level is to be used and the test is a lower-tailed test. Hence, the rejection region is in the left tail and the area is 0.01.

Step 3: Identify the test statistic.

Because the population standard deviations are not known, the t distribution is used as the test statistic. Since the standard deviations can not be assumed to be equal, text formula [11-8] is used to approximate the degrees of freedom as follows:

$$df = \frac{\left[(5.5)^2/25 + (5.2)^2/22\right]^2}{\dfrac{\left((5.5)^2/25\right)^2}{25-1} + \dfrac{\left((5.2)^2/22\right)^2}{22-1}} = \frac{5.949}{.1329} = 44.76.$$

Note that 5 minutes and 30 seconds is 5.5 minutes and 5 minutes and 12 seconds is 5.2 minutes. Round down to 44 degrees of freedom.

Step 4: Formulate a decision rule based on the selected test statistic and level of significance.

The t value for a lower-tailed test with 44 degrees of freedom and a significance level of 0.01 is -2.414, obtained from Excel. To explain, the t statistic is negative since the test is lower-tailed. The d.f. of 44 can not be found in the usual table of probabilities for the t distribution, such as the one shown in Appendix B.2. However, software such as MINITAB or Excel can be used to obtain t values corresponding to any number of degrees of freedom. The decision rule is to reject the null hypothesis if t calculated from the sample is less than -2.414.

Step 5: Make a decision to reject or not to reject the null hypothesis and interpret the results.

First, note that 48 minutes and 36 seconds is 48.6 minutes and 48 minutes and 54 seconds is 48.9 minutes. The computed value of t is $-.192$, found by formula [11-7] as follows:

$$t = \frac{\bar{X}_1 - \bar{X}_2}{\sqrt{\dfrac{s_1^2}{n_1} + \dfrac{s_2^2}{n_2}}} = \frac{48.6 - 48.9}{\sqrt{\dfrac{(5.5)^2}{25} + \dfrac{(5.2)^2}{22}}} = -\frac{-.30}{1.56} = -.192$$

The computed value of t is not less than -2.414. Thus H_0 is not rejected. We conclude that the mean race time for the Yancey County 10 K is not less than the mean race time of the Micahville 10K race. The difference of .3 minutes (48.6-48.9) can be attributed to sampling error (chance).

Exercise 11.4

Check your answers against those in the ANSWER section.

A recent MBA graduate is trying to decide between two job offers, one in Omaha and one in Kansas City. One factor affecting his decision is the cost of a new home in each city. A recent study sampled 88 new home sales in the Omaha area and found that the mean selling price of a new home was $183,900 with a standard deviation of $35,800. A similar Kansas City study based on a sample of 65 new home sales found that the mean selling price was $178,500 with a standard deviation of $29,850. Conduct a test at the .05 level of significance to determine if there is any difference in the mean selling price of new homes in Omaha versus Kansas City. You can not assume that the population standard deviations are equal.

Problem 5

The Dean of the College of Business at Kingsport University wants to determine if the Grade Point Average (GPA) of business college students decreases during the last semester of their senior year. A sample of six students is selected. Their GPAs for the fall and spring semesters of their senior year are:

At the 0.05 significance level, can the Dean conclude that the GPA of graduating seniors declined during their last semester?

Student	Fall Semester	Spring Semester
A	2.7	3.1
B	3.4	3.3
C	3.5	3.3
D	3.0	2.9
E	2.1	1.8
F	2.7	2.4

Solution 5

Let μ_d be the mean difference between the fall and spring semester grades for all business students at Kingsport U. in their senior year. Since we want to explore whether grades decrease, a one-tailed test is appropriate.

$$H_0: \mu_d \leq 0$$
$$H_1: \mu_d > 0$$

There are six paired observations; therefore, there are $(n - 1) = (6 - 1) = 5$ degrees of freedom. Using Appendix B.2 with 5 degrees of freedom, the 0.05 significance level and a one-tailed test, the critical value of t is 2.015. H_0 is rejected if the computed value of the test statistic exceeds 2.015.

The value of the test statistic is determined from formula [11-7]. $t = \dfrac{\bar{d}}{s_d / \sqrt{n}}$

Where:
$\bar{d}$ is the mean of the differences between fall and spring GPAs.
s_d is the standard deviation of those differences.
n is the number of paired observations.

First, subtract Spring semester grades from fall semester grades. If this difference is positive, then a decline has occurred. The sample data is shown below and the values of d and s_d computed:

Student	Fall	Spring	d	$(d - \bar{d})$	$(d - \bar{d})^2$
A	2.7	3.1	−0.4	−0.5	0.25
B	3.4	3.3	0.1	0	0
C	3.5	3.3	0.2	0.1	0.01
D	3.0	2.9	0.1	0	0
E	2.1	1.8	0.3	0.2	0.04
F	2.7	2.4	0.3	0.2	0.04
			0.6		0.34

$$\bar{d} = \frac{\Sigma d}{N} = \frac{0.6}{6} = 0.10$$

$$s_d = \sqrt{\frac{\Sigma (d - \bar{d})^2}{n - 1}} = \sqrt{\frac{0.34}{6 - 1}} = 0.2608$$

The t statistic is computed by: $t = \dfrac{\bar{d}}{s_d / \sqrt{n}} = \dfrac{0.10}{0.2608 / \sqrt{6}} = \dfrac{0.10}{0.1065} = 0.94$

Since the computed value of t (0.94) is less than the critical value of 2.015, H_0 is not rejected. The evidence does not suggest a reduction in grades from the fall to the spring semester. The decrease in GPAs can be attributed to chance. The p-value is greater than 0.10.

Exercise 11.5

Check your answers against those in the ANSWER section.

An independent government agency is interested in comparing the heating cost of all- electric homes and those of homes heated with natural gas. A sample of eight all-electric homes is matched with eight homes of similar size and other features that use natural gas. The heating costs for last January are obtained for each home.

At the 0.05 significance level is there reason to believe there is a difference in heating costs?

Matched Pair	Electric Heat	Gas Heat
1	265	260
2	271	270
3	260	250
4	250	255
5	248	250
6	280	275
7	257	260
8	262	260

CHAPTER 11 ASSIGNMENT

TWO-SAMPLE TESTS OF HYPOTHESIS

Name _____   Section _____   Score _____

Part I   Select the correct answer and write the appropriate letter in the space provided.

_____ 1. The test statistic for testing a hypothesis when the population standard deviation is not known is
     a. the t distribution.   **b.** the F distribution.
     c. the z distribution.   **d.** the μ distribution.

_____ 2. We want to test a hypothesis for the difference between two population proportions. The null and alternate hypothesis are indicated:
$$H_0 : \pi_1 \le \pi_2$$
$$H_1 : \pi_1 > \pi_2$$
     a. A left-tailed test should be applied
     b. A right-tailed test should be applied
     c. A two-tailed test should be applied
     d. We cannot determine whether a left, right or two-tailed test to apply without more information

_____ 3. In a upper-tailed test of means where the population standard deviations are unknown but assumed to be equal, the sample sizes for population one is 12 and population two is 14. The value of the test statistic for a significance level of 0.01 is:
     a. 2.056   **b.** 2.787
     c. 2.492   **d.** 2.330

_____ 4. In a two-sample test of means for independent samples, $n_1 = 12$ and $n_2 = 10$. How many degrees of freedom are in the test?
     a. 22   **b.** 21
     c. 20   **d.** none of the above

_____ 5. In the paired t-test, we assume in the null hypothesis that the distribution of the differences between the paired observation has a mean
     a. equal to 1.   **b.** equal to $n - 1$.
     c. equal to 0.   **d.** none of the above

_____ 6. For a particular significance level and sample size the value of the t for a one-tailed test is
     a. always less than z.   **b.** always more than z.
     c. equal to 0.   **d.** equal to z.

_____ 7. Which of the following is **not** an assumption for the two-sample t-test?
     a. equal *sample* variances   **b.** independent samples
     c. normal populations   **d.** equal *population* standard deviations

_____ 8. For dependent samples, we assume the distribution of the differences in the populations has a mean of:
     a. 30   b. 0
     c. 25   d. none of the above

_____ 9. An upper-tailed two sample means test is to be conducted at the .02 significance level. The populations standard deviations are unknown and can not be assumed equal. The degrees of freedom for the test statistic if $n_1 = 10$ and $n_2 = 8$ is:
     a. 18   b. 17
     c. 16   d. less than 16

_____ 10. To determine if a diet supplement is useful for increasing weight, patients are weighed at the start of the program and at the end of the program. This is an example of a(n)
     a. test of paired differences.   b. independent sample.
     c. one-sample test for means.   d. two-sample test for means.

Part II Answer the following questions. Be sure to show essential work.

11. A financial planner wants to compare the yield of income- and growth-oriented mutual funds. Fifty thousand dollars is invested in each of a sample of 35 income-oriented and 40 growth-oriented funds. The mean increase for a two-year period for the income funds is $1100. For the growth-oriented funds the mean increase is $1090. At the 0.01 significance level is there a difference in the mean yield of the two funds? Assume that $\sigma_1 = \$45$ and $\sigma_2 = \$55$.

a. State the null and alternate hypotheses.

H_0: _____ H_1: _____

b. State the decision rule.

_____

c. Compute the value of the test statistic.

                                                              c.

d. Compute the p-value.   d.

e. What is your decision regarding the null hypothesis?

_____

12. Is the mean salary of accountants who have reached partnership status higher than that for accountants who are not partners? A sample of 15 accountants who have the partnership status showed a mean salary of $82,000 with a standard deviation of $5,500. A sample of 12 accountants who were not partners showed a mean of $78,000 with a standard deviation of $6,500. At the 0.05 significance level can we conclude that accountants at the partnership level earn larger salaries?

a. State the null and alternate hypotheses.

H_0: _____ H_1: _____

b. State the decision rule.

_____

c. Compute the value of the test statistic.

                                                         c.

d. Compute the *p*-value.

                                                         d.

e. What is your decision regarding the null hypothesis?

_____

13. A study was conducted to determine if there is a difference, on average, in the mean starting salaries of men and women graduating with a degree in chemical engineering. A sample of 35 men who graduated with a degree in chemical engineering from Barna College resulted had a mean starting salary of $54 thousand with a standard deviation of $4 thousand. A sample of 22 women graduating from Barna College that same year with a degree in chemical engineering had a mean starting salary of $50 thousand with a standard deviation of $2 thousand. Conduct a test at the .05 level of significance. The population standard deviations can not be assumed to be equal.

a. State the null and alternate hypotheses.

H_0: _____ H_1: _____

b. Find the value of the test statistic.

c. State the decision rule.

_____

d. Compute the value of the test statistic.

e. What is your decision regarding the null hypothesis?

_____

14. The Human Resources Director for a large company is studying absenteeism among hourly workers. A sample of 120 day shift employees showed 15 were absent more than five days last year. A sample of 80 afternoon employees showed 18 to be absent five or more times. At the 0.01 significance level can we conclude that there is a higher proportion of absenteeism among afternoon employees?

a. State the null and alternate hypotheses.

H_0: _____ H_1: _____

b. State the decision rule.

_____

c. Compute the value of the test statistic.

c.

d. Compute the *p*-value.

d.

e. What is your decision regarding the null hypothesis?

_____

15. The President and CEO of Cliff Hanger International Airlines is concerned about high cholesterol levels of the pilots. In an attempt to improve the situation a sample of seven pilots is selected to take part in a special program, in which each pilot is given a special diet by the company physician. After six months each pilot's cholesterol level is checked again. At the 0.01 significance level

Pilot	Before	After	d	$(d - \bar{d})$	$(d - \bar{d})^2$
1	255	210			
2	230	225			
3	290	215			
4	242	215			
5	300	240			
6	250	235			
7	215	190			

can we conclude that the program was effective in reducing cholesterol levels?

a. State the null and alternate hypotheses.

H_0: _____ H_1: _____

b. State the decision rule.

_____

c.   Compute the value of the test statistic.

                                                       c.

d.   Compute the p-value.

                                                       d.

e.   What is your decision regarding the null hypothesis?

_____

CHAPTER 12
ANALYSIS OF VARIANCE

Chapter Goals

After completing this chapter, you will be able to:

1. List the characteristics of the F distribution.

2. Conduct a test of hypothesis to determine whether the variances of two populations are equal.

3. Discuss the general idea of analysis of variance.

4. Organize data into a one-way and a two-way ANOVA table.

5. Conduct a test of hypothesis among three or more treatment means.

6. Develop confidence intervals for the difference in two treatment means.

7. Conduct a test of hypothesis among treatment means using a blocking variable.

8. Conduct a two-way ANOVA with interaction

Introduction

In Chapter 11 we developed methods to determine whether there is a difference between two population means. What if we wanted to compare more than two population means? The two-sample tests used in Chapter 11 require that the population means be compared two at a time. This would be very time consuming, but more importantly there would be a build-up of Type I error. That is, the total value of α would become quite large as the number of comparisons increased. In this chapter, we will describe a technique that is efficient when simultaneously comparing several sample means to determine if they come from the same or equal populations. This technique is known as *Analysis of Variance (ANOVA)*.

> *Analysis of Variance (ANOVA).* A statistical technique for testing whether several populations have the same mean.

A second test compares two sample variances to determine if the populations are equal. This test is particularly useful for validating a requirement of the two-sample t test presented in Chapter 11. This test assumed that the population standard deviations were equal but unknown (see text formulas [11-5] and [11-6]).

The *F* Distribution

The *F distribution* can be used to test whether two samples are from populations having equal variances. It can also be used to compare several population mean simultaneously (*ANOVA*).

> *F Distribution.* A continuous probability distribution where F is always 0 or positive. The distribution is positively skewed. It is based on two parameters, the number of degrees of freedom in the numerator and the number of degrees of freedom in the denominator.

The major characteristics of the F distribution are:

1. **There is a family of F distributions**. A particular member of the family is determined by two parameters: the degrees of freedom in the numerator and the degrees of freedom in the denominator.

2. **The F distribution is continuous.** This means that it can assume an infinite number of values between 0 and plus infinity.

3. **The F distribution cannot be negative.** The smallest value F can assume is 0.

4. **It is positively skewed.** The long tail of the distribution is to the right-hand side. As the number of degrees of freedom increases in both the numerator and denominator, the distribution approaches a normal distribution.

5. **It is asymptotic**. As the values of X increase, the F curve approaches the X-axis but never touches it. This is similar to the behavior of the normal distribution described in Chapter 7.

Comparing Two Populations Variances

The F distribution is used to test the hypothesis that the variance of one normal population equals the variance of another normal population. The F distribution can also be used to validate assumptions with respect to certain statistical tests. Regardless of whether we want to determine if one population has more variation than another population does or validate an assumption with respect to a statistical test, we still use the usual five-step hypothesis testing procedure. The value of the test statistic is determined using text formula [12-1].

$$\boxed{\text{Test Statistic for Comparing Two Variances} \quad F = \frac{s_1^2}{s_2^2} \qquad [12-1]}$$

Where:

s_1^2 is the variance of the first sample.

s_2^2 is the variance of the second sample.

The usual practice is to determine the F ratio by putting the larger of the two sample variances in the numerator. This forces the F ratio to be larger than 1.00. This in turn allows us to always use the upper tail of the F statistic and avoid the need for more extensive F tables.

Again, the F distribution is used to determine if the variance from one normal population is the same as the variance obtained from another normal population.

For example, if you were comparing the mean starting salaries for this year's marketing graduates to this year's computer science graduates, an assumption required of the two-sample t test using text formula [11-6] is that both populations have the same standard deviation. Therefore, before conducting the test for means, it is essential to show that the two population variances are equal.

The idea behind the test for standard deviations is that if the null hypothesis is true that the two sample variances are equal, then their ratio will be approximately 1.00. If the null hypothesis is false, then the ratio will be much larger than 1.00 (recall that we always put the larger sample variance in the numerator of the F ratio). The F distribution provides a decision rule to let us know when the departure from 1.00 is too large to have happened by chance. Details of the steps of the hypothesis test for equal variances is presented below:

Step 1: State the Null and Alternate Hypothesis

$$H_0 : \sigma_1^2 = \sigma_2^2$$
$$H_1 : \sigma_1^2 \neq \sigma_2^2$$

Step 2: **State the level of significance**. Usually the value is $\alpha = .05$ or $.01$.

Step 3: Determine the test statistic. The F distribution is the appropriate test statistic.

Step 4: Find the critical value of the test statistic. The critical value is obtained from Appendix B.4. Suppose that we are testing at $\alpha = .10$. Since the test is a two-tailed test and $\alpha/2 = .05$, we can use the $.05$ page of Appendix B.4 to obtain the critical value. The degrees of freedom for the numerator is n_1-1. The degrees of freedom for the denominator is n_2-1. To find the critical value, move horizontally along the top until the value corresponding to n_1-1 is found. Then move down that column until you are opposite to the value corresponding to n_2-1. For example, if $n_1-1 = 5$ and $n_2-1 = 8$, the critical value would be 3.69 for a test of equal variances at the $\alpha = .10$ level. The decision rule is to reject the null hypothesis if the ratio of the two sample variances, s_1^2/s_2^2, is greater than 3.69.

Step 5: **Calculate s_1^2/s_2^2 and compare it to the critical value of F to reach a decision.** If s_1^2/s_2^2 is greater than the critical value, then we reject the null hypothesis, the population variances do not appear to be equal. If s_1^2/s_2^2 is less than or equal to the critical value, we can not reject the null hypothesis.

ANOVA Assumptions

Another use of the F distribution is an analysis of variance (ANOVA) where we compare three or more population means to determine whether they could be equal. To employ ANOVA, three conditions must be met:

1. The populations follow the normal distribution.

2. The populations have equal standard deviations (σ).

3. The populations are independent.

When these conditions are met, F is used as the test statistic to measure the variance among means.

The ANOVA Test

The ANOVA test is used to determine if the various sample means came from a single population or populations with different means. For example, is the mean unemployment rate the same for the food service, light industrial, and telecommunication industries? Are sales of pickup trucks the same, on average, in the fall, winter, spring, and summer sales quarters? The underlying strategy is to assume that there are no differences in the population, that is, assume that there is just one population. Then the population variance is estimated two ways and the ratio of these two estimates is calculated. If the sample means come from populations with the same mean, then the two methods for estimating the population variance are the same and the F ratio will be about one (1). In this case, we conclude that the population means are the same. If the ratio is quite different from 1, then we conclude that the population means are not the same. The F distribution tells when the ratio is too much larger than 1 to have occurred by chance.

The same hypothesis testing procedure used with the standard normal distribution (z) and Student's t is also employed with analysis of variance. The test statistic is the F distribution.

The hypothesis testing procedure for one-way ANOVA is shown below.

Step 1. State the null hypothesis and the alternate hypothesis.

When three population means are compared, the null and alternate hypotheses are written:

$$H_0: \mu_1 = \mu_2 = \mu_3$$
$$H_1: \text{not all means are equal}$$

Note that rejection of the null hypothesis does not identify which populations differ significantly. It merely indicates that a difference between at least one pair of means exists.

Step 2. Select the level of significance. The most common values selected are 0.01 or 0.05.

Step 3. Determine the test statistic. For an analysis of variance problem the appropriate test statistic is F. The F statistic is the ratio of two variance estimates and is computed by the formula:

$$F = \frac{\text{Estimate of the population variance based on the differences among the sample means}}{\text{Estimate of the population variance based on the variation within samples}}$$

There are $(k-1)$ degrees of freedom associated with the numerator of the formula for F, and $(n-k)$ degrees of freedom associated with the denominator, where k is the number of populations and n is the total number of sample observations.

Step 4. Formulate the Decision Rule.

The critical value is determined from the F table found in Appendix B.4. To illustrate how the decision rule is established, suppose a package delivery company purchased 14 trucks at the same time. Five trucks were purchased from Ford, four from General Motors (GM), and five from DaimlerChrysler. All the trucks were used to deliver packages. The cost of maintaining the trucks for the first year is shown. Is there a significant difference in the mean maintenance cost of the three manufacturers?

Maintenance Cost, By Manufacturer		
Ford	Daimler Chrysler	GM
$ 914	$933	$1,004
1,000	874	1,114
1,127	927	1,044
988	983	1,100
947		1,139

The three different manufacturers are called *treatments.*

Treatments. A specific source of variation in a set of data.

The term *treatments* is borrowed from agricultural research, where much of the early development of the ANOVA technique took place.

In the study comparing truck manufacturers there are three treatments. Therefore, there are two degrees of freedom in the numerator, found by $(k-1) = (3-1) = 2$. How is the number of degrees of freedom for the denominator determined? Note that in the three samples there are a total of 14 observations. Thus the total number of observations, designated by n, is 14. The number of degrees of freedom in the denominator is 11, found by $(n-k) = (14-3) = 11$.

The critical value of F can be found in Appendix B.4. There are tables for both the 0.01 and the 0.05 significance levels. Using the 0.05 significance level, the degrees of freedom for the numerator are at the top of the table and for the denominator in the left margin. To locate the critical value, move horizontally at the top of the table to 2 degrees of freedom in the numerator, then down that column to the number opposite 11 degrees of freedom in the left margin (denominator). That number is 3.98, which is the critical value of F.

The decision rule is to reject the null hypothesis if the computed value of F exceeds 3.98; otherwise it is not rejected. To reject the null hypothesis and accept the alternate hypothesis allows us to conclude that there is a significant difference between at least one pair of means. If the null hypothesis is not rejected, this implies the differences between the sample means could have occurred by chance. Portrayed graphically, the decision rule is shown at the right.

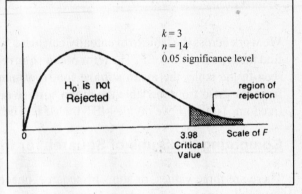

Step 5. Select the sample, perform the calculations, and make a decision.

The value of F is computed from the sample information and a decision is made regarding the null hypothesis. If the computed value of F is 1.98, for example, the null hypothesis is not rejected. If it is greater than 3.98, say 4.26, then the null hypothesis is rejected and the alternate accepted.

The ANOVA Table

A convenient way of organizing the calculations for F is to put them in a table referred to as an ANOVA table.

ANOVA Table				
Source of Variation	Sum of Squares	Degrees of Freedom	Mean Square	*F*
Treatments	SST	$k - 1$	$SST/(k - 1) =$ MST	MST / MSE
Error	SSE	$n - k$	$SSE/(n - k) =$ MSE	
Total	SS Total	$n - 1$		

Note in the ANOVA Table that there are three values, called **Sum of Squares**, that are required to compute F. The three values are determined by first calculating *SS total*. SS total is the total variation in the data.

> *Total Variation*: The sum of the squared differences between each observation and the overall mean.

SSE, is then calculated. SSE is a measure of random variation in the data. It is often called *within* treatment variation.

Random Variation: The sum of squared differences between each observation and its treatment mean.

SST is then found by subtraction. SST is the variation due to differences in the treatment means. It is often called *between* treatment variation.

Treatment Variation: The sum of squared differences between each treatment mean and the grand or overall mean.

We work across the table to eventually calculate F. The degrees of freedom are the same as those used to find the critical value of F. The term **mean square** is another expression for estimate of the variance. As seen in the table, the **mean square for treatments** (written MST) is SST divided by the degrees of freedom. Also from the table the **mean square error** (written MSE) is SSE divided by the degrees of freedom. To find F we divide MST by MSE. The entire process is explained in Problem 1.

Computing the Sums of Squares for the ANOVA Table

There are three values, or sums of squares, needed to compute the test statistic, F. These values are obtained using the computation formulas for SS total and SSE shown below, and then finding SST by:

$$SST = SS\ total - SSE.$$

The calculations needed for SS total a as follows.

To calculate the **SS total** we use text formula [12–2]:

$$SS\,total = \sum\left(X - \bar{X}_G\right)^2 \qquad [12-2]$$

Where:

X is each sample observation.

n is the total number of observations.

$\bar{X}_G$ is the grand mean, calculated by summing up all the data values and dividing by n.

SSE is the sum of the squared differences between each observation and its respective treatment mean. To calculate SSE we use text formula [12-3]:

$$SSE = \sum(X - \bar{X}_c)^2 \qquad [12-3]$$

SSE is also referred to as variation *within* the treatments.

Where:

X is each sample observation.
$\bar{X}_c$ is the sample mean for each treatment c .

SST can then be found by: $\qquad$ SST = SS total – SSE $\qquad$ [12-4]

SST is also referred to as variation *between* the treatments.

MST is found by dividing SST by its degrees of freedom, k-1. MSE is found by dividing SSE by its degrees of freedom, n-k. If the population means are equal, then MST and MSE are equivalent formulas for estimating the population variance. Their ratio, MST/MSE, should not differ significantly from 1.0. The F statistic with k-1 numerator and n-k denominator is the appropriate test statistic for comparison. If the population means are not equal, then the ratio MST/MSE should exceed the critical value of F and the null hypothesis of no difference in population means rejected.

Confidence Intervals for the Difference in Treatment Means

If the results of the ANOVA leads us to reject the null hypothesis, this indicates that the population means differ. It does not, however, tell us which mean differences are significant nor the size of the differences. If we want to answer these questions we can construct confidence intervals for the mean differences. Text formula [12-5] is used for this purpose:

Confidence Interval for the Difference in Treatment Means	$\left(\bar{X}_1 - \bar{X}_2\right) \pm t\sqrt{MSE\left(\dfrac{1}{n_1} + \dfrac{1}{n_2}\right)}$	[12 – 5]

Where:

$\bar{X}_1$ is the mean of the first treatment or sample.

$\bar{X}_2$ is the mean of the second treatment or sample.

t is obtained from the t table in Appendix B.2. The degree of freedom is equal to $(n-k)$.

MSE is the mean square error term, which is obtained from the ANOVA table. It is equal to SSE/$(n-k)$ and is an estimate of the common population variance.

n_1 is the number of observations in the first sample.

n_2 is the number of observations in the second sample.

If the confidence interval includes 0, there is not a difference in the treatment means. However, if both end points of the confidence interval are on the same side of 0, the pair of means differs.

Two-Way Analysis of Variance

In a one-way ANOVA, we divided the total variation in the data into two sources. The first was the variation that could be attributed to differences *between* the treatments, or SST. The second was variation *within* the treatments, or SSE. However, there could be other sources of variation in the data. For example, a one-way ANOVA could be conducted to determine if there is a difference, on average, in the mean time to assemble three different models of cedar dog houses. It is believed that the mean time is different for the three models. However, the individuals assembling the dog houses might also have a significant effect on the assembly times. If so we would want to account for assembler effects. To determine if there are assembler effects we could conduct a study in which each assembler put together each model of dog house. Including a second source of variation in the model—assembler effect, reduces random variation, or SSE. If assembler effects are significant, MSE will be reduced and we are more likely to detect significant differences in the mean times for the different models. A second factor included in the ANOVA model for the purpose of reducing MSE in order to more easily detect differences between treatment means is known as a ***blocking. variable***.

> **Blocking Variable**: A second treatment that when included in the ANOVA analysis will have the effect of reducing the SSE term.

In a two-way ANOVA the sums of squares due to blocks is found using text formula [12-6]:

$$SSB = k\sum \left(\bar{X}_b - \bar{X}_G \right)^2 \qquad [12-6]$$

The SS total and SST are found as before, and SSE is now found by subtraction:

$$SSE = SS\ total - SST - SSB \qquad [12\text{-}7].$$

Whether we conduct a hypothesis test to determine if there are differences in block means is a matter of disagreement. If the only purpose for including the blocking variable is to reduce MSE, we should not conduct a test of the block means. On the other hand, if we are also interested in studying the effect of the blocking variable it can be argued that the blocking variable is a second *factor* and we are actually conducting a *two-way ANOVA*, or a *two-factor experiment*.

> **Two-way Anova**: A statistical technique that partitions the total variation in the data into three sources of variation—SSE, SSA, and SSB. The purpose is to determine whether there are differences between the means of Factor A and also whether there are differences between the means of Factor B.

The Two-way ANOVA Table

A two-way ANOVA table is similar to a one-way ANOVA table. It is constructed as follows:

ANOVA Table				
Source of Variation	**Sum of Squares**	**Degrees of Freedom**	**Mean Square**	**F**
Treatments	SST	$k-1$	$SST/(k-1) = MST$	MST / MSE
Blocks	SSB	$b-1$	$SSB/(n-b) = MSB$	MSB / MSE
Error	SSE	$(k-1)(b-1)$	$SSE/(k-1)(b-1) = MSE$	
Total	SS Total	$n-1$		

Block effects appear in the row beneath treatment effects. If block effects are considered important enough to be considered a second effect, the F statistic can be computed as shown in the table and compared to the critical value of F with $b-1$ numerator and $(k-1)(b-1)$ denominator degrees of freedom.

Two-way ANOVA with Interaction

When there are two independent variables, or *factors*, in the model there is the possibility that there is an *interaction effect* between the two variables. Two factors interact when the effect of one factor on the response variable depends on the value of the other factor.

> *Interaction:* The effect of one factor on a response variable differs depending on the value of another factor.

There are two ways to detect an interaction. One way is to construct an *interaction plot*. In order to construct an interaction plot we first calculate the mean response for each combination of factors. For example, in a two factor study of the effects of model type and assembler on the mean assembly time for cedar dog houses, suppose that we have four assemblers and three models of cedar dog houses. Suppose that each assembler puts together each model of dog house on two separate occasions. We could plot the mean time it took each assembler to put together each dog house as shown in the plot below:

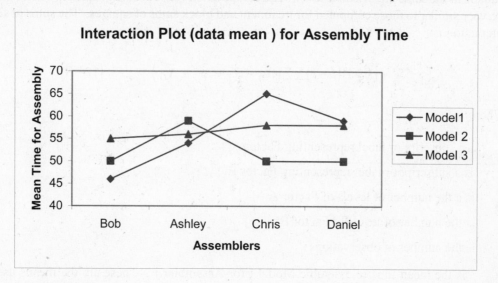

This plot helps us understand the interaction between assembler and model. If the three lines were close to parallel, then this would indicate that no interaction effect exists. On the other hand, line segments that do not appear parallel or cross indicate an interaction between the two factors. The above plot suggests an interaction between assembler and model since some of the line segments are not parallel and some even cross.

Hypothesis Tests for a Two-way ANOVA with Interactions

The interaction plot shown above indicates that an interaction is probably present between assembler and model. The next step is to conduct hypothesis tests to further investigate possible interactions. In a two-way ANOVA there is the potential for two main effects (model and assembler) and the interaction between them. In order to test for each of these effects it is necessary to *replicate* the experiment. That is, there must be at least two observations for each combination of the factors. In the above example, each assembler assembled each model of dog house twice. This allows us to estimate the error sums of squares for the F tests.

Suppose that the following data was obtained for the dog house assembly experiment:

	Model1	Model 2	Model 3
Bob	44, 48	55, 45	58, 52
Ashley	55, 53	63, 55	57, 55
Chris	68, 62	47, 53	60, 56
Daniel	60, 58	52, 48	56, 50

There are three hypotheses that are tested in the model:

H_0: There is no interaction between assemblers and models

H_0: The mean assembly times are the same for each model.

H_0: The mean assembly times are the same for each assembler.

The model effect is Factor A and the assembler effect is Factor B. Each hypothesis is tested using an F statistic at the same significance level. The computation for sums of squares for Factor A and Factor B are very similar to those computed for treatment and block sums of squares. The sums of squares for the interaction is:

$$SSI = (k-1)(b-1)\sum\sum\left(\bar{X}_{ij} - \bar{X}_{i.} - \bar{X}_{.j} + \bar{X}_G\right)^2 \qquad [12-8]$$

Where:

i is a subscript or label representing Factor A

j is a subscript or label representing Factor B

k is a the number of levels of Factor A

b is the number of levels of Factor B

n is the number of observations

$\bar{X}_{ij}$ is the mean time to assemble Model i for Assembler j . These are the means used to plot the interaction
    plot.

$\bar{X}_{i.}$ is the mean for Factor A.

$\bar{X}_{.j}$ is the mean for Factor B.

$\bar{X}_G$ is the grand mean.

Once SSA, SSB, and SSI are computed, SSE is computed by:

$$SSE = SS\ total - SSA - SSB - SSI . \qquad [12-9]$$

Two-way ANOVA Table with Interaction

The table below is used to construct the F tests for a two-way ANOVA model with interaction.

ANOVA Table				
Source of Variation	Sum of Squares	Degrees of Freedom	Mean Square	F
Factor A	SSA	$k - 1$	SST/ $(k - 1)$ = MST	MST / MSE
Factor B	SSB	$b - 1$	SSB/ $(n - b)$ = MSB	MSB / MSE
Interaction	SSI	$(k-1)(b-1)$	SSI/$(k-1)(b-1)$	MSI/MSE
Error	SSE	n-kb	SSE/ $(k-1)(b-1)$ = MSE	
Total	SS Total	$n - 1$		

MINITAB was used to analyze the cedar dog house data given in the above data table. The MINITAB output for the data is:

Analysis of Variance for Y

Source	DF	SS	MS	F	P
A	3	185.83	61.94	4.04	0.034
B	2	66.33	33.17	2.16	0.158
A*B	6	349.67	58.28	3.80	0.023
Error	12	184.00	15.33		
Total	23	785.83			

How do we interpret the results of the ANOVA table? Assume that we are testing at $\alpha = .05$. The p-value for interaction effects is less than the significance level of .05, so we conclude that the interaction between model and assembler is significant. When interactions are not significant it is appropriate to conduct F tests for each of the main effects using the ANOVA table for a two-way model with interaction. When interactions are significant, the results of the F tests for main effects are complicated. One approach is to conduct a one-way ANOVA to test differences in the factor means for each level of the other factor. Other approaches have been suggested and can be found in more advanced textbooks.

Glossary

Analysis of Variance (ANOVA): A statistical technique for determining whether several populations have the same mean. This is accomplished by comparing the sample variances.

Blocking Variable: A second variable included in an ANOVA model to reduce random variation.

Factor: An independent variable included in the ANOVA model to explain a source or cause of variation. Also called a treatment in a one-way ANOVA.

F Distribution: A continuous probability distribution where F is always 0 or positive. The distribution is positively skewed. It is based on two parameters, the number of degrees of freedom in the numerator and the number of degrees of freedom in the denominator.

Interaction: An effect that occurs when one factor in the ANOVA model changes the effect that another factor has on the response variable.

Random Variation: Variation in the response variable that is not accounted for by one or more factors in an ANOVA model.

Replicate: Repeat observations at each combination of the levels of two factors in a two-way ANOVA.

Total Variation: The total amount of variation in the response variable.

Treatments: A treatment is a specific source, or cause, of variation in a set of data.

Chapter Problems

Problem 1

Master Card	Visa	Store
$61	$85	$61
28	56	25
42	44	42
33	72	31
51	98	29
56	56	
	72	

Tiedke's Department Store accepts three types of credit cards, MasterCard, Visa, and their own store card. The sales manager is interested in finding out whether there is a difference in the mean amounts charged by customers on the three cards. A random sample of 18 credit card purchases (rounded to the nearest dollar) revealed these credit card amounts. At the 0.05 significance level, can we conclude there is a difference in the mean amounts charged per purchase on the three cards?

Solution 1

We follow the usual five-step hypothesis testing procedure.

Step 1. State the null hypothesis and the alternate hypothesis

There are three populations involved, the three credit cards. The null and alternate hypotheses are:

$$H_0: \mu_1 = \mu_2 = \mu_3$$
H_1: the means are not all equal

Step 2. Select the level of significance.

We have selected 0.05.

Step 3. Determine the test statistic.

For an analysis of variance problem the appropriate test statistic is F.

Step 4. Formulate the Decision Rule.

There are three "treatments" or columns. Hence, there are $(k-1) = (3-1) = 2$ degrees of freedom in the numerator. There are 18 observations, therefore $n = 18$. The number of degrees of freedom in the denominator is 15, found by $(n-k) = (18-3)$. The critical value is found in Appendix B.4. Find the table for the 0.05 significance level and the column headed by 2 degrees of freedom. Then move down that column to the margin row with 15 degrees of freedom and read the value. It is 3.68.

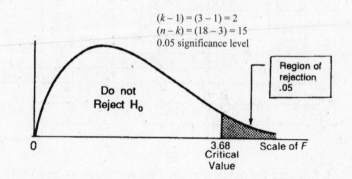

The decision rule is: Reject the null hypothesis if the computed value of F exceeds 3.68, otherwise do not reject H_0. Shown graphically, the decision rule is shown at the right.

Step 5. Select the sample, perform the calculations, and make a decision.

There are two sources of variation in an analysis of variance study. These sources occur between treatments (designated SST) and within treatments (designated SSE). The sum of SST and SSE is the total amount of variation, written SS total; n refers to the number of observations in each column (treatments).

The calculations needed for SS total, SSE, and SST are as follows.

1. To calculate the **SS total** we use text formula [12–2]. $SS\ total = \sum \left(X - \bar{X}_G \right)^2$

   We start by determining the overall grand mean $\bar{X}_G$. The formula is: $\bar{X}_G = \dfrac{\sum all\ the\ X\ values}{n}$, Where: $\bar{X}_G$ is the grand mean, X is each sample observation, and n is the total number of observations.

   Using Table I, columns **A, D, & G**: $\bar{X}_G = \dfrac{\sum all\ the\ X\ values}{n} = \dfrac{271 + 483 + 188}{6 + 7 + 5} = \dfrac{942}{18} = 52.33$

2. Find the deviations of each observation from the grand mean. For the MC observation of $61, the deviation is $(61 - 52.33) = 8.67$. See Table I, columns **B, E, & H**.

Table I

	A	B	C	D	E	F	G	H	I	J
	MC			Visa			Store			
	X	$(X-\bar{X}_G)$	$(X-\bar{X}_G)^2$	X	$(X-\bar{X}_G)$	$(X-\bar{X}_G)^2$	X	$(X-\bar{X}_G)$	$(X-\bar{X}_G)^2$	**Totals**
	$61	8.67	75.17	$85	32.67	1067.33	$61	8.67	75.17	
	28	−24.33	591.95	56	3.67	13.47	25	−27.33	746.93	
	42	−10.33	106.71	44	−8.33	69.39	42	−10.33	106.71	
	33	−19.33	373.65	72	19.67	386.91	31	−21.33	454.97	
	51	−1.33	1.77	98	45.67	2085.75	29	−23.33	544.29	
	56	3.67	13.47	56	3.67	13.47				
				72	19.67	386.91				
Σ	271			483			188			942
Σ			1162.72			4023.23			1928.07	7114.02
N	6			7					18	

3. Square the deviations from the grand mean. See Table I, columns **C, F, & I**.

4. The **SS total** is found using text formula [12–2]. We summed the totals for columns **C, F, & I**.

$$SS\,total = \sum \left(X - \bar{X}_G\right)^2 = \left(1162.72 + 4023.23 + 1928.07\right) = 7114.02$$

5. Compute **SSE** or the sum of the squared errors. This is the sum of the squared differences between each observation and its respective treatment mean.

Using Table II, For the MasterCard observations in column **A**, the mean is: $\bar{X} = \dfrac{\sum X}{n} = \dfrac{271}{6} = 45.17$

In Column **B**, We subtract each observation from the mean 45.17 and then square this difference as shown in Column **C**. Then compute the sum. It is 854.84.

This process is repeated for the other two treatments or sets of observations Visa and Store in the remaining columns **D** to **I**.

The mean for Visa is $\bar{X} = \dfrac{\sum X}{n} = \dfrac{483}{7} = 69.00$ and for Store it is $\bar{X} = \dfrac{\sum X}{n} = \dfrac{188}{5} = 37.60$

Table II

	A	B	C	D	E	F	G	H	I
	MC	$\bar{X} = 45.17$		Visa	$\bar{X} = 69.00$		Store	$\bar{X} = 37.60$	
	X	$(X-\bar{X})$	$(X-\bar{X})^2$	X	$(X-\bar{X})$	$(X-\bar{X})^2$	X	$(X-\bar{X})$	$(X-\bar{X})^2$
	$61	15.83	250.59	$85	16.00	256.00	$61	23.40	547.56
	28	−17.17	294.81	56	−13.00	169.00	25	−12.60	158.76
	42	−3.17	10.05	44	−25.00	625.00	42	4.40	19.36
	33	−12.17	148.11	72	3.00	9.00	31	−6.60	43.56
	51	5.83	33.99	98	29.00	841.00	29	−8.60	73.96
	56	10.83	117.29	56	−13.00	169.00			
				72	3.00	9.00			
Σ	271			483			188		
Σ			854.84			2078.00			843.20
n	6			7			5		

The **sum of squared errors** (SSE) is computed using text formula [12–3]. We summed the totals for columns **C, F, & I**.

$$SSE = \sum (X - \bar{X}_c)^2 = (854.84 + 2078.00 + 843.20) = 3776.04$$

6. Now we need to compute the **sum of squares due to treatment** (SST) using text formula [12–4]

$$SST = SS\, total - SSE = (7114.02 - 3776.04) = 3337.98$$

7. The next step is to insert these values into the ANOVA table.

Source Variation	Sum of Squares	Degrees of Freedom	Mean Squares
Treatment	SST = 3,337.98	$(k-1)=(3-1)=2$	$MST = \dfrac{SST}{(k-1)} = \dfrac{3,337.98}{2} = 1,668.99$
Error	SSE = 3,776.04	$(n-k)=(18-3)=15$	$MSE = \dfrac{SSE}{(n-k)} = \dfrac{3,776.04}{15} = 251.736$
Total	SS Total = 7,114.02	17	

8. The "degrees of freedom" for the treatment is $(k-1)$, where (k) is the number of treatments. The mean square for the treatments is SST divided by it degrees of freedom and is written as MST.

The "degrees of freedom" for the error is $(n-k)$, where (n) is the number of observations and (k) is the number of treatments. The mean square error is SSE divided by its degrees of freedom and is written MSE.

9. Computing F using the formula:

$$F = \frac{MST}{MSE} = \frac{1,668.98}{251.73} = 6.63$$

Since the computed value of F (6.63) exceeds the critical value of 3.68, the null hypothesis is rejected at the 0.05 level and the alternate hypothesis is accepted. It is concluded that mean amounts charged by Tiedke's Department Store customers are not the same for the three credit cards.

There are many computer software packages that will perform the ANOVA calculations and output the results. MINITAB, SAS, SPSSX, and Excel are examples. The following output is from the MINITAB system. Notice that computed F is the same as determined previously.

```
                        Individual 95% CIs For Mean Based on
                        Pooled StDev
Level   N    Mean   StDev   -----+---------+---------+---------+----
1       6   45.17   13.08        (--------*--------)
2       7   69.00   18.61                         (--------*--------)
3       5   37.60   14.52   (---------*---------)
                            -----+---------+---------+---------+----
                             30        45        60        75
Pooled StDev = 15.8
```

Check your answers against those in the ANSWER section.

The accelerating cost of electricity and gas has caused the management at Arvco Electronics to lower the heat in the work areas. The instructor conducting night classes for employees is concerned that this may have an adverse effect on the employees' test scores. Management agreed to investigate. The employees taking the basic statistics course were randomly assigned to three groups. One group was in a classroom having a temperature of 60°, another group was placed in a room having a temperature of 70°, and the third group was in a room having a temperature of 80°. At the completion of the chapters on tests of hypotheses a common examination was given consisting of ten questions. The number correct for each of the 20 employees is shown in the table. At the 0.05 significance level can management conclude that there is a difference in achievement with respect to the three temperatures? (Use the table to aid in the computations).

Table I

60 Degrees			70 Degrees			80 Degrees		
X			X			X		
3			7			4		
5			6			6		
4			8			5		
3			9			7		
4			6			6		
			8			5		
			8			4		
						3		

Problem 2

In Problem 1 it was concluded that there was a difference between the mean amounts charged for the three different credit cards, MasterCard, Visa, and the Tiedke's Store card. Between which credit cards is there a significant difference? Use the 0.05 level of significance.

Solution 2

From the MINITAB Output shown above for the credit card data, note that the mean amount charged using the VISA card was $69.00 and $37.60 for the Department Store card. Since these means have the largest difference, let's determine if this pair of means differ significantly.

To determine if the means differ, we develop a confidence interval for the difference between the two population means. This confidence interval employs the t distribution and the mean square error (MSE) term. Recall that one of the assumptions for ANOVA is that the standard deviations (or variances) in the sampled populations must be the same. The MSE term is an estimate of this common variance. It is obtained from the MINITAB output. Text formula [12-5] is used:

| Confidence Interval for the Difference in Treatment Means | $\left(\bar{X}_1 - \bar{X}_2\right) \pm t \sqrt{MSE\left(\dfrac{1}{n_1} + \dfrac{1}{n_2}\right)}$ | [12–5] |

Where:

$\bar{X}_1$ is the mean of the first treatment or sample.

$\bar{X}_2$ is the mean of the second treatment or sample.

t is obtained from the t table in Appendix B.2. The degree of freedom is equal to $(n - k)$.

MSE   is the mean square error term, which is obtained from the ANOVA table. It is equal to SSE/$(n - k)$ and is an estimate of the common population variance.

n_1 is the number of observations in the first sample.

n_2 is the number of observations in the second sample.

If the confidence interval includes 0, there is not a difference in the treatment means. However, if both end points of the confidence interval are on the same side of 0 the pair of means differs.

$$\left(\bar{X}_1 - \bar{X}_2\right) \pm t \sqrt{MSE\left(\frac{1}{n_1} + \frac{1}{n_2}\right)}$$

$$(69.00 - 37.60) \pm 2.131 \sqrt{252\left(\frac{1}{7} + \frac{1}{5}\right)}$$

$$31.40 \pm 19.81$$

$$\$11.59 \text{ to } \$51.21$$

Where:

$\bar{X}_1$ equals 69.00

$\bar{X}_2$ equals 37.60

n_1 equals 7

n_2 equals 5

t is 2.131 from Appendix B.2 with 15 degrees of freedom and the 95 percent level of confidence.

MSE   is 252, which is in the ANOVA table constructed to calculate F.

Since both end points have the same sign, positive in this case, we conclude that there is a difference in the mean amount charged on VISA and the store card.

Similarly, approximate results can be obtained directly from the MINITAB Output. In the lower right corner of the Output a confidence interval was developed for each mean. The * indicates the mean of the treatment and the parentheses ( ) symbols indicate the endpoints of the confidence interval. In comparing treatment means, if there is any common area between the two, they do not differ. If there is not any common area between the treatment means, they differ. For the credit card example, MasterCard and VISA have common area and do not differ. MasterCard and the store card do not differ, but the store and VISA do differ.

Check your answers against those in the ANSWER section.

In Exercise 12.1 it was concluded that there was a difference between the mean number correct for the three different temperatures in the work area. The mean score for the 60^0 group is 3.8 and the mean score for the 70^0 group is 7.4. Determine if this pair of means differs significantly.

Problem 3

Lens Grinders, Inc. is an innovative company in terms of employee scheduling. Recently several employees were asked to take only one long break during the day while others requested several short breaks. In addition, some workers requested to work four-day weeks, others flex time, and still others at random times. The Human Resources Department has decided to conduct a study to

Schedule Type	Number of Breaks			
	1	2	3	4
Regular	94	105	96	98
Flex time	97	106	91	90
Four day	96	100	88	88
Random	92	104	86	84

determine if the different schedule types and the number of breaks has an effect on output. A sample of 16 employees was obtained. Each employee was randomly assigned to one of the combinations of work schedules and number of breaks. The total output for each worker for a week was then recorded. At the 0.05 significance level is there a difference in the mean output for the various number of breaks and for the different schedules?

Solution 3

This is an example of a two-factor ANOVA, also referred to as two-way ANOVA. We are considering variation from three sources: the number of breaks, the type of schedule, and random causes. Two sets of hypotheses are established—one hypothesis regarding breaks and the other hypothesis regarding the type of schedules. The breaks are the treatments and the second source of variation, type of schedule, is called the "blocking variable."

Breaks: H_0:   The treatment means are the same.
                     $\mu_1 = \mu_2 = \mu_3 = \mu_4$
         H_1:   The treatment means are not the same.
Schedules: H_0:   The block means are the same.
                     $\mu_1 = \mu_2 = \mu_3 = \mu_4$
         H_1:   The block means are not the same.

The Excel Data Analysis ANOVA program was used to perform the calculations. The output from this problem is shown at the right.

There are four different schedules, so b = 4; there are also four different breaks so k = 4. Let's

ANOVA				
Source of Variation	SS	df	MS	F
Schedule	109.69	3	36.56	3.80
Breaks	495.19	3	165.06	17.16
Error	86.56	9	9.62	
Total	691.44	15		

consider the treatments, or breaks, first. There are $(k - 1) = (4 - 1) = 3$ degrees of freedom in the numerator and $(b - 1)(k - 1) = (4 - 1)(4 - 1) = 9$ degrees of freedom in the denominator. Using the 0.05 significance level, the critical value of 3.86 is obtained from Appendix B.4. That is, the null hypothesis that the mean output is the same for the number of breaks is rejected if the computed F exceeds 3.86. The value of F is computed as follows.

$$F = \frac{SST/(k-1)}{SSE/(b-1)(k-1)} = \frac{495.19/3}{86.56/9} = 17.16 \text{ or } F = \frac{MST}{MSE} = \frac{165.06}{9.62} = 17.16$$

Since the computed value of 17.16 exceeds the critical value of 3.86, the null hypothesis is rejected. The mean output is not the same for the various number of breaks.

The hypothesis regarding the blocking variable, the schedules, is considered next. There are $(b-1) = (4-1) = 3$ degrees of freedom in the numerator and $(b-1)(k-1) = (4-1)(4-1) = 9$ degrees of freedom in the denominator. Using the 0.05 significance level and Appendix B.4, the critical value is 3.86. The computed value of F is 3.80.

$$F = \frac{SSB/(b-1)}{SSE/(b-1)(k-1)} = \frac{109.69/3}{86.56/9} = 3.80 \text{ or } F = \frac{MSB}{MSE} = \frac{36.56}{9.62} = 3.80$$

The decision is not to reject the null hypothesis. However, 3.80 is very close to the critical value of 3.86. The conclusion is that there is no difference in the output using the various schedules.

Exercise 12.3			
Check your answers against those in the ANSWER section.	SOURCE	DF	SS	MS

Combined below:

Check your answers against those in the ANSWER section.

The following two-way ANOVA table was developed using the MINITAB system. Use the 0.05 significance level.

SOURCE	DF	SS	MS
TREATMENTS	3	45	15
BLOCKS	4	200	50
ERROR	12	144	12

a. How many treatments are there?

b. How many blocks are there?

c. What is the total sample size?

d. Is there a significant difference in the treatment means?

e. Is there a significant difference in the block means?

Problem 4

A study was conducted to determine the effects of price and location on the number of cups of coffee sold each morning from a canteen truck on a college campus. Three locations were chosen (library, College of Business, and College of Nursing) and three prices ($1.15, $1.25, and $1.40) were selected for study. Three days were used for each price-location combination. The data and ANOVA results follow. Construct an interaction plot. Does the plot indicate that there is an interaction between location and price? Conduct tests to determine if an interaction or main effects are present.

Chapter 12

Analysis of Variance

	Library	Business	Nursing
Price			
$1.10	115	89	90
	90	94	93
	88	102	104
$1.25	78	90	90
	85	99	89
	75	86	82
$1.40	68	95	88
	77	94	78
	80	85	86

```
Analysis of Variance for y

Source   DF       SS       MS      F      P
a         2   790.22   395.11   7.74   0.004
b         2    16.89     8.44   0.17   0.849
a*b       4    78.22    19.56   0.38   0.818
Error    18   919.33    51.07
Total    26  1804.67
```

Solution 4

This interaction plot below shows roughly parallel price lines which indicates that interaction effects probably do not exist.

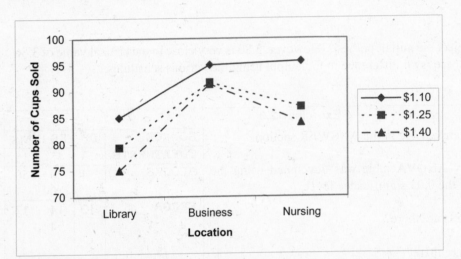

The ANOVA output from MINITAB confirms that interaction effects are not significant since the p-value = .818 which is not less than α = .05. Since interactions are not significant, tests for main effects can be performed. For Factor A (location) we see that the effects are highly significant (p-value = .004 < α = .05). However, price effects are not significant (p-value = .849 > α = .05).

Exercise 12.4

Check your answers against those in the ANSWER section.

The data set below displays the results of an experiment designed to measure the effects of two levels of temperature and two levels of catalyst on percentage increase in yield of a chemical compound.

a. Construct an interaction plot for the data. Do interaction effects appear to be present?

b. Conduct a two-way ANOVA model using a statistical software package. Use the output to test whether
there are significant interaction or main effect using α = .05. What are your conclusions?

Catalyst	Temperature	
	low	high
low	12	26
	24	16
high	18	101
	28	113

Problem 5

Teledko Associates is a marketing research firm that specializes in comparative shopping. Teledko is hired by Ford Motor Company to compare the selling price of the Ford Excape with the Honda CRV. Posing as a potential customer, a representative of Teledko visited 8 Ford dealerships in Metro City and 6 Honda dealerships and obtained quotes on comparable cars. The standard deviation for the selling prices of 8 Ford Escapes is $350 and on the six CRVs, $290. At the 0.01 significance level is there a difference in the variation in the quotes of the Pontiacs and Chevrolets?

Solution 5

Let the Escape be population 1 and the CRV be population 2. A two-tailed test is appropriate because we are looking for a difference in the variances. We are not trying to show that one population has a larger variance than the other. The null and alternate hypotheses are:

$$H_o : \sigma_1^2 = \sigma_2^2$$
$$H_1 : \sigma_1^2 \neq \sigma_2^2$$

The F distribution is the appropriate test statistic for comparing two sample variances. For a two-tailed test, the larger sample variance is placed in the numerator. The critical value of F is found by dividing the significance level in half and then referring to Appendix B.4 and the appropriate degrees of freedom. There are $(n - 1) = (8 - 1) = 7$ degrees of freedom in the numerator and $(n - 1) = (6 - 1) = 5$ degrees of freedom in the denominator. From Appendix B.4, using the 0.01 significance level, the critical value of F is 10.5. If the ratio of the two variances exceeds 10.5, the null hypothesis is rejected and the alternate hypothesis is accepted. The computed value of the test statistic is determined by:

$$F = \frac{s_1^2}{s_2^2} = \frac{(350)^2}{(290)^2} = 1.46$$

The null hypothesis is not rejected. There is no difference in the variation in the price quotes of Ford Escapes and Honda CRVs, because the computed value of F (1.46) is less than the critical F value (10.5).

Exercise 12.5

Check your answers against those in the ANSWER section.

Thomas Economic Forecasting, Inc. and Harmon Econometrics have the same mean error in forecasting the stock market over the last ten years. However, the standard deviation for Thomas is 30 points and 60 points for Harmon. At the 0.05 significance level can we conclude that there is more variation in the forecast given by Harmon Econometrics?

CHAPTER 12 ASSIGNMENT

ANALYSIS OF VARIANCE

Name _____ Section _____ Score _____

Part I   Select the correct answer and write the appropriate letter in the space provided.

_____ 1.   The analysis of variance technique is a method for
  a. comparing three or more means.   b. comparing F distributions.
  c. measuring sampling error.   d. none of the above.

_____ 2.   A treatment is
  a. a normal population.   b. the explained population.
  c. a source of variation.   d. the amount of random error.

_____ 3.   In a one-way ANOVA, k refers to the
  a. number of observations in each column. b. the number of treatments.
  c. the total number of observations.   d. none of the above.

_____ 4.   The F distribution is
  a. a continuous distribution.   b. based on two sets of degrees of freedom.
  c. never negative.   d. all of the above

_____ 5.   In an ANOVA test there are 5 observations in each of three treatments. The degrees of freedom in the numerator and denominator of the F statistic for treatments respectively are:
  a. 2, 4   b. 3, 15   c. 3, 12   d. 2, 12

_____ 6.   Which of the following assumptions is **not** a requirement for ANOVA?
  a. dependent samples   b. normal populations
  c. equal population variances   d. independent samples

_____ 7.   The mean square error term (MSE) is the
  a. estimate of the common population variance.   b. estimate of the population means.
  c. estimate of the sample standard deviation.   d. treatment variation.

_____ 8.   In a one-way ANOVA, the null hypothesis indicates that the treatment means
  a. are all the same or from equal populations.   b. are not from the same populations.
  c. in at least one pair of means are the same.   d. are all different.

_____ 9.   The appropriate test statistic for comparing two sample variances to find out if they came from the same or equal populations is the
  a. t distribution.   b. z distribution.
  c. F distribution.   d. binomial distribution.

_____ 10. In a two-way ANOVA with interaction effects there are 3 levels of Factor A and 4 levels of Factor B. The degrees of freedom for interaction sum of squares is:

    a. 2   b. 12

    c. 6   d. 5

Part II   Record your answer in the space provided. Show essential calculations.

11. The NPC, Inc. is a large mail order company that ships men's shirts all over the United States and Canada. They ship a large number of packages from their warehouse in Delta, Ohio. Their goal is to have 95 percent of the shipments delivered in 4 days. For many years they have used Brown Truck Inc., but recently there have been complaints about slow and inconsistent delivery. A sample of 10 recent shipments handled by Brown Truck showed a standard deviation in delivery time of 1.25 days. A sample of 16 shipments by Rapid Package Service showed a standard deviation in their delivery time of 0.45 days. At the 0.05 significance level is there more variation in the Brown Truck delivery time?

    a. State the null and alternate hypotheses.

    H_0: _____

    H_1: _____

    b. State the decision rule.

    _____

    c. Compute the value of the test statistic.

                                                                            c.

    d. What is your decision regarding the null hypothesis? Interpret the result.

    _____

12. Jim Ray, an avid golfer, keeps records on his scores for 18 holes of golf. When the temperature is above 65 degrees, the standard deviation of his scores is 5.75 for 25 rounds. When the temperature is below 65 degrees, the standard deviation of his scores is 7.35 for a sample of 21 rounds. At the 0.05 significance level, is there more variation in his scores when the temperature is below 65 degrees?

    a. State the null and alternate hypotheses.

    H_0: _____

    H_1: _____

b. State the decision rule.

_____

c. Compute the value of the test statistic.

c.

d. What is your decision regarding the null hypothesis? Interpret the result.

_____

13. The County Executive for Monroe County is concerned about the response time for the three fire companies in the county. Samples of the response times (in minutes) for each company follow. At the 0.05 significance level is there a difference in the mean response time?

Youngsville	Northeast	Corry
2.2	2.3	0.9
1.2	1.5	0.8
1.9	1.2	1.1
3.1	1.4	1.2
1.8	2.2	0.7
1.5		

a. State the null and alternate hypotheses.

H_0: _____

H_1: _____

b. State the decision rule.

_____

c. Compute the value of the test statistic (use the tables).

c.

d. What is your decision regarding the null hypothesis? Interpret the result.

_____

_____

14. A dentist is trying to decide if there is a difference in the number of weeks three different toothbrushes last. Fifteen patients were randomly assigned to three brands of toothbrushes and the number of weeks that the toothbrushes lasted is given. At the 0.05 significance level, is there a difference in the mean length of time the toothbrushes lasted?

Brand	Weeks of Wear				
A	3	4	6	3	4
B	2	3	2	5	2
C	5	7	5	4	6

a. State the null and alternate hypotheses.

H_0: _____

H_1: _____

b. State the decision rule.

_____

c. Compute the value of the test statistic.

c.

```
Analysis of Variance
Source    DF    SS      MS
Factor    2     16.93   8.47
Error     12    18.00   1.50
Total     14    34.93
```

d. What is your decision regarding the null hypothesis? Interpret the result.

---

15. A chain of stores that sells athletic shoes and athletic clothing is concerned about delivery times for its most popular athletic shoes. They believe that there may be differences between different brands and they also think that there may be differences according to order size. Understanding the effects of brand and order size on delivery times would help them determine when they should place orders. They collected data from the past year for the three brands of athletic shoe—Nike, Adidas, and Reebok. They also divided their orders into two sizes—large and small. The delivery times for orders are shown in the table below:

	Nike	Adidas	Reebok
Small	9,14,13	15,17,19	16,15,20
Large	12,15.15	20, 18, 25	22, 28,25

a. Construct an interaction plot for delivery times. Does an interaction appear to be present?

b. Conduct a two-way ANOVA. Is there an interaction between brand and size of order? If not, conduct F tests for Brand and Size effects. What are your conclusions? Use the p-value approach to hypothesis testing and a significance level of $= .01$ for all tests.

```
Analysis of Variance for Y
Source      DF      SS        MS       F       P
Brand       2     208.000   104.000   14.51   0.001
Size        1      98.000    98.000   13.67   0.003
Brand*Size  2      28.000    14.000    1.95   0.184
Error       12     86.000     7.167
Total       17    420.000
```

CHAPTER 13
LINEAR REGRESSION AND CORRELATION

Chapter Goals

After completing this chapter, you will be able to:

1. Understand and interpret the terms *dependent variable* and *independent variable*.

2. Calculate and interpret the *coefficient of correlation*, the *coefficient of determination*, and the *standard error of estimate*.

3. Conduct a test of hypothesis to determine whether the coefficient of correlation in the population is zero.

4. Calculate the least squares regression line.

5. Construct and interpret confidence intervals and prediction intervals for the dependent variable.

Introduction

We studied hypothesis testing concerning means and proportions where only a single feature of the sampled item was considered. For example, based on sample evidence we concluded that the beginning annual mean salary for accounting graduates is $26,000. With this chapter we begin our study of the relationship between two variables. We may want to determine if there is a relationship between the number of years of company service and the income of executives. Or we may want to explore the relationship between crime in the inner city and the unemployment rate.

What is Correlation Analysis?

To study the relationship between two variables we use two techniques: *correlation analysis* and *regression analysis*.

> *Correlation analysis*: A group of techniques to measure the association between two variables.

The purpose of correlation analysis is to find the relationship between two variables. One way of looking at the relationship between two variables is to portray the information in a *scatter diagram*.

> *Scatter diagram*: A chart that portrays the relationship between two variables.

The values of the *independent variable* are portrayed on the horizontal axis (*X*-axis) and the *dependent variable* along the vertical axis (*Y*-axis).

> *Dependent variable*: The variable that is being predicted or estimated.
>
> *Independent variable*: A variable that provides the basis for estimation. It is the predictor variable.

Note in Figure A that as the length of service increases so does income. In Figure B, as employment rises, the crime rate in the inner city declines.

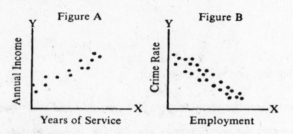

The Coefficient of Correlation

A measure of the linear (straight-line) strength of the relationship between two sets of interval-scaled or ratio-scaled variables is given by the *coefficient of correlation*. The coefficient of correlation is also called **Pearson's product moment correlation coefficient** or **Pearson's** *r* after its founder Karl Pearson.

> *Coefficient of correlation*: A measure of the strength of the linear relationship between variables.

The characteristics of the coefficient of correlation are:

1. The sample coefficient of correlation is identified by the lower case letter *r*.

2. It measures the linear (straight line) relationship between two interval of ratio scale variables.

3. It ranges from -1 up to and including 1.

4. A value near 0 indicates there is little association between the variables.

5. A value near 1 indicates a direct or positive association between the variables.

6. A value near -1 indicates inverse or negative association between the variables.

The following scatter diagrams depict correlations of 0, +1.0, and -1.0.

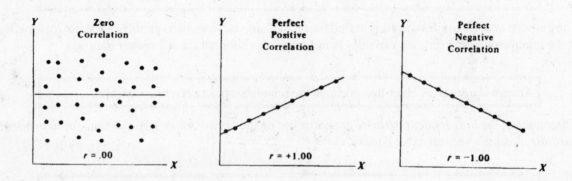

The degree of strength of the relationship is not related to the sign (direction – or +) of the coefficient of correlation. For example, an *r* value of –0.60 represents the same degree of correlation as +0.60. An *r* of

−0.70 represents a stronger degree of correlation than 0.40. An r of −0.90 represents a strong negative correlation and +0.15 a weak positive correlation.

The coefficient of correlation is computed by text formula [13-1].

$$\text{Correlation coefficient} \qquad r = \frac{\sum (X - \bar{X})(Y - \bar{Y})}{(n-1)(s_x s_y)} \qquad [13-1]$$

Where:

r	is the coefficient of correlation.
n	is the number of paired observations.
$\bar{X}$	is the mean for the X variable.
$\bar{Y}$	is the mean for the Y variable.
s_x	is the standard deviation of the X values.
s_y	is the standard deviation of the Y values.

The Coefficient of Determination, r^2

The values of the coefficient of determination are interpreted as being strong, moderate, or weak. A measure that has a more precise interpretation can be constructed by squaring the coefficient of correlation, r. The square of the correlation coefficient is called r^2, the coefficient of determination. It is interpreted at the proportion of the variation in the dependent variable, y, that can be explained by y's linear relationship with x.

> *Coefficient of Determination*: The proportion of the variation in y that can be explained by the linear relationship between x and y.

Testing the Significance of the Correlation Coefficient

A test of significance for the coefficient of correlation may be used to determine if the computed r could have occurred in a population in which the two variables are not related. To put it in the form of a question: Is the correlation in the population zero?

For a two-tailed test the null hypothesis and the alternate hypothesis are written as follows:

$$H_0 : \rho = 0 \ \left(\text{The correlation in the population is zero}\right)$$

$$H_1 : \rho \neq 0 \ \left(\text{The correlation in the population is different from zero}\right)$$

The Greek lower case rho, ρ, represents the correlation in the population. The null hypothesis is that there is no correlation in the population, and the alternate that there is a correlation.

From the way H_1 is stated, we know that the test is two tailed. The alternate hypothesis can also be set up as a one-tailed test. It could read, "The correlation coefficient is greater than zero."

The test statistic follows the t distribution with $(n-2)$ degrees of freedom. Text formula [13-2] is used.

t Test for the Coefficient of Correlation	$t = \dfrac{r\sqrt{n-2}}{\sqrt{1-r^2}}$	[13 – 2]

Regression Analysis

We have an equation that shows the linear (straight line) relationship between two variables. The equation is used to estimate Y based on X and is referred to as the ***regression equation***.

> ***Regression Equation***: An equation that expresses the linear relationship between two variables.

The linear relationship between two variables is given by the general form of the regression equation. Text formula [13-3] is used.

General Form of Linear Regression Equation	$\hat{Y} = a + bX$	[13 – 3]

Where:

$\hat{Y}$ (read Y hat) is the estimated value of the Y variable for a selected X value.

a is the Y intercept. It is the estimated value of Y when $X = 0$.

b is the slope of the line. It measures the change in $\hat{Y}$ for each unit change in X. It will always have the same sign as the coefficient of correlation.

X is any value of the independent variable that is selected.

The value of **b** is the slope of the **regression line** and is computed using formula [13-4].

Slope Of The Regression Line	$b = r\dfrac{s_y}{s_x}$	[13-4]

Where:

r is the correlation coefficient.

s_x is the standard deviation of the X values (the dependent variable).

s_y is the standard deviation of the Y values (the independent variable).

The value of **a** is the **Y intercept** and is computed using formula [13-5].

$a = \bar{Y} - b\bar{X}$	[13 – 5]

Where:

$\bar{Y}$ is the mean of the Y – values (the dependent variable).

$\bar{X}$ is the mean of the X – values (the independent variable).

How do we get these values? They are developed mathematically using the ***least squares principle***.

> **Least squares principle**: Determining a regression equation by minimizing the sum of the squares of the vertical distances between the actual Y values and the predicted values of Y, which are the $\hat{Y}$ values.

Suppose the least squares principle was used to develop an equation expressing the relationship between annual salary and years of work experience. The equation is:

$$\hat{Y} = a + bX$$
$$= 30,000 + 1000\,X \text{ (in dollars)}$$

In the example, annual income is the dependent variable, Y, and is being predicted on the basis of the employee's years of work experience, X, the independent variable. The value of 1000, which is b, means that for each additional year of work experience the employee's salary increases by $1,000. Thus, we would expect an employee with 40 years of work experience to earn $10,000 more than one with 30 years of work experience.

What does the 30,000 dollars represent? It is the value for $\hat{Y}$ when $X = 0$. Recall that this is the point where the line intersects the Y-axis. The values of a and b in the regression equation are usually referred to as the regression coefficients.

The Standard Error of Estimate

Rarely does the predicted value of $\hat{Y}$ agree exactly with the actual Y value. That is, we expect some prediction error. One measure of this error is called the ***standard error of estimate***. It is written $s_{y \cdot x}$.

> ***Standard error of estimate***: A measure of the scatter, or dispersion, of the observed values around the line of regression.

A small standard error of estimate indicates that the independent variable is a good predictor of the dependent variable.

The standard error, as it is often called, is similar to the standard deviation described in Chapter 4. Recall that the standard deviation was computed by squaring the difference between the actual value and the mean. This squaring was performed for all n observations. For the standard error of estimate, the difference between the predicted value $\hat{Y}$ and the actual value of Y is obtained and that difference squared and summed over all n observations. The text formula [13-6] is:

Standard Error of Estimate	$s_{y \cdot x} = \sqrt{\dfrac{\Sigma \left(Y - \hat{Y}\right)^2}{n-2}}$	[13 – 6]

Assumptions Underlying Linear Regression

Linear regression is based on these four assumptions:

1. For each value of X, there is a group of Y values. These Y values follow the normal distribution.

2. The means of these normal distributions of Y values all lie on the line of regression.

3. The standard deviations of these normal distributions are all the same. The best estimate we have of this common standard deviation is the standard error of estimate $\left(s_{y \cdot x}\right)$.

4. The Y values are statistically independent. This means in selecting a sample, a particular X does not depend on any other value of X. This assumption is particularly important when data are collected over a period of time. In such situations, the errors for a particular time period are often correlated with those of other time periods.

Confidence Intervals and Prediction Intervals

The standard error is also used to set confidence intervals for the predicted value of $\hat{Y}$. When the sample size is large and the scatter about the regression line is approximately normally distributed, then the following relationships can be expected:

$\hat{Y} \pm 1\, s_{y \cdot x}$ encompasses about 68% of the observed values.

$\hat{Y} \pm 2\, s_{y \cdot x}$ encompasses about 95% of the observed values.

$\hat{Y} \pm 3\, s_{y \cdot x}$ encompasses virtually all of the observed values.

Two types of *confidence intervals* may be set. The first for the mean value of $\hat{Y}$ for a given value of X and the other, called a *prediction interval,* for an individual value of $\hat{Y}$ for a given value of X. To explain the difference between the mean predicted value and the individual prediction, suppose we are predicting the salary of management personnel who are 40 years old. In this case we are predicting the mean salary of all management personnel age 40. However, if we want to predict the salary of a particular manager who is 40, then we are making a prediction about a particular individual.

The formula for the confidence interval for the mean value of Y for a given X is:

Confidence Interval for the mean of Y, given X	$\hat{Y} \pm t\left(s_{y \cdot x}\right)\sqrt{\dfrac{1}{n}+\dfrac{\left(X-\bar{X}\right)^{2}}{\Sigma(X-\bar{X})^{2}}}$	[13 – 7]

Where:
$\hat{Y}$ is the predicted value for a selected value of X.
X is any selected value of the independent variable.
$\bar{X}$ is the mean of the independent variable X, found by $\Sigma X \div n$.
n is the sample size or number of observations.
t is the value of the Student t distribution from Appendix B.2, with $(n-2)$ degrees of freedom and the given level of significance for a two-tailed test.
$s_{y \cdot x}$ is the standard error of estimate.

The formula is modified slightly for a prediction interval. The number 1 (one) is placed under the radical and the formula becomes:

Prediction Interval for Y, given X	$\hat{Y} \pm t\left(s_{y \cdot x}\right)\sqrt{1+\dfrac{1}{n}+\dfrac{\left(X-\bar{X}\right)^{2}}{\Sigma(X-\bar{X})^{2}}}$	[13 – 8]

The Relationship Among Various Measures of Association

The standard error of estimate measures how closely the actual values of Y are to the predicted values of $\hat{Y}$. When the values are close together the standard error is "small." When they are spread out, the standard error will be large. In the calculation of the standard error, the key term is: $\Sigma(Y - \hat{Y})^2$

When this term is small, the standard error is also small.

Recall that the coefficient of correlation measured the strength of the association between two variables. When the points on a scatter diagram are close to a straight line, the correlation coefficient tends to be "large." Thus the standard error and the coefficient of correlation reflect the same information but use a different scale to report it. The standard error is in the same units as the dependent variable. The correlation coefficient has a range of -1.00 to $+1.00$.

Recall that the *coefficient of determination* also reports the strength of the association by measuring the proportion of the variation in the dependent variable, Y, that is explained by the linear relationship between X and Y. It is the square of the correlation coefficient and has a range 0.00 to 1.00.

A convenient means of showing the relationships among these measures is an ANOVA Table. This is similar to the table developed in the previous chapter. The total variation $\Sigma(Y - \bar{Y})^2$ is divided into two components.

1.   The component explained by the regression.
2.   The error or unexplained variation.

These two categories are identified in the source column of the following ANOVA table. The column headed DF refers to the degrees of freedom associated with each category. The total degrees of freedom is $(n-1)$. The degrees of freedom in the regression is 1 because there is one independent variable. The degrees of freedom associated with the error term is $(n-2)$. The term SS, located in the middle of the table, refers to the variation. These terms are computed as follows:

$$\text{Total variation} = \text{SS total} = \Sigma\left(Y - \bar{Y}\right)^2$$

$$\text{Error variation} = \text{SSE} = \Sigma\left(Y - \hat{Y}\right)^2$$

$$\text{Regression} = \text{SSR} = \Sigma\left(\hat{Y} - \bar{Y}\right)^2$$

The format for the ANOVA table is:

Source	DF	SS	MS
Regression	1	SSR	SSR/1
Error	n – 2	SSE	SSE/(n – 2)
Total	n – 1	SS total*	

*SS total = SSR + SSE

The coefficient of determination, r^2 can be computed directly from the ANOVA table.

| Coefficient of Determination | $r^2 = \dfrac{SSR}{SS\,\text{total}} = 1 - \dfrac{SSE}{SS\,\text{total}}$ | [13 – 10] |

Note that as SSE decreases r^2 increases. The coefficient of correlation is the square root of this value. Hence, both of these values are related to SSE. The standard error of estimate is obtained using the following equation.

| Standard Error of Estimate | $s_{y \cdot x} = \sqrt{\dfrac{SSE}{n-2}}$ | [13 – 11] |

Note again the role played by the SSE term. A small value of SSE will result in a small standard error of estimate.

Transforming Data

The coefficient of correlation, r, measures the strength of the *linear* relationship between X and Y. A value of r near zero implies no *linear* relationship exists, but other forms of a relationship, such as a quadratic, might exist. When the relationship between X and Y is nonlinear one option is to transform one of the variables. For example, instead of using Y as the dependent variable, we could use its log, reciprocal, or squareroot. Other transformations are possible, but these are the most common.

Glossary

Coefficient of correlation: A measure of the strength of the linear relationship between two sets of interval-scaled or ratio-scaled variables.

Coefficient of determination: The proportion of the total variation in the dependent variable Y that is explained, or accounted for, by the variation in the independent variable X.

Correlation analysis: A group of techniques used to measure the strength of the association between two variables.

Dependent variable: The variable that is being predicted or estimated.

Independent variable: A variable that provides the basis for estimation. It is the predictor variable.

Least squares principle: Determining a regression equation by minimizing the sum of the squares of the vertical distances between the actual Y values and the predicted values of Y'.

Regression equation: An equation that defines the linear relationship between two variables.

Scatter diagram: A chart that portrays the relationship between two variables.

Standard error of estimate: A measure of the scatter, or dispersion, of the observed values around the line of regression.

Chapter 13
Linear Regression and Correlation

Chapter Problems

Problem 1

It is believed that the annual repair cost for the fuel-efficient automobile Sparta is related to its age. A sample of 10 automobiles revealed the results in the table at the right.

a. Plot these data in a scatter diagram. Does it appear there is a relationship between repair cost and age?
b. Compute the coefficient of correlation.
c. Determine at the 0.05 significance level whether the correlation in the population is greater than zero.

Repair Cost (in dollars) Y	Age (in years) X
$170	1
130	1
180	2
205	2
220	3
243	3
290	4
275	4
404	5
380	5

Solution 1

a. The repair cost is the dependent variable and is plotted along the Y-axis. Age is the independent variable and is plotted along the X-axis. To plot the first point, move horizontally on the X-axis to 2 and then go vertically to 72 on the Y-axis and place a dot. This procedure is continued until all paired data are plotted. Note that it appears there is a positive relationship between the two variables. That is, as X, the age of the automobile increases, so does the repair cost. But, the relationship is not perfect as evidenced by the scatter of dots.

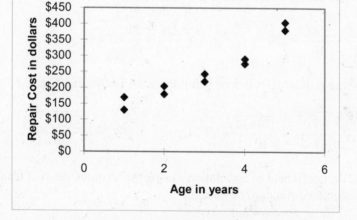

b. The degree of association between age and repair cost is measured by the coefficient of correlation. It is computed by formula [13-1]. Note that we also need to compute the mean and the standard deviation using Formula [3-2] and [3-11].

$$r = \frac{\sum \left(X - \bar{X} \right)\left(Y - \bar{Y} \right)}{(n-1)(s_x\, s_y)} \quad [13-1] \qquad \bar{X} = \frac{\sum X}{n} \quad [3-2] \qquad s = \sqrt{\frac{\sum (X - \bar{X})^2}{n-1}} \quad [3-11]$$

The calculations in the table below are needed to compute the various totals.

	A	B	C	D	E	F	G
	Repair Cost			Age			
	Y	$(Y-\bar{Y})$	$(Y-\bar{Y})^2$	X	$(X-\bar{X})$	$(X-\bar{X})^2$	$(X-\bar{X})(Y-\bar{Y})$
	$170	-80	6400	1	-2	4	160
	130	-120	14400	1	-2	4	240
	180	-70	4900	2	-1	1	70
	205	-45	2025	2	-1	1	45
	220	-30	900	3	0	0	0
	243	-7	49	3	0	0	0
	290	40	1600	4	1	1	40
	278	28	784	4	1	1	28
	404	154	23716	5	2	4	308
	380	130	16900	5	2	4	260
n	10			10			
Σ	2500	0.00	71674	30	0.00	20	1151

Step 1. Compute the means using sums in Column **A** and **D**:

$$\bar{Y} = \frac{\Sigma Y}{n} = \frac{2500}{10} = 250 \qquad\qquad \bar{X} = \frac{\Sigma X}{n} = \frac{30}{10} = 3.0$$

Step 2. Compute the standard deviations using the sums in Column **C** and **F**:

$$s_y = \sqrt{\frac{\Sigma(Y-\bar{Y})^2}{n-1}} = \sqrt{\frac{71674}{10-1}} = 89.24 \qquad\qquad s_x = \sqrt{\frac{\Sigma(X-\bar{X})^2}{n-1}} = \sqrt{\frac{20}{10-1}} = 1.49$$

Step 3. Compute the coefficient of correlation r using the formula, the sum from Column **G** in the table, and the calculated standard deviations.

$$r = \frac{\Sigma(X-\bar{X})(Y-\bar{Y})}{(n-1)(s_x\,s_y)} = \frac{1151}{9(1.4907)(89.24)} = \frac{1151}{1196.71} = 0.9613 = 0.961$$

Recall that 0 indicates no correlation and 1.00 perfect correlation. The r of 0.961 suggests a strong positive correlation between the age of this fuel efficient car and annual repair costs. As the age of the car increases, so does the annual repair cost.

c. A test of hypothesis is used to determine if the correlation in the population could be zero. In this instance, suppose we want to show that there is a positive association between the variables. Recall that the Greek letter ρ refers to the correlation in the population. The null and alternate hypotheses are written as follows:

$$H_0{:}\rho \le 0$$
$$H_1{:}\rho > 0$$

If the null hypothesis is not rejected, it indicates that the correlation in the population could be zero. If the null hypothesis is rejected, the alternate is accepted. This indicates there is correlation in the population between the two variables and it is positive.

The test statistic follows the Student's t distribution with $(n-2)$ degrees of freedom. The alternate hypothesis given above specifies a one-tailed test in the positive direction. There are 8 degrees of freedom, found by $(n-2) = (10-2)$. The critical value for a one-tailed test using the 0.05 significance level is 1.860 (Appendix B.2). The decision rule is to reject the null hypothesis if the computed value of t exceeds 1.860. The computed value of t is 4.99, found by using formula [13–2.]

$$t = \frac{r\sqrt{n-2}}{\sqrt{1-r^2}} = \frac{0.96\sqrt{10-2}}{\sqrt{1-(0.96)^2}} = \frac{2.7153}{0.28} = 9.697$$

Since the computed value (9.70) exceeds the critical value of t, namely 1.860, the null hypothesis is rejected and the alternate accepted. It is concluded that there is a positive association between the age of the automobile and the annual repair cost. The p-value is less than 0.001.

Exercise 13.1			
Check your answers against those in the ANSWER section. A major oil company is studying the relationship between the daily traffic count and the number of gallons of gasoline pumped at company stations. A sample of eight company owned stations is selected and the following information obtained:	**Location**	**Total Gallons of Gas Pumped (000)**	**Traffic count of vehicles (000)**
	West St.	120	4
a. Develop a scatter diagram with the amount of gasoline pumped as the dependent variable.	Willouhby St.	180	6
	Mallard Rd.	140	5
b. Compute the coefficient of correlation	Pheasant Rd.	150	5
c. Compute the coefficient of determination.	I-75	210	8
d. Interpret the meaning of the coefficient of determination.	Kinzua Rd.	100	3
e. Test to determine whether the correlation in the population is zero, versus the alternate hypothesis that the correlation is greater than zero. Use the 0.05 significance level.	Front St.	90	3
	Indiana Ave.	80	2

Problem 2

In Problem 1 we examined the relationship between the annual repair cost of the Sparta and its age. The correlation between the two variables was 0.96, which we considered to be a strong relationship. We conducted a test of hypothesis and concluded that the relationship between the two variables in the population was greater than zero. The same sample data is repeated below.

a. Use the least squares principle to determine the regression equation.

b. Compute the standard error of estimate.

c. Develop a 95 percent confidence interval for the mean repair cost for all 4-year-old Spartas.

d. Develop a 95 percent prediction interval for the repair cost for Ms. Paul's 4-year-old Sparta.

Repair Cost (in dollars)	Age (in years)
$170	1
130	1
180	2
205	2
220	3
243	3
290	4
278	4
404	5
380	5

Solution 2

a. The first step is to compute the regression equation using formula [13-4] for b, formula [13-5] for a.

In Problem 1, we computed: $r = 0.961$, $s_y = 32.8$, and $s_x = 2.51$. Thus:

$$[13\text{-}4] \quad b = r\frac{s_y}{s_x} = 0.96\left(\frac{86.24}{1.4907}\right) = 57.47$$

In Problem 1, we computed: $\bar{Y} = 250$ and $\bar{X} = 3$. Thus

$$[13-5] \quad a = \bar{Y} - b\bar{X}$$
$$= 250 - [(57.47)(3)]$$
$$= 77.59$$

Thus, the regression equation is:

$$\hat{Y} = a + bX = 77.59 + 57.47X \quad \text{(in dollars)}$$

Interpreting, repair costs can be expected to increase $57.47 a year on the average. Stated differently, the repair cost of a 4-year-old Sparta can be expected to cost $57.47 more a year than a 3-year-old Sparta.

b. The standard error of estimate is a measure of the dispersion about the regression line. It is similar to the standard deviation in that it uses squared differences. The differences between the value of $\hat{Y}$ and Y are squared and summed over all n observations and then divided by $(n-2)$. The standard error is the positive square root of this value. A small value indicates a close association between the dependent and independent variable. The standard error is measured in the same units as the dependent variable. The symbol for the standard error of estimate is $s_{y\cdot x}$.

The standard error is computed using formula [13-6] and the table shown.

$$s_{y\cdot x} = \sqrt{\frac{\Sigma(Y-\hat{Y})^2}{n-2}} = \sqrt{\frac{5434.078}{10-2}}$$
$$= \sqrt{679.26} = 26.063$$

c. The regression equation is used to estimate the repair cost of a 4-year-old Sparta. The value of 4 is inserted for X in the equation.

X	bX	$\hat{Y}$	Y	$(Y-\hat{Y})$	$(Y-\hat{Y})^2$
1	57.47	135.06	$170	34.94	1220.8036
1	57.47	135.06	130	-5.06	25.6036
2	114.94	192.53	180	-12.53	157.0009
2	114.94	192.53	205	12.47	155.5009
3	172.41	250	220	-30	900
3	172.41	250	243	-7	49
4	229.88	307.47	290	-17.47	305.2009
4	229.88	307.47	278	-29.47	868.4809
5	287.35	364.94	404	39.06	1525.6836
5	287.35	364.94	380	15.06	226.8036
				SUM	5434.078

$$\hat{Y} = 77.59 + 57.47X$$
$$= 77.59 + 57.47(4)$$
$$= 307.47 \quad \text{(in dollars)}$$

Thus the expected repair cost for a 4-year-old Sparta is $307.47.

Formula [13-7] is used if we want to develop a 95 percent confidence interval of the repair cost for all four-year-old Spaartas.

$$\hat{Y} \pm t(s_{y \cdot x}) \sqrt{\frac{1}{n} + \frac{(X - \bar{X})^2}{\Sigma(X - \bar{X})^2}}$$

The necessary information for the formula is:

$\hat{Y}$ is 307.47 as previously computed.

t is 2.306. There are $(n - 2)$ degrees of freedom, or $(n - 2) = (10 - 2) = 8$. From Appendix B.2, using a 95% confidence level, move down the column to 8 df and read the value of t.

n is 10. It is the sample size.

$s_{y \cdot x}$ is \$26.06, as computed in an earlier section of this problem.

X is 4, the age of the Sparta.

$\bar{X}$ is the mean age of the sampled cars. It is 3.0, found by $\bar{X} = 30/10$.

$\Sigma(X - \bar{X})^2$ is 20.0, found from the earlier computations.

Solving for the 95 percent confidence interval:

$$\hat{Y} \pm t(s_{y \cdot x}) \sqrt{\frac{1}{n} + \frac{(X - \bar{X})^2}{\Sigma(X - \bar{X})^2}} = \$307.47 \pm 2.306(\$26.06) \sqrt{\frac{1}{10} + \frac{(4 - 3.0)^2}{20}}$$

$$= \$307.47 \pm \$23.27$$

$$= \$284.20 \text{ to } \$330.74$$

The 95 percent confidence interval for the mean amount spent on repairs to a 4-year-old Sparta is between \$284.20 and \$330.74. About 95 percent of the similarly constructed intervals would include the population value.

d. Recall that Ms. Paul owns a 4-year-old Sparta. The 95 percent prediction interval for her repair costs is computed as follows using formula [13-8].

$$\hat{Y} \pm t(s_{y \cdot x}) \sqrt{1 + \frac{1}{n} + \frac{(X - \bar{X})^2}{\Sigma(X - \bar{X})^2}} = \$307.47 \pm 2.306(\$26.06) \sqrt{1 + \frac{1}{10} + \frac{(4 - 3.0)^2}{20}}$$

$$= \$307.47 \pm \$64.44$$

$$= \$243.03 \text{ to } \$371.91$$

Interpreting we would conclude that Ms. Paul will spend between \$243.03 and \$371.91 on repairs this year to her four-year-old Sparta. About 95 percent of the similarly constructed intervals would include the population value.

Exercise 13.2

Check your answers against those in the ANSWER section.

In Exercise 13.1 we studied the relationship between the gasoline pumped in thousands of gallons, and the traffic count at eight company owned stations. The data are repeated at the right.

a. Compute the regression equation.
b. Compute the standard error of estimate.
c. Develop a 95 percent confidence interval for the mean amount of gasoline pumped for all stations where the traffic count is 4.
d. Develop a 95 percent prediction interval for the amount of gasoline pumped at the station at Dowling Rd. and I-60, which has a count of 4 (actually 400 cars).

Location	Total Gallons of Gas Pumped (000)	Traffic count (hundreds of cars)
West St.	120	4
Willouhby St.	180	6
Mallard Rd.	140	5
Pheasant Rd.	150	5
I-75	210	8
Kinzua Rd.	100	3
Front St.	90	3
Indiana Ave.	80	2

Problem 3

Use the information from Problem 1 to:

a. Develop an ANOVA Table.

b. Compute the coefficient of determination.

c. Compute the coefficient of correlation.

d. Compute the standard error of estimate.

Solution 3

a. The MINITAB System was used to develop the following output.

```
            Analysis of Variance

     SOURCE      DF      SS         MS
     Regression   1    7,293.4    7,293.4
     Error        8    2,400.2      300.0
     Total        9    9,693.6
```

b. The coefficient of determination is computed using Formula [13-10] as follows.

$$r^2 = \frac{SSR}{SS\,Total} = \frac{7293.4}{9693.6} = 0.752 \quad OR \quad r^2 = \left(1 - \frac{SSE}{SS\,Total}\right) = \left(1 - \frac{2,400.2}{9,693.6}\right) = (1 - 0.248) = 0.752$$

c. The correlation coefficient is 0.867, found by taking the square root of 0.752. These two coefficients (0.867 and 0.752) are the same as computed earlier.

d. The standard error of estimate is computed using Formula [13-11] as follows:

$$s_{y \cdot x} = \sqrt{\frac{SSE}{n-2}} = \sqrt{\frac{2,400.2}{10-2}} = 17.32$$

Note again the role played by the SSE term. A small value of SSE will result in a small standard error of estimate.

Exercise 13.3

Check your answers against those in the ANSWER section.

Refer to Exercise 1, regarding the relationship between the amount of gasoline pumped and the traffic count. The following output was obtained from MINITAB.

Analysis of Variance

SOURCE	DF	SS	MS
Regression	1	14,078	14,078
Error	6	310	51.67
Total	7	14,388	

a. Compute the coefficient of determination.
b. Compute the coefficient of correlation.
c. Compute the standard error of estimate.

CHAPTER 13 ASSIGNMENT

LINEAR REGRESSION AND CORRELATION

Name _____   Section _____   Score_____

Part I   Select the correct answer and write the appropriate letter in the space provided.

_____ 1. Which of the following statements is **not** correct regarding the coefficient of correlation.
   a. It can range from −1 to 1.
   b. Its square is the coefficient of determination.
   c. It measures the percent of variation explained.
   d. It is a measure of the association between two variables.

_____ 2. The coefficient of determination
   a. is usually written as r^2.
   b. cannot be negative.
   c. is the square of the coefficient of correlation.
   d. all of the above.

_____ 3. The coefficient of correlation was computed to be −0.60. This means
   a. the coefficient of determination is $\sqrt{0.6}$.
   b. as X increase Y decreases.
   c. X and Y are both 0.
   d. as X decreases Y decreases.

_____ 4. Which of the following is a stronger correlation than −0.54?
   a. 0.67   b. 0.45
   c. 0.0   d. −0.45

_____ 5. A regression equation is used to
   a. measure the association between two variables.
   b. estimate the value of the dependent variable based on the independent variable.
   c. estimate the value of the independent variable based on the dependent variable.
   d. estimate the coefficient of determination.

_____ 6. A regression equation was computed to be $Y= = 35 + 6X$. The value of the 35 indicates that
   a. the regression line crosses the Y-axis at 35.
   b. the coefficient of correlation is 35.
   c. the coefficient of determination is 35.
   d. an increase of one unit in X will result in an increase of 35 in Y.

_____ 7. The standard error of estimate
   a. is a measure of the variation around the regression line.
   b. cannot be negative.
   c. is in the same units as the dependent variable.
   d. all of the above.

_____ 8. The variable plotted on the horizontal or X-axis in a scatter diagram is called the
  a. scatter variable.   b. independent variable.
  c. dependent variable.   d. correlation variable.

_____ 9. The least squares principle means that
  a. $\Sigma\left(Y - \hat{Y}\right)^2 = 0$.   b. $\Sigma\left(Y - \overline{Y}\right)^2$ is maximized.

  c. $\Sigma\left(Y - \hat{Y}\right)^2$ is minimized.   d. $\Sigma\left(Y - \overline{Y}\right)^2$ is minimized.

_____ 10. If all the points are on the regression line, then
  a. the value of b is 0.   b. the value of a is 0.
  c. the correlation coefficient is 0.   d. the standard error of estimate is 0.

Part II Record your answers in the space provided. Show all essential work.

11. The correlation between the number of police on the street and the number of crimes committed, for a sample of 15 comparable sized cities, is 0.45. At the 0.05 significance level is there a positive association in the population between the two variables?

  a. State the null and alternate hypotheses.

  H_0: _____

  H_1: _____

  b. State the decision rule.

  _____

  c. Compute the value of the test statistic.

  ┌─────────┐
  │ c.   │
  │   │
  └─────────┘

  d. What is your decision regarding the null hypothesis? Interpret the result.

  _____

12. A study is conducted concerning automobile speeds and fuel consumption rates. The following data is collected:

a. Plot these data in a scatter diagram.

Speed	MPG
44	22
51	26
48	21
60	28
66	33
61	32

b. Compute the coefficient of correlation.

	A	B	C	D	E	F	G
	MPG			Speed			
	Y			X			
	22			44			
	26			51			
	21			48			
	28			60			
	33			66			
	32			61			
n							
Total							

b.

c. Determine at the 0.05 significance level whether the correlation in the population is greater than zero.

c.

13. Tem Rousos, president of Rousos Ford, believes there is a relationship between the number of new cars sold and the number of sales people on duty. To investigate he selects a sample of eight weeks and determines the number of new cars sold and the number of sales people on duty for that week.

Week	Sales staff	Cars sold
1	5	53
2	5	47
3	7	48
4	4	50
5	10	58
6	12	62
7	3	45
8	11	60

a. Plot these data in a scatter diagram.

b. Determine the coefficient of correlation.

	A	B	C	D	E	F	G
	Number of Cars Sold			Number of Sales Staff			
	Y			X			
	53			5			
	47			5			
	48			7			
	50			4			
	58			10			
	62			12			
	45			3			
	60			11			
n							
Total							

b.

c. Determine the coefficient of determination. Comment on the strength
of the association between the two variables.

c.

_____

_____

d. Determine the regression equation.

d.

e. Interpret the regression equation. Where does the equation cross the Y-axis? How many
additional cars can the dealer expect to sell for each additional salesperson employed?

_____

_____

f. Determine the standard error of estimate.

X			Y		
5			53		
5			47		
7			48		
4			50		
10			58		
12			62		
3			45		
11			60		

f.

g. Develop a 95 percent confidence interval for all the mean car sales for weeks when the sales staff is at 10.

g.

h. In checking the work schedules for next week, Tem finds there are 10 people scheduled. Develop a 95 percent prediction interval for the number of cars sold next week.

h.

CHAPTER 14
MULTIPLE REGRESSION AND CORRELATION ANALYSIS

Chapter Goals

After completing this chapter, you will be able to:

1. Describe the relationship between several independent variables and a dependent variable using a multiple regression equation.

2. Setup, interpret and apply an ANOVA table.

3. Compute and interpret the multiple standard error of estimate, the coefficient of multiple determination, and the adjusted coefficient of multiple determination.

4. Conduct a hypothesis test to determine whether regression coefficients differ from zero.

5. Conduct a hypothesis test on each of the regression coefficients.

6. Use residual analysis to evaluate the assumptions of multiple regression analysis.

7. Evaluate the effects of correlated independent variables.

8. Use and understand qualitative independent variables.

9. Understand and interpret the stepwise regression method.

10. Understand and interpret possible interactions among independent variables.

Introduction

In the last chapter we began our study of regression and correlation analysis. However, the methods presented considered only the relationship between one dependent variable and one independent variable. The possible effect of other independent variables was ignored. For example, we described how the repair cost of a car was related to the age of the car. Are there other factors that affect the repair cost? Does the size of the engine or the number of miles driven affect the repair cost? When several independent variables are used to estimate the value of the dependent variable it is called *multiple regression*.

> *Multiple Regression*: A set of techniques used to analyze the relationship between two or more independent variables and a dependent variable.

Multiple Regression Analysis

Recall that for one independent variable, the linear regression equation [13-3] from the text, has the form:

$$\hat{Y} = a + bX$$

For more than one independent variable, the equation is extended to include the additional variables. For k independent variables we use text formula [14-1]:

| **Multiple Regression Equation** | $\hat{Y} = a + b_1 X_1 + b_2 X_2 + b_3 X_3 + \ldots + b_k X_K$ | [14-1] |

Where:

X_1 is one of the independent variables.

X_2 is the second independent variable.

X_3 is the third independent variable.

X_k is the kth independent variable.

a is the Y-intercept, the value of Y when all the X's are zero.

b_j is the net change in $\hat{Y}$ for each unit change in X_j, holding all other $X's$ constant.

j the subscript can assume values between 1 and k, which is the number of independent variables.

The values of b_1, and b_2, etc. are called the ***regression coefficients***. They indicate the change in the estimated value of the dependent variable for a unit change in one of the independent variables, when the other independent variables are held constant.

This equation can be extended for any number of independent variables.

For example, suppose the National Sales Manager of General Motors wants to analyze regional sales using the number of autos registered in the region (X_1), the average age of the automobiles registered in the region (X_2), and the personal income in the region (X_3). A sample of 50 regions was taken and the relevant information recorded. A portion of the sample data set follows:

Region	Sales ($ millions)	Number of autos In region (thousands)	Average age of autos (years)	Personal Income in Region ($ billions)
	Y	X_1	X_2	X_3
1	$9.20	842	5.6	$29.50
2	46.8	2,051	5.1	182.6
.	.	.	.	.
.	.	.	.	.
50	26.2	1,010	5.8	190.7

Suppose the multiple regression equation was computed to be:

$$\hat{Y} = 41.0 + 0.0071 X_1 + (-3.19) X_2 + 0.01611 X_3$$

In April of this year the automobile registration bureau announced that in a particular region 1,542,000 autos were registered, and their average age was 6.0 years. Another agency announced that personal income in the region was $150 billion. The sales manager could then estimate, as early as April, annual sales for this year by inserting the value of these independent variables in the equation and solving for $\hat{Y}$

$$\hat{Y} = 41.0 + 0.0071(1,542) - 3.19(6.0) + 0.01611(150)$$

$$= \$35.2 \text{ million}$$

What is the meaning of the regression coefficients? The 0.0071 associated with number of autos in the region (in thousands) indicates that for each additional 1,000 autos registered, sales will increase 0.0071 (million), if the other independent variables are held constant. That is, the regression coefficients show change in the dependent variable when the other independent variables are not allowed to change.

Multiple Standard Error of Estimate

It is likely that there is some error in the estimation. This can be measured by the *multiple standard error of estimate*.

> *Multiple standard error of estimate*: Measures the error in the predicted value of the dependent variable.

Like the standard error of estimate described in the previous chapter, it is based on the squared deviations between Y and $\hat{Y}$. Text formula [14-2] is used.

Multiple Standard Error of Estimate $\qquad s_{y\cdot12\cdots k} = \sqrt{\dfrac{\Sigma\left(Y - \hat{Y}\right)^2}{n - (k+1)}} \qquad [14-2]$

Where:

Y is the observation.

$\hat{Y}$ is the value estimated from the regression equation.

n is the number of observations in the sample.

k is the number of independent variables.

$s_{y\cdot12\cdots k}$ is the standard error of estimate. The subscripts indicate the number of independent variables being used to estimate the value of Y.

The ANOVA Table

A convenient means of showing the regression output is to use an ANOVA table. This table was first described in Chapter 12 and also mentioned in Chapter 13. The variation in the dependent variable is separated into two components: (1) that explained by the *regression*, that is, the independent variable and (2) the *residual error* or unexplained variation.

These two categories are identified in the source column of the following ANOVA table. The column headed "*DF*" refers to the degrees of freedom associated with each category. The total degrees of freedom is $(n-1)$.

The degrees of freedom for regression is k, the number of independent variables. The degrees of freedom associated with the error term is $n - (k+1)$. The SS in the middle of the top row of the ANOVA table refers to the sum of squares, or the variation.

$$\text{Total variation} = SS\,total = \Sigma\left(Y - \bar{Y}\right)^2$$

$$\text{Error variation} = SSE = \Sigma\left(Y - \hat{Y}\right)^2$$

$$\text{Regression variation} = SSR = \Sigma\left(\hat{Y} - \bar{Y}\right)^2 = \left(SS\,Total - SSE\right)$$

The column headed MS refers to the mean square and is obtained by dividing the SS term by the *df* term. Thus, MSR, the mean square regression, is equal to SSR/k, and MSE equals SSE/$[n - (k + 1)]$. The general format of the ANOVA table is:

Analysis of Variance

Source	df	SS	MS	F
Regression	K	SSR	MSR = SSR/k	MSR / MSE
Error	$n - (k + 1)$	SSE	MSE = SSE/$[n - (k + 1)]$	
Total	$n - 1$	SS total		

Notice that the multiple standard error of the estimate can be readily computed from the ANOVA table using

$$s_{y.123..k} = \sqrt{\frac{MSE}{n - (k + 1)}}\;.$$

Another measure of the effectiveness of the regression equation is the *coefficient of multiple determination*.

> *Coefficient of multiple determination*: The proportion of the variation in the dependent variable, Y, that is explained by the set of independent variables x_1, x_2, x_3,...x_k.

The coefficient of multiple determination, written R^2 or R square, may range from 0 to 1.0. It is the percent of the variation explained by the regression. The ANOVA table is used to calculate the coefficient of multiple determination. It is the sum of squares due to the regression divided by the sum of squares total.

Coefficient of Multiple Determination $\qquad R^2 = \dfrac{SSR}{SS\,total}\qquad$ [14 – 3]

R^2 must always be between 0 and 1.0, inclusive. That is, $0 \le R^2 \le 1.0$. The closer R^2 is to 1.0, the stronger the association between Y and the set of independent variables, x_1, x_2, x_3,...x_k.

In the Automobile Sales example, if the coefficient of multiple determination were 0.81, it would indicate that the three independent variables, considered jointly, explain 81 percent of the variation in millions of sales dollars.

Adjusted Coefficient of Determination

As the number of independent variables in the regression model increases, the coefficient of multiple determination, R^2, increases. Even if the additional independent variable is not a good predictor, its inclusion in the model decreases SSE which in turn increases SSR and R^2. Because of this, another measure of the effectiveness of a multiple regression model, called R^2_{adj}, should be considered.

R_{adj}^2 : the proportion of the variation in Y explained by $X_1, X_2, \ldots X_k$, adjusted for the number of predictors in the model.

The adjusted coefficient of determination, R_{adj}^2, is computed using the following equation:

$$\textbf{Adjusted Coefficient of Determination} \quad R_{adj}^2 = 1 - \frac{\dfrac{SSE}{n-(k+1)}}{\dfrac{SStotal}{n-1}} \quad [14-4]$$

SSE and SStotal are divided by their respective degrees of freedom. Notice that the addition of a new independent variable simultaneously decreases both SSE and the degrees of freedom for SSE. The net effect is that R_{adj}^2 will not necessarily increase when a new variable is added to the model.

Global Test: Testing Whether the Multiple Regression Model is Valid

The overall ability of the independent variables $X_1, X_2, \ldots X_k$, to explain the behavior of the dependent variable Y can be tested. Two tests of hypotheses are considered in this chapter. The first one is called the *global test*.

> *Global test*: An overall test of the regression model. It investigates the possibility that all the regression coefficients are equal to zero.

It tests the overall ability of the set of independent variables to explain differences in the dependent variable. The null hypothesis is that all of the population regression coefficients are zero. If accepted, it would imply that the set of coefficients is of no value in explaining differences in the dependent variable. The alternate hypothesis is that *at least* one of the coefficients is not zero. This test is written in symbolic form for three independent variables as:

$$H_0: \beta_1 = \beta_2 = \beta_3 = 0$$
$$H_1: \text{Not all the } \beta s = 0$$

Rejecting H_0 and accepting H_1 implies that one or more of the independent variables is useful in explaining differences in the dependent variable. However, a word of caution, it does not suggest how many or identify which regression coefficients are not zero. Note also that β_i denotes the population value of the slope, whereas b_j, a point estimate of β_j, is computed from sample data.

The test statistic used is the F distribution, which was first described in Chapter 12, the ANOVA chapter.

Recall these characteristics of the F distribution:

1. There is a family of F distributions. A change in the numerator degrees of freedom or the denominator degrees of freedom results in a new F distribution.

2. The F distribution cannot be negative. The smallest possible value is 0.

3. It is a continuous distribution.

4. It is positively skewed.

5. It is asymptotic. As the values of X increase, the F curve will approach but never touch the horizontal axis.

To employ the F distribution, two sets of degrees of freedom are required. The degrees of freedom for the numerator are equal to k, the number of independent variables. The degrees of freedom in the denominator are equal to $n - (k + 1)$ where n refers, as usual, to the total number of observations.

The value of F is found using text Formula [14-5]:

$$\boxed{\textbf{Global Test} \quad F = \frac{MSR}{MSE} = \frac{SSR/k}{SSE/[n - (k + 1)]} \qquad [14-5]}$$

Where:
SSR is the sum of the squares "explained by" the regression.
k is the number of independent variables.
SSE is the sum of squares error.
n is the number of observations.

Evaluating Individual Regression Coefficients

The second test of hypothesis identifies which of the set of independent variables are significant predictors of the dependent variable. That is, it tests the independent variables individually rather than as a unit. This test is useful because unimportant variables can be eliminated from the regression model.

The test statistic is the Student t distribution with $n - (k + 1)$ degrees of freedom. For example, suppose we want to test whether the hypothesis that the coefficient for the second independent variable in the model was equal to zero versus the alternative hypothesis that it was not equal to zero. The null and alternate hypotheses would be written as follows.

$$H_0: \beta_2 = 0$$

$$H_1: \beta_2 \neq 0$$

Rejection of the null hypothesis and acceptance of the alternate hypothesis would imply that variable number two is significant and that it has an inverse relationship with the dependent variable. Obviously its sign is negative.

$$\boxed{\textbf{Testing Individual Regression Coefficients} \qquad t = \frac{b_i - 0}{s_{b_i}} \qquad [14-6]}$$

If the hypothesis test finds that the null hypothesis cannot be rejected, then the variable should be dropped from the model. However, the above test only supports removing one variable at a time from the model. After a variable is removed, a new regression model is constructed using the remaining variables and a new t-test can be conducted for each of the remaining variables.

Assumptions About Multiple Regression and Correlation

As noted in previous chapters, it is generally considered good practice to identify the assumptions related to a topic because if the assumptions are not met fully, the results might be biased. There are five assumptions that must be met in multiple regression and correlation.

1. There is a linear relationship between the dependent variable and each independent variable. Linearity may be evaluated by constructing a scatter diagram for each independent variable and examining the diagrams to determine whether a linear relationship appears to exist. *Linearity* can

also be assessed graphically by constructing a ***residual plot***. A residual plot is constructed by plotting the ***residuals***, $\left(Y - \hat{Y}\right)$, against $\hat{Y}$.

> ***Residual***. The difference between the actual and predicted value of the dependent variable.

The residuals should be scattered randomly about the horizontal line, $\hat{Y} = 0$, and show no obvious pattern. If the plot ***does not*** show a random pattern, the assumption of a linear relationship between Y and one of more of the predictors may not be reasonable.

2. The variation in the residuals is the same for all fitted values of Y. That is, $\left(Y - \hat{Y}\right)$ must be approximately the same for all values of $\hat{Y}$. When this is the case, the residuals exhibit ***homoscedasticity***.

> ***Homoscedasticity***: The variation around the regression equation is the same regardless of the values of the independent variables.

Homoscedasticity may be evaluated using the same residual plot used to evaluate linearity.

3. The ***residuals*** are normally distributed with a mean of 0. The assumption of normality is necessary for the validity of the inferences that we make based on the global and individual hypothesis tests. If the number of observations used to construct the regression line is large, normality can be evaluated by constructing a histogram for the residuals. If the histogram of residuals has a bell shape, then the assumption of normality is reasonable. If the data set is not large, normality of the residuals can be evaluated using a normal probability plot. Briefly, and without detailing the calculations, a normal probability plot indicates normality of the residuals if the plotted points are fairly close to a straight line extending from the lower left to the upper right of the graph. Most computer software packages that support multiple regression analysis offer normal probability plots.

4. ***Mulitcollinearity*** exists when the independent variables are correlated.

In practice, it is nearly impossible to select a set of independent variables that are not correlated to some degree. However, if an independent variable is highly correlated with the other variables in the model, it should be removed. Multicollinearity makes it difficult to draw inferences about the individual regression coefficients and their effects on the dependent variable.

> ***Multicollinearity***: Correlation among the independent variables

To assess the degree to which the independent variables are correlated we can compute the ***variance inflation factor, VIF***.

> ***Variance Inflation Factor***: A measure of the degree to which an independent variable is correlated with the other independent variables in the regression model.

The variance inflation factor is computed for each independent variable, X_j, by first regressing X_j on all the other independent variables in the model to obtain R_j^2. The VIF for each independent variable, X_j, is then calculated using

> **Variance Inflation Factor** $\quad VIF = \dfrac{1}{1 - R_j^2} \qquad [14 - 7]$.

A VIF greater than 10 is unsatisfactory and indicates that the independent variable should be removed from the model. A VIF of ten or greater is equivalent to an R_j^2 of .90 or higher.

5. Successive residuals should be independent. This means that there is not a pattern to the residuals, the residuals are not highly correlated, and that there are not long runs of all positive or all negative residuals. When successive residuals are correlated we refer to this condition as ***autocorrelation***.

> ***Autocorrelation***: Correlation of successive residuals. Autocorrelation frequently occurs when data are collected over a period of time.

Residual plots can be used to detect autocorrelation by examining the plot for patterns such as a long run of residuals either above or below the horizontal line at $\hat{Y} = 0$. A formal test for autocorrelation exists and may be found in more advanced textbooks such as *Applied Linear Models* by Kutner, Nachtsheim, Wasserman, and Li, 5th Ed., McGraw-Hill, Irwin, 2006.

Seldom in a real world example are all of the conditions met fully. However, the technique of regression still works effectively. If there is concern regarding the violation of one or more of the assumptions, remedial measures can be taken to correct the problem. In such instances, a more advanced statistics book should be consulted.

Qualitative Independent Variables

Until now, the variables used in regression analysis have been ***quantitative variables.*** Recall that a quantitative variable is a variable that is numerical in nature, such as, the number of hours worked by employees, the number of traffic accidents in Bamberg in a week, and the distance traveled to work.

However, frequently we want to use nominal-scale variables such as gender, whether a home has a swimming pool, or whether an answer is yes or no. These are called ***qualitative variables.*** To use a qualitative variable in a regression model we use a scheme of ***dummy variables*** in which one of the two possible conditions is coded 0 and the other 1.

> ***Dummy variable***: A variable in which there are only two possible outcomes. For analysis, one of the outcomes is coded a 1 and the other a 0.

For example, imagine that we are interested in estimating the selling price of a used automobile based on its age. Selling price is the dependent variable and age is one independent variable. Another variable is whether or not the car has an automatic transmission. Note that a particular car can assume only two conditions: either it has an automatic transmission or it does not. Cars with automatic transmission are coded using a 1 and those without automatic transmissions are coded using a 0. Suppose that a regression analysis to predict selling price of a used automobile (Y) based on age (X_1) and whether or not the car has an automatic transmission (X_2) was conducted with the following results:

$$\hat{Y} = 15,000 - 2,000X_1 + 1,200X_2 .$$

This model predicts, for example, that a three year old car with an automatic transmission will sell for $15,000 - 2,000(3) + 1,200(1) = $10,200 and that a four year old car without an automatic transmission will sell for $15,000-2,000(4)+1,200(0)= $7,000.

Stepwise Regression

Previously, we used a global test of hypothesis and individual tests of regression coefficients to determine which predictor variables should be included in the regression model. When there are many potential predictor variables, a systematic procedure known as *stepwise regression* can be a more efficient method for determining the regression equation.

> *Stepwise Regression*. A step-by-step method to determine a regression equation that begins by introducing a single independent variable and adds or deletes independent variables one by one. Only independent variables with non-zero regression coefficients are included in the regression equation.

Stepwise regression begins with no predictor variables in the model. The first variable added to the model is the one that explains the largest percentage of the variation in Y. The next variable in the model is the X_j that explains the largest percentage of variation in Y not explained by the X variable already in the model. Whenever a new variable is added to the model, the regression equation changes. Previously significant X variables may become insignificant. When this happens the insignificant predictor variable is removed from the model. The process continues in this way, adding and deleting variables as necessary, until all the significant predictor variables have been included in the model.

Other selection procedures can also be used to determine the regression equation. The stepwise procedure described above is also called *forward selection* because we begin with no variables in the model and may add a variable with each iteration. *Backward elimination* begins with all predictor variables in the model and may remove one variable at each iteration. The *best subsets regression* finds the best model with one predictor, the best with two predictors, and so on. The criterion for "best" is the model with the largest value of R^2.

Regression Models with Interaction

For any multiple regression model, there is the possibility of an *interaction* between two or more of the independent variables. An interaction between two variables is present if the total effect of both variables on Y is different from the sum of the individual effects.

> *Interaction*: The combined effect of two independent variables on the dependent variable. An interaction between two independent variables exists if the total effect of both variables differs from the sum of the individual effects.

For example, suppose that the organizers of an annual 10 kilometer running event have observed that the winning time for the race increases by 15 seconds (.25 minute) for every one degree Fahrenheit in temperature above $80°$ at the start of the race. It has also been observed that the winning time increases by 10 seconds (.167 minute) for each percentage point in humidity above 85 percent. The race organizers proposed the following model based on data collected for the race over many years:

$$\hat{Y} = 29 + .25X_1 + .167X_2$$

Where:

X_1 is degrees Fahrenheit above $80°$;
X_2 is percent humidity above 85%.

They found that the model did not work well when *both* temperature and humidity were high. For those races when the temperature exceeded $80°$ *and* the humidity exceeded 85%, the winning times increased at a much higher rate than the sum of the individual effects, $.25X_1 + .167X_2$. There appeared to be an *interaction* between high temperature and high humidity. The combined effect of high temperature and high humidity was different (greater in this case) than the sum of their individual effects.

In a regression analysis, the interaction between two independent variables can be modeled separately by an *interaction term*. The interaction term is created by multiplying the values of X_1 and X_2 to create a third independent variable, $X_1 X_2$. The two variable models that include the interaction term are:

$$Y = \alpha + \beta_1 X_1 + \beta_2 X_2 + \beta_3 X_1 X_2$$

The interaction term can be tested for significance using the individual test for predictor variables previously described.

Glossary

Adjusted coefficient of determination: The proportion of the variation in the Y explained by X_1, $X_2, \ldots X_k$, adjusted for the the number of predictors in the model.

Autocorrelation: Correlation of successive residuals. This condition frequently occurs when time is involved in the analysis.

Coefficient of multiple determination: The proportion of the variation in the dependent variable, Y, that is explained by the independent variables $X_1, X_2, \ldots X_k$.

Dummy variable: A variable in which there are only two possible outcomes. For analysis, one of the outcomes is coded a 1 and the other a 0.

Global test: An overall test of the regression model. It investigates whether all of the independent variables have regression coefficients equal to zero.

Homoscedasticity: The residuals are approximately the same for all estimated values of the dependent variable.

Interaction: The combined effect of two (or more) independent variables on the dependent variable. An interaction between two independent variables exists if the total effect of the variables differs from the sum of the individual effects.

Multicollinearity: Correlation among the independent variables.

Multiple Regression: A set of techniques used to analyze the relationship between two or more independent variables and a dependent variable.

Multiple standard error of estimate: Measures the error in the predicted value of the dependent variable.

Qualitative variable: A nonnumeric variable measured on the nominal or ordinal scale.

Quantitative variable: A numeric variable that is at least interval scale.

Residual: The difference between the actual and the predicted value of the dependent variable.

Stepwise Regression: A step-by-step method to determine a regression equation that begins by introducing a single independent variable into the model and adds or deletes independent variables one by one until only significant independent variables remain in the model.

Variance Inflation Factor: A measure of the degree to which and independent variable is correlated with the other independent variables in the model.

Chapter Problems

Problem 1

The Skaff Appliance Company currently has over 1,000 retail outlets throughout the United States and Canada. They sell name brand electronic products, such as TVs, stereos, VCRs, DVD players, cell phones, and microwave ovens. Skaff Appliance is considering opening several additional stores in other large metropolitan areas. Paul Skaff, president, would like to study the relationship between the sales at existing locations and several factors regarding the existing store or its region. The factors are the population and the % unemployed in the region, and the advertising expense of the store. Another variable considered is "mall." Mall refers to whether the existing store is located in an enclosed shopping mall or not. A "1" indicates a mall location; a "0" indicates the store is not located in a mall. A random sample of 30 stores is selected.

Problem 1

Use EXCEL to find the

a. multiple regression equation using all four independent variables

b. multiple standard error of the estimate

c. coefficient of multiple determination,

d. adjusted coefficient of multiple determination.

Sales (000)	Population (000,000)	Percent Unemployed	Advertising Expense (000)	Mall Location
5.17	7.50	5.1	59.0	0
5.78	8.71	6.3	62.5	0
4.84	10.00	4.7	61.0	0
6.00	7.45	5.4	61.0	1
6.00	8.67	5.4	61.0	1
6.12	11.00	7.2	12.5	0
6.40	13.18	5.8	35.8	0
7.10	13.81	5.8	59.9	0
8.50	14.43	6.2	57.2	1
7.50	10.00	5.5	35.8	0
9.30	13.21	6.8	27.9	0
8.80	17.10	6.2	24.1	1
9.96	15.12	6.3	27.7	1
9.83	18.70	0.5	24.0	0
10.12	20.20	5.5	57.2	1
10.70	15.00	5.8	44.3	0
10.45	17.60	7.1	49.2	0
11.32	19.80	7.5	23.0	0
11.87	14.40	8.2	62.7	1
11.91	20.35	7.8	55.8	0
12.60	18.90	6.2	50.0	0
12.60	21.60	7.1	47.6	1
14.24	25.25	0.4	43.5	0
14.41	27.50	4.2	55.9	0
13.73	21.00	0.7	51.2	1
13.73	19.70	6.4	76.6	1
13.80	24.15	0.5	63.0	1
14.92	17.65	8.5	68.1	0
15.28	22.30	7.1	74.4	1
14.41	24.00	0.8	70.1	0

Solution 1

a. From the EXCEL regression output , the multiple regression model is:

$$\hat{Y} = -1.669 + .552(pop) + .203(\%unemp) + 0.031(adv) + 0.220(mall)$$

	Coefficients	Standard Error	t Stat	P-value
Intercept	-1.66853987	1.408315529	-1.18478	0.247247
pop	0.551907307	0.050629062	10.901	5.47E-11
%unemp	0.203162643	0.117086169	1.735155	0.095027
Exp	0.031354963	0.016062075	1.952112	0.062211
Mall	0.219790323	0.540028513	0.406998	0.687473

The Anova table from the regression output can be used to answer b., c., and d,

ANOVA					
	df	SS	MS	F	Significance F
Regression	4	270.461	67.615	34.707	7.22088E-10
Residual	25	48.705	1.948		
Total	29	319.166			

b. The multiple standard error of the estimate is obtained by finding the square root of the mean square error The mean square error is found by dividing SSE, the sum of the squared errors ,by the degrees of freedom for SSE. The degrees of freedom for SSE = n-(k+1) = 30 – (4+1) = 25.

Multiple standard error of the estimate $= \sqrt{\dfrac{\sum(Y - \hat{Y})^2}{n - (k+1)}} = \sqrt{\dfrac{SSE}{n - (k+1)}} = \sqrt{MSE}$

$$= \sqrt{\dfrac{270.461}{30 - (4+1)}} = \sqrt{67.615} = 8.223.$$

c. The coefficient of multiple determination measures the proportion of the variation in Y explained by the independent variables. It is computed by dividing the sum of squared regession (SSR) by the sum of squared total (SStotal).

$$R^2 = \dfrac{SSR}{SStotal} = \dfrac{270.461}{319.416} = .847.$$

84.7% of the variation in Y can be explained by the independent variables in the model.

d. R^2_{adj} measures the proportion of the variation in Y explained by the independent variables, but adjusts downward for the number of variables in the model. This measure discourages inclusion of independent variables that do not have a significant relationship with Y. It is calculated using the following formula:

$$R_{adj}^2 = 1 - \frac{\dfrac{SSE}{n-(k+1)}}{\dfrac{SStotal}{n-1}} \cdot$$

Using the appropriate SS's and df from the Anova table, we obtain: $R_{adj}^2 = 1 - \dfrac{\dfrac{67.615}{25}}{\dfrac{319.416}{29}} = .823$.

82.3% of the variation in Y is explained by the independent variables in the model and is adjusted for the number of variables included in the model. Note that $R_{adj}^2 = .823$ is less than $R^2 = .847$

Exercise 14.1

Check your answers against those in the ANSWER section.

Todd Heffren, President of Heffren Manufacturing Co., is studying the power usage at his Vanengo Plant. He believes that the amount of electrical power used is a function of the outside temperature during the day, and the number of units produced that day. A random sample of ten days is selected. The power usage in thousands of kilowatt hours of electricity and the production on that date is obtained. The National Weather Service is contacted to obtain the high temperature for the selected dates.
EXCEL was used to compute a correlation matrix and ANOVA table for the Heffren Manufacturing Co. data.

Power Used	Temperature (F)	Units Produced
12	83	120
11	79	110
13	85	128
9	75	101
14	87	105
10	81	108
12	84	110
11	77	107
14	85	112
11	84	119

ANOVA			
	df	SS	MS
Regression	2	17.069	8.534
Residual	7	7.031	1.004
Total	9	24.100	

a. Regress sales on all the predictor variables in the data set. Write out the multiple regression model.

b. Compute the multiple standard error of the estimate.

c. Calculate R^2.

d. Calculate R_{adj}^2.

Problem 2

Refer to Problem 1. The President of Skaff Appliance Company would like to develop a regression model to predict sales. Use EXCEL to carry out computations required for the following questions.

a. Interpret the simple coefficients of correlation between sales and each of the independent variables.

b. Conduct a global test of hypothesis to determine if at least one regression coefficient is non-zero.

c. Conduct a hypothesis test for each of the four predictor variables to determine which, if any, should be dropped from the model.

Solution 2

a. The simple coefficients of correlation show that population has the strongest correlation with sales. The negative sign between sales and % unemployed indicates that, as the % unemployed rate increases, sales decrease.

	Sales
pop	0.89400
% unemp	-0.19836
adv	0.27869
mall	0.15508

b. We want to test the overall ability of the set of independent variables to explain the behavior of the dependent variable. Do the independent variables, population, percent unemployed, advertising expense, and mall explain a significant amount of the variation in sales? This question can be answered by conducting a global test of the regression coefficients. The null and alternate hypotheses are

$$H_0 : \beta_1 = \beta_2 = \beta_3 = \beta_4 = 0$$
$$H_1 : \text{At least one of the } \beta\text{'s is not zero.}$$

The null hypothesis states that the regression coefficients are all zero. If they are all zero, this indicates they are of no value in explaining differences in the sales of the various stores. If the null hypothesis is rejected and the alternate accepted the conclusion is that at least one of the regression coefficients is not zero. Hence, we would conclude that at least one of the variables is significant in terms of explaining differences in sales.

The F distribution introduced in Chapter 12 is used as the test statistic. The F distribution is based on the degrees of freedom in the numerator and in the denominator. The degrees of freedom associated with the regression, which is the numerator, is equal to the number of independent variables. In this case there are four independent variables, so there are 4 degrees of freedom in the numerator. The degrees of freedom in the error row is $n - (k + 1) = 30 - (4 + 1) = 25$. There are 25 degrees of freedom in the denominator. The critical value of F is obtained from Appendix B.4. Find the column with 4 degrees of freedom and the row with 25 degrees of freedom in the table for the 0.05 significance level. The value is 2.76. The null hypothesis is rejected if the computed F is greater than 2.76 or if the reported probability value (p-value) is less than .05.

The output from EXCEL required for the test is shown again:

ANOVA

	df	SS	MS	F	Significance F
Regression	4	270.461	67.615	34.707	7.22088E-10
Residual	25	48.705	1.948		
Total	29	319.166			

…ue of F is 34.71 as shown above. It is also computed using formula [14-4].

$$F = \frac{\dfrac{SSR}{k}}{\dfrac{SSE}{[n-(k+1)]}} = \frac{\dfrac{270.461}{4}}{\dfrac{48.705}{[30-(4+1)]}} = \frac{67.615}{1.948} = 34.71$$

…ion and Correlation Analysis

Since the computed value of 34.71 exceeds the critical value of 2.76 (or the p-value =*Significance F* is less than .05), the null hypothesis is rejected and the alternate accepted. The conclusion is that at least one of the regression coefficients does not equal zero.

c. We will conduct hypothesis tests for each of the four predictor variables to determine which, if any, should be dropped from the model. In each case we will conduct a two-sided test of hypothesis to see if the coefficients for the predictor variables is different from zero. If we cannot reject the null hypothesis that the coefficient is equal to zero, we will consider eliminating that variable from the regression equation. The four tests of hypotheses are:

For Population	For % Unemployed	For Advertising	For Mall
$H_0 : \beta_1 = 0$	$H_0 : \beta_2 = 0$	$H_0 : \beta_3 = 0$	$H_0 : \beta_4 = 0$
$H_1 : \beta_1 \neq 0$	$H_1 : \beta_2 \neq 0$	$H_1 : \beta_3 \neq 0$	$H_1 : \beta_4 \neq 0$

We will use the 0.05 significance level. In each test, the test statistic is the t distribution with $n - (k + 1) = 30 - (4 + 1) = 25$ degrees of freedom. The decision rule is to reject the null hypothesis if the computed value of t is less than -2.060 or greater than 2.060.

From the EXCEL output, the column labeled "Coefficients" reports the regression coefficients (slopes). The standard error column reports the standard deviation of the coefficients. The "t-stat" column reports the computed value of the test statistic.

The t-ratio for population (10.90) exceeds the critical value, but the computed values for percent unemployed, (1.74) advertising expense (1.95), and mall (0.41) are not in the rejection region. This indicates that the independent variable population should be retained and the other three dropped.

However, there is a problem that occurs in many real situations. Note that both percent unemployed and advertising expense are close to being significant. In fact, advertising expense would be significant if we increased the level of significances to 0.10. (The critical value would be -1.708 and 1.708, and 1.95 is outside the critical region.) Also, we should be cautious about dropping more than one variable from the regression model at the same time. When a predictor variable is dropped from the model, the significance of the remaining variables change. Formerly insignificant variables can become significant.

Exercise 14.2

Check your answers against those in the ANSWER section.

Refer to Exercise 14.1 The output is for the Heffren Manufacturing problem. The table of simple coefficients of correlation, anova table, and regression coefficients are shown below.

Correlations

	Power	Temp	Units
Power	1.0000	0.8384	0.3612
Temp	0.8384	1.0000	0.5057
Units	0.3612	0.5057	1.0000

Regression Coefficients

	Coeff	Standard Error	t Stat	P-value
Intercept	-16.8	7.162	-2.346	0.051
Temp	0.371	0.0996	3.723	0.007
Units	-0.02	0.04791	-0.3563	0.732

ANOVA					
	df	SS	MS	F	Significance F
Regression	2	17.06870075	8.534350376	8.49636	0.013414203
Residual	7	7.031299249	1.004471321		
Total	9	24.1			

a. Interpret the simple coefficients of correlation between sales and each of the independent variables.

b. Conduct a global test of hypothesis to determine if at least one regression coefficient is non-zero. Use $\alpha = .05$.

c. Conduct a hypothesis test for each of the predictor variables to determine which, if any, should be dropped from the model.

Problem 3

The multiple regression and correlation data for Problem 2 were rerun using the two most significant variables—population and advertising expense.

	Coefficients	Standard Error	t Stat	P-value
Intercept	-0.078741938	1.086382342	-0.07248	0.942753
Pop	0.520747156	0.048062131	10.83487	2.47E-11
Exp	0.033471615	0.015903475	2.104673	0.044766

ANOVA					
	df	SS	MS	F	Significance F
Regression	2	264.1210773	132.0605	64.7767	4.95984E-11
Residual	27	55.04501937	2.038704		
Total	29	319.1660967			

a. What is the new multiple regression equation?

b. What is the $\hat{Y}$ value for the first store?

c. What is the coefficient of multiple determination? Interpret.

Regression Statistics	
Multiple R	0.909689441
R Square	0.827534879
Adjusted R Square	0.814759685
Standard Error	1.42783207
Observations	30

d. Construct a residual plot to graphically evaluate the model assumptions of linearity and homoscedasticity.

e. Construct a histogram of the residuals to assess whether the residuals appear to be normally distributed.

f. Calculate the variance inflation factors (VIF's) to determine whether multicollinearity a problem for this model.

Solution 3

a. The regression equation is: Sales $= -\ 0.08 + 0.521\ pop + 0.0335\ exp$

$$\hat{Y} = -0.08 + 0.521 X_1 + 0.0335 X_3$$

b. $\hat{Y}$ for the first store is found by substituting the value: $X_1 = 7.5$ and $X_3 = 59.0$ into the $\hat{Y}$ equation.

$$\hat{Y} = -0.0787 + 0.5207 X_1 + 0.0335 X_3$$
$$= -0.0787 + 0.5207(7.5) + 0.0335(59) = 5.802$$

c. The coefficient of multiple determination is *R Square* on the printout. It is .8275. A total of 82.8% of the variation in sales is explained by the population and the advertising expense. It can also be found by: $R^2 = \dfrac{SSR}{SStotal} = \dfrac{264.12}{319.17} = 0.828$.

d. EXCEL was used to develop the predicted values of $\hat{Y}$ and the residuals. The predicted values are obtained by substituting the actual values of population and advertising expense in the regression equation. For example, the first store was in a city having 7.5 million populations and advertising expense of 59.0 thousand dollars. We substituted these values in the regression equation and the estimated, or "fitted" values of $\hat{Y}$ obtained was 5.802.

The residual is the difference between the actual and the predicted value. For the first store it is −0.6317, found by $(Y - \hat{Y}) = (5.17 - 5.8017)$. The residuals are computed for the other 29 stores in a similar fashion. EXCEL will perform these time-consuming calculations for us.

A plot of the residuals versus $\hat{Y}$, shown below, can be used to assess both linearity and homoscedasticity. The assumption of a linear relationship between Y and each of the X's is reasonable if the residuals appear in a random pattern around $\hat{Y}=0$ and shows no obvious pattern. The residual plot indicates that the assumption of linearity is reasonable for our model. A residual plot demonstrates homoscedasticity if the scatter of residuals around $\hat{Y}$ is approximately the same over the

Observation	Predicted Y	Residuals
1	5.8017	-0.6317
2	6.5489	-0.7689
3	7.1705	-2.3305
4	5.8426	0.1574
5	6.4779	-0.4779
6	6.0679	0.0521
7	7.983	-1.583
8	9.1177	-2.0177
9	9.3502	-0.8502
10	6.327	1.173
11	7.7342	1.5658
12	9.6327	-0.8327
13	8.7221	1.2379
14	10.4625	-0.6325
15	12.3549	-2.2349
16	9.2153	1.4847
17	10.7332	-0.2832
18	11.0019	0.3181
19	9.5187	2.3513
20	12.3862	-0.4762
21	11.437	1.163
22	12.7626	-0.1626
23	14.5261	-0.2861
24	16.1129	-1.7029
25	12.5707	1.1593
26	12.7439	0.9861
27	14.606	-0.806
28	11.3919	3.5281
29	14.0242	1.2558
30	14.7655	-0.3555

length of $\hat{Y}$. The residual plot indicates that the scatter of residuals is about equal over the length of $\hat{Y}$. The residual for observation number 28 seems unusually large, however, and may be cause for concern.

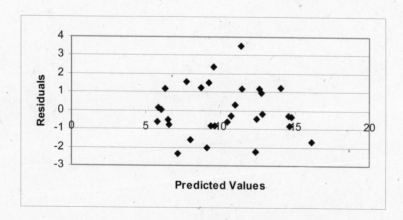

e. The assumption of normality can be assessed by constructing a histogram of the residuals. The histogram shows that the residuals are roughly symmetrically distributed and clustered around zero. One residual is unusually large and should be investigated.

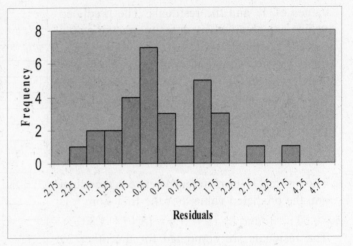

f. The variance inflation factor (*VIF*) can be calculated by regressing each X in the model on the remaining X's and calculating R^2. Equation 14-7 is then used to find the *VIF* for each X. We regress X_1 (population) on X_3 (advertising expense) and find that $R_1^2 = .01564$. Since there are only two predictor variables in the model, R^2 will be the same for both regressions ($R_1^2 = R_3^2 = .01564$). The *VIF* for each variable is 1.016. Since this value is less than 10, we would conclude that X_1 and X_3 are not highly correlated and multicollinearity and not a concern for this model.

$$VIF = \frac{1}{1 - R_j^2} = \frac{1}{1 - .01564} = 1.016$$

Exercise 14.3

Check your answers against those in the ANSWER section.

The multiple regression and correlation data for Exercise 13.1 and 13.2 were rerun using the most significant variable *temperature*. Use the EXCEL output shown below and on the next page to answer the following questions:

a. What is the new multiple regression equation?

b. What is the $\hat{Y}$ value for the first item in the sample?

c. What is the coefficient of multiple determination? Interpret.

d. Do the residuals approximate a normal distribution?

e. Are the residuals constant for all fitted values of $\hat{Y}$?

Multiple R	0.838423
R Square	0.702953
Adjusted R Square	0.665823
Standard Error	0.945967
Observations	10
Multiple R	0.838423

ANOVA					
	df	SS	MS	F	Significance F
Regression	1	16.94118	16.94118	18.9318	0.002442
Residual	8	7.158824	0.894853		
Total	9	24.1			

	Coefficients	Standard Error	t Stat	P-value
Intercept	-17.2412	6.658233	-2.58945	0.03214
Temperature	0.352941	0.081116	4.351069	0.002442

Continued on next page

The following two plots were obtained. Comment on the normality assumption, the linearity assumption, and the condition of homoscedasticity.

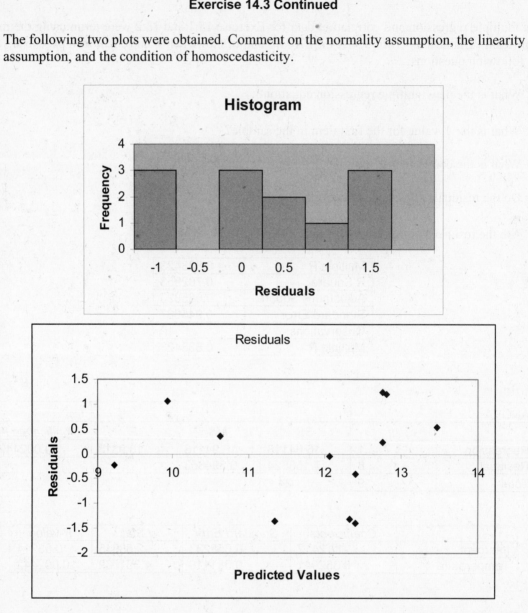

Problem 4

A manufacturer of tractors has decided to reduce the size of its U.S. workforce. In order to avoid layoffs, the manufacturer decides to offer "buyouts"—lump-sum payments given at the time a worker terminates his or her employment. They expect the size of the offer and the location of the plant to affect the number of people who accept the offer. The manufacturer has a large plant in the northeast and a large plant in the southeast. The manufacturer randomly selects 100 employees at each plant and asks them if they would accept a buyout of $100, $140, $170, $200 or $240 thousand dollars. The results of the survey are shown in the table.

a. Construct a regression model using both independent variables, *offer* and *region*. Write out the model.

b. Conduct a global test of hypothesis that at least one of is not zero. Use $\alpha = .05$.

c. Run a separate hypothesis test for the significance of each of the independent variables. Use $\alpha = .05$ for both tests.

d. Construct another regression model that includes the interaction between offer and region. Write out the model and determine if the interaction term should be included in the regression equation.

Number of Employees who Accept	Offer ($1,000s)	Region
70	100	1
40	100	0
75	140	1
50	140	0
80	170	1
60	170	0
90	200	1
70	200	0
95	250	1
80	250	0

Solution 4

The results of the analysis for the first model using EXCEL are:

Multiple R	0.98362
R Square	0.967509
Adjusted R Square	0.958226
Standard Error	3.50053
Observations	10

ANOVA

	df	SS	MS	F	Significance F
Regression	2	2554.224	1277.112	104.2224	6.18253E-06
Residual	7	85.77599	12.25371		
Total	9	2640			

	Coefficients	Standard Error	t Stat	P-value
Intercept	21.0107	4.038354	5.202788	0.001249
Offer	0.226682	0.021643	10.47374	1.58E-05
Region	22	2.21393	9.937081	2.23E-05

a. The regression model is: $\hat{Y} = 21.01 + .227 X_1 + 22 X_2$

b. A global test of hypothesis tests for at least one $\beta_j \neq 0$

$H_0 : \beta_1 = \beta_2 = 0$

H_1 : At least one of the β's is not zero.

To find the critical value of the test statistic note that we use an F statistic with a significance level of .05. The numerator degrees of freedom $= k = 2$. The denominator degrees of freedom $= n-(k+1) = 10 - (2+1) = 7$. we have . From Appendix B.4 we have F $= 4.74$. From the Anova table from the Excel output, we have

$$F = \dfrac{\dfrac{SSR}{k}}{\dfrac{SSE}{[n-(k+1)]}} = \dfrac{\dfrac{2554.22}{2}}{\dfrac{85.78}{[10-(2+1)]}} = \dfrac{1277.11}{12.25} = 104.22$$

Since the calculated value of F $= 104.22 > 4.74$, we reject the null hypothesis and conclude that at least one $\beta_j \neq 0$.

c. We will conduct a hypothesis test for both predictor variables to determine which, if either, should be dropped from the model. In both cases we will conduct a two-sided test of hypothesis to see if the coefficients for the predictor variables is different from zero. If we cannot reject the null hypothesis that the coefficient is equal to zero, we will consider eliminating that variable from the regression equation. The four tests of hypotheses are:

For Offer	For Region
$H_0 : \beta_1 = 0$	$H_0 : \beta_2 = 0$
$H_1 : \beta_1 \neq 0$	$H_1 : \beta_2 \neq 0$

We will use the 0.05 significance level. In each test, the test statistic is the t distribution with $n - (k + 1) = 10 - (2 + 1) = 7$ degrees of freedom. The decision rule is to reject the null hypothesis if the computed value of t is less than -2.365 or greater than 2.365.

From the EXCEL output, the column labeled "Coefficients" reports the regression coefficients (slopes). The standard error column reports the standard deviation of the coefficients. The "t-stat" column reports the computed value of the test statistic.

The t-stat for offer (10.47) exceeds the critical value and the t-stat for region (9.94) also exceeds the critical value. This indicates that both variables should be retained in the model.

d. We run the model again, this time with the interaction term created by multiplying the values of *offer* with the corresponding values of *region*. The new variable *offer* × *region* appears to be significant. The results from EXCEL are:

ANOVA					
	df	SS	MS	F	Significance F
Regression	3	2615.879	871.9597	216.8983	1.66272E-06
Residual	6	24.1208	4.020133		
Total	9	2640			

Individual hypothesis tests for the three independent variables are:

Offer	Region	RegionxOffer
$H_0 : \beta_1 = 0$	$H_0 : \beta_2 = 0$	$H_0 : \beta_3 = 0$
$H_1 : \beta_1 \neq 0$	$H_1 : \beta_2 \neq 0$	$H_1 : \beta_3 \neq 0$

Again we use a t statistic, but now with n - (k+1) = 10-(3+1) =6 degrees of freedom. Using the .05 level of significance and the tables in Appendix B.2, we find that the critical values of t are -2.447 and 2.447. From the Excel table, we find that all three variables are significant with the t-stat of 15.70 for *offer*, 8.70 for *region*, and -3.92 for *offer x region*.

	Coefficients	Standard Error	t Stat	P-value
Intercept	12.66055	3.145895	4.024467	0.006924
Offer	0.275229	0.017531	15.69923	4.23E-06
Region	38.70031	4.448968	8.698716	0.000127
Offer x Region	-0.09709	0.024793	-3.9162	0.007836

It appears that the interaction term should be included in the model. The multiple regression equation is:

$$\hat{Y} = 21.01 + .275 X_1 + 38.70 X_2 + -.10 X_3 \quad \text{where} \quad X_3 = X_1 X_2.$$

CHAPTER 14 ASSIGNMENT

MULTIPLE REGRESSION AND CORRELATION ANALYSIS

Name _____   Section _____   Score_____

Part I   Select the correct answer and write the appropriate letter in the space provided.

_____1. In a multiple regression equation there is more than one
   a.   independent variable.   **b.**   dependent variable.
   c.   coefficient of correlation.   **d.** R^2 value.

_____2. If the coefficient of multiple determination is 1, then the
   a.   net regression coefficients are 0.   **b.**   standard error of estimate is 0.
   c. X values are equal to 0.   **d.**   standard error of estimate is also 1.

_____3. A dummy variable
   a.   is a qualitative variable.   **b.**   can only assume one of two values.
   c.   is used as an independent variable.   **d.**   all of the above.

_____4. In the global test of hypothesis
   a.   we use the t distribution as the test statistic.
   b.   we test to see if all of the regression coefficients are 0.
   c.   we test to insure that each of the independent variables is 0.
   d.   all of the above.

_____5. A residual is
   a.   the independent variable.
   b.   the dependent variable.
   c.   the difference between the actual value and the fitted value of the dependent variable.
   d.   equal to R^2.

_____6. The test for individual variables determines which independent variables
   a.   have the most value in determining R^2.
   b.   have nonzero regression coefficients.
   c.   are used to compute the coefficients of correlation.
   d.   are highly correlated with other independent variables.

_____7. A correlation matrix shows the
   a.   coefficients of correlation among all the variables.
   b.   regression coefficients.
   c.   stepwise regression coefficients.
   d.   residuals.

_____8. Homoscedasticity refers to
   a.   residuals that are correlated.
   b.   independent variables that are correlated.
   c.   a nonlinear relationship.
   d.   residuals that are the same for all fitted values of $\hat{Y}$.

_____9. Multicollinearity means that
   a. the independent variables are correlated.
   b. time is involved with one of the independent variables.
   c. the dependent variable is correlated with the independent variables.
   d. the residuals do not have a constant variance.

_____10. When successive residuals are correlated we refer to this as
   a. multicollinearity.   b. a dummy variable.
   c. autocorrelation.   d. homoscedasticity.

_____11. A measure used to evaluate multicollinearity is:
   a. R^2 b. R^2_{adj}
   c. VIF   d. slope

_____12. In the forward stepwise procedure
   a. we begin with no variables in the model
   b. the variable with the largest R^2 enters the model first.
   c. a variable already entered in the model may be removed at a later stage.
   d. all of the above.

_____13. The best subsets procedure for model selection does *not*
   a. examine 2^{k-1} possible regression models.
   b. find the best model for each number of predictors.
   c. ensure that each variable in the best model has a non-zero regression coefficient.
   d. use R^2 to measure the best model.

_____14. An interaction between two independent variables
   a. means that they are highly correlated
   b. is constructed by multiplying corresponding observations for the two variables
   c. is present when the total effect the two variables have on Y is different from the sum of the individual effects.
   d. both **b.** and **c.**

Part II Record your answer in the space provided. Be sure to show essential calculations.

The information at the right is used for Problems 15 to 17:

William Clegg is the owner and CEO of Clegg QC Consulting. Mr. Clegg is concerned about the salary structure of his company and has asked the Human Relations Department to conduct a study. Mr. Stan Holt, an analyst in the department, is assigned the project. Stan selects a random sample of 15 employees and gathers information on the salary, number of years with Clegg Consulting, the employee=s performance rating for the previous year, and the number of days absent last year.

Salary ($1000)	Years with Firm	Performance Rating	Days Absent
50.3	6	60	8
69.0	9	85	3
50.7	7	60	8
46.9	4	78	12
44.2	5	70	6
50.3	6	73	6
49.2	6	83	6
54.6	5	74	5
52.1	5	85	5
58.3	6	85	4
54.8	4	88	5
63.0	8	78	5
50.1	5	61	6
52.1	4	74	5
36.5	3	65	7

15. The correlations in the table at the right were computed using EXCEL.

	Salary	Years	Perform
Years	0.768		
Perform	0.514	0.130	
Absent	−0.587	−0.370	−0.435

   a. Which independent variable has the strongest correlation with salary?

a.

   b. Does the correlation matrix suggest any problems with the relationship among the variables?

   c. Calculate the VIF for each predictor variable. What are your findings?

16. Conduct a test of hypotheses to determine if any of the regression coefficients are not equal to 0. This analysis of variance table was computed as part of the output. Use the 0.05 significance level.

Analysis of Variance

	df	SS	MS	F	Significance F
Regression	3	641.10	213.70	13.91	0.00046
Residual	11	168.94	15.36		
Total	14	810.04			

a. H_0: _____

_____

H_1: _____

_____

b. The decision rule is to reject H_0 if _____

_____

c. What is your decision?

Interpret it.

_____

_____

d. Determine the R-square value.

Interpret it.

_____

_____

17. Additional information was obtained from EXCEL. Conduct a test of hypothesis to determine if any of the regression coefficients do not equal 0. Use the 0.05 significance level. The regression equation is:

Salary = 19.2 + 3.10 *Years* + 0.269 *Perform* - 0.704 *Absent*

	Coefficients	Standard Error	t Stat	P-value
Intercept	19.186	12.146	1.580	0.143
Years	3.096	0.706	4.385	0.001
Perform	0.269	0.120	2.252	0.046
Absent	-0.704	0.586	-1.202	0.255

a. H_0: _____

_____

H_1: _____

_____

H_0: _____

_____

H_1: _____

_____

H_0: _____

_____

H_1: _____

_____

b. The decision rules are to reject H_0 if _____

: _____

c. What is your decision? Interpret.

_____

_____

18. Mr. Stan Holt thinks that there might be an interaction between the two independent variables year with firm and performance rating. He runs the regression analysis again, this time with days absent excluded from the model and the interaction term between years with firm and performance rating included. The additional EXCEL is shown below. Conduct a hypothesis test to determine if the interaction term should be included in the model.

	Coefficients	Standard Error	t Stat	P-value
Intercept	1.171	35.383	0.033	0.974
Years	4.747	6.139	0.773	0.456
Perform	0.429	0.461	0.930	0.372
Yrs x Perform	-0.018	0.079	-0.222	0.829

a. H_0: _____

_____

H_1: _____

_____

b. The decision rules are to reject H_0 if _____

: _____

c. What is your decision? Interpret.

_____

_____

CHAPTER 15
INDEX NUMBERS

Chapter Goals

After completing this chapter, you will be able to:

1. Describe the term *index*.

2. Understand the difference between a weighted and an unweighted index.

3. Construct and interpret a Laspeyres Price index.

4. Construct and interpret a Paasche Price index.

5. Construct and interpret a value index.

6. Explain how the Consumer Price index is constructed and interpreted.

Introduction

There are thousands of indexes published on a regular basis by the federal government, foreign governments, the United Nations, magazines devoted to business such as *Forbes*, universities, and so on. You have most likely heard of such *index numbers* as the **Consumer Price Index**, the **Dow Jones Industrial Average**, and **Nasdaq**. What is an index number?

> *Index number*: A number that expresses the relative change in price, quantity, or value compared to a base period.

The main use of index numbers is to describe the percent change in price, quantity, or value from one time period (called the *base period*) to another time period.

> *Base period*: Usually one year, such as 1995, which is used as a reference period. Changes in price, quantity, or value are measured from the base period to another period, called the given period.

The *base* of most indexes is 100.

> *Base*: The number in the denominator used to compute the index. Most indexes have the base of 100.

At this writing, the base period for the Consumer Price Index (CPI) is the period 1993 – 95. It is written 1993-95 = 100. If the CPI for this month is 149.2, it indicates that the overall price of goods and services purchased by American consumers increased 49.2 percent from the 1993-95 base to the present month. Likewise, if the index measuring the quantity of pig iron exported is presently 90.0 with a base in 1986 of 100, it indicates that the quantity of exports decreased 10 percent from 1986 to the present.

Construction of Index Numbers

Simple indexes are calculated by dividing the number in the given period by the number in the base period. For a price index, P is found by formula [15-1].

$$\text{Simple Index} \qquad P = \frac{p_t}{p_o}(100) \qquad [15-1]$$

Where:

P is the price index for any given period.

p_t is the price in the given period (any period other than the base period).

p_o is the price in the base period.

As an example, suppose the wholesale price of tomatoes in 1988 (selected as the base period and written 1988 = 100), was \$0.32 a pound, and currently they are \$1.29 a pound. The index of tomato prices for the given period is 309.4, found by

$$P = \frac{p_t}{p_o}(100) = \frac{1.29}{0.32}(100) = 403.125 = 403.1$$

This reveals that the price of tomatoes increased 303.1 percent from 1988 to the present time.

Unweighted Indexes

In many situations we wish to combine several items and develop an index to compare the cost of a group of items in two different time periods. We might be interested in an index for the items that relate to the cost of driving a sport utility vehicle. This index would include items such as insurance prices, fuel prices, cost of oil changes, license fees, and so on.

Simple Average of the Price Indexes

The simple average of the price indexes is an arithmetic mean of the simple indexes for a group of items. It is computed using text formula [15-2].

$$\text{Simple Average of the Price Indexes} \qquad P = \frac{\Sigma P_i}{n} \qquad [15-2]$$

Where:

ΣP_i is the sum of the indexes for each of the items.

n is the number of items.

To illustrate, suppose the prices of several items for 1985 and 2006 and the simple index for each item is as shown.

Commodity	Unit	1985	2006	Simple Index
Battery	Each	$60.00	$80.00	133.3333
Tires	Set of 4	240	400	166.6667
Gasoline	Gallon	1.23	2.79	226.8293
			Total	526.8293

The simple average of the price indexes is found using formula [15-2].

$$P = \frac{\Sigma P_i}{n} = \frac{526.8293}{3} = 175.6098 = 175.61$$

This indicates that the mean of the group of indexes increased 75.61 percent from 1985 to 2006. A distinct advantage of the simple average of the price indexes is that the impact an item has on the average is not related to the units. A negative feature of this index is that it does not consider the relative importance of the items included in the index.

Simple Aggregate Index

A slightly more complex problem would be to compute the **simple aggregate index** for several commodities. The formula is text formula [15-3]

Simple Aggregate Index	$P = \dfrac{\Sigma p_t}{\Sigma p_o} \times 100$	[15 – 3]

Where:

Σp_t is the sum of the prices for the given period.

Σp_o is the sum of the prices for the base period.

To illustrate using the previous example, suppose the prices of several items for 1985 and 2006 are shown in the table at the right:

Commodity	Unit	1985	2006
Battery	Each	$ 60.00	$ 80.00
Tires	Set of 4	240.00	400.00
Gasoline	Gallon	1.23	2.79
Total		$301.23	$482.79

A simple aggregate price index is computed using formula [15-3].

$$P = \frac{\Sigma p_t}{\Sigma p_o}(100) = \frac{\$482.79}{\$301.23}(100) = 160.2729 = 160.27$$

This indicates there has been a 49.9 percent increase in the prices over the 21-year period from 1985 to 2006.

This method of computing a price index has two major disadvantages. It fails to consider the relative importance (weights) of the items, and it does not take into account the differing units. The index would be different, for example, if we considered one tire instead of a set of four tires.

Weighted Price Index

In the previous example we indicated that relative importance or weights of the items were not taken into account. A way to appropriately weight various items is with a **weighted price index**. There are two common methods of computing a weighted price index.

Laspeyres Price Index

The most commonly used weighted price index is the *Laspeyres Price Index* named after its originator.

> *Laspeyres Price Index*: A weighted aggregate price index that uses the quantities in the *base* period as weights.

It uses *base-year* quantities as weights. In essence, it assumes that consumption of the items selected for the index does not change from the base period to the current period. Thus, only price is allowed to change and the index for the current period reflects this price change.

Text formula [15-4] is used:

$$\text{Laspeyres' Price Index} \qquad P = \frac{\Sigma p_t q_o}{\Sigma p_o q_o}(100) \qquad [15-4]$$

Where:
P is the price index.
p_t is the price in the current period.
p_o is the price in the base period.
q_o is the quantity consumed in the base period.

The Laspeyres method, with some modifications, is the method used for most weighted price indexes.

Paasche Price Index

Another weighted price index is the *Paasche Price Index*, which uses the current quantity weights and adjusts the base each time a new period is considered.

> *Paasche Price Index*: A weighted aggregate price index that uses the quantities in the *current* year as the weights.

Text formula [15-5] is used:

$$\text{Paasche's Price Index} \qquad P = \frac{\Sigma p_t q_t}{\Sigma p_o q_t}(100) \qquad [15-5]$$

Where:
P is the price index.
p_t is the price in the current period.
p_o is the price in the base period.
q_t is the quantity consumed in the current period.

How do we decide which index to use? Both the Laspeyres index and the Paasche's index have limitations, as indicated in the following table:

	Advantages	Disadvantages
Laspeyres	Requires quantity data from only the base period. This allows a more meaningful comparison over time. The changes in the index can be attributed to changes in the price.	Does not reflect changes in buying patterns over time, thus may overweight goods whose prices increase over time.
Paasche's	Uses quantities from the current period, thus reflects current buying habits.	Requires quantity data for each year, which may be difficult to obtain. Because different quantities are used each year, it is impossible to attribute changes in the index to changes in price alone. Tends to overweight the goods whose prices have declined. Requires the prices to be recomputed each year.

Fisher's Ideal Index

Fisher's Ideal Index is an index that attempts to overcome the shortcomings of both the Laspeyres and Paasche's index.

Fisher's Ideal Index: The geometric mean of the Laspeyres and Paasche's indexes.

Recall that a geometric mean is calculated by taking the kth root of the product of k positive integers.

Fisher's ideal index is computed using formula [15-6] from the text.

$$\text{Fisher's Ideal Index} = \sqrt{\left(\text{Laspeyres' Index}\right)\left(\text{Paasche's Index}\right)} \qquad [15-6]$$

It appears that Fishers Ideal Index is perfect since it combines the best features of both Laspeyres and Paasche, however it has the same basic flaws as the Paasche index. It requires a new set of quantities each year.

Value Index

A *value index* is an index computed for a group of items, such as computers, software, printers, and paper from one time period to another.

Value index: Measures the changes in both the price and quantities involved.

Text formula [15-7] is used:

$$\text{Value Index} \qquad V = \frac{\Sigma p_t q_t}{\Sigma p_o q_o}(100) \qquad [15-7]$$

Where:

p_t is the price in the current period.
q_t is the quantity consumed in the current period.
p_o is the price in the base period.
q_o is the quantity consumed in the base period.

Note that we need the original base year prices, the base year quantities, the current year prices, and the current year quantities.

The Consumer Price Index

The *Consumer Price Index* (CPI) is the most well-known price index.

> *Consumer Price Index*: Measures the change in the price of a fixed market basket of goods and services from one period to another.

Actually there are currently two consumer price indexes being published by the federal government every month. The Consumer Price Index—All Urban Consumers is applicable for about 87 percent of the total population. The other CPI, the Consumer Price Index for City Wage Earners and Clerical Worker Families covers about 32 percent of the population in the United States.

They are designed to measure the price changes in a fixed "market basket" of goods and services purchased by most American consumers using the base period 1982-84. Included are such diverse items as the price of gasoline, bread, dental fees, taxes, and soft drinks. It has been published regularly since 1921.

The CPI is not just one index. Separate indexes are published for food and beverages, transportation, medical care, entertainment, rent, and apparel. In addition, there are CPIs for most large cities, such as Dallas, Detroit, and Seattle.

Real Income

Both consumer price indexes have a number of other applications. The CPI can be used to determine *real income.*

> *Real income*: A person's income adjusted for changes in price. It allows a person to determine whether his or her standard of living has increased, stayed the same, or decreased since the base period.

The computation of real income allows a person to evaluate whether his or her take-home pay has been keeping up with price increases. If prices are rising faster than the increase in take-home pay (called money income), a person's standard of living is decreasing, meaning that she or he cannot purchase the same amount of goods and services as in the base period. Text formula [15-8] for real income is:

| Real Income | $\text{Real Income} = \dfrac{\text{Money income}}{\text{CPI}}(100)$ | $[15-8]$ |

Purchasing Power of the Dollar

The CPI can also be used to compute the *purchasing power of the dollar.*

> *Purchasing power of the dollar:* The value of one dollar in a given period compared with the value of a dollar in the base period.

As the name implies, it shows how much purchasing power the dollar has today compared with the base period. For a particular time period it is computed using text formula [15-10]:

| Using an Index to Find Purchasing Power | $\text{Purchasing power of dollar} = \dfrac{\$1}{\text{CPI}}(100)$ | $[15-10]$ |

Glossary

Base: The number in the denominator used to compute the index. Most indexes have the base of 100.

Base period: Usually one year, such as 1982, which is used as a reference period. Changes in price, quantity, or value are measured from the base period to another period, called the given period.

Consumer Price Index: Measures the change in the price of a fixed market basket of goods and services from one period to another.

Fisher's Ideal Index: The geometric mean of the Laspeyres and Paasche's indexes.

Index number: A number that expresses the relative change in price, quantity, or value from one time period to another.

Laspeyres Price Index: A weighted aggregate price index that uses the quantities in the *base* period as weights.

Paasche Price Index: A weighted aggregate price index that uses the quantities in the *current* year as the weights.

Purchasing power of the dollar: The value of one dollar in a given period compared with the value of a dollar in the base period.

Real income: A person=s income adjusted for changes in price. It allows a person to determine whether his or her standard of living has increased, stayed the same, or decreased since the base period.

Value Index: Measures the changes in both the price and quantities involved.

CHAPTER PROBLEMS

Problem 1

The average hourly earnings for pharmacists reported for the years 1997—2004 are shown in the table. Using 1997 as the base period, develop an index that shows the changes in average hourly earnings during the period. Interpret.

Year	Average Hourly Earnings
1997	$26.20
1998	27.35
1999	27.17
2000	30.33
2001	32.81
2002	37.01
2003	39.32
2004	41.27

Solution 1

The wage in a selected period is divided by the wage in the base period and the result is multiplied by 100 (formula [15-1]). The calculations are shown below. The usual practice is to report the index either to the nearest tenth or the nearest hundredth.

The average hourly earnings of pharmacists increased 57.52% percent from 1997 to 2004, found by (157.52 − 100.0).

Year	Hourly Earnings	Index	Found by
1997	$26.20	100.00	($26.20/$26.20)(100)
1998	27.35	104.39	($27.35/$26.20)(100)
1999	27.17	104.08	($27.17/$26.20)(100)
2000	30.33	115.76	($30.33/$26.20)(100)
2001	32.81	125.23	($32.81/$26.20)(100)
2002	37.01	141.26	($37.01/$26.20)(100)
2003	39.32	150.08	($39.32/$26.20)(100)
2004	41.27	157.52	($41.27/$26.20)(100)

Exercise 15.1

Check your answers against those in the ANSWER section.

The federal minimum hourly wage has not changed since 1997. The federal minimum hourly wage rates for selected years between 1975 and 1997 are shown. Using 1975 as the base period, develop an index that shows the changes in hourly wages.

Year	Hourly Wage
1975	$2.10
1980	3.10
1985	3.35
1990	3.80
1995	4.25
1996	4.75
1997	5.15

Problem 2

An index is to be constructed to show the changes in the price of selected hardware items sold from 1986 to 2006. The prices and quantities consumed in the two periods are shown at the right. Using 1986 as the base period, compute:

Item	1986		2006	
	Price	Quantity	Price	Quantity
Hammer (each)	$6.00	100	$12.50	120
Linseed oil (qt.)	2.00	1,000	8.00	1,100
Sandpaper (sheet)	0.10	800	0.90	900
½ hp. motor (each)	30.00	10	100.00	15

a. A simple aggregate price index.

b. The Laspeyres price index.

c. The Paasche price index,

Solution 2

a. First the simple aggregate price index is computed. The prices of the four items for the base year (1986) and the current year are totaled.

The formula for the simple price index is:

$$P = \frac{\Sigma p_t}{\Sigma p_o}(100) = \frac{\$121.40}{\$38.10}(100) = 318.64$$

Item	1986	2006
	Price	Price
Hammer (each	$6.00	$12.50
Linseed oil (qt.)	2.00	8.00
Sandpaper (sheet)	0.10	0.90
½ hp. motor (each)	30.00	100.00
Total	$38.10	$105.80

The simple aggregate index shows the price has increased 218.6 percent in the twenty-year period.

b. The simple, or unweighted index, does not take into account any of the quantities involved. For example, the price of sandpaper increased by $0.80, but this will have little impact compared to the $6.50 increase in hammers or the $70.00 increase in the motor. A more meaningful measure is to consider the quantities consumed. The Laspeyres index assumes that the quantities in the base period are still representative in the current period and uses them as weights. Recall that the formula [15-4] for the Laspeyres price index is:

$$P = \frac{\Sigma p_t q_o}{\Sigma p_o q_o}(100)$$

The calculations for the Laspeyres weighted-price index are shown.

Item	1986 Price	Quantity		2006 Price	
	p_o	q_o	$p_o\, q_o$	p_t	$p_t\, q_o$
Hammer (each)	$6.00	100	$600	$12.50	$1,250
Linseed oil (qt.)	2.00	1,000	2,000	8.00	8,000
Sandpaper (sheet)	0.10	800	80	0.90	720
½ hp. motor (each)	30.00	10	300	100.00	1000
Total	$38.10		$2,980		$10,970

Applying formula [15-4]:

$$P = \frac{\Sigma p_t q_o}{\Sigma p_o q_o}(100) = \frac{\$10,970}{\$2,980}(100) = 368.1$$

The quantity sold in the base period q_o is held constant, that is, it appears both in the denominator and in the numerator. Since the quantity sold is held constant, the only factor affecting the index is price. The price of these selected hardware items increased 268.1 percent between 1986 and 2006.

c. Note in the following table involving hammers, linseed oil, etc. that the quantities sold changed from 1986 to 2006. Paasche's index reflects these changes. Computing the price index using the Paasche method gives 353.6. The percent change is 253.6.

Item	1986 Price	Quantity		2000 Price	Quantity	
	p_o	q_t	$p_o\, q_t$	p_t	q_t	$p_t\, q_t$
Hammer (each	$6.00	120	$720.00	$12.50	120	$1,500.00
Linseed oil (qt.)	2.00	1,100	2,200.00	8.00	1,100	8,800.00
Sandpaper (sheet)	0.10	900	90.00	0.90	900	810.00
½ hp. motor (each)	30.00	15	450.00	100.00	15	1500.00
Total			$3,460.00			$12,610.00

Formula [15-5] is used and the essential calculations are:

$$P = \frac{\Sigma p_t q_t}{\Sigma p_o q_t}(100) = \frac{\$12,610}{\$3,460}(100) = 364.45$$

Thus, the price of these selected items using current quantities consumed as weights increased 264.45 percent between 1986 and 2006. The Paasche method has one serious drawback. As the time period changes from 1998, 1999, 2000, etc., the quantity consumed for each one of those years must be collected and all the calculations redone.

	Exercise 15.2						
		1991				**2006**	
		Price	Quantity		Price	Quantity	
Item	p_o	q_o	p_oq_o	p_t	q_t	p_tq_t
Battery	$25	32		$90	30	
Cable	22	8		40	8	
Bimini top	325	2		600	2	
Depth finder	300	2		500	2	
Total	$672			$1,230		

Check your answers against those in the ANSWER section.

The manager of a small marine discount store believes that prices of marine products have risen dramatically since 1991. Others disagree. To investigate, he selected a few items and recorded the prices and quantities sold the first week of April, 1991 and the first week of April, 2006.

a. Compute a simple aggregate price index.
b. Determine the weighted price index using the Laspeyres method.
c. Determine the weighted price index using the Paasche method

Problem 3

Hannah Simpson, an accountant, graduated from college in 1988 and received a starting salary of $22,000. By 2006 her salary had increased to $77,000. The consumer price index (1982 – 84 = 100) in 1988 was 107.6 and in 2006 it was 202.5. Convert her salary to 1988 dollars and determine her real income. What conclusion would you make?

Solution 3

By converting her actual yearly income of $22,000 and $77,000 to real incomes, changes in her standard of living between two time periods can be evaluated. If money income is increasing faster than the consumer price index, then a person's standard of living is higher than the base period. This would mean, in Hannah's case, she could buy more goods and services in 2006 than in 1988. Conversely, if consumer prices are rising at a faster rate than her money income, then her standard of living is declining. That is, she could buy less. Real income is computed using formula [15-8], which is:

$$\text{Real Income} = \frac{\text{Money income}}{\text{CPI}}(100)$$

$$\text{For 1988 Real Income} = \frac{\$22,000}{107.6}(100) = \$20,446.09 = \$20,446$$

$$\text{For 2006 Real Income} = \frac{\$77,000}{202.5}(100) = \$38,024.69 = \$38,025$$

Thus in terms of constant 1982-84 base period dollars, Hannah's salary increased $17,579, found by ($38,025 – $20,446). This is an increase in real income of 86.0%, found by ($17,579/$20,446)(100).

Problem 4

The Consumer Price Index in the base period of 1993-95 is set at 100. The CPI was 202.5 in May, 2006. What is the purchasing power of the dollar for the base period and May 2006?

Solution 4

The purchasing power of the dollar for a particular time period is found by.

$$\text{Purchasing power of the dollar} = \frac{\$1}{\text{CPI}}(100)$$

$$\text{For the base period} = \frac{\$1}{100.0}(100) = \$1.00$$

$$\text{For May 2006} = \frac{\$1}{202.5}(100) = \$0.4938 = \$0.49$$

Assume that a hamburger cost $1 in the base period of 1993-95. Thus if you had $1,000 you could buy 1,000 hamburgers. However, in May 2006 that same $1,000 could only purchase 490 orders (because the price of a hamburger had increased).

Exercise 15.3

Check your answers against those in the ANSWER section.

Carl Eger had an annual income in the base period of $40,000 and by 2006 his income had increased to $65,000. During the same period the consumer price index rose from 100 to 202.5

a. What was Carl's real income in 2006?

b. Did his income keep pace with inflation?

c. Compare the value of $1.00 in the base period with that of the year 2006.

CHAPTER 15 ASSIGNMENT

INDEX NUMBERS

Name _____ Section _____ Score _____

Part I   Select the correct answer and write the appropriate letter in the space provided.

_____1.   The base period is
    a.   always 1982-84.
    b.   usually a year such as 1990, or a group of years such as 1982-84.
    c.   always reported as dollars.
    d.   a number such as 104.67

_____2.   A given period refers to
    a.   any other period than the base period.
    b.   the year 1967.
    c.   a dollar value such as $25,000.
    d.   the smaller of two values.

_____3.   A Laspeyres Price Index uses as its weights
    a.   given period quantities.
    b.   base period quantities.
    c.   base period prices.
    d.   given period prices.

_____4.   In an aggregate price index
    a.   the prices of several commodities are added.
    b.   no consideration is given to the units.
    c.   it does not consider the quantities involved.
    d.   all of the above.

_____5.   The Paasche Price index uses as its weights the
    a.   given period quantities.
    b.   base period quantities.
    c.   base period prices.
    d.   given period prices.

_____6.   The current base period for the Consumer Price Index is
    a.   1982-84.
    b.   1993-95.
    c.   1982.
    d.   1984.

_____7.   The Index of Industrial Production is 135.4, (1982-84 = 100). This means that production
    a.   increased $35.40 in 1996.   b.   declined 35.4 percent since 1982.
    c.   increased 35.4 percent since 1982-84.   d.   decreased 35.4 percent in 1996.

_____8. A firm sold $50,000 of a particular product in 1995 and $120,000 in 2005. Using 1995 as the base, what is the index for 2001?
   a. $70,000   b. 240 percent
   c. 140 percent.   d. 41.7 percent

_____9. An index has 1980 as its base. The index reported in 1993 was 127.2 and in 2005 it was 186.7. The percent increase from 1993 to 2005 is
   a. 46.8 percent.   b. 27.2 percent.
   c. 59.5 percent.   d. none of the above.

_____10. Which of the following price indexes uses *current* period quantities in its base?
   a. a value index   b. a simple index
   c. Laspeyres Price Index   d. Paasche Price Index

Part II: Record your answer in the space provided. Show essential work.

11. The earnings per share for General Electric from the 2002 Annual Report are given at the right. Develop an index showing the change in earnings for the given years. Use 1998 as the base period.

Year	Earnings per share	Index
1998	$0.95	
1999	1.09	
2000	1.29	
2001	1.41	
2002	1.51	
2003	1.52	
2004	1.62	
2005	1.55	

12. Professor Jim Martin had an annual income in the base period of $30,000. In 2005 his annual income was $75,100. During the same period the CPI rose from 100 to 184.6. What was his real income in 2005?

12. _____

13. The following table shows the prices and quantities consumed by a family of four for selected food commodities for 1990 and 2006. Use 1990 as the base period.

	1990		2006	
Commodity	Price	Quantity	Price	Quantity
Ground beef (per lb)	$1.39	80	$2.09	110
Milk (1 gallon)	1.69	100	2.75	120
Cookies (dozen)	1.29	95	2.59	100
Steak (per pound)	4.99	50	9.49	40

a. Determine the simple index for steak for 2006.

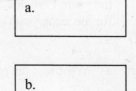

a.

b. Determine the simple aggregate price index for 2006.

b.

c. Determine the Laspeyres price index for 2006.

c.

d.

d. Determine the Paasche price index for 2006.

e. Determine a value index for 2006.

e.

14. The table reports the net profit for Heban Tool and Die, Inc. for the years 1996 and 2006. Also reported is the tool and die index for the same years (1985 = 100).

Year	Net profit	Index
1996	$45,380	136.3
2006	65,035	150.2

a. What was the percent increase in the index from 1996 to 2006?

a.

b. Convert the index to a 1996 base. What is the new index for 2006?

b.

c. Determine the net profit for 2006 in terms of the 1996 base. Comment on the change.

c.

CHAPTER 16
TIME SERIES AND FORECASTING

Chapter Goals

After completing this chapter, you will be able to:

1. Define the four components of a time series.

2. Compute a moving average

3. Determine a linear trend equation.

4. Compute a trend equation for a nonlinear trend.

5. Use a trend equation to forecast future time periods and to develop seasonally adjusted forecasts.

6. Determine and interpret a set of seasonal indexes.

7. Deseasonalize data using a seasonal index.

Introduction

It is often necessary to analyze past sales, and/or production data, in order to estimate future events. A collection of data over a period of time is called a *time series*.

> *Time series*: A collection of data recorded over a period of time — weekly, monthly, quarterly, or annually.

The collection of time series data is generally done yearly, quarterly, monthly, or weekly. As an example of time series, Tasco, a petroleum refinery, reports sales of petroleum products into final local markets each month. Another example is quarterly foreign car sales in the U.S. over the last twenty years. Analysis of historical data is useful to management in current decision making as well as intermediate and long-range estimates.

Components of a Time Series

A time series value consists of four components: the *secular trend*, the *cyclical variation*, the *seasonal variation*, and the *irregular variation*.

Secular Trend

The first component of a time series is the *secular trend*.

> *Secular Trend*: The smooth long-term direction of a time series.

The trend or direction may be upward, such as the sales of GPS's (geographic positioning systems). The trend may be downward. The manager of your bookstore would attest that the sales of slide rules have declined since 1975 to virtually zero today (because calculators and home computers have replaced slide rules in business and universities).

Cyclical Variation

The second component of a time series is the *cyclical variation*.

> *Cyclical variation*: The rise and fall of a time series over periods longer than one year.

While the long-run direction of the time series may be increasing, there may be "ups and downs" that seem to follow the business cycle. These periods of prosperity and recession are referred to as cyclical variation.

Seasonal Variation

The third component of a time series is the *seasonal variation*.

> *Seasonal variation*: Patterns of change in a time series within a year. These patterns tend to repeat themselves each year.

Many sales, production, and other time series fluctuate with the season. Sales of toys are highest during the Christmas season, and rentals of skis at a ski resort are higher in February and nonexistent in July.

Irregular Variation

The fourth component of a time series, **irregular variation**, may be divided into two components, *episodic fluctuations* and *residual fluctuations*.

> *Episodic fluctuations*: Unpredictable variation in a time series that is due to unusual causes that can be identified such as strikes, tornado damage, or fire.

Episodic variations are unpredictable, but they can be identified. Major floods, hurricanes, or strikes are examples of unpredictable events but it is possible to identify the time period in which they happened.

> *Residual fluctuations*: Unpredictable variation in a time series that cannot be identified.

Residual variation is the random variation that is present in a time series after the episodic variations have been removed from the data.

A Moving Average

A *moving average method* is useful in smoothing a time serious to see its trend.

> *Moving Average Method*: Used to smooth the fluctuations in the data.

It is the basic method used in measuring the seasonal fluctuation in the data. This is accomplished by "moving" the arithmetic mean values through the time series. (See Problem 3).

Weighted Moving Average

A *weighted moving average* is a natural extension of the weighted average discussed in Chapter 3. Calculating a weighted moving average involves selecting a different weight for each data value and then computing a weighted average of the most recent n values as the smoothed value. The smoothed value is used as a forecast of the future.

Types of Trend Equations

Linear Trend

If sales, employment, production, and other business series increase or decrease over a period of time and approximate a *straight line*, the equation for this growth is given by formula [16-1], the linear trend equation.

$$\boxed{\text{Linear Trend Equation} \quad \hat{Y} = a + bt \qquad [16-1]}$$

Where:

$\hat{Y}$ is the projected value of the Y variable for a selected value of t.

a is the Y-intercept. It is the estimated value of Y when $t = 0$.

b is the slope of the line, or the average change in $\hat{Y}$ for each change of one unit (increase or decrease) in t.

t is any value of time that is selected.

Least Squares Method

In Chapter 13, we discussed simple linear regression. We showed how the *least squares method* of computing the equation for a straight line through the data of interest gives the "best fitting" line. In forecasting methods, time is the independent variable and the value of the time series is the dependent variable.

If the sales, production, or other data tend to approximate a linear trend, the equation developed by the least squares method can be used to estimate sales, etc. for some future period.

Nonlinear Trends

If the general trend of a time series does not follow a straight line when plotted on arithmetic graph paper, the least squares trend equation should not be used to approximate past trends or to estimate future values. A series that appears curvilinear when plotted on arithmetic graph paper should be fitted with a logarithmic trend equation. The general equation for the logarithmic trend equation is:

$$\boxed{\text{Logarithmic Trend Equation} \quad \log \hat{Y} = \log a + \log b(t) \qquad [16-2]}$$

There are many other types of equations that may be fitted to the data, such as second and third degree polynomials. A good first step in determining which equation to use is to plot the data with time on the horizontal axis and to plot the data with sales, production, or the variable of interest on the vertical axis.

Seasonal Variation

Seasonal variations is another component of time series. Businesses such as lawn care service firms, automobile sales, and highway construction, have periods of above average and below average activities each year. A *seasonal index* is used for analysis of the trends of seasonally affected businesses.

> *Seasonal index*: A value that identifies the effects of various seasons. The index is usually reported monthly or quarterly.

As the name *seasonal* implies, climatic conditions are often responsible for the variation in the time series. Construction activities, sales of skis and suntan lotion, and the production of corn are examples of products whose production and consumption are related to the weather. Retail sales increase around holidays such as Easter, Christmas, and the start of the new school year. Techniques are available to isolate the seasonal component of a time series in order to make better estimates. One reason for measuring a seasonal pattern is to understand the pattern and to compare it to other years.

For example, we may want to compare the sales this March with the sales in March for previous years. Another reason for determining an index is to use it for short-term planning. A firm in the lawn care business in the Great Lakes region, for example, will want to begin hiring seasonal employees early in April when the weather starts to get warm. The ratio-to-moving-average method of isolating the seasonal component will be examined in the Problem section.

Glossary

Cyclical variation: The rise and fall of a time series over periods longer than one year.

Episodic fluctuations: Unpredictable variation in a time series that is due to unusual causes that can be identified such as strikes, tornado damage, or fire.

Moving Average Method: Used to smooth the fluctuations in the data.

Residual fluctuations: Unpredictable variation in a time series that cannot be identified

Seasonal index: A value that identifies the effects of various seasons. The index is usually reported monthly or quarterly.

Seasonal variation: Patterns of change in a time series within a year. These patterns tend to repeat themselves each year.

Secular trend: The smooth, long-term direction of a time series.

Time series: A collection of data recorded over a period of time — weekly, monthly, quarterly, or annually.

CHAPTER PROBLEMS

Problem 1

The sales (in $ millions) for the years 2001 to 2006 of Grape Juice, Inc. are shown.

a. Plot the data on a chart.

b. Estimate the linear trend equation by drawing a line through the data.

c. Determine the least squares trend equation.

d. Estimate the sales for 2008, using the trend equation.

Year	Sales ($ million)
2001	740
2002	780
2003	890
2004	940
2005	970
2006	1000

Solution 1

a. and **b.** The data plot and trend equation are shown.

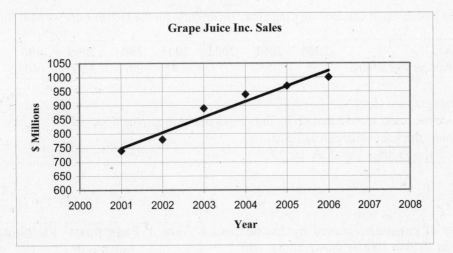

c. The least squares trend equation is of the form $\hat{Y} = a + bt$, where $\hat{Y}$ is the estimated sales, a is the Y intercept, b is the slope of the trend equation, and t is the coded time value (t=1 for 2001, t=2 for 2002,..t=6 for 2006). EXCEL was used to compute the equation for the least squares regression line.

ANOVA					
	df	SS	MS	F	Significance F
Regression	1	52662.86	52662.86	73.38553	0.00102
Residual	4	2870.476	717.619		
Total	5	55533.33			

	Coefficients	Standard Error	t Stat	P-value
Intercept	694.6667	24.93865	27.85502	9.88E-06
t	54.85714	6.403655	8.566536	0.00102

The least squares regression line is: $\hat{Y} = 694.67 + 54.86t$.

How do we interpret this equation? The value of 694.67 is the intersection with the Y-axis. This is the estimated sales when the coded year is 0 (Year =2000). The value 54.86 is the rate of change. That is, sales are increasing at a rate of $54.86 million dollars per year.

d. To estimate sales for 2008, the first step is to determine the code for that year. The code is 8 found by subtracting: (2008 – 2000). Note that 2000 would be year zero in the coding system. Next 8 is substituted for t in the trend equation and the value of $\hat{Y}$ determined.

$$\hat{Y} = 694.67 + 54.86t = 694.67 + 54.86(8) = 1133.547$$

The estimated sales for 2008 are $1,134 million.

Exercise 16.1

Check your answers against those in the ANSWER section.

The following table reports the earnings per share (in dollars) for the Heban Lumber Mill from 2000 to 2006.

Year	2000	2001	2002	2003	2004	2005	2006
Earnings Per Share	1.56	1.86	2.17	2.41	2.67	2.97	3.40

a. Plot the data on a chart.
b. Estimate the linear trend equation by drawing a line through the data.
c. Determine the least squares trend equation.
d. Estimate the earnings per share for 2008.

Problem 2

The number of passengers carried by Northeastern Airlines from 2000 to 2006 is shown at the right.

a. Plot the data on a chart.

b. Determine a trend equation.

c. Estimate the number of passengers for 2008.

Year	Passengers (millions))	Log₁₀(passengers)
2000	3.3	6.5185
2001	4.1	6.6128
2002	4.9	6.6902
2003	6.4	6.8062
2004	9.0	6.9542
2005	12.8	7.1072
2006	16.9	7.2279

Solution 2

a. The data on the number of passengers carried by Northeastern Airlines is shown in the chart. The number of passengers is increasing, but not in a linear fashion. In fact, the number of passengers not only increased but the amount of the increase was larger each year. This suggests the trend is not linear, and a logarithmic equation is appropriate.

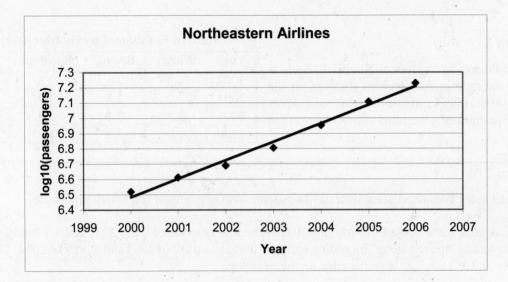

Northeastern Airlines

EXCEL is used to determine the logarithmic equation. The output is shown at the right:

The number of passengers for 2007 can be estimated using the logarithmic equation. The code for 2008 is 9, found by 2008 – 1999. Substituting $t = 9$ into the equation:

ANOVA					
	df	SS	MS	F	Significance F
Regression	1	0.40826	0.40826	406.7522	5.54E-06
Residual	5	0.005019	0.001004		
Total	6	0.413278			

$$\hat{Y} = 6.36229 + 0.120751t$$
$$= 6.36229 + 0.120751(9)$$
$$= 6.36229 + 1.086759$$
$$= 6.449049$$

	Coefficients	Standard Error	t Stat	P-value
Intercept	6.362285	0.026776	237.6149	2.51E-11
X Variable 1	0.120751	0.005987	20.1681	5.54E-06

Since $\hat{Y}$ is a logarithmic equation, we need the antilog of 6.449049. It is 2,812,218.

Thus, the estimated number of passengers in 2008 is 28,121,637.

Exercise 16.2		
Check your answers against those in the ANSWER section.	**Year**	**Imports (000,000)**
The imports in millions of dollars, for the Zeta Company are shown at the right. Develop a logarithmic trend equation and predict imports for 2007.	2002	$2.0
	2003	3.0
	2004	4.4
	2005	6.0
	2006	8.5

Problem 3

The enrollment by quarter at Starbrick Tech is given at the right in thousands of students for the years 2000 to 2003. Compute the seasonal indexes for each quarter using the ratio-to-moving-average method.

Student Enrollment by Quarter (000)				
Year	Winter	Spring	Summer	Fall
2003	3.2	2.8	0.8	3.2
2004	3.0	2.8	0.9	3.5
2005	3.5	3.4	0.9	4.1
2006	4.0	3.8	1.0	4.3

Solution 3

A seasonal index computed using the ratio-to-moving-average method is a 6-step procedure.

Step 1. Calculate a four-quarter moving total. Add the four quarters of $3.2 + 2.8 + 0.8 + 3.2 = 10.0$ for 2003. The total is "moved along" by adding spring, summer, and fall of 2003 and winter of 2004. That is $2.8 + 0.8 + 3.2 + 3.0 = 9.8$. Note the table on the next page.

A convenient way to do this on a hand calculator is to subtract the winter quarter of 2003, namely 3.2, from the total 10.0 and then add the winter quarter of 2004, namely 3.0. The result is 9.8. Continuing, 2.8 is subtracted from 9.8 and the Spring 2004 enrollment of 2.8 is added to obtain the next moving total. This subtraction and addition to the moving total is continued until all quarter enrollments are used. This procedure can also be easily accomplished using an EXCEL spreadsheet.

Step 2. Divide the moving totals by 4. Each moving total in column 2 is divided by four to give a four-quarter average and the result reported in column 3. This value is called the moving average.

Step 3. The moving averages are then centered. This step is required because the four-quarter moving average does not have the same center as any of the quarterly values. To explain further, the winter quarter data is centered at 2/15/03, the spring quarter at 5/15/03, the summer at 8/15/03, and the fall at 11/15/03. When these four periods are totaled and then averaged, the resulting value is centered at 7/1/03. Thus the value of 2.5, the first value in column 3, is centered at 7/1/03, which does not correspond to the center of any of the quarters. By averaging consecutive moving averages, the average is then adjusted to the proper time. For the first two values in column 3, the 2.5, centered at 7/1/03, is averaged with 2.450, which is centered at 10/1/03, to obtain 2.475, which is centered at 8/15/03.

Step 4. Determine the specific seasonal index. The specific seasonal index for each quarter is then computed by dividing the quarterly enrollment in column 1 by the centered four-quarter moving average in column 4 and multiplying the result by 100. The specific seasonal for the summer quarter of 2003 is 32.3, found by $(0.8/2.4750)(100)$. The specific seasonals are in column 5.

		1	2	3	4	5
Year	Quarter	Enrollment	Four quarter moving total	Four-quarter moving average	Centered moving average	Specific Seasonal
2003	Winter	3.2				
	Spring	2.8				
			10.0	2.500		
	Summer	0.8			2.4750	32.3
			9.8	2.450		
	Fall	3.2			2.4500	130.6
			9.8	2.450		
2004	Winter	3.0			2.4625	121.8
			9.9	2.475		
	Spring	2.8			2.5125	111.4
			10.2	2.550		
	Summer	0.9			2.6125	34.4
			10.7	2.675		
	Fall	3.5			2.7500	127.3
			11.3	2.825		
2005	Winter	3.5			2.8250	123.9
			11.3	2.825		
	Spring	3.4			2.9000	117.2
			11.9	2.975		
	Summer	0.9			3.0375	29.6
			12.4	3.100		
	Fall	4.1			3.1500	130.2
			12.8	3.200		
2006	Winter	4.0			3.2125	124.5
			12.9	3.225		
	Spring	3.8			3.2500	116.9
			13.1	3.275		
	Summer	1.0				
	Fall	4.3				

Step 5. Determine the mean of the specific seasonals. The specific seasonals are organized into a table and the mean specific seasonal for each quarter is determined. For the winter quarter the mean is 123.4.

Quarter					
Year	Winter	Spring	Summer	Fall	
2003			32.3	130.6	
2004	121.8	111.4	34.4	127.3	
2005	123.9	117.2	29.6	130.2	
2006	124.5	116.9	_____	_____	
Total	370.2	345.5	96.3	388.1	**Total**
Mean	123.4	115.2	32.1	129.4	400.1
Typical Index	123.37	115.17	32.09	129.37	400.0

Step 6. Adjust the means. The total of the four means should theoretically be 400.0 because the average of the four quarters is designated as 100.0. However, the total may not be equal to 400.0 due to rounding. A correction factor, therefore, is applied to each mean to arrive at the typical seasonal indexes. It is computed by.

$$\text{Correction factor} = \frac{400.0}{\text{Total of means}}$$

$$\text{For this problem} = \frac{400.0}{400.1} = 0.99975$$

Multiplying each of the means by the correction factor of 0.99975 gives the four typical seasonal indexes

Winter	123.37
Spring	115.17
Summer	32.09
Fall	129.37

Note that enrollment is traditionally high in the fall and winter, and drops off sharply in the summer. The summer enrollment is typically only 32.09 percent of the mean enrollment, or nearly 70 percent below the mean enrollment for the year.

Exercise 16.3

Check your answers against those in the ANSWER section.

The quarterly sales for the Norton Company are given in millions of dollars for four years. Compute the quarterly seasonal index using the ratio-to-moving-average method

	Quarter			
Year	I	II	III	IV
2003	2	8	10	2
2004	4	10	10	4
2005	4	12	14	4
2006	6	16	20	4

Problem 4

The Kinzua Boat Rental Company estimates that 24,000 boat rentals will be made this coming year. The seasonal index for the month of July is 130. What are the estimated rentals for July?

Solution 4

If there were no seasonal variation, 2,000 boats would be rented each month, found by 24,000/12. However, the index of 130 for July indicates that rentals are 30 percent above average for that month. To determine the projected rentals for July, we increase the average rental by 30 percent. This is computed by 2,000 (1.30) [or 2,000 (130/100)] which equals 2,600 rentals.

Exercise 16.4

Check your answers against those in the ANSWER section.

Refer to Problem 4. Suppose the seasonal index for June was computed to be 120 and 47 for November.

a. Determine the seasonally adjusted sales for June.

b. Determine the seasonally adjusted sales for November.

Problem 5

The Director of Admissions at Starbrick Tech needs an estimate of enrollment for each quarter of 2007.

a. Use the enrollment data for the years 2003 to 2006 and the seasonal indexes determined in Problem 3 to find a trend equation for enrollment.

b. Use the trend equation and the seasonal values to estimate enrollment for each quarter of 2007.

Year	Quarter	Code	Students	Index	Deseasonalized
2003	Winter	1	3.2	1.2337	2.59382
	Spring	2	2.8	1.1517	2.43119
	Summer	3	0.8	0.3209	2.49299
	Fall	4	3.2	1.2937	2.47353
2004	Winter	5	3.0	1.2337	2.43171
	Spring	6	2.8	1.1517	2.43119
	Summer	7	0.9	0.3209	2.80461
	Fall	8	3.5	1.2937	2.70542
2005	Winter	9	3.5	1.2337	2.83699
	Spring	10	3.4	1.1517	2.95216
	Summer	11	0.9	0.3209	2.80461
	Fall	12	4.1	1.2937	3.16920
2006	Winter	13	4.0	1.2337	3.24228
	Spring	14	3.8	1.1517	3.29947
	Summer	15	1.0	0.3209	3.11624
	Fall	16	4.3	1.2937	3.32380

Solution 5

a. First we need to determine the seasonally adjusted trend equation. In the following table the actual enrollment for each quarter is shown in the "Students" column and the seasonal index is shown in the "Index" column. To determine the deseasonalized trend value, the actual enrollment is divided by the seasonal index. For example, the actual enrollment in the winter quarter of 2003 was 3.2 students (in thousands) and the seasonal index is 123.37 for the winter quarter. The deseasonalized enrollment is 2.5938, found by $3.2 \div 1.2337$.

In the chart on the next page, EXCEL is used to determine the trend equation with the seasonal effect removed. Also shown is the Regression Plot.

	Coefficients	Standard Error	t Stat	P-value
Intercept	2.278712	0.071322	31.94957	1.75E-14
Code	0.063602	0.007376	8.622833	5.66E-07

From the EXCEL output above, the deseasonalized trend equation is $\hat{Y}$ = 2.27871 + 0.0636017 t. This trend equation indicates that over the 16 quarters the deseasonalized growth rate was about 64 students per quarter. (Recall that the enrollment data was reported in thousands.)

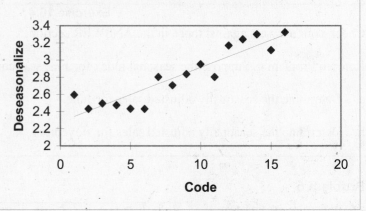

Regression Plot, Deseasonalized Data

b. Assuming that the 16 periods of historical data are reasonably good predictors of future enrollment at Starbrick Tech, we can use the trend equation to project 2007 enrollment. The winter quarter of 2007 is period 17, so t = 17 is substituted in the trend equation.

$$\hat{Y} = 2.27871 + 0.0636017\,t = 2.27871 + 0.0636017(17) = 3.3599389$$

The estimated enrollment for the winter quarter is 3.3599389, or 3,360 students, without considering the seasonal effect. The index for winter is 123.37, which indicates that winter is 23.37 percent above the typical quarter, so the actual enrollment

Estimated Enrollment for 2007 by Quarter				
Quarter	Code	Deseasonalized Enrollment	Seasonal Index	Forecast
Winter	17	3.3599	123.37	4,145
Spring	18	3.4235	115.17	3,943
Summer	19	3.4871	32.09	1,119
Fall	20	3.5507	129.37	4,594

for the winter quarter is estimated at 4.145, or 4,145 students, found by 3.3599389 (1.2337). The estimates for the other quarters are determined in a similar fashion and this information is summarized in the table at the right.

The enrollment for the fall quarter is normally the highest, and the enrollment is normally smallest for the summer. This is also true for the estimates in 2007.

Exercise 16.5

Check your answers against those in the ANSWER section.
The quarterly sales for the Norton Company were reported in Exercise 16.3 and a seasonal index was computed for each quarter.
a. Deseasonalize the data and determine the trend equation.
b. Estimate the seasonally adjusted sales for the four quarters of 2007.

TIME SERIES AND FORECASTING

Name _____ Section _____ Score _____

Part I   Select the correct answer and write the appropriate letter in the space provided.

_____ 1. A listing of values over a period of time is called a
     a. trend.   b. time series.
     c. seasonal index.   d. residual.

_____ 2. The long-term behavior of a variable over an extended period of time is called
     a. the seasonal index.   b. the cyclical variation.
     c. the trend.   d. episodic variation.

_____ 3. A period of prosperity followed by recession is called the
     a. cyclical variation.   b. trend.
     c. seasonal variation.   d. irregular variation.

_____ 4. When we plot a trend equation, the variable plotted along the horizontal axis is
     a. the dependent variables. b. sales.
     c. time.   d. log of time.

_____ 5. The variation within a year, such as retail sales during the Christmas holidays, is called the
     a. trend.   b. seasonal variation.
     c. irregular variation.   d. cyclical variation.

_____ 6. In June the Youngsville TrueValue Hardware store suffered severe damage to its contents during a flood. This is an example of
     a. residual variation.   b. cyclical variation.
     c. episodic variation.   d. seasonal variation because it happened during the summer.

_____ 7. The purpose of determining the ratio-to-moving average when computing a seasonal index is to eliminate the
     a. random variation.   b. trend.
     c. episodic variation.   d. none of the above.

_____ 8. The reason for centering a moving average is to
     a. convert the average to an index.   b. remove the random variation.
     c. find the correction factor.   d. align the time periods.

_____ 9. A monthly index is being developed for the company sales. The moving total will consist of
     a. four quarterly sales values.   b. logs of sales.
     c. logs of quarters.   d. twelve monthly sales values.

_____ 10. The index for October for imports by Wines, Inc. is 90. The actual imports for October were $450,000. The seasonally adjusted imports are
    a. $405,000.   b. $450,000.
    c. $500,000.   d.   none of the above.

Part II   Record the answers in the space provided. Show essential calculations.

   11. Shown below are the net sales for the J. M. Smucker Company, a leading marketer of jams and jellies.
     a.   Plot the data on a chart and estimate the linear trend equation by drawing a line through the data.

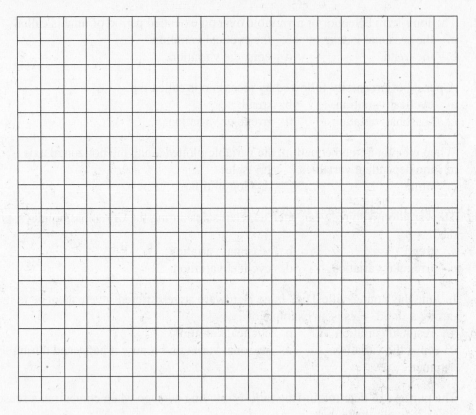

Smucker's Net Sales	
Year	Sales (millions)
1993	345
1994	399
1995	425
1996	454
1997	462
1998	478
1999	511
2000	529
2001	524
2002	565
2003	602
2004	632
2005	651
2006	687

b. Determine the least squares trend equation.

b.

c. Estimate the sales for 2007, using the trend equation. Code the year 1993 as 1.

c.

12. The following table shows the number of homes built by Custom Builders, Inc. in the last four years by quarter. Develop a seasonal index for each quarter using the ratio-to-moving average method. (Use the forms on the next page).

Year	I	II	III	IV
2003	5	9	8	8
2004	6	9	9	8
2005	6	10	10	7
2006	6	10	9	8

Year	Qtr.	Homes	4-Qtr. Moving Total	4-Qtr. Moving Avg.	Centered Moving Avg.	Specific Seasonal
2003	I					
	II					
	III					
	IV					
2004	I					
	II					
	III					
	IV					
2005	I					
	II					
	III					
	IV					
2006	I					
	II					
	III					
	IV					

	Quarter				
Year	**I**	**II**	**III**	**IV**	
2003					
2004					
2005					
2006					
Total					Total
Mean					
Typical Index					

CHAPTER 17
NONPARAMETRIC METHODS: CHI-SQUARE APPLICATIONS

Chapter Goals

After completing this chapter, you will be able to:

1. List the characteristics of the Chi-square distribution.

2. Conduct a test of hypothesis comparing an observed set of frequencies to an expected distribution.

3. Conduct a hypothesis test to determine whether two classification criteria are related.

Introduction

Recall that in Chapters 9 through 12, the data was interval or ratio scale such as weights of shipments of computers, income of McDonald's employees, or number of years on the job. The population from which the sample was drawn was assumed to be normally distributed. What if these conditions cannot be met?

Recall that the nominal scale of measurement requires only that the sample information be categorized, with no order implied. As an example, students are classified by major, such as, business, history, computer science, etc.

This chapter considers a new test statistic, a chi-square distribution, where only the nominal level of measurement is required.

The Chi-Square Distribution

In the previous chapters the standard normal, the t distribution, and the F distributions were used as the test statistics. Recall that a test statistic is a quantity, determined from the sample information, used as a basis for deciding whether to reject the null hypothesis. In this chapter another distribution, called chi-square and designated χ^2, is used as the test statistic. It is similar to the t and F distributions in that there is a family of χ^2 distributions, each with a different shape, depending on the number of degrees of freedom. When the number of degrees of freedom is small the distribution is positively skewed, but as the number of degrees of freedom increases it becomes symmetrical and approaches the normal distribution. Chi-square is based on squared deviations between an observed frequency and an expected frequency and, therefore, it is always positive.

Goodness-of-Fit Tests

In the *goodness-of-fit test* the χ^2 distribution is used to determine how well an "observed" set of observations "fit" an "expected" set of observations.

> *Goodness-of-fit test:* A test designed to compare an observed distribution to an expected distribution.

The purpose of the goodness-of-fit test is to determine if there is a statistical difference between the two sets of data, one of which is observed and the other expected.

For example, an instructor told a class that the grading system would be "uniform." That is, that the same number of A's, B's, C's, D's and F's would be given. Suppose that the grades shown at the right were recorded at the end of the semester:

Grade	Number
A	12
B	24
C	23
D	30
F	11
	100

The question to be answered is: Do these final grades depart significantly from those that could be expected if the instructor had in fact graded uniformly? The null and alternate hypotheses are:

H_0: The distribution is uniform.
H_1: The distribution is not uniform.

The sampling distribution follows the χ^2 distribution and the value of the test statistic is computed by text formula [17-1]:

$$\textbf{Chi-Square Test Statistic} \quad \chi^2 = \Sigma \left[\frac{(f_o - f_e)^2}{f_e} \right] \qquad [17-1]$$

Where:
f_o is the observed frequency in a particular category.
f_e is the expected frequency in a particular category.
k is the number of categories with ($k - 1$) degrees of freedom.

It is not necessary that the expected frequencies be equal to apply the goodness-of-fit test. For example, at Scandia Technical Institute, over the years, 50 percent of the students were classified as freshmen, 40 percent sophomores, and 10 percent unclassified.

A sample of 200 students this past semester revealed that 90 were freshmen, 80 were sophomores, and 30 were unclassified. The null and alternate hypotheses are:

H_0: The distribution of students has not changed.
H_1: The distribution of students has changed.

Characteristics of the Chi-Square Distribution

The chi-square distribution has the following characteristics:

1. **Chi-square is never negative**. This is because the difference between f_o and f_e is squared, that is, $(f_o - f_e)^2$.

2. **There is a family of chi-square distributions.** There is a chi-square distribution for one degree of freedom, another for two degrees of freedom, another for three degrees of freedom, and so on.

3. **The chi-square distribution is positively skewed.** However, as the number of degrees of freedom increases, the distribution begins to approximate the normal probability distribution.

Recall that the value of the test statistic is computed by formula [17-1].

$$\chi^2 = \Sigma \left[\frac{(f_o - f_e)^2}{f_e} \right]$$

The value of the test statistic is determined by first taking the difference between the observed frequency and the expected frequency (Col. 3). Next these differences are squared (Col. 4). Then the result is divided by the expected frequency (Col. 5). This result is then summed over the five locations. The total is 19.18. The value of 19.18 is compared to the critical value of 13.277. Since 19.18 is greater than the critical value, H_0 is rejected and H_1 accepted. We conclude that sales are not uniformly distributed among the five locations.

Exercise 17.1

Check your answers against those in the ANSWER section.

A tire manufacturer is studying the position of tires in blowouts. It seems logical that the tire blowouts will be uniformly distributed among the four positions. For a sample of 100 tire failures, is there any significant difference in that tire's position on the car? Use the 0.05 significance level.

Location of Tire on the Car

Left Front	Left Rear	Right Front	Right Rear
28	20	29	23

Problem 2

From past experience the manager of the parking facilities at a major airport knows that 58 percent of the customers stay less than one hour, 23 percent between one and two hours, 10 percent between two and three hours, and nine percent three hours or more.

The manager wants to update this study. A sample of 500 stamped parking tickets is selected. The results showed 300 stayed less than one hour, 100 from one to two hours, 60 from two to three hours, and 40 parked three hours or more. At the 0.01 significance level does the data suggest there has been a change in the distribution of the length of time customers use the parking facilities?

Solution 2

The first step is to state the null hypothesis and alternate hypothesis.

H_0: There has been no change in the distribution of parking times.
H_1: There has been a change in the distribution of parking times

The next step is to determine the decision rule. (Note in the table below that there are four categories). The number of degrees of freedom is the number of categories minus 1. In this problem it is $(4 - 1) = 3$ degrees of freedom.

Referring to Appendix B.3, the 0.01 level and 3 degrees of freedom, the critical value of chi-square is 11.345, so H_0 is rejected if χ^2 is greater than 11.345.

The value of the test statistic is computed as follows:

The observed frequencies from the sample are shown In Column 2 of the following table. Recall that based on past experience 58 percent of the customers parked their car less than one hour. If the null hypothesis is true, then 58% × 500 (in the sample) = 290, the expected frequency. Likewise, 23 percent stayed from one to two hours. Thus, 23% × 500 gives the expected frequency of 115. The complete set of expected frequencies is given in Column 3. Chi-square is computed to be 4.86.

Time in Parking Lot	Col. 1 Percent of Total	Col. 2 Number in Sample f_o	Col. 3 f_e	Col. 4 $f_o - f_e$	Col. 5 $\left(f_o - f_e\right)^2$	Col. 6 $\dfrac{\left(f_o - f_e\right)^2}{f_e}$
Less than 1 hour	58	300	290	10	100	100/290 = 0.34
1 up to 2 hours	23	100	115	−15	225	225/115 = 1.96
2 up to 3 hours	10	60	50	10	100	100/50 = 2.00
3 hours or more	9	40	45	−5	25	25/45 = 0.56
Total	100	500	500	0		$\chi^2 = 4.86$

Since the computed value of chi-square (4.86) is less than the critical value (11.345), the null hypothesis is not rejected. There has been no change in the distribution of the lengths of parking time at the airport.

Exercise 17.2

Check your answers against those in the ANSWER section.

In recent years, 42 percent of the American made automobiles sold in the United States were manufactured by General Motors, 33 percent by Ford, 22 percent by Damlier-Chrysler, and 3 percent by all others.
A sample of the sales of American-made automobiles conducted last week revealed that 190 were manufactured by DamlierChrysler, 240 by Ford, 325 by GM, and 45 by all others.

Test the hypothesis at the 0.05 level that there has been no change in the sales pattern.

Problem 3

A study is made by an auto insurance company to determine if there is a relationship between the driver's age and the number of automobile accident claims submitted during a one-year

No. of Accidents	Age (Years)			Total
	Less than 25	25-50	Over 50	
0	37	101	74	212
1	16	15	28	59
2 or more	7	9	13	29
Total	60	125	115	300

period. From a sample of 300 claims, the sample information on the right was recorded.

Use the 0.05 significance level to determine if there is any relationship between the driver's age and the number of accidents.

Solution 3

The question under investigation is whether the number of auto accidents is related to the driver's age. The null and alternate hypotheses are.

H_0: There is no relationship between age and the number of accidents.
H_1: There is a relationship between age and the number of accidents.

The critical value is obtained from the chi-square distribution in Appendix B.3. The number of degrees of freedom is equal to the number of rows minus one, times the number of columns minus one. Hence, the degrees of freedom are $(3 - 1)(3 - 1) = 4$. The significance level, as stated in the problem, is 0.05. The critical value from Appendix B.3 is 9.488. The null hypothesis is rejected if the computed value of χ^2 is greater than 9.488.

Formula [17-1], as cited earlier, is used to determine χ^2.

$$\chi^2 = \Sigma \left[\frac{(f_o - f_e)^2}{f_e} \right]$$

Where:
f_o is the frequency observed.
f_e the expected frequency.

The first step is to determine the expected frequency for each corresponding observed frequency. If the null hypothesis is true (the number of accidents is not related to age), we can expect 212 out of the 300 sampled, or 70.67 percent of the drivers to have had no accidents. Thus, we can expect 70.67 percent of the 60 drivers under 25 years, or 42.40 drivers, to have had no accidents.

Likewise, if the null hypothesis is true, 70.67 percent of the 125 drivers in the 25 to 50 age bracket, or 88.33 drivers, should have had no accidents.

The table at the right shows the complete set of observed and expected frequencies. Note that some totals were rounded.

No. of Accidents	Age						
	Less than 25		25-50		Over 50		
	f_o	f_e	f_o	f_e	f_o	f_e	Total
0	37	42.40	101	88.33	74	81.27	212
1	16	11.80	15	24.58	28	22.62	59
2 or more	7	5.80	9	12.08	13	11.12	29
Total	60	60.00	125	124.99	115	115.01	300

Note: The f_e values were calculated without rounding the percents. Ex: 212/300 = 70.666666%

The expected frequency for any category is found by text formula [17-2]:

$$\text{Expected frequency} = \frac{(\text{row total})(\text{column total})}{\text{grand total}}$$

The value for the first row and column is used as an example. There are 212 people who did not have any accidents, 60 persons are less than 25 years old, and there is a total of 300 people. These values are inserted into the formula:

$$f_e = \frac{(\text{row total})(\text{column total})}{\text{grand total}} = \frac{(212)(60)}{300} = 42.40$$

This is the same value computed previously.

The computed value of χ^2 is 11.03.

$$\chi^2 = \Sigma \left[\frac{(f_o - f_e)^2}{f_e} \right] = \frac{(37.00 - 42.40)^2}{42.40} + \frac{(101.00 - 88.33)^2}{88.33} + \ldots + \frac{(13 - 11.12)^2}{11.12} = 11.03$$

Since the computed value of χ^2 is greater than the critical value of 9.488, the null hypothesis is rejected and the alternate accepted. We conclude that there is a relationship between age and the number of accidents.

Exercise 17.3

Check your answers against those in the ANSWER section.

A random sample of 480 male and female adults was asked the amount of time each person spent watching TV last week. Their responses are shown at the right. At the 0.05 significance level, does it appear that the amount of time spent watching TV is related to the gender of the viewer?

Hours	Gender of Viewer		Total
	Male	Female	
Under 8	70	90	160
8 to 15	100	60	160
15 or more	55	105	160
	225	255	480

CHAPTER 17 ASSIGNMENT

NONPARAMETRIC METHODS: CHI-SQUARE APPLICATIONS

Name _____ Section _____ Score _____

Part I   Select the correct answer and write the appropriate letter in the space provided.

_____1. In a goodness-of-fit test
   a.   the sample size must be at least 30.
   b.   no assumption is made regarding the shape of the population.
   c. σ is always known.
   d.   the interval scale of measurement is required.

_____2. The level of measurement required for the goodness-of-fit test is
   a.   nominal.   b.   ordinal.
   c.   interval.   d.   ratio.

_____3. The chi-square distribution is
   a.   positively skewed.   b.   a continuous distribution.
   c.   based on the number of categories.   d.   all of the above.

_____4. A two-way classification of the data is called a
   a.   chi-square distribution.   b.   normal distribution.
   c.   contingency table.   d.   none of the above.

_____5. In a goodness-of-fit test where f_e values are the same in all four categories
   a.   the degrees of freedom is 3.
   b. $k = 4$.
   c.   the null hypothesis is that the proportion in each category is the same.
   d.   all of the above.

_____6. A sample of 100 undergraduate students is classified by major (3 groups) and gender. How
   many degrees of freedom are there in the test?
   a.   2   b.   3   c.   4   d.   99

_____7. In a chi-square test the $df = 4$. At the 0.05 significance level the critical value of the chi-
   square is
   a.   7.779   b.   7.815   c.   9.488   d.   13.388

_____8. The shape of the chi-square distribution is
   a.   based on the degrees of freedom.   b.   based on the level of measurement.
   c.   based on the shape of the population.   d.   based on at least 30 observations.

_____9. In a test to find out if the two criteria of classification are related, the expected cell
   frequencies should be
   a.   all less than 5.   b.   at least one less than 5.
   c.   at least 5 percent of the population.   d.   at least 5.

_____10. The sum of the observed and the expected frequencies are
   a.   always at least 30.   b.   always the same.
   c.   always less than 5 percent.   d.   always less than 5.

Part II Record your answer in the space provided. Show essential work.

11. The manager of a Farmer Jack Super Market would like to know if there is a preference for the day of the week on which customers do their shopping. A sample of 420 families revealed the following. At the 0.05 significance level, is there a difference in the proportion of customers that prefer each day of the week?

Day of the week	Number of persons
Monday	20
Tuesday	30
Wednesday	20
Thursday	60
Friday	80
Saturday	130
Sunday	80

a. State the null and alternate hypotheses.

H_0: _____

H_1: _____

b. State the decision rule.

_____

c. Compute the value of the test statistic.

c.				

Day of week				
Monday				
Tuesday				
Wednesday				
Thursday				
Friday				
Saturday				
Sunday				
Total				

d. What is your decision regarding the null hypothesis? Interpret the result.

_____

_____

12. A charity solicits donations by phone. From long experience the charity's director reports that 60 percent of the calls will result in refusal to donate, 30 percent will request more information via the mail, and 10 percent will result in an immediate credit card donation. For a sample of 200 calls last week, 140 refused to donate, 50 requested additional information, and 10 made an immediate donation. At the 0.10 significance level was the sample result different from the usual pattern?

a. State the null and alternate hypotheses.

H_0: _____

H_1: _____

b. State the decision rule.

_____

_____

c. Compute the value of the test statistic.

c.

d. What is your decision regarding the null hypothesis? Interpret the result.

_____

_____

_____

13. There are three loan officers at Farmer National Bank. All decisions on mortgage loans are made by one of these officers. The president of the bank would like to be sure that the rejection rate is about the same for the three officers. A sample of 200 recent applications yielded the following results. Is the rejection rate related to the officer that processes the loan? Use the 0.05 significance level.

	Loan Officer		
	Felix	Otis	Foxburrow
Approved	50	70	55
Rejected	10	10	5
Total	60	80	60

a. State the null and alternate hypotheses.

H_0: _____

H_1: _____

b. State the decision rule.

_____

_____

c. Compute the value of the test statistic.

c.

d. What is your decision regarding the null hypothesis? Interpret the result.

_____

_____

CHAPTER 18
NONPARAMETRIC METHODS:
ANALYSIS OF RANKED DATA

CHAPTER GOALS

After completing this chapter, you will be able to:

1. Conduct the sign test for dependent samples using the binomial and standard normal distribution as the test statistics.

2. Conduct a test of hypothesis for dependent samples using the Wilcoxon signed-rank test.

3. Conduct and interpret the Wilcoxon rank-sum test for independent samples.

4. Conduct and interpret the Kruskal-Wallis test for several independent samples.

5. Compute and interpret Spearman's coefficient of rank correlation.

6. Conduct a test of hypothesis to determine whether the correlation among the ranks in the population is different from zero.

Introduction

This chapter continues our study of nonparametric tests of hypotheses. Recall that for nonparametric tests no assumption regarding the shape of the population is required. The data is either the nominal or ordinal scale. Chapter 17 presented applications of the chi-square distribution, which require only the nominal scale of measurement. In this chapter several tests based on the ordinal scale of measurement are examined.

The first two tests require paired or dependent samples. The sign test is based on only the sign of the difference between paired observations. The Wilcoxon matched-pair signed rank test considers both the sign of the difference and also the magnitude of the difference. The Wilcoxon rank-sum test and the Kruskal-Wallis test are applied to independent samples. Also we look at a coefficient of correlation especially designed for ranked data.

The Sign Test

The *sign test* is based on the sign of a difference between two related observations.

> *Sign test*: A test based on the sign of a difference between two related observations. We usually designate a plus sign (+) for a positive difference between observations and a minus sign (−) for a negative difference between observations.

The sign test has many applications. One is for before and after experiments. It is an alternative to the paired *t* test presented in Chapter 12. The paired *t* test requires that the distribution of the differences in paired observations have a normal probability distribution. If this normality assumption cannot be met, the sign test is employed as an alternative.

The underlying assumption for the sign test is that the number of positive differences should be about the same as the number of negative differences, assuming the treatment or pairing has no effect. The null hypothesis is that the pairing has no effect. If H_0 is true, then any difference in the number of positive and negative differences is due to chance. If the treatment has an effect, then there will be significantly more positive (or negative) differences.

Testing a Hypothesis about a Median

We have concentrated so far on testing a hypothesis about a mean or means. We can also apply the ideas of the sign test to conduct a *median test*, that is, a hypothesis test about the median of a population.

> *Median test*: A test to determine whether the median of a set of sample data is equal to a hypothesized value.

Recall that the median is a value above which half of the observations lie and the other half lie below it.

For example, we might want to find out whether the median annual salary of quality assurance managers is $56,000, meaning that half the managers earn more than $56,000 and the other half of the managers earn less. In our sample, an annual salary of more than $56,000 is assigned a plus sign and a salary below $56,000 is assigned a minus sign. A salary exactly equal to $56,000 is omitted from further analysis.

The Human Relations Director wants to explore the annual salary of quality assurance managers further. So she first sets up the following null and alternate hypotheses.

$$H_0: \text{Median salary is } \$56,000$$
$$H_1: \text{Median salary is not } \$56,000$$

The way the alternate hypothesis is stated signifies a two-tailed test. The solution to this problem is presented in the Chapter Problem section.

The binomial distribution, discussed in Chapter 6, is the test statistic. Recall that there are four conditions for the binomial: only two outcomes, independent trials, a constant probability of success, and a fixed sample size. The null hypothesis, stated in terms of the binomial, is that $\pi = 0.50$. π is the probability of a success. The normal approximation to the binomial is used if both $n\pi$ and $n(1-\pi)$ are greater than 5.

The Wilcoxon Signed-Rank Test

The sign test considers only the sign of the difference between paired observations. Any information regarding the magnitude of the difference is not used. The *Wilcoxon Signed-Rank Test* not only considers the sign of the difference but also the magnitude of the difference.

> *Wilcoxon Signed-Rank Test*: A nonparametric test for determining whether there is a difference between paired or related observations.

The *Wilcoxon Signed-Rank Test* is also a replacement for the paired t test when the normality assumption cannot be met. When information on the magnitude of the paired difference is available, the Wilcoxon test is a stronger or a more powerful test because it makes more effective use of the data.

The Wilcoxon Rank-Sum Test

This test is the nonparametric alternative to the Student t test described in Chapter 11. The purpose of Student's t was to determine if two independent populations had the same mean. Recall we assumed the two independent random samples were selected from populations with a normal distribution with equal standard deviations. What if the equal standard deviation or the normality assumption cannot be met? The Student t is not appropriate and we use the ***Wilcoxon Rank-Sum Test*** as an alternative.

> ***Wilcoxon Rank-Sum Test***: A test to determine whether two independent samples came from equivalent populations. No assumption is made regarding the normality of the populations.

The Wilcoxon rank-sum test is based on the average of ranks of independent samples. If the populations are the same, then the combined rankings of the two samples will be nearly evenly divided between the two samples and the average of the ranks will be about the same. If the populations are not the same, one of the samples will have more of the lower ranks and its average will be lower. The other sample will have more of the higher ranks and, therefore, a larger average. When both samples contain at least 8 observations, the standard normal distribution is used as the test statistic. Text formula [18–4] is used:

$$\text{Wilcoxon Rank-Sum Test} \qquad z = \frac{W - \dfrac{n_1(n_1 + n_2 + 1)}{2}}{\sqrt{\dfrac{n_1 n_2 (n_1 + n_2 + 1)}{12}}} \qquad [18-4]$$

Where:
W is the sum of the ranks from the first population
n_1 is the number of observations from the first population
n_2 is the number of observations from the second population.

The Kruskal-Wallis Test – Analysis of Variance by Ranks

The Wilcoxon rank-sum test compares two independent populations. The ***Kruskal-Wallis test*** allows for the simultaneous comparison of more than two independent populations. It is an alternative to the ANOVA, described in Chapter 12, for comparing more than two population means.

> ***Kruskal-Wallis test***: A test to determine whether there is a difference between more than two populations. No assumption regarding the shape of the populations is necessary.

Recall from Chapter 12 that to apply ANOVA it was necessary that:

1. The samples be independent

2. The populations have a normal distribution

3. The populations have equal standard deviations

The Kruskal-Wallis test should be used if one or more of these assumptions cannot be met. It requires at least five observations in each sample. To employ the Kruskal-Wallis test, we substitute the rankings of the sampled items for the actual values.

The test statistic, designated by H, is computed using formula [18-5].

$$\text{Kruskal-Wallis Test} \qquad H = \frac{12}{n(n+1)}\left(\frac{(\Sigma R_1)^2}{n_1} + \frac{(\Sigma R_2)^2}{n_2} + \ldots \frac{(\Sigma R_k)^2}{n_k}\right) - 3(n+1) \qquad [18-5]$$

Where:

$\Sigma R_1, \Sigma R_2 \ldots \Sigma R_k$ are the sum of the ranks for the samples designated $1, 2, \ldots, k$.

$n_1, n_2, \ldots n_k$ are the sizes of samples $1, 2, \ldots k$.

n is the combined number of observations for all samples.

There are $(k-1)$ degrees of freedom (k is the number of populations).

The distribution of the sample H statistic is very close to the Chi-square distribution with $(k-1)$ degrees of freedom *if every sample size is at least 5*. Therefore we use chi-square in formulating the decision rule.

Rank-Order Correlation

Pearson's coefficient of correlation assumes the data to be of at least interval scale. Charles Spearman, a British statistician, introduced a measure of correlation for ordinal-level data known as *Spearman's coefficient of rank correlation*.

> ***Spearman's Coefficient of rank correlation:*** A measure of the relationship between two sets of ranked data.

Spearman's coefficient of rank correlation, designated r_s, may range between -1.0 and $+1.0$ inclusive with -1.0 and $+1.0$ representing perfect rank correlation. Zero indicates there is no association between the ranks of the two variables.

Text formula [18-6] is used to compute r_s.

$$\text{Spearman's Coefficient of Rank Correlation} \qquad r_s = 1 - \frac{6(\Sigma d^2)}{n(n^2 - 1)} \qquad [18-6]$$

Where:

n is the number of paired observations.

d is the difference between the ranks for each pair.

Testing the Significance of r_s

The value of r_s is tested to rule out the possibility that the association is due to chance. For a two-tailed test, the null and alternate hypotheses are stated as follows:

H_0:   The rank correlation in the population is zero.
H_1:   The rank correlation in the population is not zero.

For large samples where n is 10 or more, the Student's t distribution can be used as the test statistic. There are $(n - 2)$ degrees of freedom and the computed t value is found by:

Hypotheses Test, Rank Correlation	$t = r_s \sqrt{\dfrac{n - 2}{1 - r_s^2}}$ [18 – 7]

GLOSSARY

Kruskal-Wallis test: A test to determine whether there is a difference between more than two populations. No assumption regarding the shape of the populations is necessary.

Median test: A test to determine whether the median of a set of sample data is equal to a hypothesized value.

Sign test: A test based on the sign of a difference between two related observations. We usually designate a plus sign (+) for a positive difference between observations and a minus sign (–) for a negative difference between observations.

Spearman's Coefficient of rank correlation: A measure of the relationship between two sets of ranked data.

Wilcoxon Rank-Sum test: A test to determine whether there is a difference between two independent populations. No assumption is made regarding the normality of the populations.

Wilcoxon Signed-Rank Test: A nonparametric test for determining whether there is a difference between paired or related observations.

CHAPTER PROBLEMS

Problem 1

The steep rise in gasoline prices may be influencing the type of new vehicles being purchased. A small study was conducted to investigate whether sales of full-size sports utility vehicles may be declining. The number of full-size sports utility vehicles sold in the first quarter of 2005 and in the first quarter of 2006 were recorded for a sample of ten car dealerships in the southeast. The data are shown in the following table. At the 0.05

Dealership	No. SUVs Sold 1st Quarter 2005	No. SUVs Sold 1st Quarter 2006
Steivers Dodge	83	72
Midlands Ford	125	140
Hudson Automart	110	95
Bob Hale Toyota	80	71
Camden Honda	102	95
Hagler's Airport GMC	105	83
Ron Berry Chrysler	137	98
Heritage Cadillac-Olds	112	87
Capital City Chevrolet	124	99
Walterboro Dodge-Jeep	90	71

level of significance, can we conclude that the number of full-size sports utility vehicles sold in the southeast is less for the first quarter of 2006 compared to the first quarter of 2005?

Solution 1

First, note that the samples are dependent. That is, we have number of SUVs sold for Steivers Dodge in the first quarter of 2005 and the first quarter of 2006. We are concerned with the distribution of the differences and are not willing to assume these differences follow the normal probability distribution. Thus the paired t test, described in Chapter 11, which requires the normality assumption, cannot be used.

The null hypothesis and the alternate hypothesis are as follows:

H_0: There was no change in demand for full-size SUVs ($\pi \leq 0.50$)
H_1: The demand for full-size SUVs has declined.($\pi > 0.50$)

Why is the alternate hypothesis $\pi > 0.50$? We subtract the number sold in the first quarter of 2006 from the number sold in the first quarter of 2005. Hence, a positive number indicates that the demand for full-size SUVs has declined.

If the null hypothesis is true that there is no change in the demand for full-size SUVs, then there should be about as many positive differences in the number sold as negative differences. If demand has declined, there should be significantly more positive differences. The binomial distribution is used as the test statistic. Recall that to apply the binomial distribution:

1. Each outcome is classified into one of two possible outcomes. A difference can only be positive or negative. (If a difference is 0, that observation is dropped from the study.)

2. The probability of a success remains the same from trial to trial. If the null hypothesis is true, that demand has not changed, the probability of the positive difference is 0.50.

3. There are a fixed number of trials. In this case "trials" refers to the sample size. There are ten dealerships (trials).

4. Each trial is independent. This means, for example, the sales of SUVs for Steivers Dodge are not related to Capital City Chevrolet sales.

The table below shows that of the ten dealerships, 9 out of 10 sold more full-size SUVs in the first quarter of 2005 compared to the first quarter of 2006.

Dealership	No. SUVs Sold X 1st Quarter 2005	No. SUVs Sold Y 1st Quarter 2006	X-Y Sign of Difference
Steivers Dodge	83	72	+
Midlands Ford	140	125	+
Hudson Automart	110	95	+
Bob Hale Toyota	71	80	-
Camden Honda	102	95	+
Hagler's Airport GMC	105	83	+
Ron Berry Chrysler	137	98	+
Heritage Cadillac	112	87	+
Capital City Chevy	124	99	+
Manning Dodge	90	71	+

If the number of observations in the sample is greater than 10, the normal probability distribution can be used to approximate the binomial. In this case, n = 10, so the binomial distribution will be used as the test statistic. The binomial table is found in Appendix B.9.

How is the critical value determined? Recall that the alternate hypothesis indicated a one-tailed test. The binomial probability distribution, when n = 10 and π = 0.50, is shown below.

Binomial Probabilities when n = 10, π = 0.50, alpha = 0.05		
Number of Successes	Probability of Success	Cumulative Probability
0	0.001	
1	0.010	
2	0.044	
3	0.117	
4	0.205	
5	0.246	
6	0.205	
7	0.117	
8	0.044	0.055
9	0.010	↑ 0.011
10	0.001	0.001

The decision rule is formulated by adding the probability starting with ten successes (+ signs) in ten trials, then nine successes, and so on, until we come as close to the significance level as possible without exceeding it. In this instance the probability of ten successes in ten trials is 0.001, the probability of nine successes is 0.010, and so on.

The cumulative probabilities are shown in the right-hand column. The probability of nine or more successes is 0.011, and the probability of eight or more successes is 0.055. Since 0.055 is greater than the significance level, of 0.05, the decision rule is to reject the null hypothesis if nine or more plus signs are obtained in the sample.

There are nine plus signs, indicating that nine of the ten dealerships had higher first quarter sales of full-size SUVs in 2005 compared to the first quarter of 2006. So the null hypothesis is rejected. It is concluded that first quarter sales of full-size SUVs declined in 2006 compared to 2005.

Exercise 18.1			
Check your answers against those in the ANSWER section.	Student	Before SAT Score	After SAT Score
Before and after SAT scores for a sample of 8	L. Bratton	1240	1300
high school students who participated in a course	S. Mantini	1030	1080
designed to help students improve their SAT	V. Haj	1150	1120
scores are shown at right.	E. Sosa	1090	1000
	B. Harvey	1110	1200
At the 0.05 significance level, can we conclude	J.Redding	1100	1230
that the SAT scores have improved?	C. Papalia	1090	1150
	V. Suppa	1130	1260

Problem 2

After reviewing the results in Problem 1, a larger study was conducted to determine if the demand for full-size SUVs has declined in the southeast. A sample of $n = 50$ dealerships in the southeastern United States was taken and the number of full-size SUVs sold in the first quarter of 2005 and in the first quarter of 2006 recorded. A total of 37 dealerships out of the 50 in the sample reported lower sales of full-size SUVs in the first quarter of 2006. At the 0.05 significance level, can we conclude that sales of full-size SUVs in the southeastern United States declined during the first quarter of 2006 compared to the first quarter of 2005?

Solution 2

The null hypothesis and the alternate hypothesis are stated as follows:

$$H_0: \pi \leq 0.50$$
$$H_1: \pi > 0.50$$

Rejection of the null hypothesis and acceptance of the alternate hypothesis allows us to conclude that first-quarter sales of full-size SUVs declined in the southeast in 2006.

The normal approximation to the binomial is used since $n > 10$. The continuity correction, discussed in Chapter 7, is appropriate when a continuous distribution, such as the normal, is used to describe a discrete distribution (the binomial). The continuity correction factor included a value of 0.50, which is either added to or subtracted from X. If the number of plus signs is greater than $n/2$, then 0.50 is subtracted for

X. If the number of plus signs is less than *n*/2, then 0.50 is added. In this sample, there are 37 pluses which is more than *n*/2 = 50/2 =25. Thus, the formula for the test statistic is:

Sign Test, *n* > 10, + Signs More Than n/2	$z = \dfrac{(X - 0.50) - \mu}{\sigma} = \dfrac{(X - 0.50) - 0.50n}{0.50\sqrt{n}}$	[18 – 2]

Where:

X is the number of plus (or minus) signs.

n is the number of paired observations (disregarding ties).

μ is the population mean, found by $n\pi$

σ is $0.50\ \sqrt{n}$.

z is the *z* value.

The decision rule is to reject the null hypothesis if the computed value of *z* exceeds 1.65. This decision rule is based on a one-tailed test, the standard normal distribution, and the 0.05 significance level.

The value of *z* is computed to be 3.47.

$$z = \frac{(X - 0.50) - \mu}{0.50\sqrt{n}} = \frac{(37 - 0.50) - 50(0.50)}{0.50\sqrt{50}} = \frac{11.5}{3.536} = 3.25$$

Since the computed value of 3.25 exceeds the critical value of 1.65, the null hypothesis is rejected. It is concluded that first-quarter sales of full-size SUVS in the southeast declined in 2006.

Exercise 18.2

Check your answers against those in the ANSWER section.

Before and after SAT scores for a sample of 30 students who participated in a course designed to improve SAT scores were obtained in order to determine if the course was effective. It was found that nineteen students showed an increase in their scores and 11 showed a decrease. At the 0.05 significance level can we conclude that the scores for students participating in the course have increased?

Problem 3

The Human Relations Director at ARCO is wondering whether the median age of executives is 45 years. She selects a sample of 228 executives at random. Of the 228 selected, 3 were exactly 45 years old, 120 were over 45 years, and 105 were less than 45 years of age. At the 0.10 significance level, can we conclude that the median age is different from 45 years?

Solution 3

The null and the alternate hypotheses are:

$$H_0: \text{Median} = 45$$
$$H_1: \text{Median} \neq 45$$

The three executives who were exactly 45 years old were omitted from the analysis, so the sample size is reduced from 228 to 225. Using a two-tailed test, the 0.10 significance level, and the standard normal distribution (Appendix B.1) as the test statistic, the decision rule is to reject H_0 if the computed value of z is less than -1.65 or greater than $+1.65$.

We will conduct the test for the number of observations greater than 45 years of age. Because the number of observations above the median is more than $n/2$, we use formula [18-2]. There are 120 observations larger than the hypothesized median and $n/2 = 225/2 = 112.5$. The value of z is 0.93, found by

$$z = \frac{(X - 0.50) - 0.50n}{0.50\sqrt{n}} = \frac{(120 - 0.50) - 0.50(225)}{0.50\sqrt{225}} = 0.93$$

Because 0.93 is not in the region beyond 1.65, the null hypothesis is not rejected. We cannot reject the hypothesis that the median age of ARCO executives is 45 years.

Problem 4

Use the Wilcoxon signed-rank test and the sample data in Problem 1 regarding sales of full-size SUVs to determine if the number of SUVs sold in the first quarter of 2005 is higher than for the first quarter of 2006. Again, use the 0.05 significance level.

Solution 4

The sign test considers only the sign of the difference between paired observations. The Wilcoxon signed-rank test not only considers the sign of the difference between paired observations but also the magnitude of the difference. The null and alternate hypotheses are stated as follows.

H_0: There was no change in demand for full-size SUVs.
H_1: Demand for full-size SUVs was higher in the first quarter of 2005.

9The steps to complete the Wilcoxon signed-rank test are as follows.

1. Compute the difference between each pair of observations. Eliminate any difference of 0 and reduce the size of the sample by the number of zero (0) differences.

2. Determine the absolute value for the values in the difference column.

3. These differences are ranked from lowest to highest, without regard to their signs. If ties occur, the ranks involved are averaged and each tied observation is awarded the mean value.

4. The ranks with a positive difference are assigned to one column and those with a negative difference to another.

5. The sums of the positive (R^+) and negative (R^-) ranks are determined.

6. The smaller of the two sums (R^+) and (R^-) is compared with the critical values found in Appendix B.7. This critical value is called T.

Appendix B.7 is used to formulate the decision rule. First locate the column headed by 0.05 using a one-tailed test. Next move down that column to the row where $n = 10$. The critical value is 10. The decision is to reject H_0 if the smaller of R^+ and R^- is 10 or less.

The values for R^+ and R^- are as follows:

Dealership	1st Qtr. 2005	1st Qtr. 2006	Difference	Absolute	Rank	R^+	R^-
Steivers Dodge	83	72	11	11	3.0	3.0	
Midlands Ford	125	140	−15	15	4.5		4.5
Hudson Automart	110	95	15	15	4.5	4.5	
Bob Hale Toyota	80	71	9	9	2.0	2.0	
Camden Honda	102	95	7	7	1.0	1.0	
Hagler's Airport	105	83	22	22	7.0	7.0	
R. Berry Chrysler	137	98	39	39	10.0	10.0	
Heritage Cadillac	112	87	25	25	8.5	8.5	
Cap.City Chevy	124	99	25	25	8.5	8.5	
Manning Dodge	90	71	19	19	6.0	6.0	
						50.5	4.5

Since $R^- = 4.5$, H_0 is rejected and H_1 accepted. It is concluded that demand for full-size SUVs was higher in the first quarter of 2005.

Exercise 18.3

Check your answers against those in the ANSWER section.

Before and after SAT scores for a sample of 8 high school students who participated in a course designed to help students improve their SAT scores are shown below.

At the 0.05 significance level, can we conclude that the SAT scores have improved? Use the Wilcoxon signed-rank test.

Student	Before SAT Score	After SAT Score					
L. Bratton	1240	1300					
S. Mantini	1030	1080					
V. Haj	1150	1120					
E. Sosa	1090	1000					
B. Harvey	1110	1200					
J.Redding	1100	1230					
C. Papalia	1090	1150					
V. Suppa	1130	1260					

Problem 5

A manufacturer of candy, gum and other snacks wants to compare the daily amounts spent by men and women. To investigate, samples of nine men and ten women are selected. Each person is asked to keep a record of the amount spent for a week. The results are as follows:

Assume the distribution of the amounts spent for men and women does not follow the normal distribution. At the 0.05 significance level can we conclude that men spend more?

Amount Spent by Men	Amount Spent by Women
$4.32	$2.81
6.05	3.45
7.21	4.16
8.57	4.32
9.80	5.54
10.10	6.93
12.76	7.54
13.65	8.32
15.87	10.76
	11.21

Solution 5

The first step is to determine which test to use. Because the populations do not follow the normal distributions, the t test for independent samples is not appropriate. The Wilcoxon rank-sum test allows for two independent samples and does not require any assumptions regarding the shape of the population, so it is appropriate.

The next step is to state the null and the alternate hypotheses. A one-tailed test is used because we want to show that the distribution of the amounts spent by the men is larger, or to the right of, that of the women. To put it another way, the median amount spent by the men is larger than the median amount spent by the women.

H_0: The distributions are the same.
H_1: The distribution of the amount spent by men is larger than for women.

When the two independent samples both have at least eight observations, the test statistic is the standard normal distribution. Formula [18-4] for z is:

$$z = \frac{W - \dfrac{n_1(n_1 + n_2 + 1)}{2}}{\sqrt{\dfrac{n_1 n_2 (n_1 + n_2 + 1)}{12}}}$$

Where:
n_1 is the number of observations from the first population.
n_2 is the number of observations from the second population.
W is the sum of the ranks from the first population .

At the 0.05 significance level the null hypothesis is rejected if z is greater than 1.65.

The test is based on the mean of the ranks. The two samples are ranked as if they belonged to a single sample. If the null hypothesis is true – that the two populations are the same – then the mean of the ranks for the two groups would be about the same. The low, medium, and high ranks would be about evenly divided between the two samples. If the null hypothesis is not true, then one of the samples will have more of the lower ranks and thus a smaller rank average. The other sample will have more of the higher ranks and, therefore, a larger rank average.

The data on the amounts spent by both the men and the women are ranked in the following table and the rank sums determined.

Amount Spent by Men		Amount Spent by Women	
Dollars	Rank	Dollars	Rank
$4.32	4.5	$2.81	1.0
6.05	7.0	3.45	2.0
7.21	9.0	4.16	3.0
8.57	12.0	4.32	4.5
9.80	13.0	5.54	6.0
10.10	14.0	6.93	8.0
12.76	17.0	7.54	10.0
13.65	18.0	8.32	11.0
15.87	19.0	10.76	15.0
		11.21	16.0
	113.5		76.5

The value of z is computed where $W = 113.5$, $n_1 = 9$ and $n_2 = 10$. Note that there was a man and a woman who each spent $4.32. That is, there is a tie for this position. To resolve the tie, the ranks involved are averaged. That is, the ranks of 4 and 5 are averaged and the value of 4.5 is assigned to those involved.

$$z = \frac{W - \frac{n_1(n_1 + n_2 + 1)}{2}}{\sqrt{\frac{n_1 n_2 (n_1 + n_2 + 1)}{12}}} = \frac{113.5 - \frac{9(9 + 10 + 1)}{2}}{\sqrt{\frac{9(10)(9 + 10 + 1)}{12}}} = 1.92$$

Because the computed value of z (1.92) is greater than the critical value of 1.65, the null hypothesis is rejected. The distribution of the amounts spent by men is larger than that of women. To say it another way, the median of the distribution of the amounts spent by men is larger than the median of the amounts spent by women.

Exercise 18.4		
Check your answers against those in the ANSWER section.	**Tough Muffler**	**Long Last Muffler**
	24	35
The Continental Muffler Company manufactures two different mufflers, the	31	46
Tough Muffler and the Long Last Muffler. As an experiment, they installed	37	49
Tough Mufflers on eight of their employees' automobiles and the Long Last on	44	52
nine automobiles. The number of miles driven before a muffler needed	36	41
replacing is recorded at the right (in thousands of miles).	30	40
	28	32
Assume the miles driven do not follow the normal distributions. Does the	21	29
evidence suggest a difference in the number of miles driven using the two		27
mufflers before replacement? Use the 0.05 significance level.		

Problem 6

A study is made regarding the reaction time (in seconds) to danger among four groups of professional drivers: cab drivers, bus drivers, truck drivers, and race car drivers. The results are as follows:

Assume that the reaction times do not follow the normal distributions. At the 0.05 significance level, is there a difference in reaction times?

Reaction Time (seconds)			
Cab Drivers	Bus Drivers	Truck Drivers	Race Car Drivers
3.4	4.5	3.7	2.8
3.3	4.0	3.0	2.7
1.9	2.9	2.1	3.8
3.1	3.1	2.9	2.2
2.5	3.7	1.8	1.7
	4.4	3.6	

Solution 6

The ANOVA technique described in Chapter 12 for comparing several population means assumed that the populations have a normal distribution. In this case the normality assumption cannot be made. Hence a nonparametric alternative, the Kruskal-Wallis test, is used. The null and alternate hypotheses are:

H_0: The distributions of reaction times are the same.
H_1: The distributions of reaction times are not the same.

The χ^2 distribution is the test statistic. For this test there are $(k-1)$ degrees of freedom, where $k = 4$ is the number of treatments (groups of professional drivers), so the degrees of freedom is $(k-1) = (4-1) = 3$. The critical value from Appendix B.3 is 7.815 given a significance level of 0.05.

The value of the test statistic is computed using formula [18-5].

$$H = \frac{12}{n(n+1)} \left(\frac{\Sigma R_1^2}{n_1} + \frac{\Sigma R_2^2}{n_2} + \ldots \frac{\Sigma R_k^2}{n_k} \right) - 3(n+1)$$

Where:
$\Sigma R_1, \Sigma R_2 \ldots \Sigma R_k$ are the sum of the ranks for the sample designated $1, 2, \ldots, k$.
$n_1, n_2, \ldots .n_k$ are the sizes of samples $1, 2, \ldots k$.
n is the combined number of observations for all samples.
There are $(k-1)$ degrees of freedom (k is the number of populations).

The value of the test statistic is computed by first ranking the reaction times of the four groups as though they were a single group. Note that there are several instances involving tied ranks. The third bus driver and the fourth truck driver each had a reaction time of 2.9 seconds. These two drivers involve the 9th and 10th ranks. To resolve the tie, the ranks involved are averaged and the average rank assigned to each. Hence both drivers are assigned the rank of 9.5, found by (9 + 10)/2. The other ties are resolved in a similar fashion.

Reaction Times and Ranks for Professional Drivers							
Cab Drivers		Bus Drivers		Truck Drivers		Race Car Drivers	
Time	Rank	Time	Rank	Time	Rank	Time	Rank
3.4	15	4.5	22	3.7	17.5	2.8	8
3.3	14	4.0	20	3.0	11	2.7	7
1.9	3	2.9	9.5	2.1	4	3.8	19
3.1	12.5	3.1	12.5	2.9	9.5	2.2	5
2.5	6	3.7	17.5	1.8	2	1.7	1
		4.4	21	3.6	16		
Total	50.5		102.5		60		40

Next, these results are substituted into the formula for H and its value is computed:

$$H = \frac{12}{n(n+1)}\left[\frac{\left(\Sigma R_1\right)^2}{n_1} + \frac{\left(\Sigma R_2\right)^2}{n_2} + \frac{\left(\Sigma R_3\right)^2}{n_3} + \frac{\left(\Sigma R_4\right)^2}{n_4}\right] - 3(n+1)$$

$$= \frac{12}{22(22+1)}\left[\frac{(50.5)^2}{5} + \frac{(102.5)^2}{6} + \frac{(60)^2}{6} + \frac{(40)^2}{5}\right] - 3(22+1)$$

$$= \frac{12}{506}(510.05 + 1751.04 + 600 + 320) - 69 = (75.44 - 69) = 6.44$$

Since the computed value (6.44) is less than the critical value of 7.815, the null hypothesis cannot be rejected. The evidence does not suggest a difference in the distribution of reaction times to emergency situations among various types of professional drivers.

Exercise 18.5

Check your answers against those in the ANSWER section.

A travel agency selected a sample of flights from each of three major airlines and recorded the "load factors"—the percentage of available seats sold. The results are shown in the table at the right.

Do these data suggest any difference in the load factors? Use the 0.05 level of significance. Assume that the load factors do not follow a normal distribution.

US Airways	Delta	Northwest
98%	89%	92%
87	87	90
97	92	94
93	89	84
91	97	86
94		

Problem 7

A supervisor ranked a sample of 12 auto mechanics by their mechanical ability and their social compatibility. The results are given at the right:

Compute the coefficient of rank correlation. Can we conclude that there is a positive association in the population between the ranks of mechanical ability and social compatibility? Use the 0.05 significance level.

Worker	Mechanical Ability	Social Compatibility
1	1	4
2	2	3
3	3	2
4	4	6
5	5	1
6	6	5
7	7	8
8	8	12
9	9	11
10	10	9
11	11	7
12	12	10

Solution 7

The steps in finding the coefficient of rank correlation are:

(1) compute the difference between each set of ranks and then (2) square these differences. The difference is designated d.

Worker	Mechanical Ability	Social Compatibility	d	d^2
1	1	4	−3	9
2	2	3	−1	1
3	3	2	1	1
4	4	6	−2	4
5	5	1	4	16
6	6	5	1	1
7	7	8	−1	1
8	8	12	−4	16
9	9	11	−2	4
10	10	9	1	1
11	11	7	4	16
12	12	10	2	4
			0	74

Applying formula [18-6]:

$$r_s = 1 - \frac{6\left(\Sigma d^2\right)}{n\left(n^2 - 1\right)} = 1 - \frac{6(74)}{12\left(12^2 - 1\right)} = 0.741$$

The value 0.741 indicates a fairly strong positive association between the ranks of mechanical ability and social compatibility. It appears those workers with more mechanical ability also show more social compatibility.

Could this association be due to chance? Use the 0.05 significance level. To answer this question we first state the null and alternate hypotheses.

H_0: The rank correlation in the population is zero.
H_1: The rank correlation in the population is greater than zero.

The alternate hypothesis suggests a one-tailed test. There are ten degrees of freedom, found by $(n-2) = (12-2) = 10$. To locate the critical value refer to Appendix B.2. For the 0.05 level the critical value of t is 1.812. H_0 is rejected if the computed value of t is greater than 1.812. Using formula [18-7], the computed t is 3.490.

$$t = r_s \sqrt{\frac{n-2}{1-r_s^2}} = 0.741 \sqrt{\frac{12-2}{1-(0.741)^2}} = 0.741\sqrt{22.177} = 0.741(4.7092) = 3.4895 = 3.490$$

Since the computed value of 3.490 exceeds the critical value of 1.812, H_0 is rejected and H_1 accepted. It is concluded that there is a positive association between the ranks of social compatibility and mechanical ability among auto mechanics.

Exercise 18.6				
	Team	News	Free Press	
Check your answers against those in the ANSWER section.	Penn State	1	2	
	Ohio State	2	1	
The sports editors of the two daily Detroit newspapers predicted the order of finish for the upcoming BigTen football season:	Michigan	3	5	
	Iowa	4	6	
	Wisconsin	5	3	
	Michigan State	6	7	
	Indiana	7	8	
Compute the coefficient of rank correlation. Interpret.	Minnesota	8	9	
	Purdue	9	10	
	Illinois	10	4	
Could the value that you calculated by due to chance? Test at significance level 0.01.	Northwestern	11	11	

NONPARAMETRIC METHODS: ANALYSIS OF RANKED DATA

Name _____   Section _____   Score_____

Part I   Select the correct answer and write the appropriate letter in the space provided.

_____1. For nonparametric tests
    a. the population must be normal.
    b. there cannot be more than two populations.
    c. the populations must be independent.
    d. assumptions regarding the shape of the population are not necessary.

_____2. Which of the following is not an example of a nonparametric test?
    a. sign test   b. median test
    c. one-way ANOVA   d. Kruskal-Wallis test

_____3. Which of the following tests require paired observations or dependent samples?
    a. sign test and Kruskal-Wallis
    b. Wilcoxon's rank-sum and signed-rank tests
    c. coefficient of rank correlation and Wilcoxon rank-sum test
    d. sign test and Wilcoxon signed-rank test

_____4. The Wilcoxon signed-rank test is stronger than the sign test because the
    a. Wilcoxon uses interval scale.
    b. sign test actually uses independent observations.
    c. sign test has fewer observations.
    d. Wilcoxon considers the magnitude of the differences.

_____5. Which of the following conditions must be met for the sign test?
    a. independent samples   b. at least 30 observations
    c. dependent samples   d. all of the above

_____6. The z distribution is used as the test statistic for the Wilcoxon rank-sum test when
    a. each sample has at least 8 observations.
    b. the populations are normal.
    c. the populations have equal standard deviations.
    d. the samples are dependent.

_____7. The binomial distribution is used as the test statistic for which of the following tests?
    a. sign test   b. Wilcoxon signed-rank test
    c. Wilcoxon rank-sum test   d. Kruskal-Wallis test

_____8. Which of the following nonparametric tests can be used when comparing more than two populations?
    a. sign test   b. Kruskal-Wallis test
    c. median test   d. Wilcoxon signed-rank test

_____9. What is the difference between Pearson's and Spearman's coefficients of correlation.
   a. Spearman cannot be negative.
   b. Pearson requires that n be at least 10.
   c. Spearman uses ranked data.
   d. Pearson uses nominal data.

_____10. The Kruskal-Wallis is a nonparametric alternative to
   a. the chi-square tests.
   b. the paired t test.
   c. the independent t test.
   d. ANOVA

Part II   Record your answer in the space provided. Show essential work.

11. The National Association of Certified Public Accountants selected a sample of taxpayers with gross incomes of more than $100,000. They asked two major accounting firms, Sheet Tax Service and Square Deal, to compute the income tax liability for each sampled taxpayer. Use the sign test and the 0.10 significance level to determine if there is a difference in the tax liability.

Taxpayer	Sheet Tax Service	Square Deal					
Schwind	18.9	28.0					
Gankowski	33.1	24.8					
Virost	38.2	28.0					
Williamson	30.2	38.0					
Govito	30.7	31.7					
Trares	30.9	25.7					
Willbond	28.1	30.7					
Fowler	27.2	29.9					
Hawley	30.2	31.0					
Hall	26.2	34.5					
Sanchez	33.4	35.3					
Naymik	33.6	28.2					

a. State the null and the alternate hypotheses.

   H_0: _____

   H_1: _____

b. State the decision rule.

   _____

c. Compute the value of the test statistic. (Use the space provided in the data table)

   c.

d.   What is your decision regarding the null hypothesis? Interpret the result.

_____

12.   Refer to Problem 11. Rework the problem using the Wilcoxon signed-rank test.

  a.   State the null and the alternate hypotheses.

    H_0: _____

    H_1: _____

  b.   State the decision rule.

_____

  c.   Compute the value of the test statistic. (Use the space provided in the data
       table)

c.

  d.   What is your decision regarding the null hypothesis? Interpret the result.

_____

13.   A large Publishing Company wants to compare the annual operating costs of two brands of copying
      machines. The chief accountant gathered the following information. At the 0.05 significance level
      is there a difference in the operating costs of the two machines? The costs do not follow the normal
      distributions.

Copier A		Copier B	
12,965		4,462	
13,145		4,990	
13,504		5,106	
13,603		5,844	
13,727		7,470	
13,833		7,740	
13,925		8,429	
14,438		9,954	
14,948		10,957	
15,202		12,532	
		13,338	
		14,828	
		21,641	
		23,045	
		28,110	

a. State the null and the alternate hypotheses.

H_0: _____

H_1: _____

b. State the decision rule.

_____

c. Compute the value of the test statistic. (Use the space provided in the data table)

c.

d. What is your decision regarding the null hypothesis?

_____

e. Interpret the result.

_____

14. A retired husband and wife were asked to rate their favorite daytime soaps on a scale of 1 to 20. Their ratings are:

Show	Husband		Wife			
General Hospital	1		3			
Port Charles	20		18			
All My Children	3		2			
Days of Our Lives	5		7			
Guiding Light	4		5			
As the World Turns	16		19			
One Life to Live	10		11			
Passions	3		4			
The Young & the Restless	9		9			
Bold and Beautiful	6		4			

a. Rank each of the shows for the husband and the wife.

b. Compute the coefficient of rank correlation.

b.

CHAPTER 19
STATISTICAL QUALITY CONTROL

Chapter Goals

After completing this chapter, you will be able to:

1. Discuss the role of quality control in production and service operations.
2. Define and understand the terms: *chance cause*; *assignable cause*; *in control*, *out of control*, *attribute*, and *variable*.
3. Construct and interpret a *Pareto chart*.
4. Construct and interpret a *fishbone diagram*.
5. Construct and interpret a *mean* and *range* chart.
6. Construct and interpret a *percent defective* and a *c-bar chart*.
7. Discuss *acceptance sampling*.
8. Construct an *operating characteristic curve* for various sampling plans.

Introduction

Prior to the Industrial Revolution, a craftsman was in complete charge of the quality of the finished product. Before selling a buggy, the craftsman made sure the wheels were round, all the bolts were tight, etc. The Industrial Revolution changed the way clothing, furniture, farm implements, shoes, and other consumer items were manufactured. Employees were organized in assembly lines and each employee performed one or two tasks. To control the quality of the output, all of the finished products were inspected, that is, there was 100 percent inspection after the manufacturing operation was completed.

During the 1930s and 1940s the concept of **statistical process control** or **SPC,** also called **statistical quality control** was developed.

> **Statistical process control**: A collection of strategies, techniques, and actions taken by an organization to ensure they are producing a quality product or providing a quality service.

Instead of 100 percent inspection, a sample of the parts produced is selected and inspected during production and a decision made regarding the quality of the production. The goal is to minimize the amount of defective material produced.

Causes of Variation

On a production line there is no such thing as two identical parts or products. The difference between two parts may be very small but they are different. The tensile strength of a roll of steel wire varies throughout the length of wire, and not every McDonald's Quarter Pounder has exactly 0.25 lbs. of meat. There are two general categories of variation in a process: **chance variation** and **assignable variation** causes.

> ***Chance variations***: Variation that is random in nature. This type of variation cannot be completely eliminated unless there is a major change in the techniques, technologies, methods, equipment or materials used in the process.

A few examples of chance variation include, temperature, humidity, dust in the air, variations in materials, and vibrations from a passing forklift. Chance causes are large in number and random in nature and usually cannot be eliminated. The amount of material or "shot" of plastic used in the injection molding of a plastic product varies due to many conditions. Conditions such as temperature, dust and dirt, etc. are not always constant causing the amount of plastic to vary slightly.

> ***Assignable variation***: Variation that is not random. It can be eliminated or reduced by investigating the problem and finding the cause.

An assignable cause of variation is nonrandom variation which can usually be eliminated or greatly reduced. Suppose the sample boxes of breakfast cereal are significantly overweight. An investigation revealed that the lever controlling the weight of the cereal had become loose. Thus, the assignable cause is a loose lever, and it can be easily reset and tightened.

In recent years competition from foreign manufacturers, especially in the automotive industry, has caused American firms to revamp and strengthen their quality control programs.

Diagnostic Charts

The ***Pareto chart*** and a ***Fishbone diagram*** are two popular and very useful tools for investigating quality problems to insure that a product is manufactured properly.

> ***Pareto chart***: An analysis technique for tallying the number and type of defects that happen within a product or service.

Pareto, an Italian scientist, noted that most of the "activity" in a process is caused by relatively few of the "factors." His concept, called the 80-20 rule, is that 80 percent of the activity is caused by 20 percent of the factors. The point he makes is that if management concentrates its efforts on 20 percent of the factors, they can attack 80 percent of the problem.

> ***Fishbone diagram***: A cause and effect diagram to emphasize the relationship between an effect and a set of possible causes that produce the particular effect.

The fishbone diagram is useful to help organize ideas and to identify relationships that can help us determine factors that are a cause of variability in our process. The usual approach to a fishbone diagram is to consider four problem areas namely: methods, materials, equipment, and personnel.

Fishbone Diagram

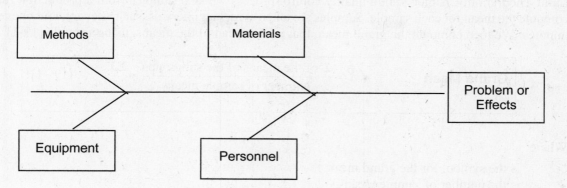

Purposes and Types of Quality Control Charts

A useful tool for insuring that a product is manufactured properly is a *quality control chart*.

> ***Quality control charts***: Portray graphically the results of samples taken during the production period. They are used to identify when assignable causes of variation or changes have entered the process.

Control charts are based on the theory of sampling. We select random samples of the product during the production process and portray the results in chart form. These control charts are useful for separating random causes of variation from those that are assignable to some particular condition.

There are two types of control charts, namely a *variable control chart* and an *attribute control chart*.

> ***Variable control chart***: A control chart that portrays interval or ratio scale measurements.

The variable control chart portrays measurements such as amount of liquid in a container, length of a steel bar, and the time it takes to pack a computer for shipping.

> ***Attribute control chart***: A control chart that classifies a product or service as acceptable or unacceptable and is based on the nominal scale of measurement.

The attribute control chart portrays measurements such as the rating of a software program as acceptable or not acceptable.

In order to develop control charts we rely on the sampling theory discussed in connection with the Central Limit Theorem in Chapter 8. In a quality control process we take samples from a production run and compute the mean for each sample. Samples are taken at regular intervals, such as every hour or every 30 minutes. We then compute the grand mean, that is, the mean of the means, using formula [19-1].

$$\overline{\overline{X}} = \frac{\Sigma \text{ of the means of the subgroups}}{\text{Number of sample means}} = \frac{\Sigma \overline{X}}{k} \qquad [19-1]$$

Grand Mean

Where:
$\overline{\overline{X}}$ is the symbol for the grand mean.
k is the number of sample means.
$\Sigma \overline{X}$ is the sum of the means for each sample.

The standard error of the distribution of the individual sample means is designated $s_{\overline{x}}$ and is computed using formula [19-2].

$$\textbf{Standard Error of the Mean} \quad s_{\overline{x}} = \frac{s}{\sqrt{n}} \qquad [19-2]$$

Where:
s is the sample standard deviation
n is the sample size.

On a chart there is an *in control area* and an *out of control* area. If the plot on the chart representing production is in the "in control" area, it is assumed that the production is satisfactory. If the plot on the chart is in the "out of control" area, it is assumed that the production is unsatisfactory. There is an upper control limit (UCL), and a lower control limit (LCL).

> ***Upper control limit and lower control limit:*** These two limits are the two points (lines on the control chart) which separate the in control area from the out of control area.

A typical chart before any plots are made appears as:

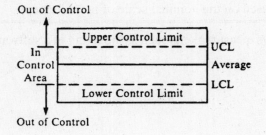

If we are concerned with the mean outside diameter of a pipe and if the manufacturing process is "in control," the sample mean will fall between the UCL and LCL 99.74 percent of the time by chance. This is the same as ± three standard deviations from the arithmetic mean.

Types of Control Charts

There are two basic types of control charts. We use control charts for **_variables_** when the characteristic under investigation can be measured, such as the outside diameter of a pipe or the weight of the contents of a bottle of cola.

> **_Variable_**: A reading or measurement obtained on the product or service.

Two types of control charts for variables are _the_ **_mean chart_** and the **_range chart_**.

> **_Mean chart_**: The purpose is to portray the fluctuation in the sample means and to identify sample means that indicate that the process is out of control.

The mean chart shows management, production, engineers, machine operators, and others whether the arithmetic mean weight, length, outside diameter, inside diameter, etc., is in control (satisfactory), or out of control (unsatisfactory).

A mean chart has two limits, an upper control limit (UCL) and a lower control limit (LCL). These are computed using formula [19-3].

Control Limits for the Mean	$UCL = \overline{\overline{X}} + 3\dfrac{s}{\sqrt{n}}$ and $LCL = \overline{\overline{X}} - 3\dfrac{s}{\sqrt{n}}$	[19 – 3]

Where:

s is an estimate of the standard deviation of the population σ.

n is the sample size.

Note that the number 3 appears in both formulas. It represents the 99.74 percent confidence limits. Other levels of confidence can be used.

Rather than calculate the standard deviation from each sample as a measure of variation, it easier to use the range. For small fixed size samples there is a constant relationship between the range and the standard deviation, so we can use the following formulas to determine the 99.74 percent control limits for the mean. It can be shown mathematically that the term $3\dfrac{s}{\sqrt{n}}$ from formula [19-3] is equivalent to $A_2\overline{R}$ in the following formula [19-4].

Control Limits for the Mean	$UCL = \overline{\overline{X}} + A_2\overline{R}$ and $LCL = \overline{\overline{X}} - A_2\overline{R}$	[19 – 4]

Where:

A_2 is a constant used in computing UCL and LCL and is based on the average range, $\overline{R}$. See Appendix B.8.

$\overline{\overline{X}}$ is the grand mean or the mean of the sample means, formula [19-1]: $\overline{\overline{X}} = \dfrac{\Sigma\overline{X}}{k}$.

$\overline{R}$ is the mean of the sample ranges, found by $\overline{R} = \dfrac{\Sigma R}{k}$.

A *range chart* has a similar purpose to that of the means chart.

> **Range chart**: Shows the variation in the sample ranges and is used to identify sample ranges that indicate the process is out of control.

The range chart shows the fluctuation in the sample ranges and makes it easy to identify sample ranges that indicate the process is out of control. It has been shown that, according to chance, the range of the samples will fall within the limits 99.7 percent of the time (997 out of 1000). When the range falls above the limits we conclude that an assignable cause has affected the operation and an adjustment in the process is needed. Note that for small samples the lower limit is often zero.

As examples, the two charts for variables might appear as shown on the right.

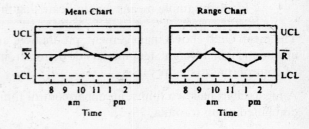

An analysis of the two charts reveals that both the arithmetic mean length of a piece of steel and the range of the lengths of the pieces are satisfactory (in control).

The upper and lower limits of a range chart are computed using formula [19-5]:

> **Control Limits for Ranges** $UCL = D_4\overline{R}$ $LCL = D_3\overline{R}$ $\left[19-5\right]$

The values D_3 and D_4 reflect the usual three σ (sigma) limits and can be found in Appendix B.8.

Attribute Control Charts

Some data we collect is the result of counting, rather than measuring. We may have a product or situation, such as a bank loan, that is either granted (acceptable) or not granted (unacceptable). Some products can only be classified as being "acceptable" or "unacceptable." Charts developed for these products are called *attribute charts*.

> **Attributes:** A product or service is classified as acceptable or unacceptable. No reading or measurement is obtained.

For example, a light bulb is either defective or not defective. When this type of classification is used, control charts for these attributes include *the percent defective chart* and *c-bar chart*.

Percent defective chart

When the item recorded is the fraction of unacceptable parts made in a group of parts, the appropriate control chart is the percent defective chart.

> **Percent defective chart**: Shows the percent of production that is defective.

The percent defective chart was drawn to show the percent defective for the manufacturing process for a ball bearing.

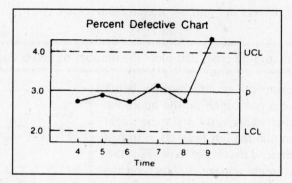

The process was in control from 4 p.m. until 8 p.m. The 9 p.m. check revealed that the percent defective exceeded the upper control limit of 4 percent. The quality control engineer would no doubt take steps to bring the process back into control (below 4 percent). A percent defective chart is also known as a *p* chart.

The percent defective chart is based on the binomial distribution, discussed in Chapter 6, and proportions, discussed in Chapters 9. The centerline of the chart is at *p*, the mean proportion defective. Formula [19-6] is used.

Mean Proportion Defective $p = \dfrac{\text{Total number defective}}{\text{Total number of items sampled}}$ $[19-6]$

The variation in the sample proportion is described by the standard error of a proportion. Formula [19-7] is used.

Standard Error of the Proportion $s_p = \sqrt{\dfrac{p(1-p)}{n}}$ $[19-7]$

The standard error of the proportion is used to compute the *UCL* and *LCL* Formula [19-8] is used.

Control Limits for Proportions $LCL, UCL = p \pm 3\sqrt{\dfrac{p(1-p)}{n}}$ $[19-8]$

c–Bar Chart

It is difficult for many processes to manufacture all the units without a defect appearing. A chart designed to portray the number of defects per unit is called a **c-bar chart**.

> **c-bar chart**: An attribute chart that plots the number of defects or failures per unit.

For example, the exterior of an automobile being manufactured might have a paint glob on the hood, the trunk lid might not be centered correctly, and there might be a steel sliver protruding on the left front door. In that case, there would be three defects per unit. For this example, the c–bar chart might appear as shown on the right.

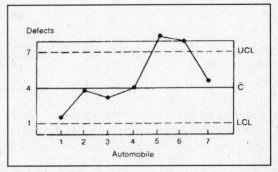

Based on the chart, between 1 and 7 defects per car is expected. The mean is 4. However, the number of defects in car 5 and car 6 exceeded the upper control limit and the process would be declared "out of control." It was brought under control for car 7. That is, the process was back "in control." The purpose of the c-bar chart is to show how many defects are in a unit of production.

We let $\bar{c}$ be the mean number of defects per unit. Recall from Chapter 6 that the standard deviation of a Poisson distribution is the square root of the mean. Thus we can determine the 99.74 percent confidence limits on a c–bar chart by formula [19-9].

> **Control Limits for the Number of Defects Per Unit** $\qquad LCL, UCL = \bar{c} \pm 3\sqrt{\bar{c}} \qquad [19-9]$

Acceptance Sampling

In any business situation there is concern over the quality of an incoming shipment of a product. For example, a cola manufacturer purchases plastic 2-liter bottles from a blow-molding supplier. The plastic bottles are received in lots of 2,400. The manufacturer does not expect each bottle to be perfect, but the manufacturer has an agreement with the supplier regarding the percent of the bottles that are defective. The usual procedure is to check the quality of the incoming product using a statistical sampling plan called **acceptance sampling**.

> **Acceptance sampling**: A method for determining whether an incoming lot of a product meets specified standards.

A random sample of n units is selected from the lot of N units. If c or less units are found defective among the n sampled units, the lot is accepted, otherwise it is rejected. The inspection will determine the number of defective parts in the sample. This number is compared to the predetermined number called the **acceptance number**. If the number of defects exceeds the acceptance number, the lot is rejected and returned to the supplier.

> ***Acceptance number***: The maximum number of defective units allowed in a sample before the lot is rejected. The number is usually designated as c.

As an example, the cola manufacturer selects a random sample of 30 bottles and inspects each. If 3 or less are defective, the entire lot of bottles is accepted. Otherwise, the shipment is returned to the supplier.

Acceptance sampling is a decision-making process. According to the specific sampling plan, the lot is either acceptable or unacceptable. So there are two decisions that can be made. In addition, there are two states of nature. If the lot is acceptable and the sampling process reveals it to be good, or the lot is unacceptable and the sampling process shows the lot to be unacceptable, then a correct decision has been made. However, there are two additional possibilities. The lot may actually contain more defects than it should, but the sampling process reveals it to be acceptable. This is called ***consumer's risk***.

> ***Consumer's risk***: The likelihood that a lot that should not be accepted is actually accepted.

If the lot is actually within agreed upon limits, but the sampling process reveals that it should be rejected, this is called the ***producer's risk***.

> ***Producer's risk***: The likelihood that an acceptable lot is rejected.

The following table summarizes the possibilities for the acceptance decisions:

Decision	States of Nature	
	Good Lot	**Bad Lot**
Accept Lot	Correct	Consumer's Risk
Reject Lot	Producers Risk	Correct

An **operating characteristic** curve is developed to show the probabilities of accepting incoming lots with various quality levels. The binomial distribution is used to determine the probabilities corresponding to the various quality levels.

Glossary

Acceptance number: The maximum number of defective units allowed in a sample before the lot is rejected. The number is usually designated as c.

Acceptance sampling: A method for determining whether an incoming lot of a product meets specified standards.

Assignable variation: Variation that is not random. It can be eliminated or reduced by investigating the problem and finding the cause.

Attributes: A product or service is classified as acceptable or unacceptable. No reading or measurement is obtained.

Attribute control chart: A control chart that classifies a product or service as acceptable or unacceptable and is based on the nominal scale of measurement

***c-bar* chart**: An attribute chart that plots the number of defects or failures per unit.

Chance variation: Variation that is random in nature. This type of variation cannot be completely eliminated unless there is a major change in the equipment or material used in the process.

Consumer's risk: The likelihood that a lot that should not be accepted is actually accepted.

Fishbone diagram: A cause and effect diagram to emphasize the relationship between an effect and a set of possible causes that produce the particular effect.

Mean chart: The purpose is to portray the fluctuation in the sample means and to identify sample means that indicate that the process is out of control.

Pareto chart: An analysis technique for tallying the number and type of defects that happen within a product or service.

Percent defective chart: Shows the percent of production that is defective.

Producer's risk: The likelihood that an acceptable lot is rejected.

Quality control charts: Portray graphically the results of samples taken during the production period. They are used to identify when assignable causes of variation or changes have entered the process.

Range chart: Shows the variation in the sample ranges and is used to identify sample ranges that indicate the process is out of control.

Statistical process control: A collection of strategies, techniques, and actions taken by an organization to ensure they are producing a quality product or providing a quality service.

Upper control limit and lower control limit: These two limits are the two points (lines on the control chart) which separate the in control area from the out of control area.

Variable: A reading or measurement obtained on the product or service.

Variable control chart: A control chart that portrays interval or ratio scale measurements

CHAPTER PROBLEMS

Problem 1

Custom Comp sells special order computers by taking orders, assembling the computers, and then delivering them to the customer. Each delivery is followed up with a survey seeking to identify ways to improve the service to the customers. Last month's survey showed these results:

a. Develop a Pareto chart.

b. What complaints should management focus on for improved customer satisfaction?

Type of Complaint	Number
Wrong hardware configuration	30
Late delivery	38
Poor technical support	22
Error on invoice	20
Component failure	15
Wrong software package	25

Solution 1

a. To develop a Pareto chart follow these steps:

Step 1. Calculate the total number of responses. The total is 150

Step 2. Determine what percent each category is of the total by dividing the number in each category by the total. See chart.

Type of Complaint	No.	%	Rank	Complaints in rank order	%	Cum. %
Wrong hardware configuration	30	20.0	2	Late delivery	25.3	25.3
Late delivery	38	25.3	1	Wrong Hardware	20.0	45.3
Poor technical support	22	14.7	4	Wrong Software	16.7	62.0
Error on invoice	20	13.3	5	Poor support	14.7	76.7
Component failure	15	10.0	6	Error on invoice	13.3	90.0
Wrong software package	25	16.7	3	Component failure	10.0	100.0

Step 3. Rank the frequencies from largest to smallest. Note that late delivery and wrong hardware account for 45.3 percent of the complaints.

Step 4. Draw the Pareto chart:

Pareto Chart - Type of Complaint

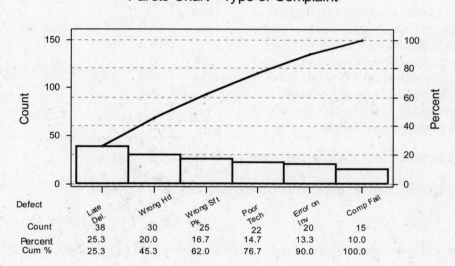

b. Management should focus on late deliveries and wrong hardware to improved customer satisfaction.

Check your answer against those in the ANSWER section.

Return Code*	Number
01	75
2	38
03	12
04	35
05	7
06	11
07	14
08	8

Azure Bay is a large mail-order and online clothing retailer. Recently, there has been an increase in the amount of merchandise that has been returned by the customers. When a customer returns an item, they are required to fill out a returned merchandise form and check the reason the item is being returned. The following table was constructed from information obtained from the last 200 receipts of returned merchandise.

* 01 = too small 02 = too big 03 = too short 04 = too long 05 = not what was ordered
  06 = poor fit   07 = not what was expected 08 = defective

a. Construct a Pareto Chart for the 'reason for return' data.

b. Which reasons should the retailer focus on first to reduce the incidence of returned merchandise?

Problem 2

A machine set to fill a bottle with 60.0 grams of liquid was started at 7 a.m. today. Slight variations (called chance variations) were expected. The quality control inspector made her initial check of the weights at 8 a.m. She selected five bottles from the first hour of production and weighed the contents of each bottle. The results of the first seven inspections follow:

Time	1	2	3	4	5
8 a.m.	60.0	59.9	60.0	60.0	60.1
9 a.m.	60.0	60.2	60.1	60.2	60.0
10 a.m.	60.1	60.1	60.0	59.8	60.0
11 a.m.	60.0	59.8	60.0	60.0	60.2
12 noon	60.2	60.0	59.8	60.1	59.8
1 p.m.	60.3	60.1	59.9	60.1	59.8
2 p.m.	60.1	59.8	59.7	59.9	59.8

a. Develop a control chart for the sample means.

b. Develop a control chart for the sample ranges.

Solution

a. The upper and lower control limits for the mean are determined using formula [19-3].

$$UCL \text{ and } LCL = \overline{\overline{X}} \pm A_2\overline{R}$$

Where:

$\overline{\overline{X}}$ is the mean of the sample means.
$\overline{R}$ is the mean of the sample ranges.
A_2 is a factor which is related to the standard deviation. A_2 is based on the number of observations taken each hour, that is, the sample size.

Statistical theory has shown that there is a constant relationship between the range and the standard deviation for a given sample size. A_2 expresses this constant relationship. To obtain the specific value for A_2, refer to Appendix B.8. Move down the "Number of items in the sample" column to 5. Read across the row to the A_2 column and read the value. It is 0.577.

To find the mean and the average range, refer to the table below. The sample values for 8 a.m. are 60.0, 59.9, 60.0, 60.0 and 60.1 grams, respectively. The sum of those five values is 300.0, so the mean is 60.0 grams (found by 300.0 / 5). The means for all remaining hours are computed. The sum of the seven means is 419.98 and the mean of these seven means $\left(\overline{\overline{X}}\right)$ is 59.997, found

by: $\overline{\overline{X}} = \dfrac{\Sigma \overline{X}}{n} = \dfrac{419.98}{7} = 59.997.$

For the 8 a.m. check, the highest weight is 60.1 grams, the lowest 59.9 grams. The difference between the highest and lowest (the range) is 0.2. The sum of the seven ranges is 2.4 and the mean is 0.343, found by (2.4 / 7) = 0.343. This information is summarized in the following table.

Time	1	2	3	4	5	ΣX	$\overline{X}$	R	
8 a.m.	60.0	59.9	60.0	60.0	60.1	300.0	60.00	0.2	$\overline{\overline{X}} = \dfrac{419.98}{7} = 59.997$
9 a.m.	60.0	60.2	60.1	60.2	60.0	300.5	60.10	0.2	
10 a.m.	60.1	60.1	60.0	59.8.	60.0	300.0	60.00	0.3	$\overline{R} = \dfrac{2.4}{7} = 0.343$
11 a.m.	60.0	59.8	60.0	60.0	60.2	300.0	60.00	0.4	
12 noon	60.2	60.0	59.8	60.1	59.8	299.9	59.98	0.4	
1 p.m.	60.3	60.1	59.9	60.1	59.8.	300.2	60.04	0.5	
2 p.m.	60.1	59.8.	59.7	59.9.	59.8.	299.3	59.86	0.4	
							419.98	2.4	

As noted, the control limits for the hourly sample means are determined using formula [19-3].

$$UCL \text{ and } LCL = \overline{\overline{X}} \pm A_2 \overline{R}$$
$$= 59.997 \pm 0.577(0.343)$$
$$= 59.997 \pm 0.198$$

So the lower control limit is set at 59.799 and the upper control limit is set at 60.195.

The MINITAB software system was used to generate the following control chart. Note that subgroup 1 is 8:00 a.m., subgroup 2 is 9:00 a.m., etc. There is a small difference in the limits due to rounding, but it is clear that the process is in control until 2 p.m. At that time the sample mean drops to 59.86 grams. This is still greater than the lower limit on the chart of 59.80 grams. However, this rather dramatic downward shift is likely an indicator of trouble and should be investigated.

Control Chart for Bottle Weight

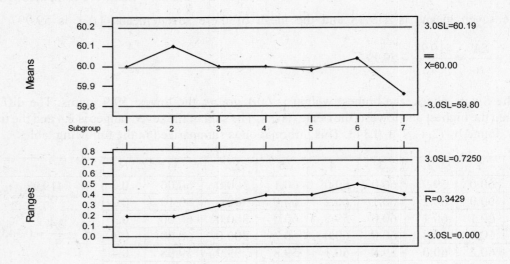

b. For the 8 a.m. check, the highest weight is 60.1 grams, the lowest 59.9. The difference between the highest and lowest (the range) is 0.2. The sum of the seven ranges is 2.4 and the mean 0.343, found by (2.4/7)=0.343. This information is summarized in the previous table.

The LCL and UCL of the control chart for ranges is constructed using formula [19-4].

$$\text{Upper control limit UCL} = D_4 \overline{R}$$

$$\text{Lower control limit LCL} = D_3 \overline{R}$$

The factors D_3 and D_4 (like A_2) are developed from the constant relationship between the range and the standard deviation. The factors D_3 and D_4 are also obtained from Appendix B.8. To locate the values go down the left column to the number in the sample (5) and then go across to the columns headed D_3 and D_4. The factor D_4. = 2.115 and $D_3 = 0$. To determine the UCL and LCL for the range chart:

$$\text{Upper control limit UCL} = D_4 \overline{R} = 2.115(0.343) = 0.725$$

$$\text{Lower control limit LCL} = D_3 \overline{R} = 0(0.343) = 0$$

The process appears to be in control for variability.

Problem 3

The Administration at Rossford General Hospital is investigating the quality of meals served to patients. A ten-day survey is conducted by submitting a questionnaire to 50 patients with the noon meal each day. The patients are required only to indicate whether the meal was satisfactory or unsatisfactory. The results are shown in the table on the right:

Construct a control chart for the proportion of the patients dissatisfied with their meal.

Date	Sample Size	Number of Unsatisfactory Meals
May 1	50	2
2	50	3
3	50	1
4	50	4
5	50	8
6	50	2
7	50	5
8	50	4
9	50	7
10	50	4

Solution 3

This problem requires the use of an attribute chart because a meal is classified only as satisfactory or unsatisfactory. No "measurement" is obtained.

The upper and lower control limits are determined using formula [19-8].

$$UCL \text{ and } LCL = p \pm 3\sqrt{\frac{p(1-p)}{n}}$$

Where:
p is the proportion defective over all the samples.

n is the number in each sample.

The value of p, the proportion unsatisfactory, is computed by first determining the proportion of unsatisfactory meals for each sample.

To compute the mean percent defective:

$$p = \frac{\text{Sum of percent defective}}{\text{Number of samples}}$$

$$= \frac{0.80}{10} = 0.08$$

$$UCL \text{ and } LCL = p \pm 3\sqrt{\frac{p(1-p)}{n}}$$

$$= 0.08 \pm 3\sqrt{\frac{0.08(1-0.08)}{50}}$$

$$= 0.08 \pm 0.115$$

$$= 0 \text{ and } 0.195$$

Date	Sample Size	Number of Unsatisfactory Meals	Proportion of Unsatisfactory Meals
May 1	50	2	0.04
2	50	3	0.06
3	50	1	0.02
4	50	4	0.08
5	50	8	0.16
6	50	2	0.04
7	50	5	0.10
8	50	4	0.08
9	50	7	0.14
10	50	4	0.08
			0.80

Thus, the control limits for the proportion of unsatisfactory meals are set at 0 and 0.195. The lower control limit could not logically be a negative number. The following MINITAB chart indicates that the proportion of unsatisfactory meals is well within the control limit.

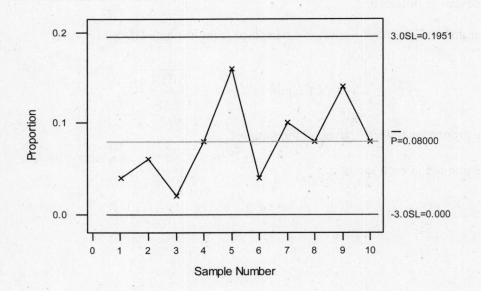

Control Chart for Unsatisfactory Meals

Check your answers against those in the ANSWER section.

The manager of the campus Subway Sandwich Shop is investigating the quality of the noon special sandwich for the week of April 1. The five-day survey requested that customers indicate if a sandwich is satisfactory or unsatisfactory. The results are shown at the right.

Day	Sample Size	Number Unsatisfactory
1	40	2
2	40	3
3	40	1
4	40	2
5	40	4

Develop a control chart for the proportion of customers dissatisfied with the sandwich.

Problem 4

A new automobile assembly line was put into operation. The number of defects on the exterior of the first ten cars off the assembly line was 3, 5, 4, 6, 2, 3, 5, 4, 2, and 4. Construct a $\bar{c}$ chart for the number of defects per unit.

Solution 4

The upper and lower limits for a $\bar{c}$ chart are determined using formula [19-7].

$$UCL \text{ and } LCL = \bar{c} \pm 3\sqrt{\bar{c}}$$

The total number of defects in the first ten cars is 38, found by $(3 + 5 + 4 + 6 + 2 + 3 + 5 + 4 + 2 + 4) =$ 38. The mean number of defects per car ($\bar{c}$) is:

$$\bar{c} = \frac{\Sigma \text{ of the number of defects}}{\text{Total number of cars}}$$

$$= \frac{38}{10} = 3.8$$

The upper and lower control limits are:

$$UCL \text{ and } LCL = \bar{c} \pm 3\sqrt{\bar{c}}$$

$$= 3.8 \pm 3\sqrt{3.8}$$

$$= 3.8 \pm 5.848$$

$$UCL = 9.648$$

$$LCL = 0 \text{ (since number of defects cannot be less than 0)}$$

Based on the sample data for the $\bar{c}$ bar chart, more than 99 percent (99.73% to be more precise) of the cars will have between 0 and 9.648 defects. The process is in control.

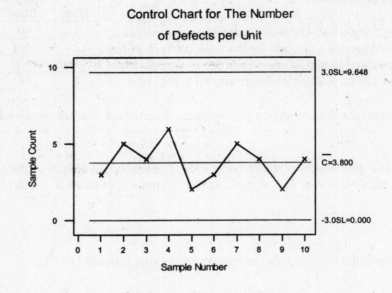

Control Chart for The Number of Defects per Unit

3.0SL=9.648

C̄=3.800

-3.0SL=0.000

Exercise 19.4

Check your answers against those in the ANSWER section.

| 2 | 4 | 5 | 3 | 2 |
| 1 | 5 | 2 | 3 | 1 |

A new injection-molding machine at Fulton Plastics was put into operation. After
fine tuning the machine, the number of defects on the exterior of the first ten items produced is shown on the right.

Construct a $\bar{c}$ chart for the number of defects per unit.

Problem 5

The Berry Cola Company processes a soft drink with a blueberry flavor added to the cola. It is packaged in 2-liter plastic bottles. The bottles are purchased from Persall Plastics in lots of 2,400. Berry Cola has agreed to select a sample of 25 incoming bottles and inspect them for all quality characteristics. If 2 or less defective bottles are found in the sample, the lot is considered acceptable. Suppose we want to develop an operating characteristic curve showing the likelihood that lots will be accepted that are 5%, 10%, or 20% defective.

Solution 5

This is an example of attribute sampling, because each bottle sampled is classified as either acceptable or not acceptable. No measurement or "reading" is obtained on the bottle.

The binomial distribution is used to compute the various probabilities. Recall that to employ the binomial distribution four requirements must be met.

1. There are only two possible outcomes. A bottle is either acceptable or not acceptable.

2. There are a fixed number of trials. The number of trials is the sample size, 25 in this case.

3. There is constant probability of success. A success is the probability of finding a defective part. In this case, Berry Cola is concerned about lots that are 5 percent, 10 percent and 20 percent defective.

4. The trials are independent. The probability the fifth bottle is defective is not related to the probability the eighth bottle is defective.

The binomial probabilities are given in Appendix B.9.

First, let's assume the lot is actually 5% defective, so $\pi = 0.05$, n, the size of the sample, is 25, and the acceptance number is 2. We usually let c refer to the acceptance number, so here $c = 2$.

Next, to find the probability turn to Appendix B.9, an n of 25, and the column where $\pi = 0.05$. Berry Cola will allow 0, 1, or 2 defects in the sample of 25.

Then, find the row where x, the number of defects, is 0 and read the probability. It is 0.277. The probability of 1 defect in a sample of 25 where $\pi = 0.05$ is 0.365. The probability of 2 defects is 0.231.

Adding these three probabilities (0, 1, and 2) gives the probability of accepting a lot that is actually 5 percent defective. The result is 0.873, found by (0.277 + 0.365 + 0.231). Hence, the probability of accepting a lot that is actually 5 percent defective is 0.873. This is often written in the following shorthand form.

$$P\left(x \le 2 \mid \pi = 0.05 \text{ and } n = 25\right) = 0.873$$

Where:
x is the number of defects.
| means "given that."

To find the probability of 2 or fewer defects, when $\pi = 0.10$:

$$P\left(x \le 2 \mid \pi = 0.10 \text{ and } n = 25\right) = \left(0.072 + 0.199 + 0.266\right) = 0.537$$

The probability of 2 or fewer defects when $\pi = 0.20$ is 0.099, found by (0.004 + 0.024 + 0.071). The points for 5, 10, and 20 percent defective are plotted in the following graph. The points are connected with a smooth line.

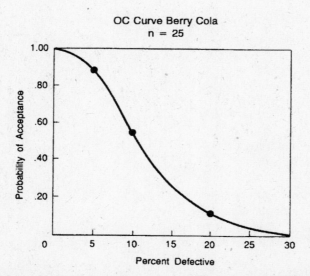

The above OC curve shows the various values of π and their corresponding probability of accepting a lot of that quality. The management of Berry Cola will be able to quickly evaluate the acceptance probabilities for the various quality levels. Other probabilities can be developed by using the normal approximation to the binomial distribution (not discussed here).

Exercise 19.5

Check your answers against those in the ANSWER section.

Use the sampling plan developed above and compute the probability that a lot which is 30% defective is accepted

---

CHAPTER 19 ASSIGNMENT

STATISTICAL QUALITY CONTROL

Name _____ Section _____ Score _____

Part I   Select the correct answer and write the appropriate letter in the space provided.

_____ 1.   Which of the following actions is recommended by statistical quality control?
    a.   inspecting all members of the population.
    b.   inspecting a sample of the population.
    c.   limiting the size of the population.
    d.   finding every defective item in the population.

_____ 2.   Chance causes are
    a.   random in nature.
    b.   due to some specific cause, like a worn tool.
    c.   the result of the use of control charts.
    d.   used in hypothesis testing.

_____ 3.   A variable control chart is
    a.   based on a measurement or reading.
    b.   used to estimate the probability of acceptance.
    c.   based on whether the product is acceptable or unacceptable.
    d.   used to estimate the standard deviation.

_____ 4.   Which of the following is a variable control chart?
    a. c-bar chart   b.   percent defective chart
    c.   mean and range chart   d.   all of the above

_____ 5.   In acceptance sampling
    a.   the sample size is n.   b.   the binomial distribution is used.
    c.   the letter c is the acceptance number.   d.   all of the above

_____ 6.   How far away from the mean are the upper and lower control limits?
    a.   99.73 percent   b.   plus or minus two standard deviations
    c.   plus or minus three standard deviations   d.   half the range

_____ 7.   A particular sampling plan consists of 20 items. The lot is considered acceptable if there are 0 or 1 defects found in the sample.
    a. c is equal to 1   b.   the probability of accepting a lot 20 percent defective is 0.070
    c. n is equal to 20   d.   all of the above

_____ 8.   Refer to question 7. If the acceptance number is increased from 1 to 2, the probability of accepting a lot 20 percent defective will
    a.   stay the same.   b.   increase.
    c.   decrease.   d.   cannot tell from the information given

_____ 9. An operating characteristic curve shows the probability of
   a. finding a particular sample size.
   b. finding a particular value for c.
   c. rejecting a lot.
   d. accepting a lot with a given percent defective.

_____ 10. The consumer's risk is
   a. the likelihood a defective lot is rejected.
   b. a new value for c.
   c. the likelihood a defective lot is accepted.
   d. the size of the sample.

Part II   Record the answers in the space provided. Show essential calculations.

.11. *SkyBlue*, a no-frills airline, is reviewing its data on customer complaints in order to improve customer service. Data from the last quarter is shown in the table.

a. Construct a Pareto chart for the data.

b. Based on the information in the Pareto chart, which categories should SkyBlue focus their efforts on first?

Category	Number
In-flight Service	46
Flight Delays	123
Ticketing	40
Reservations	51
Flight Safety/Security	57
Lost or Mishandled Luggage	240
Flight Cancellations	95
Other	48

12.   The North Central Insurance Company is studying recent claim history. A sample of 5 claims (in $000) for each of the last 5 months is obtained.

	Samples							
Month	1	2	3	4	5	Total	Mean	Range
Jan	1.1	0.9	1.3	1.5	1.2			
Feb	0.5	1.4	1.4	1.3	1.1			
March	0.4	0.3	0.9	0.9	1.0			
April	1.3	1.6	1.6	1.5	0.6			
May	1.2	0.3	1.1	0.7	0.6			

a. Determine the upper and lower control limits for the mean.

a.

b. Determine the upper and lower control limits for the range.

b.

13. A high-speed machine produces a small plastic spacer. To check on the machine's performance, a sample of 30 spacers is selected each hour and the number of defects in the sample determined. On the basis of the samples taken yesterday, determine the control limits for the percent defective chart.

Sample Number	Number in Sample	Number of Defects
1	30	1
2	30	5
3	30	5
4	30	1
5	30	5
6	30	9
7	30	5
8	30	10
9	30	7
10	30	3

14. Dr. Sundar is chairman of the Sociology Department at Southeast State University. He is studying the number of students who drop a sociology course after they have initially registered. The following is the number of drops per section for the 15 courses offered last semester in the department:

4   9   3   4   4   4   8   6   8   2   1   2   2   3   5

What are the control limits for the c-bar chart of the number of drops?

13.

15. The Mills Hardware Company purchases various types of pliers, in lots of 5,000, for sale in the Home Improvement Department. The Purchasing Department inspects 20 pliers at random before accepting each lot. If 2 or less of the pliers are defective, the lot is accepted. If 3 or more of the sample are defective, the lot is returned to the manufacturer.

   a. Determine the probability of accepting a lot that is 10 percent defective.

a.

   b. Determine the probability of finding a lot that is 20 percent defective.

b.

16. A company produces steel rods for various machines. The rods must meet strict specifications in order to function.. Seven recent lots were examined and each rod was checked to see if it met the specifications. The data in the table at the right was observed:

   a. Determine the control limits for the percent defective chart.

Lot Number	Sample Size	Number of unusable rods
1	100	6
2	100	3
3	100	9
4	100	8
5	100	4
6	100	4
7	100	5

a.

   b. Based on this sample, what would the largest number of unusable rods per 100 be before the process is judged out of control?

b.

17. The company in problem # 15 also undergoes a daily inspection of the lengths of the steel rods produced. The data in the table at the right is collected during a daily inspection:

Sample lengths				
Time	1	2	3	4
9:00 a.m.	1.27 m	1.26 m	1.30 m	1.28 m
11:00 a.m.	1.26	1.29	1.26	1.27
1:00 p.m.	1.30	1.28	1.28	1.26
3:00 p.m.	1.26	1.29	1.26	1.28
5:00 p.m.	1.27	1.30	1.29	1.27

a. Determine the upper and lower control limits for the mean.

a.

b. Determine the upper and lower control limits for the range.

b.

CHAPTER 20
AN INTRODUCTION TO DECISION THEORY

CHAPTER GOALS

After completing this chapter, you will be able to:

1. Define the terms *state of nature, event, decision alternative*, and *payoff*.

2. Organize information into a payoff table or a decision tree.

3. Find the expected payoff of a *decision alternative*.

4. Compute *opportunity loss* and *expected opportunity loss*.

5. Assess the expected value of information.

Introduction

The approach to decision making in the earlier chapters was to set up a null hypothesis and an alternate hypothesis, formulate a decision rule, take a sample from the population, and then on the basis of the sample information make a decision about the null hypothesis. This is the classical approach to decision making. This chapter considers a slightly different approach to decision making called *statistical decision theory*. In statistical decision theory various alternative courses of action are considered. However, the monetary values of these courses of action are taken into account for the purpose of determining the optimum course of action.

Elements of a Decision

Under conditions of certainty there are several courses of action available to the decision-maker, and the decision-maker knows the result of each course of action. The purchasing agent at a hotel may need to purchase 1,000 new bed sheets. The agent checks with several suppliers and obtains prices for sheets of comparable quality and then makes the purchase from the supplier offering the best price. Note that no uncertainty regarding future events exists.

Decision making under conditions of uncertainty also entails several courses of action, but in addition there is uncertainty regarding future events. For example, a business owner has $100,000 to invest and is considering investing it in drilling oil wells.

If the well driller strikes oil, the business owner makes a profit ten times the original investment. If it is a dry well, the business owner loses money. Note, therefore, there is a condition of uncertainty. The unknown future outcomes are called the *states of nature*.

> *States of nature*: The uncontrollable future events.

The state of nature is not under the control of the decision-maker. In the oil drilling problem there are two states of nature, either the well will produce oil or it will not. The investor has two courses of action, or alternatives, either to invest or not to invest. Thus the **acts** are the courses of action available to the decision-maker.

> ***Acts***: Two or more possible actions available to the decision-maker.

For each combination of a state of nature and a course of action there is a ***payoff*** or outcome.

> ***Payoff***: The result of a particular combination of an act and a state of nature.

These terms are summarized in the following **payoff table** showing the problems facing the investor.

The payoff from the act "Investing in the oil well" and the state of nature "strike oil" is $1,000,000.

Payoff Table		
	State of Nature	
Act	**Strike Oil**	**Does Not Strike Oil**
Invest in oil well	$1,000,000	–$100,000
Do not invest in oil well	0	0

Usually the payoff table is not the only information available. In fact a decision based solely on the payoff table might, in many situations, ignore valuable historical records. In our oil-drilling problem, we might do some research and find out that only 5 of 100 drillings result in an oil strike. It could be said that the probability of striking oil is 0.05 while the probability of not striking oil is 0.95.

If we combine our payoff table with the probabilities, we can arrive at an **expected payoff**. Expected payoff is also called **expected monetary value**, shortened to EMV. It is also called the **mean payoff**. Text formula [20-1] is used to calculate EMV.

> **Expected Monetary Value** $$EMV(A_i) = \Sigma \left[P\left(S_j\right) \cdot V\left(A_i, S_j\right) \right]$$ [20-1]

Where:

$EMV(A_i)$ refers to the expected monetary value of decision alternatives. There may be several decision possibilities. We will let 1 refer to the first alternative, 2 for the second, and so on. The lowercase letter i represents the entire set of decision alternatives.

$P(S_j)$ refers to the probability of the states of nature. There can be an unlimited number, so we'll let j represent the possible outcomes.

$V(A_i, S_j)$ refers to the value of the payoffs. Note that each payoff is the result of a combination of a decision alternative and a state of nature

Opportunity Loss

The difference between what a decision-maker could have made had he /she known the state of nature and what he /she actually made is referred to as regret or *opportunity loss*.

> *Opportunity loss*: The difference between the payoff a decision-maker receives for a chosen action and the maximum that the decision-maker could have received for choosing the action yielding the highest payoff for the state of nature that occurred.

A payoff table is easily converted to an opportunity loss table by finding the maximum payoff for each state of nature and subtracting all other entries in the column from the maximum value. In the oil drilling problem if the state of nature is to strike oil, the opportunity loss for selecting the event "do not invest" is $1,000,000, found by $1,000,000 (the optimum event) minus 0 (the payoff for selecting the course of action "do not invest").

The following table is an opportunity loss table for the oil well problem.

Opportunity Loss Table		
	State of Nature	
Event	Strike Oil	Does Not Strike Oil
Invest in oil well	0	$100,000
Do not invest in oil well	$1,000,000	0

In an opportunity loss table values cannot be negative.

The calculations for expected opportunity loss are summarized in text formula [20-2].

| Expected Opportunity Loss | $EOL(A_i) = \sum \left[P(S_j) \times R(A_i, S_j) \right]$ | [20 – 2] |

where:

$EOL(A_i)$ is the expected opportunity loss for a particular decision alternative.

$P(S_j)$ is the probability associated with the states of nature j.

$R(A_i, S_j)$ refers to the regret or loss for a particular combination of a state of nature and a decision alternative.

Evaluating Courses of action

Under conditions of uncertainty the various courses of action can be compared if the probability of the various states of nature can be estimated. These estimates may be obtained from an analysis of historical data, or on the basis of subjective estimates. Suppose geological studies indicated the probability of striking oil was 0.05, and the probability of not striking oil was 0.95. That is $P(S_1) = 0.05$ and $P(S_2) = 0.95$.

The expected payoff called the EMV for the act of investing can be obtained as follows:

State of Nature	Payoff	Probability of State of Nature	Expected Value
Strike oil S_1	$1,000,000	0.05	$50,000
Do not strike oil S_2	-$100,000	0.95	-$95,000
			-$45,000

The expected payoff is the probability of each state of nature times the payoff for the particular combination of acts and state of nature. In the previous examples the expected payoff is -$45,000, a loss of $45,000 for the act of investing. The expected payoff for the act of investing is compared with that of not investing.

State of Nature	Payoff	Probability of State of Nature	Expected Value
Strike oil S_1	0	0.05	$0
Do not strike oil S_2	0	0.95	0
			0

The expected payoff for not investing is $0. Using the expected value of the various outcomes as the decision criterion, the decision rule would be to select the largest expected value. If you were the investor, would you rather lose $45,000 or lose $0. Undoubtedly you would select to lose $0.

Value of Perfect Information

The concept of **perfect information** refers to the value of knowing with certainty, which state of nature will occur. In the oil well problem, the investor would know beforehand which state of nature would happen, that is whether the oil well is dry or not. What is this advance information worth? The dollar value of this information is called the *expected value of perfect information* written EVPI.

> *Expected value of perfect information.* (EVPI) is calculated by determining the difference between the maximum payoff under conditions of certainty and the maximum payoff under uncertainty.

It may be thought of as the cost of uncertainty. In general, the expected value of perfect information is computed using text formula [20-3].

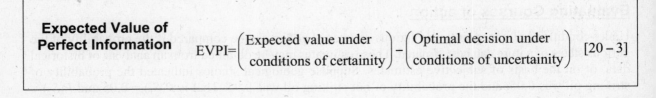

$$\text{EVPI} = \begin{pmatrix} \text{Expected value under} \\ \text{conditions of certainty} \end{pmatrix} - \begin{pmatrix} \text{Optimal decision under} \\ \text{conditions of uncertainty} \end{pmatrix} \quad [20-3]$$

Expected Value of Perfect Information

GLOSSARY

Acts: Two or more possible actions available to the decision-maker.

Expected value of perfect information: EVPI is calculated by determining the difference between the maximum payoff under conditions of certainty and the maximum payoff under uncertainty.

Opportunity loss: The difference between the payoff a decision-maker receives for a chosen action and the maximum that the decision-maker could have received for choosing the action yielding the highest payoff for the state of nature that occurred.

Payoff: The result of a particular combination of an act and a state of nature.

State of nature: The unknown future event. The state of nature is not under the control of the decision-maker.

CHAPTER PROBLEMS

Problem 1

Jan's Bake Shop is a small bakery that specializes in coffee cakes. These cakes are baked early each morning for sale that day. Any cakes not sold the same day they are baked must be discarded. Jan knows, from her records, that she can always sell between 11 and 14 cakes, but she would like to know how many to bake each day to maximize her profit. From the last

Number of Cakes Sold	Days	Probability
11	10	0.20
12	25	0.50
13	10	0.20
14	5	0.10
	50	1.00

50 business days she is able to develop the following probability distribution. The table shows that 11 cakes were sold on 10 days or 20% of the days. Also, 12 cakes were sold on 25 days, or 50% of the days, etc. Suppose each cake is sold for $10.00, and the cost to bake plus the ingredients and labor is $6.00.

a.   Develop a payoff table.

b.   Using the expected monetary value criterion make a recommendation as to the number of cakes to bake.

c.   What is the value of perfect information?

Solution 1

a.   The first step is to develop a payoff table. There are four acts, or alternative decisions, open to Jan. She can bake 11, 12, 13 or 14 cakes each day. There are also four states of nature, and one of these will happen each day. The four states of nature are that 11, 12, 13, or 14 cakes are demanded.

The payoff for the act of baking 11 cakes and the state of nature of 11 cakes being demanded is a payoff of $44, found by:

$$(\text{number sold} \times \text{selling price}) - (\text{number baked} \times \text{cost}) = (11 \times \$10) - (11 \times \$6) = \$44$$

So the entry in the first row and the first column is $44. What is the profit if the demand is 14 cakes but only 11 are baked? Only 11 cakes were baked and hence only 11 can be sold. So the profit (payoff) is $44, found by 11 × $4. How about the payoff for baking 14 cakes and a demand of 11? Note that in this case Jan has 3 unsold cakes at a value of 3 × $6 = $18, which

State of Nature (Demand)				
Act	S_1	S_2	S_3	S_4
Cakes Baked	11	12	13	14
11 A_1	$	$	$44	$
12 A_2	8	8	48	8
13 A_3	3	2	52	3
14 A_4	0	0	46	6

must be deducted from the total amount sold. The same equation is used to determine the payoff:

$$(\text{number sold} \times \text{selling price}) - (\text{number baked} \times \text{cost}) = (11 \times \$10) - (14 \times \$6) = \$26$$

The other entries in the payoff table are developed similarly.

The expected payoff or expected monetary value, written EMV (A_i) for each act (alternative course of action) is computed using the historical sales. For the act of baking 14 cakes, the expected payoff is $38, as shown.

State of Nature Demand	Payoff $V(A_4, S_j)$	Probability $P(S_j)$	Expected Value
11 cakes S_1	$26	0.20	$5.20
12 cakes S_2	36	0.50	18.00
13 cakes S_3	46	0.20	9.20
14 cakes S_4	56	0.10	5.60
		EMV(A_4)→	$38.00

These calculations are summarized as follows:

$$EMV(A_i) = \Sigma P(S_j) \cdot V(A_i, S_j) \qquad [20-1]$$

Where:

$EMV(A_i)$ refers to the expected monetary value of decision alternatives. There may be several decision possibilities. We will let 1 stand for the first alternative, 2 for the second, and so on. The lowercase letter i represents the range of decision alternatives.

$P(S_j)$ refers to the probability of the states of nature. There can be an unlimited number, so we'll let j represent the possible outcomes.

$V(A_i, S_j)$ refers to the value of the payoffs. Note that each payoff is the result of a combination of a decision alternative and a state of nature.

The $EMV(A_4)$, the expected monetary value for the decision alternative of baking 14 cakes is computed using formula [20-1].

$$EMV(A_4) = P(S_1) \cdot V(A_4 S_1) + P(S_2) \cdot V(A_4 S_2) + P(S_3) \cdot V(A_4 S_3) + P(S_4) \cdot V(A_4 S_4)$$

$$= 0.20(\$26.00) + 0.50(\$36.00) + 0.20(\$46.00) + 0.10(\$56.00)$$

$$= \$5.20 + \$18.00 + \$9.20 + \$5.60$$

$$= \$38.00$$

The expected payoffs for all four acts are shown at the right.

EMV(A_i)	Number of Cakes	Expected Payoff
1	11	$44.00
2	12	46.00
3	13	43.00
4	14	38.00

b. The act of baking 12 cakes has the largest expected profit of $46.00. In the long run, if Jan baked 12 cakes each day her profit would be the largest. We recommend that Jan bake 12 cakes.

c. Suppose an old prospector came by the bakery and said he could predict, without error, the demand (state of nature) for the day. This information would be available before she started to bake the cakes. How much should Jan be willing to pay him for the information? In essence, the old prospector is removing the uncertainty from the decision making process. The expected payoff under conditions of certainty, written in EVPI, is computed as follows:

Column 1	Column 2	Column 3	Column 4
State of Nature Demand	Payoff $V(A^*, S_j)$	Probability $P(S_j)$	Payoff $P(S_j) V(A^*, S_j)$
11 cakes	44	0.20	$8.80
12 cakes	48	0.50	24.00
13 cakes	52	0.20	10.40
14 cakes	56	0.10	5.60
			$48.80

The symbol $V(A^*, S_j)$ refers to the best alternative for a given state of nature.

If the prospector said the demand today will be 12, Jan would bake 12 cakes because that will maximize her profit. This will occur 50 percent of the time, which is obtained from Column 3 of the probability distribution. If Jan always knew her demand, she could make $48.80 per day. Using the expected value criterion she can make $46 per day.

The value of perfect information EVPI is $2.80, found by $48.80 – $46.00. Jan should be willing to pay up to $2.80 to remove the uncertainty from her decision making process.

Exercise 20.1

Check your answers against those in the ANSWER section.

A bank is trying to decide whether to make a one-year loan of $100,000 to Sharkey Chevy. Past experience has shown that one of three outcomes will occur if the loan is made:

1. The loan is repaid plus the 10 percent interest without a problem.

2. The customer, Sharkey Chevy in this case, has difficulty paying the loan. However, the bank is finally repaid with 10 percent interest, but collection fees cost the bank $2,000.

3. The customer goes bankrupt and the bank only collects 70 percent of the amount loaned.

If the bank does not make the loan it can make eight percent interest for the year elsewhere. Historical records reveal the following probabilities for the various states of nature.

States of Nature	Probability
Repaid	0.85
Repaid with difficulty	0.10
Bankrupt	0.05
	1.00

a. Develop a payoff table.

b. Determine the optimum act using the expected monetary value criterion.

c. Compute the value of perfect information

Problem 2

Using the data from Jan's Bake Shop in Problem 1, develop an opportunity loss table and compute the expected opportunity loss.

Solution 2

A loss table is generated from a payoff table. Recall the payoff table for this problem was part of Problem 1. The opportunity loss is the difference between what could have been made had the decision-maker known the state of nature and thus selected the maximum payoff, the payoff for the other acts. For Jan's Cake Shop, had she known the state of nature was that 11 cakes would be sold, designated S_1, she would have obviously selected to bake 11 cakes. Hence, $44 – $44 = $0, so the opportunity loss would have been $0. Had the state of nature been 11 and Jan decided to bake 12 cakes, the opportunity loss would be $6, found by $44 – $38.

If the demand been 13 cakes, but Jan decided to bake 11 cakes, the opportunity loss would be $8, found by $52 – $44. The full table is shown at the right.

The expected opportunity loss is determined in the same way as expected payoff. For example, the expected opportunity loss for the act of baking 13 cakes is computed as follows:

Opportunity Loss Table State of Nature (demand)			
Act	11	12	13	14
11	$0	$4	$8	$12
12	6	0	4	8
13	12	6	0	4
14	18	12	6	0

Opportunity Loss For Baking 13 Cakes			
State of Nature	Opportunity Loss	Probability of State of Nature	Expected Opportunity Loss
11 Cakes baked	$12	0.20	$2.40
12 Cakes baked	6	0.50	3.00
13 Cakes baked	0	0.20	0.00
14 Cakes baked	4	0.10	0.40
			$5.80

The calculations are summarized as follows:

$$EOL(A_i) = \Sigma \left[P(S_j) \cdot R(A_i, S_j) \right] \qquad [20-2]$$

Where:

$EOL(A_i)$ refers to the expected opportunity loss for a particular decision alternative.

$P(S_j)$ refers to the probability associated with the various states of nature.

$R(A_i, S_j)$ refers to the regret or loss for a particular combination of a state of nature and a decision alternative.

The $EOL(A_3)$, the regret or opportunity loss for selecting the alternative of baking 13 cakes, is computed as follows using text Formula [20-2].

$$EOL(A_3) = P(S_1) \cdot R(A_2, S_1) + P(S_2) \cdot R(A_2, S_2) + P(S_3) \cdot R(A_2, S_3) + P(S_4) \cdot R(A_2, S_4)$$

$$= 0.20(\$12.00) + 0.50(\$6.00) + 0.20(\$0) + 0.10(\$4.00)$$

$$= \$5.80$$

The expected opportunity loss is the smallest for the act of baking 12 cakes. In fact, it is exactly the same as the value of perfect information. The expected opportunity loss measures the uncertainty in the decision-making process.

Expected Opportunity Loss	
Act	Expected Opportunity Loss
11 cakes baked	$4.80
12 cakes baked	2.80
13 cakes baked	5.80
14 cakes baked	10.80

Exercise 20.2

Check your answers against those in the ANSWER section.

Using the bank loan problem in Exercise 1, develop an opportunity loss table and compute the expected opportunity loss for each decision alternative.

CHAPTER 20 ASSIGNMENT

AN INTRODUCTION TO DECISION THEORY

Name _____   Section _____   Score _____

Part I   Select the correct answer and write the appropriate letter in the space provided.

_____1.   In decision theory there is uncertainty regarding
  a.   course of action.
  b.   payoffs.
  c.   states of nature.
  d.   the value of perfect information.

_____2.   The term "decision theory" refers to
  a.   classical hypothesis testing.
  b.   subjective probability.
  c.   the alternate hypothesis.
  d.   two or more decision alternatives.

_____3.   The unknown future outcomes are called
  a.   courses of action.
  b.   states of nature.
  c.   the opportunity loss.
  d.   the value of perfect information.

_____4.   For each combination of course of action and state of nature there is
  a.   a payoff.
  b.   an expected value of perfect information.
  c.   an expected value.
  d.   none of the above.

_____5.   The expected value of perfect information and the expected opportunity loss
  a.   are always equal.
  b.   have no relationship with each other.
  c.   have the same standard deviation
  d.   equal the particular state of nature

_____6.   Two or more courses of action available to the decision-maker are called
  a.   states of nature.
  b.   decision alternatives or acts.
  c.   the expected value.
  d.   none of the above.

_____7.   The difference between the optimum decision and any other decision is called
  a.   an expected value.
  b.   a payoff.
  c.   an opportunity loss.
  d.   the expected value of perfect information.

_____8. A decision-maker does not have control over
   a. the payoff table.
   b. the decision alternatives.
   c. the states of nature.
   d. the opportunity loss table.

_____9. An opportunity loss table reports the amount of opportunity loss for each state of nature and
   a. course of action.
   b. payoff.
   c. expected value.
   d. expected value of perfect information.

_____10. When all the facts are known in a decision situation, it can be said that the decision was made under
   a. uncertainty.
   b. certainty.
   c. opportunity.
   d. subjectivity.

Part II Record your answer in the space provided. Show all essential work.

11. Ralph Higgins, the owner of the Spaghetti House, is considering expansion. He owns the land nearby and could build his own building on that land. If he decides to build the new building and the economy improves, he estimates that his first year profits will be $100,000. If he builds his own building and there is a recession, he will lose $40,000. He could expand the current restaurant. If he selects this alternative, he estimates he will make an additional $25,000 if the economy improves, and lose $5,000 if there is a recession. He could also do nothing, in which case there is no additional profit or loss. The probability the economy will improve is 0.25, and the probability of a recession is 0.75.

   a. Develop a payoff table for the various acts and states of nature.

	States of Nature	
Acts	**Economy improves**	**Recession**
Build new		
Expand		
Do nothing		

b. Compute the expected payoff for each alternative.

b. A_1

b. A_2

b. A_3

c. Determine the expected value of perfect information.

c.

d. Convert the payoff to an opportunity loss table.

Acts	States of Nature	
	Economy improves	Recession
Build new		
Expand		
Do nothing		

e. What course of action would you recommend?

_____

_____

_____

_____

12. *SkyBlue*, a no-frills airline, is trying to decide whether it should replace 10 of its older commercial jets with new, fuel efficient jetliners. The unit cost of the new jetliner is $140 million. However, *SkyBlue* estimates that over the next ten years it will save $300 million in fuel costs per jetliner if the price of jet fuel increases, $180 million per jetliner if the cost of jet fuel remains the same, and $90 million per jetliner if the cost of jet fuel decreases. *SkyBlue* could also choose to retrofit the engines on the 10 older jets with newer, more fuel efficient engines at a cost of $52 million per jet. Over the next ten years the retrofit is estimated to save $150 million per aircraft in fuel costs if the price of jet fuel increases, $100 million if it stays the same, and $45 million if the cost of jet fuel decreases. Suppose that experts have assessed the following probabilities that jet fuel will increase, stay the same, or decrease: P(increase) = .6, P(same) = .3, P(decrease) = .1. Assume that *SkyBlue* is using a ten-year time horizon to evaluate the alternatives.

a. Develop a payoff table for net savings for the various acts and states of nature.

Acts	States of Nature		
	Fuel Price Increases	Fuel Price Stays the Same	Fuel Price Decreases
No change			
Buy New			
Retrofit			

b. Compute the expected payoff for each alternative.

b. A_1

b. A_2

b. A_3

c. Determine the expected value of perfect information.

c.

d. What course of action would you recommend?

_____

_____

_____

_____

CHAPTER 2

DESCRIBING DATA: FREQUENCY DISTRIBUTIONS AND GRAPHIC PRESENTATION

Exercise 2.1

a. Frequency bar chart for type of car rented.

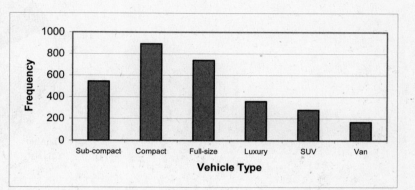

Relative frequency bar chart for type of car rented.

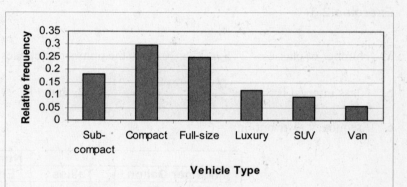

b. Pie chart for type of car rented
.

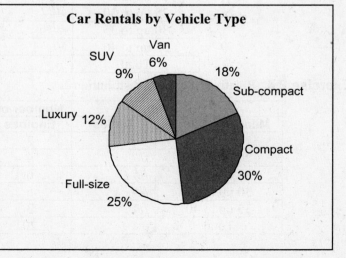

c. Number of luxury cars expected to be rented next summer = 1.20 x 360 = 432

Exercise 2.2

Pie chart for new cars sold

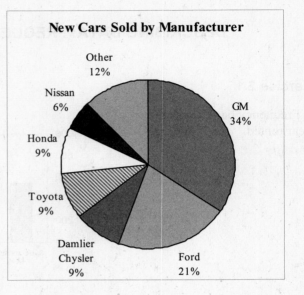

New Cars Sold by Manufacturer

Other 12%
Nissan 6%
Honda 9%
Toyota 9%
Damlier Chysler 9%
Ford 21%
GM 34%

Exercise 2.3

a. Number of classes: $2^k \geq n$, $2^5 \geq 20$, thus the number of classes is 5.

b. Class interval is 5: $i \geq \dfrac{H - L}{k}$, $\dfrac{39 - 18}{5} = \dfrac{21}{5} = 4.2$, thus i is > 4.2 (round up to 5)

c. Frequency distribution:

Miles per Gallon	Tallies	Number of Engines
15 up to 20	//	2
20 up to 25	////	4
25 up to 30	//// /	6
30 up to 35	////	5
35 up to 40	///	3
Total		20

Exercise 2.4 Relative frequency distribution

Miles per Gallon	Tallies	Number of Engines	Relative Frequency	Found By
15 up to 20	//	2	10%	2/20
20 up to 25	////	4	20%	4/20
25 up to 30	//// /	6	30%	6/20
30 up to 35	////	5	25%	5/20
35 up to 40	///	3	15%	3/20
Total		20	100%	

Exercise 2.5

Histogram

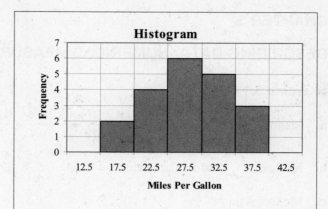

Exercise 2.6

Frequency polygon

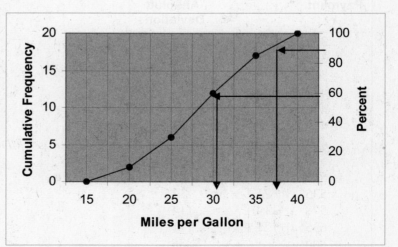

Exercise 2.7

a. Cumulative Frequency Polygon

MPG	Number	Cumulative Total
15<20	2	2
20<25	4	6
25<30	6	12
30<35	5	17
35<40	3	20

b. 60% of the automobiles are getting less than 30 miles per gallon .

c. 95% of the automobiles are getting about 37.5 miles per gallon or less.

CHAPTER 3

DESCRIBING DATA: NUMERICAL MEASURES

Exercise 3.1

a. Mean: $\overline{X} = \dfrac{\Sigma X}{n} = \dfrac{8+5+4+10+8+3+4}{7} = \dfrac{42}{7} = 6$

b. Median = 5. Middle data value. 3, 4, 4, 5, 8, 8, 10
⇑

c. Mode = 4 and 8

Exercise 3.2

Geometric mean:

$$GM = \sqrt[15]{\dfrac{2850}{475}} - 1 = (\sqrt[15]{6} - 1) = (1.1268776 - 1) = 0.1268776 = 12.7\%$$

Exercise 3.3

a. Range: Range = Highest Value − Lowest Value = $($595 − 295) = \$300$

This indicates that there is a difference of $300 between the largest and the smallest monthly rent.

b. The mean deviation:

Payment X	$\lvert X - \overline{X} \rvert$		Absolute Deviations
335	| −129 |	=	129
373	| −91 |	=	91
385	| −79 |	=	79
410	| −54 |	=	54
410	| −54 |	=	54
430	| −34 |	=	34
462	| −2 |	=	2
500	| +36 |	=	36
515	| +51 |	=	51
535	| +71 |	=	71
578	|+114 |	=	114
635	|+171 |	=	171
5,568			\$886

$\overline{X} = \dfrac{\Sigma X}{n} = \dfrac{\$5,568}{12} = \$464$

$MD = \dfrac{\Sigma \lvert X - \overline{X} \rvert}{n} = \dfrac{\$886}{12} = \$74$

The mean deviation of $74 indicates that the typical monthly rent deviates $74 from the mean of $464.

Exercise 3.4

Frequency distribution:

Mean:

$$\overline{X} = \frac{\sum fX}{n} = \frac{\$717}{50} = \$14.34$$

Wage Rate	Frequency f	Class Midpoint X	fX
$6 up to $9	2	$7.50	$15.00
$9 up to $12	8	10.50	84.00
$12 up to $15	20	13.50	270.00
$15 up to $18	14	16.50	231.00
$18 up to $21	6	19.50	117.00
Total	50		$717.00

Exercise 3.5

Weighted mean:

$$\overline{X} = \frac{w_1X_1 + w_2X_2 + w_3X_3 + w_4X_4}{w_1 + w_2 + w_{31} + w_4}$$

$$= \frac{31(\$30) + 42(\$10) + 47(\$20) + 63(\$24)}{31 + 42 + 47 + 63} = \frac{\$3802}{183} = \$20.78$$

Exercise 3.6

a. Range = $27 - $10 = $17

b. Mean $= \overline{X} = \frac{\sum X}{n} = \frac{80}{5} = \$16$

c. Variance

$$s^2 = \frac{\sum(X - \overline{X})^2}{n-1} = \frac{174}{5-1} = \frac{174}{4} = 43.5$$

d. Standard deviation $s = \sqrt{43.5} = 6.595 = \$6.60$

X	$(X - \overline{X})$			$(X - \overline{X})^2$
10	10 – 16	=	–6	36
12	12 – 16	=	–4	16
15	15 – 16	=	–1	1
16	16 – 16	=	0	0
27	27 – 16	=	11	121
80				174

Exercise 3.7

Age to the Nearest Month	f	Midpoint M	fM	Midpoint – Mean	$(M - \overline{X})$	$(M - \overline{X})^2$	$f(M - \overline{X})^2$
100 up to 150	5	125	625	125– 240 =	–115	13,225	66,125
150 up to 200	9	175	1575	175– 240 =	–65	4,225	38,025
200 up to 250	20	225	4500	225 – 240 =	–15	225	4500
250 up to 300	18	275	4950	275 – 240 =	35	1,225	22,050
300 up to 350	5	325	1625	325 – 240 =	85	7,225	36,125
350 up to 400	3	375	1125	375–240 =	135	18,225	54,675
Σ	60		14,400		0		221,500

Step 1: Find the midpoint M of each class.

For the first class it is: $M = \frac{100 + 150}{2} = \frac{250}{2} = 125$

Step 2: Multiply the frequency f by the midpoint M for each class.

For the first class it is: $fM = 5 \times 125 = 625$

Step 3: Find the sum of the fM column. $\Sigma f M = 14,400$

Step 4: Find the mean using formula [3-12] $\overline{X} = \dfrac{\Sigma f M}{n} = \dfrac{14,400}{60} = 240$

To find the standard deviation:

Step 1: Subtract the mean $\overline{X}$ from the midpoint M of each class. That is find: $(M - \overline{X})$.

For the first class it is: $(M - \overline{X}) = 125 - 240 = -115$

Step 2: Square the difference between the class midpoint and the mean. That is find: $(M - \overline{X})^2$

For the first class it is: $(M - \overline{X})^2 = (-115)^2 = 13,225$

Step 3: Multiply the squared difference between the class midpoint and the mean by the class frequency. That is find: $f(M - \overline{X})^2$

For the first class it is: $f(M - \overline{X})^2 = 5(13,225) = 66,125$

Step 4: Find the sum of the $f(M - \overline{X})^2$ column. $\Sigma f(M - \overline{X})^2 = 221,500$

Step 5: Find the standard deviation using formula [3-13]

$$s = \sqrt{\dfrac{\Sigma f(M - \overline{X})^2}{n-1}} = \sqrt{\dfrac{221,500}{60-1}} = \sqrt{\dfrac{221,500}{59}} = \sqrt{3,754.23728} = 61.27183 = 61.27$$

Note that the variance is $s^2 = 3754.23728$

Exercise 3.8

a. Percent:
$$k = \dfrac{X - \overline{X}}{s} = \dfrac{\$885 - \$990}{\$70} = -1.5$$
$$k = \dfrac{X - \overline{X}}{s} = \dfrac{\$1095 - \$990}{\$70} = 1.5$$

Applying Chebyshev's Theorem: $1 - \dfrac{1}{k^2} = (1 - \dfrac{1}{1.5^2}) = (1 - \dfrac{1}{2.25}) = (1 - 0.4444) = 0.5556 = 55.6\%$

This means that at least 56% of the salespersons earn between $885 and $1095 in commission.

b. Positive skewness since the mean 990 is larger than the median 950.

Chapter 4

DESCRIBING DATA: DISPLAYING AND EXPLORING DATA

Exercise 4.1

a. Sort

18	20	21	22	22	24	25	25	25	26	26	28	28	28	29	30	35	35	35	37

b. Dot plot.

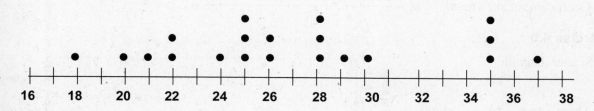

Exercise 4.2

Stem and leaf chart

Exercise 4.3

The data is first put into an ordered array.

Stem	Leaf
1	89
2	0013577899
3	00022679

25	28	39	50	61	65	81	82	85	85	85	86	90	92	120	137	140	142	148

a. First Quartile: Let $P = 25$ and

$$L_p = (n+1)\frac{P}{100} = (19+1)\frac{25}{100} = 5$$

Then locate the 5th observation in the array, which is 61. Thus $Q_1 = 61$ or $61,000.

b. Third quartile: Let $P = 75$ and

$$L_p = (n+1)\frac{P}{100} = (19+1)\frac{75}{100} = 15$$

Then locate the 15th observation in the array, which is 120. Thus $Q_3 = 120$ or $120,000.

c. The median: Let $P = 50$ and

$$L_p = (n+1)\frac{P}{100} = (19+1)\frac{50}{100} = 10$$

Then locate the 10th observation in the array, which is 85. Thus $Q_2 =$ the median $= 85$ or

$85,000.

d. Box plot: The five essential pieces of data are:

Minimum value $= 25$, $Q_1 = 61$, $Q_2 = 85$, $Q_3 = 120$,   Maximum value $= 148$

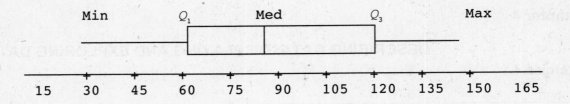

15 30 45 60 75 90 105 120 135 150 165

Exercise 4.4

a. Positive skewness, since the mean 1385 is larger than the median 1330.

b. Coefficient of skewness: $sk = \dfrac{3(\overline{X} - \text{median})}{s} = \dfrac{3(1385 - 1330)}{75} = 2.2$

Exercise 4.5

a. Scatter diagram:

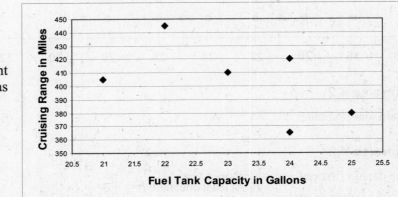

b. There may be a slight decline in cruising range as tank capacity increases.

Exercise 4.6

a. Percent males working at home $= \dfrac{8}{20} = 0.40 = 40\%$

b. Percent males working at office $= \dfrac{12}{20} = 0.60 = 60\%$

c. Percent employees working at office $= \dfrac{18}{40} = 0.45 = 45\%$

CHAPTER 5

A SURVEY OF PROBABILITY CONCEPTS

Exercise 5.1

a. Visits twice a year: $\dfrac{90}{300} = 0.30$ b. Visits: $\dfrac{60}{300} + \dfrac{90}{300} + \dfrac{120}{300} = \dfrac{270}{300} = 0.90$

Exercise 5.2
Proportion of students: $0.60 + 0.20 - 0.12 = 0.68$

Exercise 5.3

a. All three: $P(3) = (0.10)(0.10)(0.10) = 0.001$

b. None: $P(\text{none}) = (0.90)(0.90)(0.90) = 0.729$

c. At least one: $1 - P(\text{none}) = (1 - 0.729) = 0.271$

Exercise 5.4

a. Both female: $P(\text{both female}) = \dfrac{6}{10} \times \dfrac{5}{9} = 0.33$

b. At least one male: $P(\text{At least one male}) = \left(\dfrac{4}{10} \times \dfrac{3}{9}\right) + \left(\dfrac{4}{10} \times \dfrac{6}{9}\right) + \left(\dfrac{6}{10} \times \dfrac{4}{9}\right) = 0.67$

$\qquad\qquad\qquad\qquad\qquad m \quad m \qquad m \quad f \qquad f \quad m$

Exercise 5.5

a. Had Heart attack or is heavy smoker:

$P(\text{Heart attack or heavy smoker}) = \dfrac{180}{500} + \dfrac{125}{500} - \dfrac{90}{500} = \dfrac{215}{500} = 0.43$

b. Heavy Smoker and no heart attack: $P(\text{Heavy smoker and no heart attack}) = \dfrac{35}{500} = 0.07$

Exercise 5.6

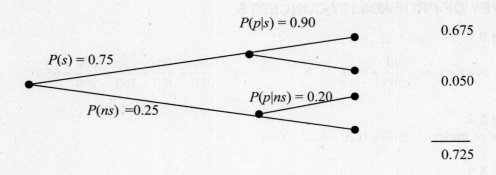

$$P(s|p) = \frac{0.75 \times 0.90}{(0.75)(0.90) + (0.25)(0.20)} = \frac{0.675}{0.725} = 0.931$$

Exercise 5.7

Number of different flights: $5 \times 10 = 50$

Exercise 5.8

Number of different ways: $_nP_r = \dfrac{n!}{(n-r)!} = \dfrac{9!}{(9-3)!} = \dfrac{9!}{6!} = \dfrac{9 \times 8 \times 7 \times 6!}{6!} = 9 \times 8 \times 7 = 504$

Exercise 5.9

Number of different trip combinations: $_nC_r = \dfrac{n!}{r!(n-r)!} = \dfrac{8!}{5!3!} = \dfrac{8 \times 7 \times 6 \times 5!}{5! \times 3 \times 2} = \dfrac{8 \times 7 \times 6}{3 \times 2} = 56$

CHAPTER 6

DISCRETE PROBABILITY DISTRIBUTIONS

Exercise 6.1

Number of Accidents per Month X	Probability P(X)	XP(X)	(X - μ)	(X - μ)² P(X)
0	0.60	0	0 – 0.5	(0.25)(0.6) = 0.150
1	0.30	0.3	1 – 0.5	(0.25)(0.3) = 0.075
2	0.10	0.2	2 – 0.5	(2.25)(0.1) = 0.225
Σ	1.00	0.5		Σ = 0.450

a. Mean: $\mu = \sum[xP(x)] = 0.5$ **b.**   Variance:

$\sigma^2 = \sum[(x - \mu)^2 P(x)] = 0.45$

Exercise 6.2

a. Rules of probability: R,R,NR $(0.60)(0.60)(0.40)$ $=$ 0.144

R,NR,R $(0.60)(0.40)(0.60)$ $=$ 0.144

b. NR,R,R $(0.40)(0.60)(0.60)$ $=$ $\underline{0.144}$

Σ $=$ 0.432

$$P(x) = \frac{n!}{x!(n-x)!}(\pi)^x(1-\pi)^{n-x} = \frac{3!}{2!(3-2)!}(0.60)^2(0.40)^1 = 0.432$$

Exercise 6.3

Use Appendix B.9 and $n = 12$

a. $P(0) = 0.014$ **b.** $P(x \geq 5) = 0.158 + 0.079 + 0.029 + 0.008 + 0.001 + 0 + 0 + 0 = 0.275$

c. $P(2 \leq x \leq 4) = 0.168 + 0.240 + 0.231 = 0.639$

Exercise 6.4

a. $\mu = n\pi = 12 \times 0.30 = 3.6$ **b.** $\sigma^2 = n\pi(1-\pi) = 12 \times 0.30 \times (1-0.30) = 2.52$

Exercise 6.5

$\mu = np = (1000)(0.002) = 2.00$ and Appendix B.5, $\mu = 2$ and $x = 0$

a. $P(0) = 0.1353$ or by formula $P(x) = \dfrac{u^x e^{-u}}{x!} = \dfrac{2^0 e^{-2}}{0!} = e^{-2} = 0.1353$

b. $P(x \geq 2) = \{1 - [P(0) + P(1)]\} = \{1 - [0.1353 + 0.2707]\} = \{1 - 0.406\} = 0.594$

Exercise 6.6

$$P(x) = \frac{u^x e^{-u}}{x!} = \frac{10^8 e^{-10}}{8!} = 0.1126$$

Exercise 6.7

Two are defective: $N = 30, \; S = 5, \; n = 4, \; x = 2$

$$P(x) = \frac{\left(_S C_x\right)\left(_{N-S} C_{n-x}\right)}{\left(_N C_n\right)} = \frac{\left(_5 C_2\right)\left(_{30-5} C_{4-2}\right)}{\left(_{30} C_4\right)} = \frac{\dfrac{5!}{2!3!} \times \dfrac{25!}{2!23!}}{\dfrac{30!}{4!26!}} = 0.109$$

CHAPTER 7

CONTINUOUS PROBABILITY DISTRIBUTION

Exercise 7.1

a. Determine the height using Formula [7 – 3]

$$P(x) = \frac{1}{(b-a)} = \frac{1}{(3-0)} = \frac{1}{3} = 0.333$$

The uniform distribution is shown.

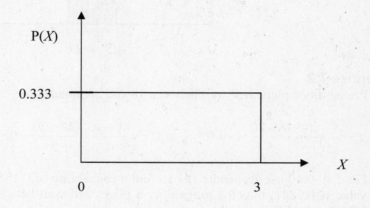

b. The mean represents the typical wait time. To determine the mean use Formula [7–1].

$$\mu = \frac{a+b}{2} = \frac{0+3}{2} = \frac{3}{2} = 1.5$$

c. To determine the standard deviation use Formula [7–2].

$$\sigma = \sqrt{\frac{(b-a)^2}{12}} = \sqrt{\frac{(3-0)^2}{12}} = \sqrt{\frac{(3)^2}{12}} = \sqrt{0.75} = 0.866$$

d. The probability a particular customer will wait less than 1 minutes is found by finding the area of the rectangle with a height of 0..333 and a base of (1 – 0).

$$P(0 < wait\ time < 1) = Height \times Base = \frac{1}{(3-0)} \times (1-0) = 0.333 \times 1 = 0.333$$

e. The probability a particular customer will wait between 1.5 and 2 minutes is found by finding the area of the rectangle with a height of 0.333 and a base of (2 – 1.5).

$$P(1.5 < wait\ time < 2) = Height \times Base = 0.333 \times (2-1.5) = 0.333 \times 0.5 = 0.1665$$

This probability is illustrated by the following graph.

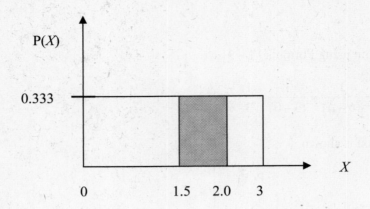

Exercise 7.2

a. Probability a plane will wait between 18 and 24 minutes:

$$z = \frac{X - \mu}{\sigma} = \frac{18 - 20}{5} = -0.40 \qquad z = \frac{X - \mu}{\sigma} = \frac{24 - 20}{5} = 0.80$$

For $z = -0.40$ use Appendix B.1 to find a probability of 0.1554. For $z = 0.80$ the Appendix B.1 value is 0.2881; thus the probability a plane will wait between 18 and 24 minutes is 0.1554 + 0.2881 = 0.4435

b. Probability a bottle will contain between 22.00 and 30.0 minutes:

$$z = \frac{22 - 20}{5} = 0.40 \quad z = \frac{30 - 20}{5} = 2.00 \qquad \text{Appendix B.1 values are 0.1554 and 0.4772}$$

Subtract 0.1554 from 0.4772 to obtain 0.3218. The probability that a plane will wait between 22 and 30 minutes is 0.3218.

c. Probability a plane will wait more than 12 minutes. $\quad z = \frac{12 - 20}{5} = -1.60$

Appendix B.1 value is 0.4452, thus (0.4452+0.5000 = 0.9452). The probability a plane will wait more than 12 minutes is 0.9452.

d. The waiting time such that only 5% of planes wait this long or longer. First subtract 0.05 from 0.50 = 0.45, then find the z value such that 0.4500 of the area is between 0 and z. That value is $z = 1.645$. Then solve for .

$$z = \frac{X - \mu}{\sigma} \qquad 1.645 = \frac{X - 20}{5} \qquad X = 1.645 \times 5 + 20 = 28.225$$

Thus the largest 5% of planes wait 28.225 minutes or more.

Exercise 7.3

The probability that more than 265 will be relieved:

$$\mu = 300 \times 0.90 = 270$$

$$\sigma = \sqrt{300(0.90)(0.10)} = \sqrt{27} = 5.20$$

$$z = \frac{265.5 - 270}{5.20} = -0.87$$

$$P(X > 265.5) = 0.3078 + 0.5000 = 0.8078$$

CHAPTER 8

SAMPLING METHODS AND THE CENTRAL LIMIT THEOREM

Exercise 8-1

a. Start with row six and column six and use the first two digits .The number is 84822. The column is repeated below with the selected numbers in bold, italics and underlined:
84, 65,32, 23, 36,66, *__17,__ __16,__* 72,77,*__05__*, 27, 35, 33, 21, 51, 28, 72, 71, 90, 69, *__00, 18.__*
We select advertiser number *00, 05, 16, 17, 18.*

b. Starting at the bottom right corner of the table. The number is 70603. The column is repeated below starting with 03 and working up with the selected numbers in bold italics and underlined:
__03,__ 89, 95, *__10,__* 43, *__00, 09,__* 26, 98, 87, 48, 49, *__18.__* We select advertisers: *00, 03, 09, 10, 18.*

c. Every fourth advertiser starting with 03 would be advertiser: 03, 07, 11, 15, 19.

d. In order to select a sample of four advertisers so that one of each type of advertiser is included we had to skip a selection when we had already selected an advertiser for that category. Starting at the top of column two. The number is 08182. Use the left two digits starting with 08. The numbers in the column are repeated below with the selected numbers in bold, italics and underlined:
__08,(S),__ 90, 78, 97, 00(S) Skip, *__19,(P),__* 04(S) Skip, 14(S) Skip, 57, 81, 26, 25, 67, 22, 19(P) Skip, 72, 90, 76, 36, 87, 97, 47, 25, *__15(A),__* 24, 86, 53, 73, 41, *__03 (R)__* We select advertisers *08(S), 19(P), 15(A), 03(R).*

Exercise 8.2

a. $_5C_3 = \dfrac{5!}{3!2!} = 10$

b.

Sample Number	Homes Sold	Total Homes Sold	Mean Number of Homes Sold
1	ABC	13	4.33
2	ABD	17	5.67
3	ABE	11	3.67
4	BCD	16	5.33
5	BCE	10	3.33
6	CDE	17	5.67
7	CDA	20	6.67
8	DEA	18	6.00
9	DEB	14	4.67
10	ACE	14	4.67

c.

Mean Sold	Frequency	Probability
3.33	1	0.1
3.67	1	0.1
4.33	1	0.1
4.67	2	0.2
5.33	1	0.1
5.67	2	0.2
6.00	1	0.1
6.67	1	0.1
	10	1.0

d.

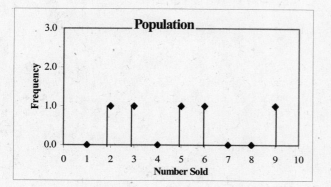

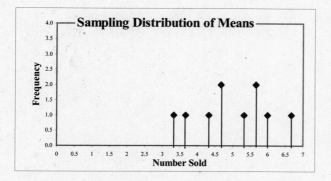

Exercise 8.3

0.7881, found by:
$$z = \frac{\overline{X} - \mu}{\sigma / \sqrt{n}} = \frac{48.45 - 48.5}{0.25 / \sqrt{16}} = \frac{-0.05}{0.0625} = -0.8$$

The probability that z is greater than -0.8 is $(0.5000 + 0.2881) = 0.7881$

Exercise 8.4

0.0023, found by:
$$z = \frac{\overline{X} - \mu}{\sigma/\sqrt{n}} = \frac{26 - 24}{5/\sqrt{50}} = \frac{2}{0.7071} = 2.83$$

Referring to Appendix B.1, the probability (area) for a z-value of 2.83 is 0.4977. The likelihood of finding a z-value greater than 2.83 is found by (0.5000 − 0.4977) = 0.0023. There is about a 0.2 % chance of finding a sample mean of 26 grams or higher from the population.

CHAPTER 9

ESTIMATION AND CONFIDENCE INTERVALS

Exercise 9.1

The z value is 2.33, found by Appendix B.1 and locating the value 0.4901 in the body of the table, and reading the corresponding row and column values.

$$\overline{X} \pm z \frac{\sigma}{\sqrt{n}} = \$150 \pm 2.33 \left(\frac{\$20}{\sqrt{36}} \right) = \$150 \pm \$7.77 = \$142.23 \, to \, \$157.77$$

Exercise 9.2

a. The sample mean is given: $\overline{X} = 5.67$. The standard deviation is given: $s = 0.57$.

b. The population mean is not known. The best estimate is the sample mean of 5.67.

c. Construct a 95 percent confidence interval for the population mean. Use formula [9-2].

$$\overline{X} \pm t \frac{s}{\sqrt{n}} = 5.67 \pm 2.262 \frac{0.57}{\sqrt{10}} = 5.67 \pm 0.408 = 5.262 \text{ and } 6.078$$

d. The t distribution is used as a part of the confidence interval because the population standard deviation is unknown.

e. It is reasonable for SkyBlue to claim that the mean flight time between New York and London is five and one half hours since 5.5 is within the 95% confidence interval.

Exercise 9.3

$$p \pm z \sqrt{\frac{p(1-p)}{n}} \left(\sqrt{\frac{N-n}{N-1}} \right) = \$150 \pm 2.33 \left(\frac{\$20}{\sqrt{36}} \right) \left(\sqrt{\frac{200-36}{200-1}} \right) = \$150 \pm \$7.05 = \$142.95 \, to \, \$157.05$$

Exercise 9.4

The z value is 1.65, found by Appendix B.1 and locating the value 0.4500 in the body of the table, and reading the corresponding row and column values. Note that 0.4500 is exactly half way between 0.4495 and 0.4505.

$$p \pm z \sqrt{\frac{p(1-p)}{n}} = 0.60 \pm 1.65 \sqrt{\frac{(0.60)(1-0.60)}{100}} = 0.60 \pm 0.08 = 0.52 \, and \, 0.68$$

Exercise 9.5

$$n = \left[\frac{zs}{E} \right]^2 = \left[\frac{(2.58)(0.25)}{0.20} \right]^2 = 10.4 = 11 \, (\text{Common practice to round up when determining sample size.})$$

Exercise 9.6

$$n = p(1-p) \left(\frac{z}{E} \right)^2 = (0.33)(1-0.33) \left(\frac{2.33}{0.04} \right)^2 = 750.2 = 751$$

CHAPTER 10

ONE-SAMPLE TESTS OF HYPOTHESES

Exercise 10.1

$H_0: \mu \leq \$30$
$H_1: \mu > \$30$

H_0 is rejected if z is greater than 1.65.

$$z = \frac{\$33 - \$30}{\$12 / \sqrt{40}} = 1.58$$

H_0 is not rejected. No increase in the mean amount spent.

p-value $= P(z > 1.58) =$
$0.5000 - 0.4429 = 0.0571$
The p-value of $0.0571 \geq 0.05$, do not reject H_0.

Exercise 10.2

Step 1: *State the null and alternate hypotheses*: The null hypothesis is that there is no change in the construction time. That is, the construction time is at least 3.5 days. The alternate hypothesis is that the construction time is less than 3.5 days. Symbolically, these statements are written as follows:

$H_0: \mu \geq 3.5$
$H_1: \mu < 3.5$

Step 2: *Select the level of significance:* It was given as 0.05.

Step 3: *Select the test statistic:* The test static is the t distribution. The distribution is said to be a normal distribution, however we do not know the value of the population standard deviation. We use text Formula [9-3]:

Thus:
$$t = \frac{\overline{X} - \mu}{s / \sqrt{n}} = \frac{3.4 - 3.5}{0.8 / \sqrt{15}} = \frac{-0.1}{0.20656} = -0.48$$

Step 4: *Develop the decision rule:* The critical values of t are given in Appendix B.2. The number of degrees of freedom is $(n - 1) = (15 - 1) = 14$. We have a one-tailed test, so we find the portion of the table labeled 'one-tailed." Locate the column for the 0.05 significance level. Read down the column until it intersects the row with 14 degrees of freedom. The value is 1.761.

Since this is a one-tailed test and the rejection region is in the left tail, the critical value is negative. The decision rule is to reject H_0 if the value of t is less than -1.761.

Step 5: *Make a decision regarding the null hypothesis, and interpret the results*: Because −0.48 lies to the right of the critical value −1.761, the null hypothesis is not rejected at the 0.05 significance level. This indicates that the use of the "precut and assembled roof trusses" does not decrease the construction time to less than 3.5 days.

Exercise 10.3

Step 1: *State the null and alternate hypotheses*: The null hypothesis is that The University of Findlay students use the computer 2.55 hours a day. The alternate hypothesis is that The University of Findlay students do not use the computer 2.55 hours a day. Symbolically, these statements are written as follows:

$$H_0 : \mu = 2.55$$
$$H_1 : \mu \neq 2.55$$

Step 2: *Select the level of significance:* We decide on the 0.05 significance level.

Step 3: *Select the test statistic:* The test static in this situation is the t distribution.

We need to calculate the mean and standard deviation of the sample. The standard deviation of the sample can be determined using either Formula [3-2] or [3-10].

X	$X - \overline{X}$	$(X - \overline{X})^2$
3.15	0.46154	0.21302
3.25	0.56154	0.31533
2.00	− 0.68846	0.47398
2.50	−0.18846	0.03552
2.65	− 0.03846	0.00148
2.75	0.06154	0.00379
2.35	− 0.33846	0.11456
2.85	0.16154	0.02610
2.95	0.26154	0.06840
2.45	− 0.23846	0.05686
1.95	− 0.73846	0.54532
2.35	− 0.33846	0.11456
3.75	1.06154	1.12687
$\sum$ 34.95	0.00000	3.09579

$$\overline{X} = \frac{\sum X}{n} = \frac{34.95}{13} = 2.68846$$

$$s = \sqrt{\frac{\Sigma(X - \overline{X})^2}{n-1}} = \sqrt{\frac{3.09579}{13-1}}$$
$$= \sqrt{0.25798} = 0.5079 = 0.51$$

The value of t is computed using Formula [10-5]:

$$t = \frac{\overline{X} - \mu}{s/\sqrt{n}} = \frac{2.69 - 2.55}{0.51/\sqrt{13}} = \frac{0.14}{0.1414} = 0.9901$$

Step 4: *Develop the decision rule:*

Remember that the significance level stated in the problem is 0.05. The critical values of t are given in Appendix B.2. The number of degrees of freedom is $(n-1) = (13-1) = 12$. We have a two-tailed test, so we find the portion of the table labeled "two-tailed." Locate the column for the 0.05 significance level. Read down the column until it intersects the row with 12 degrees of freedom. The value is 2.179.

The decision rule is: Reject the null hypothesis if the computed value of t is to the left of -2.179, or to the right of 2.179

Step 5: *Make a decision regarding the null hypothesis, and interpret the results:*

The value of t lies between the two critical values: -2.179 and 2.179. The null hypothesis is not rejected at the 0.05 significance level. We conclude the population mean hours of usage could be 2.55 hours per day. The evidence fails to show Findlay students to be different.

Exercise 10.4

$H_0 : \pi \geq 0.40 \qquad H_1 : \pi < 0.40$

The 0.10 level of significance yields a decision rule of $(0.500 - 0.100) = 0.400$ or 1.28. Thus, H_0 is rejected if z is less than -1.28.

$$z = \frac{\dfrac{60}{200} - 0.40}{\sqrt{\dfrac{(0.40)(1-0.40)}{200}}} = \frac{-0.10}{0.03464} = -2.886 = -2.89$$

Since -2.89 lies to the left of -1.28 H_0 is rejected. Less than 40% of the viewing audience watched the concert.

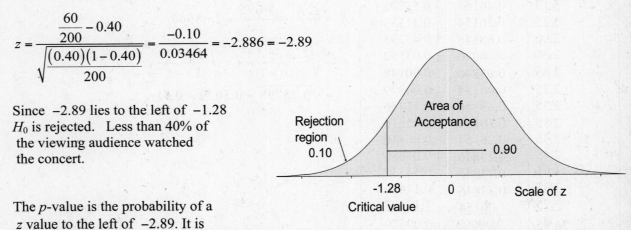

The p-value is the probability of a z value to the left of -2.89. It is $(0.5000 - 0.4981) = 0.0019$, which is less than the level of significance of 0.10; thus we reject H_0.

Exercise 10.5

We use formula [10-5] to determine the probability of a Type II error.

$$z = \frac{\bar{X}_c - \mu_1}{\sigma/\sqrt{n}} \qquad\qquad [10-5]$$

First, find the critical value of the sample mean, $\bar{X}_c$ by substituting the critical value of z, 1.65, into text formula [10-1] and solving for $\bar{X}$:

$$1.65 = \frac{\bar{X} - \mu}{\sigma/\sqrt{n}}$$

$$\bar{X}_c = \bar{X} = 1.65\left(12/\sqrt{40}\right) + 30$$

$$\bar{X}_c = 33.131.$$

Next, substitute $\bar{X}_c$ =33.131 and μ_1 = 32 into formula [10-5] and compute the z value.

$$z = \frac{\bar{X}_c - \mu_1}{\sigma/\sqrt{n}} =$$

$$\frac{33.131 - 32}{12/\sqrt{40}} = 0.596.$$

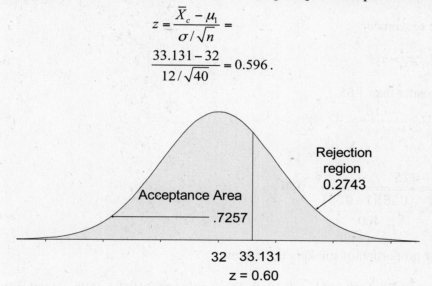

Rejection region
0.2743

Acceptance Area
.7257

32   33.131
z = 0.60

The rejection area is found by looking up a z value of 0.60 in Appendix B.1 and locating an area of 0.2257. Add 0.5000 to 0.2257 to obtain an area to the left of $\bar{X}_c$ = .7257. We accept the null hypothesis when $\bar{X}_c$ is less than or equal to 31.113. The probability of obtaining a sample mean, $\bar{X}$, of 31.113 or less when the population mean is 32 (the alternate value of the mean, μ_1) is 0.7257. Thus, the probability of a Type II error, β, when the true mean is 32 and we are testing at a significance level of 0.05 is 0.7257.

CHAPTER 11

TWO-SAMPLE TESTS OF HYPOTHESIS

Exercise 11.1

Let population 1 refer to Youngsville and population 2 refer to Claredon.

$$H_0: \mu_1 \leq \mu_2$$
$$H_1: \mu_1 > \mu_2$$

H_0 is rejected if z is greater than 1.65.

$$z = \frac{6.9 - 4.9}{\sqrt{\dfrac{(3.8)^2}{60} + \dfrac{(3.0)^2}{70}}} = 3.29$$

H_0 is rejected. It takes Youngsville longer to respond to emergency runs.

Exercise 11.2

Let population 1 refer to women.

$$H_0: \pi_1 \leq \pi_2 \qquad H_1: \pi_1 > \pi_2$$

H_0 is rejected if z is greater than 1.65.

$$\rho_c = \frac{45 + 25}{150 + 100} = 0.28$$

$$z = \frac{0.30 - 0.25}{\sqrt{\dfrac{(0.28)(1 - 0.28)}{150} + \dfrac{(0.28)(1 - 0.28)}{100}}} = 0.86$$

H_0 is not rejected. The proportion of smokers is the same.

p-value $= P(z > 0.86) = (0.5000 - 0.3051) = 0.1949$, The p-value of $0.1949 \geq 0.05$, do not reject H_0.

Exercise 11.3

Let population 1 refer to the mall and population 2 refer to downtown.

$$H_0: \mu_1 \leq \mu_2 \qquad H_1: \mu_1 > \mu_2 \qquad H_0 \text{ is rejected if } t \text{ is greater than 2.552.}$$

$$s_p^2 = \frac{(10-1)(12)^2 + (10-1)(10)^2}{10 + 10 - 2} = 122 \qquad t = \frac{40 - 36}{\sqrt{122\left(\dfrac{1}{10} + \dfrac{1}{10}\right)}} = 0.81$$

H_0 is not rejected. There is no difference in mean amount spent at the mall and downtown store. p-value is greater than 0.10.

Exercise 11.4

Let population 1 refer to Omaha and population 2 refer to Kansas City.

$H_0 : \mu_1 = \mu_2$

$H_1 : \mu_1 \neq \mu_2$

Use [11-8] to approximate $d.f.$ for t.

$$df = \frac{\left[(35,800)^2 / 88 + (29,850)^2 / 22 \right]^2}{\dfrac{\left((35,800)^2 / 88 \right)^2}{88-1} + \dfrac{\left((29,850)^2 / 65 \right)^2}{65-1}} = 148.73 \quad \text{Round } d.f. \text{ for } t \text{ down to 148.}$$

H_0 is rejected if t is greater than $+1.976$ or $t < -1.976$ (Excel used to find t).

$$t = \frac{183,900 - 178,500}{\sqrt{\dfrac{(35,800)^2}{88} + \dfrac{(29,850)^2}{65}}} = \frac{5,400}{5,317.15} = 1.02$$

H_0 is not rejected. There is no difference in mean selling prices of home in Omaha and Kansas City.

Exercise 11.5

$H_0: \mu_d = 0 \qquad H_1: \mu_d \neq 0$

Reject H_0 if t is less than -2.365 or greater than 2.365.

Electric	Gas	d	$d - \bar{d}$	$(d - \bar{d})^2$
265	260	5	3.375	11.390625
271	270	1	−0.625	0.390625
260	250	10	8.375	70.140625
250	255	−5	−6.625	43.890625
248	250	−2	−3.625	13.140625
280	275	5	3.375	11.390625
257	260	−3	−4.625	21.390625
262	260	2	0.375	0.140625
	Total	13		171.875

$$\bar{d} = \frac{13}{8} = 1.625$$

$$s_d = \sqrt{\frac{171.875}{8-1}} = 4.96$$

$$t = \frac{1.625}{4.96 / \sqrt{8}} = 0.93$$

H_0 is not rejected. There is no difference in the heating cost.

CHAPTER 12

ANALYSIS OF VARIANCE

Exercise 12.1

Step 1. State the null hypothesis and the alternate hypothesis

$H_0: \mu_1 = \mu_2 = \mu_3$; H_1: Not all means are equal.

Step 2. Select the level of significance. We have selected 0.05.

Step 3. Determine the test statistic.

For an analysis of variance problem the appropriate test statistic is F.

Step 4. Formulate the Decision Rule.

H_0 is rejected if F is greater than 3.59. Degrees of freedom in numerator $= (3 - 1) = 2$, degrees of freedom in denominator $= (20 - 3) = 17$

Step 5. Select the sample, perform the calculations, and make a decision.

Compute the grand mean and the SS total using Table I.

Use columns **A, D, & G**: $\overline{X}_G = \dfrac{\sum all\ the\ X\ values}{n} = \dfrac{19 + 52 + 40}{5 + 7 + 8} = \dfrac{111}{20} = 5.55$

Table I

	A	B	C		D	E	F		G	H	I	
	\multicolumn{3}{c}{60 Degrees}		\multicolumn{3}{c}{70 Degrees}		\multicolumn{3}{c}{80 Degrees}	
	X	$X - \overline{X}_G$	$(X - \overline{X}_G)^2$		X	$X - \overline{X}_G$	$(X - \overline{X}_G)^2$		X	$X - \overline{X}_G$	$(X - \overline{X}_G)^2$	X
	3	-2.55	6.50		7	1.45	2.10		4	-1.55	2.40	
	5	-0.55	0.30		6	0.45	0.20		6	0.45	0.20	
	4	-1.55	2.40		8	2.45	6.00		5	-0.55	0.30	
	3	-2.55	6.50		9	3.45	11.90		7	1.45	2.10	
	4	-1.55	2.40		6	0.45	0.20		6	0.45	0.20	
					8	2.45	6.00		5	-0.55	0.30	
					8	2.45	6.00		4	-1.55	2.40	
									3	-2.55	6.50	
$\sum$	19				52				40			111.00
$\sum$			18.10				32.40				14.40	64.90 SS Total
n	5				7				8			20

Use columns **C, F, & I**: $SS\,total = \sum (X - \overline{X}_G)^2 = (18.10 + 32.40 + 14.40) = 64.90$

Use Table II to compute the mean for each group.

For 60° $\bar{X} = \dfrac{\sum X}{n} = \dfrac{19}{5} = 3.8$ For 70° $\bar{X} = \dfrac{\sum X}{n} = \dfrac{52}{7} = 7.43$ For 80° $\bar{X} = \dfrac{\sum X}{n} = \dfrac{40}{8} = 5.0$

Table II

	A	B	C		D	E	F		G	H	I	
	60 Degrees				70 Degrees				80 Degrees			
	X	$X-\bar{X}$	$(X-\bar{X})^2$	X		$X-\bar{X}$	$(X-\bar{X})^2$	X		$X-\bar{X}$	$(X-\bar{X})^2$	
	3	-0.80	0.64	7		-0.43	0.18	4		-1	1.00	
	5	1.20	1.44	6		-1.43	2.04	6		1	1.00	
	4	0.20	0.04	8		0.57	0.32	5		0	0.00	
	3	-0.80	0.64	9		1.57	2.46	7		2	4.00	
	4	0.20	0.04	6		-1.43	2.04	6		1	1.00	
				8		0.57	0.32	5		0	0.00	
				8		0.57	0.32	4		-1	1.00	
								3		-2	4.00	
$\sum$	19			52				40				111.00
$\sum$			2.80				7.68				12.00	22.48
N	5			7				8				20

Use columns **C, F, & I**: $SSE = \sum(X-\bar{X}_c)^2 = (2.80 + 7.68 + 12.00) = 22.48$

$SST = SS\ total - SSE$

$\quad\quad = 64.90 - 22.48$

$\quad\quad = 42.42$

ANOVA Table

Source Variation	Sum of Squares	Degrees of Freedom	Mean Squares
Treatment	SST = 42.42	$(k-1) = (3-1) = 2$	$MST = \dfrac{SST}{(k-1)} = \dfrac{42.42}{2} = 20.65$
Error	SSE = 22.48	$(n-k) = (20-3) = 17$	$MSE = \dfrac{SSE}{(n-k)} = \dfrac{22.48}{17} = 1.32$
Total	SS Total = 64.90	19	

$F = \dfrac{20.65}{1.32} = 15.64$ H_0 is rejected since F is greater than 3.59.

There is a difference in the mean number correct (achievement).

Exercise 12.2

The means differ, found by using formula [12-5] and:

$$\overline{X}_1 = 7.4 \qquad n_1 = 7$$
$$\overline{X}_2 = 3.8 \qquad n_2 = 5$$

$t = 2.110$ from Appendix B.2: $(n - k) = (20 - 3) = 17$ degrees of freedom and the 95 percent level of confidence.

MSE = 1.32 from SSE/$(n - k)$ = 22.48/17 = 1.32.

$$\left(\overline{X}_1 - \overline{X}_2\right) \pm t\sqrt{\text{MSE}\left(\frac{1}{n_1} + \frac{1}{n_2}\right)}$$

$$\left(7.4 - 3.8\right) \pm 2.110\sqrt{1.3241\left(\frac{1}{7} + \frac{1}{5}\right)}$$

$$3.6 \pm 1.42167$$

$$2.1783 \text{ to } 5.0217$$

The means differ since both end points of the confidence interval are of the same sign, positive in this problem.

Exercise 12.3

a. There are 4 treatments, found by: If $(k - 1) = 3$, then $k = 4$

b. There are 5 blocks, found by, if $(b - 1) = 4$, then $b = 5$

c. Total sample size is 20, found by, if $(n - 1) = 19$, then $n = 20$

d. $H_0 : \mu_1 = \mu_2 = \mu_3$
    H_1 : Not all means are equal
    H_0 is rejected if $F > 3.49$

$F = \dfrac{MST}{MSE} = \dfrac{15}{12} = 1.25$ H_0 is not rejected.

No difference in the treatment means.

e. $H_0 : \mu_1 = \mu_2 = \mu_3 = \mu_4$
    H_1 : Not all means are equal
    H_0 is rejected if $F > 3.26$

$$F = \frac{MSB}{MSE} = \frac{50}{12} = 4.17 \quad H_0 \text{ is rejected. The block means differ.}$$

Exercise 12.4

a. The interaction plot on the right indicates an interaction between temperature and catalyst.

b. The analysis of variance was conducted on MINITAB and are shown below. The p-value corresponding to the interaction term (A*B) is 0.002. Since this is less than $\alpha = .05$, we conclude that interaction effects are significant. Because the interaction effect is significant, the two-way ANOVA results for the main effects temperature and catalyst are probably not meaningful

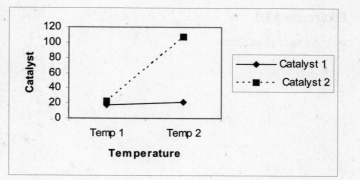

```
Analysis of Variance for Y

Source   DF       SS       MS      F       P
A         1    4140.5   4140.5   67.88   0.001
B         1    3784.5   3784.5   62.04   0.001
A*B       1    3280.5   3280.5   53.78   0.002
Error     4     244.0     61.0
Total     7   11449.5
```

Exercise 12.5

$$H_0: \sigma_H^2 \le \sigma_T^2; \qquad H_1: \sigma_H^2 > \sigma_T^2$$

At the 0.05 level of significance and 9 degrees of freedom for both the numerator and the denominator, using Appendix B.4, H_0 is rejected if $F > 3.18$.

$$F = \frac{(60)^2}{(30)^2} = 4.00$$

H_0 is rejected. There is more variation in the Harmon forecast.

CHAPTER 13

LINEAR REGRESSION AND CORRELATION

Exercise 13.1

a. Scatter diagram:

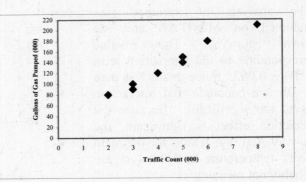

b. Coefficient of correlation:

	A	B	C	D	E	F	G
	Total Gallons			Traffic Count			
	Y	$(Y-\bar{Y})$	$(Y-\bar{Y})^2$	X	$(X-\bar{X})$	$(X-\bar{X})^2$	$(X-\bar{X})(Y-\bar{Y})$
	120	-13.75	189.06	4	-0.5	0.25	6.88
	180	46.25	2,139.06	6	1.5	2.25	69.38
	140	6.25	39.06	5	0.5	0.25	3.13
	150	16.25	264.06	5	0.5	0.25	8.13
	210	76.25	5,814.06	8	3.5	12.25	266.88
	100	-33.75	1,139.06	3	-1.5	2.25	50.63
	90	-43.75	1,914.06	3	-1.5	2.25	65.63
	80	-53.75	2,889.06	2	-2.5	6.25	134.38
n	8			8			
Total	1070		14,387.48	36		26	605.04

Step 1. Compute the means using sums in Column **A** and **D**:

$$\bar{Y} = \frac{\Sigma Y}{n} = \frac{1070}{8} = 133.75 \qquad \bar{X} = \frac{\Sigma X}{n} = \frac{36}{8} = 4.5$$

Step 2. Compute the standard deviations using the sums in Column **C** and **F**:

$$s_y = \sqrt{\frac{\Sigma(Y-\bar{Y})^2}{n-1}} = \sqrt{\frac{14,387.48}{8-1}} = \sqrt{2055.354} = 45.336 = 45.34$$

$$s_x = \sqrt{\frac{\Sigma(X-\bar{X})^2}{n-1}} = \sqrt{\frac{26}{8-1}} = \sqrt{3.714} = 1.927 = 1.93$$

Step 3. Compute the coefficient of correlation r using the formula, the sum from Column **G** in the table, and the calculated standard deviations.

$$r = \frac{\Sigma(X-\bar{X})(Y-\bar{Y})}{(n-1)(s_x\,s_y)} = \frac{605.04}{7(45.34)(1.93)} = \frac{605.04}{612.5434} = 0.9877 = 0.988$$

c. Coefficient of determination: $r^2 = (0.988)^2 = 0.976$.

d. About 97.6 percent of the variation in gasoline pumped is explained by the traffic count.

e. $H_0: \rho \leq 0$ H_0 is rejected if t is greater than 1.943.
$H_1: \rho > 0$

$$t = \frac{r\sqrt{n-2}}{\sqrt{1-r^2}} = \frac{0.988\sqrt{6}}{\sqrt{1-(0.988)^2}} = \frac{2.420}{0.15445} = 15.67$$

H_0 is rejected. There is positive correlation in the population.

Exercise 13.2

a. Regression equation: From Exercise 13.1, we know that: $r = 0.988$, $s_y = 45.34$, $s_x = 1.93$

$$b = r\frac{s_y}{s_x} = 0.988\left(\frac{45.34}{1.93}\right) = 0.988(23.49) = 23.208 = 23.21$$

In Exercise 13.1, we computed: $\bar{Y} = 133.75$ and $\bar{X} = 4.5$. Thus using Formula [13-5]:

$$a = \bar{Y} - b\bar{X}$$
$$= 133.75 - [(23.21)(4.5)]$$
$$= 133.75 - 104.45 = 29.30$$

Using the computed values the regression equation is:

$$\hat{Y} = a + bX = 29.30 + 23.21\,X \quad \text{(in dollars)}$$

b. Standard error of estimate:

X	bX	$\hat{Y}$	Y	$(Y-\hat{Y})$	$(Y-\hat{Y})^2$	Y^2	XY
4	92.84	122.14	120	-2.140	4.580	14400	480
6	139.26	168.56	180	11.440	130.874	32400	1080
5	116.05	145.35	140	-5.350	28.622	19600	700
5	116.05	145.35	150	4.650	21.623	22500	750
8	185.68	214.98	210	-4.980	24.800	44100	1680
3	69.63	98.93	100	1.070	1.145	10000	300
3	69.63	98.93	90	-8.930	79.745	8100	270
2	46.42	75.72	80	4.280	18.318	6400	160
Sum			1070		309.707	157500	5420

$$s_{y \cdot x} = \sqrt{\frac{\Sigma(Y-\hat{Y})^2}{n-2}} = \sqrt{\frac{309.707}{8-2}} = \sqrt{51.6178} = 7.18$$

c. A 95% confidence interval:

$$\hat{Y} = 29.30 + 23.21X = 29.30 + 23.21(4) = 122.14$$

$$\hat{Y} \pm t\left(s_{y \cdot x}\right)\sqrt{\frac{1}{n} + \frac{\left(X - \bar{X}\right)^2}{\Sigma(X - \bar{X})^2}} = 122.14 \pm 2.447(7.646)\sqrt{\frac{1}{8} + \frac{(4 - 4.5)^2}{26}}$$

$$= 122.14 \pm 6.8646$$

$$= 115.275 \text{ to } 129.005$$

d. A 95% prediction interval:

$$\hat{Y} \pm t\left(s_{y \cdot x}\right)\sqrt{1 + \frac{1}{n} + \frac{\left(X - \bar{X}\right)^2}{\Sigma(X - \bar{X})^2}} = 122.14 \pm 2.447(7.646)\sqrt{1 + \frac{1}{8} + \frac{(4 - 4.5)^2}{26}}$$

$$= 122.14 \pm 19.929$$

$$= 102.21 \text{ to } 142.069$$

Exercise 13.3

a. Coefficient of determination:
$$r^2 = \frac{SSR}{SS\,Total} = \frac{14,078}{14,388} = 0.9785 \quad OR \quad 1 - \frac{SSE}{SS\,Total} = 1 - \frac{310}{14,388} = (1 - 0.0215) = 0.9785$$

b. Coefficient of correlation: $\quad r = \sqrt{r^2} = \sqrt{0.9785} = 0.9892$

c. Standard error of estimate: $\quad s_{y \cdot x} = \sqrt{\frac{SSE}{n-2}} = \sqrt{\frac{310}{8-2}} = 7.188$

CHAPTER 14

MULTIPLE REGRESSION AND CORRELATION ANALYSIS

Exercise 14.1

a. The regression equation is: $\hat{Y} = -16.80 + .371temp - .017units$.

b. The multiple standard error of the estimate is $\sqrt{\dfrac{7.031}{7}} = \sqrt{1.004} = 1.002$.

c. $R^2 = \dfrac{SSR}{SStotal} = \dfrac{17.07}{24.10} = 0.708$

d. $R^2_{adj} = 1 - \dfrac{\dfrac{7.03}{7}}{\dfrac{24.1}{9}} = .625$

Exercise 14.2

a. The coefficient of correlation between power and temperature is 0.8384. This indicates a strong positive linear relationship between the two variables. The correlation between power and units is 0.3612. This indicates a moderate positive linear relationship between the two variables.

b.
$H_0 : \beta_1 = \beta_2 = 0$
$H_1 :$ At least one of the β's is not zero.

For
F has k = 2 numerator degrees of freedom and n-(k+1) = 7 denominator degrees of freedom.

$\alpha = .05$ the critical value of F is 4.74.

$F = \dfrac{MSR}{MSE} = \dfrac{8.534}{1.004} = 8.50$.   Since 8.50 > 4.74, we conclude that at least one β_j is not = 0.

c.

For Temp	For Units
$H_0 : \beta_1 = 0$	$H_0 : \beta_2 = 0$
$H_1 : \beta_1 \neq 0$	$H_1 : \beta_2 \neq 0$

The test statistic is a t with 7 d.f. . At $\alpha = .05$, t = 2.365.

From Excel, t for temperature is equal to 3.72. For units, $t = -.356$. This indicates that the variable units is not significant and should be dropped from the model. Temperature is significant, and should be kept in the model.

Exercise 14.3

a. The new regression equation is : $\hat{Y} = -17.24 + .353(temp)$

b. The first value for temperature is 83. So, $\hat{Y} = -17.24 + .353(83) = 12.05$.

c. $R^2 = .703$. 70.3% of the variation in *power* can be explained by *temperature*.

d. The histogram of the residuals does not resemble a bell-shape. However, because the sample size is small, it is difficult to make a judgment about normality of the residuals with a histogram. A normal probability plot is may be a better way to judge normality when n is small.

e. The residuals appear to be approximately the same and randomly distributed over the length of $\hat{Y}$. The assumption of constant variance is reasonable for this model. to zero.

CHAPTER 15

INDEX NUMBERS

Exercise 15.1 See table.

Year	Wage		Index	
1975	$2.10		100.00	found by (2.10/2.10) 100
1980	$3.10		147.6	found by (3.10/2.10) 100
1985	$3.35		159.5	found by (3.35/2.10) 100
1990	$3.80		181.0	found by (3.80/2.10) 100
1995	$4.25		202.4	found by (4.25/2.10) 100
1996	$4.75		226.2	found by (4.75/2.10) 100
1997	$5.15		245.2	found by (5.15/2.10) 100

Exercise 15.2

a. Simple aggregate index:

$$P = \frac{\$1,680}{\$672}(100) = 250.0$$

b. Laspeyres index:

	1989			2006		
	Price	**Quantity**		**Price**		
Item	p_0	q_0	$p_0 q_0$	p_t	$p_t q_0$	
Battery	$25	32	$800	$90	$2880	
Cable	22	8	176	40	320	
Bimini top	325	2	650	600	1200	
Depth finder	300	2	600	500	1000	
Total	$672		$2226	$1680	$5400	

Laspeyres index = 242.6 found by: $P = \dfrac{\$5,400}{\$2,226}(100) = 242.588$

b. Paasche=s index:

	1989			2006		
	Price	**Quantity**		**Price**	**Quantity**	
Item	p_0	q_t	$p_0 q_t$	p_t	q_t	$p_t q_t$
Battery	$25	30	$750	$90	30	$2700
Cable	22	8	176	40	8	320
Bimini top	325	2	650	600	2	1200
Depth finder	300	2	600	500	2	1000
Total	$672		$2176	$1680		$5220

Paasche's index: $P = \dfrac{\$5,220}{\$2,176}(100) = 239.9$

Exercise 15.3.

a. 2006 real income: $\dfrac{\$65,000}{202.5}(100) = \$32,099$

b. No. His salary decreased \$7,901 in real dollars, found by (\$32,099 − \$40,000)

c. 2006 purchasing power $\dfrac{\$1}{202.5}(100) = \$0.4938 = \$0.49$

CHAPTER 16

TIME SERIES AND FORECASTING

Exercise 16.1.

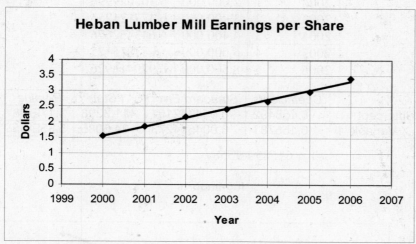

a. and **b**. The data plot and trend equation are shown.

c. Trend equation. The least squares regression line was calculated using EXCEL. It is:

$$\hat{Y} = 1.257 + .2943t \, .$$

	Coefficients	Standard Error	t Stat	P-value
Intercept	1.257143	0.04607	27.28764	1.24E-06
X Variable 1	0.294286	0.010302	28.56706	9.85E-07

d. To estimate sales for 2007, the first step is to determine the code for that year. The code is 8 found by subtracting: (2007 − 1999). Next 8 is substituted for *t* in the trend equation and the value of $\hat{Y}$ determined. $\hat{Y} = 1.257 + 0.2943t = \left[1.257 + 0.2943(8)\right] = \left(1.257 + 2.354\right) = 3.611$

The estimated earnings for 2007 are $3.611.

Exercise 16.2

a. The equation is developed using the EXCEL output.

Year	Code	Imports	log-imports
2002	1	2,000,000	6.301029996
2003	2	3,000,000	6.477121255
2004	3	4,400,000	6.643452676
2005	4	6,000,000	6.77815125
2006	5	8,500,000	6.929418926

	Coefficients	Standard Error	t Stat	P-value
Intercept	6.158492	0.014972151	411.3298	3.17E-08
X Variable 1	0.155781	0.004514273	34.5085	5.35E-05

$$\hat{Y} = 6.1585 + .1558\,t$$

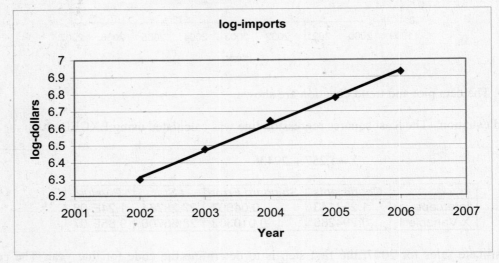

b. The prediction for 2007 is $\hat{Y} = 6.1585 + .1558\,t = 6.1585 + .1558\,(6) = 6.1585 + .9348 = 7.0933$.

The antilog of 7.0933 is 12,396,526. The prediction for 2007 is $12,396,526.

Exercise 16.3

Table for computing quarterly seasonal index.

Year	Qtr.		Moving Total	Moving Avg.	Centered Moving Avg.	Specific Seasonal
2003	I	2				
	II	8				
			22	5.50		
	III	10			5.750	173.913
			24	6.00		
	IV	2			6.250	32.000
			26	6.50		
2004	I	4			6.500	61.538
			26	6.50		
	II	10			6.750	148.148
			28	7.00		
	III	10			7.000	142.857
			28	7.00		
	IV	4			7.250	55.172
			30	7.50		
2005	I	4			8.000	50.000
			34	8.50		
	II	12			8.500	141.176
			34	8.50		
	III	14			8.750	160.000
			36	9.00		
	IV	4			9.500	42.105
			40	10.00		
2006	I	6			10.750	55.814
			46	11.50		
	II	16			11.500	139.130
			46	11.50		
	III	20				
	IV	4				

	Quarter				
Year	I	II	III	IV	
2003			173.913	32.000	
2004	61.538	148.148	142.857	55.172	
2005	50.000	141.176	160.000	42.105	
2006	55.814	139.130			
Total	167.352	428.454	476.770	129.277	Total
Mean	55.784	142.818	158.923	43.092	400.617
Typical Index	55.698	142.598	158.678	43.026	400.000

Exercise 16.4

a. June = 2,000 (1.20) = 2,400   **b.** November = 2,000 (0.47) = 940

Exercise 16.5

a. Using Excel the trend equation is:

$$\hat{Y} = 4.0434 + 0.46079\,(t),$$ First quarter of 2003 = 1, thus first quarter of 2007 is 17.

b. Seasonally adjusted sales.

Quarter	Trend	Seasonal	Forecast
17	11.87683	55.69809	6.615167
18	12.33762	142.598	17.5932
19	12.79841	158.6782	20.30829
20	13.25920	43.02563	5.704854

NOTE: SLIGHT VARIATIONS IN THE PREDICTION EQUATION MAY OCCUR DEPENDING ON THE COMPUTER SOFTWARE USED.

CHAPTER 17

NONPARAMETRIC METHODS: CHI-SQUARE APPLICATIONS

Exercise 17.1.

H_0: Tire failures are uniformly distributed.

H_1: Tire failures are not uniformly distributed.

Reject H_0 if the computed value of χ^2 is greater than 7.815, found by Appendix B.3, 0.05 level of significance and 3 df.

Location	Col. 1 f_o	Col. 2 f_e	Col. 3 $f_o - f_e$	Col. 4 $(f_o - f_e)^2$	Col. 5 $\dfrac{(f_o - f_e)^2}{f_e}$
Left Front	28	25	3	9	0.36
Left Rear	20	25	−5	25	1.00
Right Front	29	25	4	16	0.64
Right Rear	23	25	−2	4	0.16
	100	100	0		2.16

H_0 is not rejected. There is no difference in the failure rate.

Exercise 17.2

H_0: There has been no change in the distribution.

H_1: There has been a change in the distribution..

Reject H_0 if the computed value of χ^2 is greater than 7.815, found by Appendix B.3, 0.05 level of significance and 3 df.

Company	Col. 1 Percent of Total	Col. 2 Number in Sample f_o	Col. 3 f_e	Col. 4 $f_o - f_e$	Col. 5 $(f_o - f_e)^2$	Col. 6 $\dfrac{(f_o - f_e)^2}{f_e}$
GM	42	325	336	−11	121	121/336 = 0.360
Ford	33	240	264	-24	576	576/264 = 1.182
DaimlerChrysler	22	190	176	14	196	196/176 = 1.114
Other	3	45	24	21	441	441/24 = 18.375
Total	100	800	800	0		$\chi^2 = 21.031$

H_0 is rejected. There has been a change in the distribution.

Exercise 17.3

H_0: There is no relationship between gender and amount of time spent watching TV.

H_1: There is a relationship between gender and amount of time spent watching TV.

Reject H_0 if the computed value of χ^2 is greater than 5.991, found by Appendix B.3, 0.05 level of significance and 2 df.

$$f_e = \frac{(\text{row total})(\text{column total})}{\text{grand total}} = \frac{160 \times 225}{480} = 75, \ \frac{160 \times 255}{480} = 85$$

Hours	Male f_o	f_e	$\dfrac{(f_o - f_e)^2}{f_e}$	Female f_o	f_e	$\dfrac{(f_o - f_e)^2}{f_e}$	Total
Under 8	70	75	0.333	90	85	0.294	160
8 up to 15	100	75	8.333	60	85	7.353	160
15 or more	55	75	5.333	105	85	4.706	160
Total	225	225	13.999	255	255	12.353	480

$$\chi^2 = \Sigma \left[\frac{(f_o - f_e)^2}{f_e} \right] = \frac{(70-75)^2}{75} + \frac{(100-75)^2}{75} + \ldots + \frac{(105-85)^2}{85} = 26.352$$

H_0 is rejected because χ^2 is greater than 5.991. There is a relationship between gender and the amount of time spent watching television.

CHAPTER 18

NONPARAMETRIC METHODS: ANALYSIS OF RANKED DATA

Exercise 18.1

Student	After SAT Score	Before SAT Score	Sign of Difference
L. Bratton	1300	1240	+
S. Mantini	1080	1030	+
V. Haj	1120	1150	-
E. Sosa	1000	1090	-
B. Harvey	1200	1110	+
J.Redding	1230	1100	+
C. Papalia	1150	1090	+
V. Suppa	1260	1130	+

H_0: There is no change in SAT scores ($\pi \le 0.50$)
H_1: SAT scores after the course are higher than scores before the course ($\pi > 0.50$)

Binomial Probabilities when $n = 10$, $\pi = 0.50$, alpha = 0.05		
Number of Successes	Probability of Success	Cumulative Probability
x	$p(x)$	
0	0.004	
1	0.031	
2	0.109	
3	0.219	
4	0.273	
5	0.219	
6	0.109	0.144
7	0.031	0.035
8	0.004	0.004

There are 8 observations, so $n = 8$. From Appendix B.9, $n = 8$ and $\pi = 0.5$, we find $P(X \ge 7) = (0.004 + 0.031) = 0.035$ and $P(X \ge 6) = (0.004 + 0.031 + 0.109) = 0.144$. H_0 is rejected if there are 7 or more plus signs. Since there are only 6, H_0 cannot be rejected. There is not enough evidence to conclude that SAT scores have increased.

Exercise 18.2

H_0: $\pi \leq 0.50$
H_1: $\pi > 0.50$

H_0 is rejected if $z > 1.65$.

$$z = \frac{(19 - 0.50) - (30 \times 0.50)}{0.5\sqrt{30}} = \frac{3.5}{2.74} = 1.28$$

H_0 cannot be rejected. There is not enough evidence to conclude that SAT scores have increased.

Exercise 18.3

H_0: There is no difference in the SAT scores.
H_1: The SAT scores have increased.
H_0 is rejected if the smaller of R^+ and R^- is 5 or less.

Student	After SAT Score	Before SAT Score	Diff.	Absol.	Rank	R^+	R^-
L. Bratton	1300	1240	60	60	3.5	3.5	
S. Mantini	1080	1030	50	50	2.0	2.0	
V. Haj	1120	1150	-30	30	1.0		1.0
E. Sosa	1000	1090	-90	90	5.5		5.5
B. Harvey	1200	1110	90	90	5.5	5.5	
J. Redding	1230	1100	130	130	7.5	7.5	
C. Papalia	1150	1090	60	60	3.5	3.5	
V. Suppa	1260	1130	130	130	7.5	7.5	
						29.5	6.5

Since 6.5 is not less than or equal to 5, H_0 is not rejected. There is not enough evidence to conclude that there has been an increase in SAT scores.

Exercise 18.4

H_0: The two populations are the same.
H_1: The two populations are not the same.
Reject H_0 if $z < -1.65$ or $z > 1.65$.

Tough		Long Last	
Miles	Rank	Miles	Rank
24	2	35	9
31	7	46	15
37	11	49	16
44	14	52	17
36	10	41	13
30	6	40	12
28	4	32	8
21	1	29	5
	55	27	3
			98

$$z = \frac{55 - \dfrac{8(8+9+1)}{2}}{\sqrt{\dfrac{8(9)(8+9+1)}{12}}} = -1.636 = 1.64$$

H_0 is not rejected. There is not enough evidence to conclude that the distributions of miles driven are different.

Exercise 18.5

H_0: The distributions of load factors are the same.
H_1: The distributions of load factors are not the same.
H_0 is rejected if χ^2 is greater than 5.991.

Load Factors for Three Airlines							
US Airways		Delta		Northwest			
%	Rank	%	Rank	%	Rank		
98%	15.0	89	5.5	92%	9.5		
87	3.5	87	3.5	90	7.0		
100	16.0	92	9.5	94	12.5		
93	11.0	89	5.5	84	1.0		
91	8.0	97	14.0	86	2.0		
94	12.5						
	66.0		38.0		32.0		

$$H = \frac{12}{16(17)}\left(\frac{(66.0)^2}{6} + \frac{(38.0)^2}{5} + \frac{(32.0)^2}{5} \right) - 3(17)$$

$$= \frac{12}{272}(726 + 288.8 + 204.8) - 51 = (53.81 - 51) = 2.81$$

H_0 is not rejected. There is not enough evidence to conclude that the load factors are different.

Exercise 18.6

Team	News	Free Press	d	d^2
Penn State	1	2	−1	1
Ohio State	2	1	1	1
Michigan	3	5	−2	4
Iowa	4	6	−2	4
Wisconsin	5	3	2	4
Michigan State	6	7	−1	1
Indiana	7	8	−1	1
Minnesota	8	9	−1	1
Purdue	9	10	−1	1
Illinois	10	4	6	36
Northwestern	11	11	0	0
				54

$$r_s = 1 - \frac{6(54)}{11(11^2 - 1)} = 0.7545$$

There is a strong positive correlation between the ratings.

Could this association be due to chance? Use the 0.01 significance level.

H_0: The rank correlation in the population is zero.
H_1: The rank correlation in the population is greater than zero.

The alternate hypothesis suggests a one-tailed test. There are nine degrees of freedom, found by (n − 2) = (11 − 2) = 9. The critical value of the t for the 0.01 is 2.821. H_0 is rejected if the computed value of t is greater than 2.821. Using formula [18-7], the computed t is 3.490.

$$t = r_s \sqrt{\frac{n-2}{1-r_s^2}} = 0.7545 \sqrt{\frac{11-2}{1-(0.7545)^2}} = 0.7545\sqrt{22.177} = 0.7545(4.571) = 3.449$$

H_0 is rejected. There is enough evidence to conclude that there is a positive association between the two ratings for Big 10 football teams.

CHAPTER 19

STATISTICAL QUALITY CONTROL

Exercise 19.1

a. There are a total of 200 reasons. Determine the % of reasons in each category by dividing each category count by 200. Order categories in descending order by corresponding percent. Compute cumulative percent for this order as shown in the table. The Pareto Chart follows.

Return Code*	No.	%	Rank	Reasons in Rank Order	%	Cum. %
01	75	0.375	1	01	37.50	37.50
02	38	0.19	2	02	19.00	56.50
03	12	0.06	5	04	17.50	74.00
04	35	0.175	3	07	7.00	81.00
05	7	0.035	8	03	6.00	87.00
06	11	0.055	6	06	5.50	92.50
07	14	0.07	4	08	4.00	96.50
08	8	0.04	7	05	3.50	100.00

* 01 = too small 02 = too large 03 = too short 04 = too long 05 = not what was ordered
06 = poor fit   07 = not what was expected 08 = defective

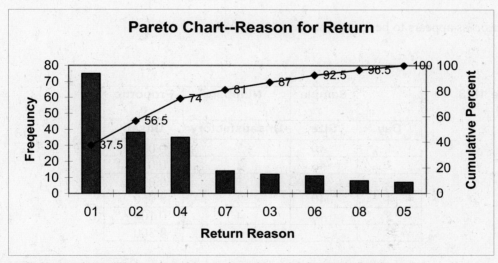

Pareto Chart--Reason for Return

01 = too small 02 = too large 03 = too short 04 = too long 05 = not what was ordered
06 = poor fit   07 = not what was expected 08 = defective

b. 74% of return reasons are caused by wrong size. The company should investigate how they size their clothing or on instructions provided to the customer for determining correct size.

Exercise 19.2.

a. Sample means

Bag								
Time	1	2	3	4	ΣX	$\overline{X}$	R	
8 a.m.	16.1	16.0	15.9	16.1	64.1	16.03	0.2	
9 a.m.	16.2	16.1	16.0	15.9	64.2	16.05	0.3	
10 a.m.	16.0	15.8	15.9	15.7	63.4	15.85	0.3	
11 a.m.	15.8	15.9	16.0	15.8	63.5	15.88	0.2	
						63.81	1.0	

$$\overline{\overline{X}} = \frac{63.81}{4} = 15.95$$

$$\overline{R} = \frac{1}{4} = 0.25$$

$$UCL \text{ and } LCL = 15.95 \pm 0.729(0.25)$$
$$= 15.95 \pm 0.18$$
$$UCL = 16.13 \text{ and } LCL = 15.77$$

b. Sample ranges:

$$UCL = D_4\overline{R} = 2.282(0.25) = 0.57$$
$$LCL = D_3\overline{R} = 0(0.25) = 0$$

c. The process appears to be in control.

Exercise 19.3

	Sample	Number	Proportion
Day	Size	Unsatisfactory	Unsat.
1	40	2	0.050
2	40	3	0.075
3	40	1	0.025
4	40	2	0.050
5	40	4	0.100
			0.300

$$p = \frac{0.3}{5} = 0.06$$

$$UCL \text{ and } LCL = p \pm 3\sqrt{\frac{p(1-p)}{n}}$$

$$= 0.06 \pm 3\sqrt{\frac{0.06(1-0.06)}{40}}$$

$$= 0.06 \pm 0.11 = 0 \text{ and } 0.17$$

Exercise 19.4

$$\bar{c} = \frac{2+4+5+3+2+1+5+2+3+1}{10} = \frac{28}{10} = 2.8$$

$$UCL \text{ and } LCL = \bar{c} \pm 3\sqrt{\bar{c}}$$
$$= 2.8 \pm 3\sqrt{2.8}$$
$$= 2.8 \pm 5.02$$
$$UCL = 7.82$$
$$LCL = 0$$

Exercise 19.5

$P(x \leq 2 \mid \pi = 0.30 \text{ and } n = 25) = 0.008$ from Appendix B.9 where

$c = 2,\, n = 25,\, \pi = 0.30$ and $(0.000 + 0.001 + 0.007 = 0.008)$

CHAPTER 20

AN INTRODUCTION TO DECISION THEORY

Exercise 20.1

a. Payoff table.

	Repaid	Difficulty	Bankrupt
Loan	$110,000	$108,000	$70,000
No loan	108,000	108,000	108,000

(Loan) $EMV(A_1) = 0.85\ (\$110,000) + 0.10\ (\$108,000) + 0.05\ (\$70,000) = \$107,800$

(No loan) $EMV(A_2) = \$108,000$

Since $108,000 is greater than $107,800 the banker should not make the loan.

b. $EMV = 0.85\ (\$110,000) + 0.10\ (\$108,000) + 0.05\ (\$108,000) = \$109,700$

c. $EVPI = \$109,700 - \$108,000 = \$1,700$

Exercise 20.2

	Repaid	Difficulty	Bankrupt
Loan	0	0	$38,000
No loan	$2,000	0	0

$EOL(A_1)$ (Loan) $= 0.05\ (\$38,000) = \$1,900$

$EOL(A_2)$ (No loan) $= 0.85\ (\$2,000) = \$1,700$

The expected opportunity loss is the smallest for the act of no loan and the same as the value of perfect information ($1,700).

APPENDIX B.1

AREAS UNDER THE NORMAL CURVE

Example:
If z = 1.96, then
0.4750 of the area is
between 0 and 1.96.

Z	0.00	0.01	0.02	0.03	0.04	0.05	0.06	0.07	0.08	0.09
0.0	0.0000	0.0040	0.0080	0.0120	0.0160	0.0199	0.0239	0.0279	0.0319	0.0359
0.1	0.0398	0.0438	0.0478	0.0517	0.0557	0.0596	0.0636	0.0675	0.0714	0.0753
0.2	0.0793	0.0832	0.0871	0.0910	0.0948	0.0987	0.1026	0.1064	0.1103	0.1141
0.3	0.1179	0.1217	0.1255	0.1293	0.1331	0.1368	0.1406	0.1443	0.1480	0.1517
0.4	0.1554	0.1591	0.1628	0.1664	0.1700	0.1736	0.1772	0.1808	0.1844	0.1879
0.5	0.1915	0.1950	0.1985	0.2019	0.2054	0.2088	0.2123	0.2157	0.2190	0.2224
0.6	0.2257	0.2291	0.2324	0.2357	0.2389	0.2422	0.2454	0.2486	0.2517	0.2549
0.7	0.2580	0.2611	0.2642	0.2673	0.2704	0.2734	0.2764	0.2794	0.2823	0.2852
0.8	0.2881	0.2910	0.2939	0.2967	0.2995	0.3023	0.3051	0.3078	0.3106	0.3133
0.9	0.3159	0.3186	0.3212	0.3238	0.3264	0.3289	0.3315	0.3340	0.3365	0.3389
1.0	0.3413	0.3438	0.3461	0.3485	0.3508	0.3531	0.3554	0.3577	0.3599	0.3621
1.1	0.3643	0.3665	0.3686	0.3708	0.3729	0.3749	0.3770	0.3790	0.3810	0.3830
1.2	0.3849	0.3869	0.3888	0.3907	0.3925	0.3944	0.3962	0.3980	0.3997	0.4015
1.3	0.4032	0.4049	0.4066	0.4082	0.4099	0.4115	0.4131	0.4147	0.4162	0.4177
1.4	0.4192	0.4207	0.4222	0.4236	0.4251	0.4265	0.4279	0.4292	0.4306	0.4319
1.5	0.4332	0.4345	0.4357	0.4370	0.4382	0.4394	0.4406	0.4418	0.4429	0.4441
1.6	0.4452	0.4463	0.4474	0.4484	0.4495	0.4505	0.4515	0.4525	0.4535	0.4545
1.7	0.4554	0.4564	0.4573	0.4582	0.4591	0.4599	0.4608	0.4616	0.4625	0.4633
1.8	0.4641	0.4649	0.4656	0.4664	0.4671	0.4678	0.4686	0.4693	0.4699	0.4706
1.9	0.4713	0.4719	0.4726	0.4732	0.4738	0.4744	0.4750	0.4756	0.4761	0.4767
2.0	0.4772	0.4778	0.4783	0.4788	0.4793	0.4798	0.4803	0.4808	0.4812	0.4817
2.1	0.4821	0.4826	0.4830	0.4834	0.4838	0.4842	0.4846	0.4850	0.4854	0.4857
2.2	0.4861	0.4864	0.4868	0.4871	0.4875	0.4878	0.4881	0.4884	0.4887	0.4890
2.3	0.4893	0.4896	0.4898	0.4901	0.4904	0.4906	0.4909	0.4911	0.4913	0.4916
2.4	0.4918	0.4920	0.4922	0.4925	0.4927	0.4929	0.4931	0.4932	0.4934	0.4936
2.5	0.4938	0.4940	0.4941	0.4943	0.4945	0.4946	0.4948	0.4949	0.4951	0.4952
2.6	0.4953	0.4955	0.4956	0.4957	0.4959	0.4960	0.4961	0.4962	0.4963	0.4964
2.7	0.4965	0.4966	0.4967	0.4968	0.4969	0.4970	0.4971	0.4972	0.4973	0.4974
2.8	0.4974	0.4975	0.4976	0.4977	0.4977	0.4978	0.4979	0.4979	0.4980	0.4981
2.9	0.4981	0.4982	0.4982	0.4983	0.4984	0.4984	0.4985	0.4985	0.4986	0.4986
3.0	0.4987	0.4987	0.4987	0.4988	0.4988	0.4989	0.4989	0.4989	0.4990	0.4990

APPENDIX B.2

STUDENT'S *t* DISTRIBUTION

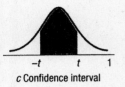

c Confidence interval

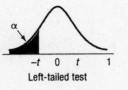

Left-tailed test

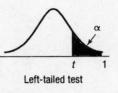

Left-tailed test

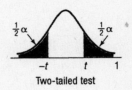

Two-tailed test

df	Confidence Intervals, *c*					
	80%	90%	95%	98%	99%	99.9%
	Level of Significance for One-Tailed Test, α					
df	0.100	0.050	0.025	0.010	0.005	0.0005
	Level of Significance for Two-Tailed Test, α					
	0.20	0.10	0.05	0.02	0.01	0.001
1	3.078	6.314	12.706	31.821	63.657	636.619
2	1.886	2.920	4.303	6.965	9.925	31.599
3	1.638	2.353	3.182	4.541	5.841	12.924
4	1.533	2.132	2.776	3.747	4.604	8.610
5	1.476	2.015	2.571	3.365	4.032	6.869
6	1.440	1.943	2.447	3.143	3.707	5.959
7	1.415	1.895	2.365	2.998	3.499	5.408
8	1.397	1.860	2.306	2.896	3.355	5.041
9	1.383	1.833	2.262	2.821	3.250	4.781
10	1.372	1.812	2.228	2.764	3.169	4.587
11	1.363	1.796	2.201	2.718	3.106	4.437
12	1.356	1.782	2.179	2.681	3.055	4.318
13	1.350	1.771	2.160	2.650	3.012	4.221
14	1.345	1.761	2.145	2.624	2.977	4.140
15	1.341	1.753	2.131	2.602	2.947	4.073
16	1.337	1.746	2.120	2.583	2.921	4.015
17	1.333	1.740	2.110	2.567	2.898	3.965
18	1.330	1.734	2.101	2.552	2.878	3.922
19	1.328	1.729	2.093	2.539	2.861	3.883
20	1.325	1.725	2.086	2.528	2.845	3.850
21	1.323	1.721	2.080	2.518	2.831	3.819
22	1.321	1.717	2.074	2.508	2.819	3.792
23	1.319	1.714	2.069	2.500	2.807	3.768
24	1.318	1.711	2.064	2.492	2.797	3.745
25	1.316	1.708	2.060	2.485	2.787	3.725
26	1.315	1.706	2.056	2.479	2.779	3.707
27	1.314	1.703	2.052	2.473	2.771	3.690
28	1.313	1.701	2.048	2.467	2.763	3.674
29	1.311	1.699	2.045	2.462	2.756	3.659
30	1.310	1.697	2.042	2.457	2.750	3.646
40	1.303	1.684	2.021	2.423	2.704	3.551
60	1.296	1.671	2.000	2.390	2.660	3.460
120	1.289	1.658	1.980	2.358	2.617	3.373
∞	1.282	1.645	1.960	2.326	2.576	3.291

APPENDIX B.3

CRITICAL VALUES OF CHI-SQUARE

This table contains the values of χ^2 that correspond to a specific right tail area and specific numbers of degrees of freedom df.

Possible Values of χ^2

DEGREES OF FREEDOM df	RIGHT-TAIL AREA			
	0.10	0.05	0.02	0.01
1	2.706	3.841	5.412	6.635
2	4.605	5.991	7.824	9.210
3	6.251	7.815	9.837	11.345
4	7.779	9.488	11.668	13.277
5	9.236	11.070	13.388	15.086
6	10.645	12.592	15.033	16.812
7	12.017	14.067	16.622	18.475
8	13.362	15.507	18.168	20.090
9	14.684	16.919	19.679	21.666
10	15.987	18.307	21.161	23.209
11	17.275	19.675	22.618	24.725
12	18.549	21.026	24.054	26.217
13	19.812	22.362	25.472	27.688
14	21.064	23.685	26.873	29.141
15	22.307	24.996	28.259	30.578
16	23.542	26.296	29.633	32.000
17	24.769	27.587	30.995	33.409
18	25.989	28.869	32.346	34.805
19	27.204	30.144	33.687	36.191
20	28.412	31.410	35.020	37.566
21	29.615	32.671	36.343	38.932
22	30.813	33.924	37.659	40.289
23	32.007	35.172	38.968	41.638
24	33.196	36.415	40.270	42.980
25	34.382	37.652	41.566	44.314
26	35.563	38.885	42.856	45.642
27	36.741	40.113	44.140	46.963
28	37.916	41.337	45.419	48.278
29	39.087	42.557	46.693	49.588
30	40.256	43.773	47.962	50.892

APPENDIX B.4

CRITICAL VALUES OF THE F DISTRIBUTION AT A 5 PERCENT LEVEL OF SIGNIFICANCE, $\alpha = 0.05$

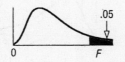

		Degrees of Freedom for the Numerator														
		1	2	3	4	5	6	7	8	9	10	12	15	20	24	30	40
	1	161	200	216	225	230	234	237	239	241	242	244	246	248	249	250	251
	2	18.5	19.0	19.2	19.2	19.3	19.3	19.4	19.4	19.4	19.4	19.4	19.4	19.4	19.5	19.5	19.5
	3	10.1	9.55	9.28	9.12	9.01	8.94	8.89	8.85	8.81	8.79	8.74	8.70	8.66	8.64	8.62	8.59
	4	7.71	6.94	6.59	6.39	6.26	6.16	6.09	6.04	6.00	5.96	5.91	5.86	5.80	5.77	5.75	5.72
	5	6.61	5.79	5.41	5.19	5.05	4.95	4.88	4.82	4.77	4.74	4.68	4.62	4.56	4.53	4.50	4.46
	6	5.99	5.14	4.76	4.53	4.39	4.28	4.21	4.15	4.10	4.06	4.00	3.94	3.87	3.84	3.81	3.77
	7	5.59	4.74	4.35	4.12	3.97	3.87	3.79	3.73	3.68	3.64	3.57	3.51	3.44	3.41	3.38	3.34
	8	5.32	4.46	4.07	3.84	3.69	3.58	3.50	3.44	3.39	3.35	3.28	3.22	3.15	3.12	3.08	3.04
	9	5.12	4.26	3.86	3.63	3.48	3.37	3.29	3.23	3.18	3.14	3.07	3.01	2.94	2.90	2.86	2.83
	10	4.96	4.10	3.71	3.48	3.33	3.22	3.14	3.07	3.02	2.98	2.91	2.85	2.77	2.74	2.70	2.66
	11	4.84	3.98	3.59	3.36	3.20	3.09	3.01	2.95	2.90	2.85	2.79	2.72	2.65	2.61	2.57	2.53
	12	4.75	3.89	3.49	3.26	3.11	3.00	2.91	2.85	2.80	2.75	2.69	2.62	2.54	2.51	2.47	2.43
	13	4.67	3.81	3.41	3.18	3.03	2.92	2.83	2.77	2.71	2.67	2.60	2.53	2.46	2.42	2.38	2.34
	14	4.60	3.74	3.34	3.11	2.96	2.85	2.76	2.70	2.65	2.60	2.53	2.46	2.39	2.35	2.31	2.27
	15	4.54	3.68	3.29	3.06	2.90	2.79	2.71	2.64	2.59	2.54	2.48	2.40	2.33	2.29	2.25	2.20
	16	4.49	3.63	3.24	3.01	2.85	2.74	2.66	2.59	2.54	2.49	2.42	2.35	2.28	2.24	2.19	2.15
	17	4.45	3.59	3.20	2.96	2.81	2.70	2.61	2.55	2.49	2.45	2.38	2.31	2.23	2.19	2.15	2.10
	18	4.41	3.55	3.16	2.93	2.77	2.66	2.58	2.51	2.46	2.41	2.34	2.27	2.19	2.15	2.11	2.06
	19	4.38	3.52	3.13	2.90	2.74	2.63	2.54	2.48	2.42	2.38	2.31	2.23	2.16	2.11	2.07	2.03
	20	4.35	3.49	3.10	2.87	2.71	2.60	2.51	2.45	2.39	2.35	2.28	2.20	2.12	2.08	2.04	1.99
	21	4.32	3.47	3.07	2.84	2.68	2.57	2.49	2.42	2.37	2.32	2.25	2.18	2.10	2.05	2.01	1.96
	22	4.30	3.44	3.05	2.82	2.66	2.55	2.46	2.40	2.34	2.30	2.23	2.15	2.07	2.03	1.98	1.94
	23	4.28	3.42	3.03	2.80	2.64	2.53	2.44	2.37	2.32	2.27	2.20	2.13	2.05	2.01	1.96	1.91
	24	4.26	3.40	3.01	2.78	2.62	2.51	2.42	2.36	2.30	2.25	2.18	2.11	2.03	1.98	1.94	1.89
	25	4.24	3.39	2.99	2.76	2.60	2.49	2.40	2.34	2.28	2.24	2.16	2.09	2.01	1.96	1.92	1.87
	30	4.17	3.32	2.92	2.69	2.53	2.42	2.33	2.27	2.21	2.16	2.09	2.01	1.93	1.89	1.84	1.79
	40	4.08	3.23	2.84	2.61	2.45	2.34	2.25	2.18	2.12	2.08	2.00	1.92	1.84	1.79	1.74	1.69
	60	4.00	3.15	2.76	2.53	2.37	2.25	2.17	2.10	2.04	1.99	1.92	1.84	1.75	1.70	1.65	1.59
	120	3.92	3.07	2.68	2.45	2.29	2.18	2.09	2.02	1.96	1.91	1.83	1.75	1.66	1.61	1.55	1.50
	∞	3.84	3.00	2.60	2.37	2.21	2.10	2.01	1.94	1.88	1.83	1.75	1.67	1.57	1.52	1.46	1.39

Note: The left axis label reads "Degrees of Freedom for the Denominator".

CRITICAL VALUES OF THE *F* DISTRIBUTION AT A 1 PERCENT LEVEL OF SIGNIFICANCE, $\alpha = 0.01$

		Degrees of Freedom for the Numerator														
		1	**2**	**3**	**4**	**5**	**6**	**7**	**8**	**9**	**10**	**12**	**15**	**20**	**24**	**30**	**40**
	1	4052	5000	5403	5625	5764	5859	5928	5981	6022	6056	6106	6157	6209	6235	6261	6287
	2	98.5	99.0	99.2	99.2	99.3	99.3	99.4	99.4	99.4	99.4	99.4	99.4	99.4	99.5	99.5	99.5
	3	34.1	30.8	29.5	28.7	28.2	27.9	27.7	27.5	27.3	27.2	27.1	26.9	26.7	26.6	26.5	26.4
	4	21.2	18.0	16.7	16.0	15.5	15.2	15.0	14.8	14.7	14.5	14.4	14.2	14.0	13.9	13.8	13.7
	5	16.3	13.3	12.1	11.4	11.0	10.7	10.5	10.3	10.2	10.1	9.89	9.72	9.55	9.47	9.38	9.29
	6	13.7	10.9	9.78	9.15	8.75	8.47	8.26	8.10	7.98	7.87	7.72	7.56	7.40	7.31	7.23	7.14
	7	12.2	9.55	8.45	7.85	7.46	7.19	6.99	6.84	6.72	6.62	6.47	6.31	6.16	6.07	5.99	5.91
	8	11.3	8.65	7.59	7.01	6.63	6.37	6.18	6.03	5.91	5.81	5.67	5.52	5.36	5.28	5.20	5.12
	9	10.6	8.02	6.99	6.42	6.06	5.80	5.61	5.47	5.35	5.26	5.11	4.96	4.81	4.73	4.65	4.57
	10	10.0	7.56	6.55	5.99	5.64	5.39	5.20	5.06	4.94	4.85	4.71	4.56	4.41	4.33	4.25	4.17
Degrees of Freedom for the Denominator	11	9.65	7.21	6.22	5.67	5.32	5.07	4.89	4.74	4.63	4.54	4.40	4.25	4.10	4.02	3.94	3.86
	12	9.33	6.93	5.95	5.41	5.06	4.82	4.64	4.50	4.39	4.30	4.16	4.01	3.86	3.78	3.70	3.62
	13	9.07	6.70	5.74	5.21	4.86	4.62	4.44	4.30	4.19	4.10	3.96	3.82	3.66	3.59	3.51	3.43
	14	8.86	6.51	5.56	5.04	4.69	4.46	4.28	4.14	4.03	3.94	3.80	3.66	3.51	3.43	3.35	3.27
	15	8.68	6.36	5.42	4.89	4.56	4.32	4.14	4.00	3.89	3.80	3.67	3.52	3.37	3.29	3.21	3.13
	16	8.53	6.23	5.29	4.77	4.44	4.20	4.03	3.89	3.78	3.69	3.55	3.41	3.26	3.18	3.10	3.02
	17	8.40	6.11	5.18	4.67	4.34	4.10	3.93	3.79	3.68	3.59	3.46	3.31	3.16	3.08	3.00	2.92
	18	8.29	6.01	5.09	4.58	4.25	4.01	3.84	3.71	3.60	3.51	3.37	3.23	3.08	3.00	2.92	2.84
	19	8.18	5.93	5.01	4.50	4.17	3.94	3.77	3.63	3.52	3.43	3.30	3.15	3.00	2.92	2.84	2.76
	20	8.10	5.85	4.94	4.43	4.10	3.87	3.70	3.56	3.46	3.37	3.23	3.09	2.94	2.86	2.78	2.69
	21	8.02	5.78	4.87	4.37	4.04	3.81	3.64	3.51	3.40	3.31	3.17	3.03	2.88	2.80	2.72	2.64
	22	7.95	5.72	4.82	4.31	3.99	3.76	3.59	3.45	3.35	3.26	3.12	2.98	2.83	2.75	2.67	2.58
	23	7.88	5.66	4.76	4.26	3.94	3.71	3.54	3.41	3.30	3.21	3.07	2.93	2.78	2.70	2.62	2.54
	24	7.82	5.61	4.72	4.22	3.90	3.67	3.50	3.36	3.26	3.17	3.03	2.89	2.74	2.66	2.58	2.49
	25	7.77	5.57	4.68	4.18	3.85	3.63	3.46	3.32	3.22	3.13	2.99	2.85	2.70	2.62	2.54	2.45
	30	7.56	5.39	4.51	4.02	3.70	3.47	3.30	3.17	3.07	2.98	2.84	2.70	2.55	2.47	2.39	2.30
	40	7.31	5.18	4.31	3.83	3.51	3.29	3.12	2.99	2.89	2.80	2.66	2.52	2.37	2.29	2.20	2.11
	60	7.08	4.98	4.13	3.65	3.34	3.12	2.95	2.82	2.72	2.63	2.50	2.35	2.20	2.12	2.03	1.94
	120	6.85	4.79	3.95	3.48	3.17	2.96	2.79	2.66	2.56	2.47	2.34	2.19	2.03	1.95	1.86	1.76
	∞	6.63	4.61	3.78	3.32	3.02	2.80	2.64	2.51	2.41	2.32	2.18	2.04	1.88	1.79	1.70	1.59

APPENDIX B.5

POISSON DISTRIBUTION

X	μ 0.1	0.2	0.3	0.4	0.5	0.6	0.7	0.8	0.9
0	0.9048	0.8187	0.7408	0.6703	0.6065	0.5488	0.4966	0.4493	0.4066
1	0.0905	0.1637	0.2222	0.2681	0.3033	0.3293	0.3476	0.3595	0.3659
2	0.0045	0.0164	0.0333	0.0536	0.0758	0.0988	0.1217	0.1438	0.1647
3	0.0002	0.0011	0.0033	0.0072	0.0126	0.0198	0.0284	0.0383	0.0494
4	0.0000	0.0001	0.0003	0.0007	0.0016	0.0030	0.0050	0.0077	0.0111
5	0.0000	0.0000	0.0000	0.0001	0.0002	0.0004	0.0007	0.0012	0.0020
6	0.0000	0.0000	0.0000	0.0000	0.0000	0.0000	0.0001	0.0002	0.0003
7	0.0000	0.0000	0.0000	0.0000	0.0000	0.0000	0.0000	0.0000	0.0000

X	μ 1.0	2.0	3.0	4.0	5.0	6.0	7.0	8.0	9.0
0	0.3679	0.1353	0.0498	0.0183	0.0067	0.0025	0.0009	0.0003	0.0001
1	0.3679	0.2707	0.1494	0.0733	0.0337	0.0149	0.0064	0.0027	0.0011
2	0.1839	0.2707	0.2240	0.1465	0.0842	0.0446	0.0223	0.0107	0.0050
3	0.0613	0.1804	0.2240	0.1954	0.1404	0.0892	0.0521	0.0286	0.0150
4	0.0153	0.0902	0.1680	0.1954	0.1755	0.1339	0.0912	0.0573	0.0337
5	0.0031	0.0361	0.1008	0.1563	0.1755	0.1606	0.1277	0.0916	0.0607
6	0.0005	0.0120	0.0504	0.1042	0.1462	0.1606	0.1490	0.1221	0.0911
7	0.0001	0.0034	0.0216	0.0595	0.1044	0.1377	0.1490	0.1396	0.1171
8	0.0000	0.0009	0.0081	0.0298	0.0653	0.1033	0.1304	0.1396	0.1318
9	0.0000	0.0002	0.0027	0.0132	0.0363	0.0688	0.1014	0.1241	0.1318
10	0.0000	0.0000	0.0008	0.0053	0.0181	0.0413	0.0710	0.0993	0.1186
11	0.0000	0.0000	0.0002	0.0019	0.0082	0.0225	0.0452	0.0722	0.0970
12	0.0000	0.0000	0.0001	0.0006	0.0034	0.0113	0.0263	0.0481	0.0728
13	0.0000	0.0000	0.0000	0.0002	0.0013	0.0052	0.0142	0.0296	0.0504
14	0.0000	0.0000	0.0000	0.0001	0.0005	0.0022	0.0071	0.0169	0.0324
15	0.0000	0.0000	0.0000	0.0000	0.0002	0.0009	0.0033	0.0090	0.0194
16	0.0000	0.0000	0.0000	0.0000	0.0000	0.0003	0.0014	0.0045	0.0109
17	0.0000	0.0000	0.0000	0.0000	0.0000	0.0001	0.0006	0.0021	0.0058
18	0.0000	0.0000	0.0000	0.0000	0.0000	0.0000	0.0002	0.0009	0.0029
19	0.0000	0.0000	0.0000	0.0000	0.0000	0.0000	0.0001	0.0004	0.0014
20	0.0000	0.0000	0.0000	0.0000	0.0000	0.0000	0.0000	0.0002	0.0006
21	0.0000	0.0000	0.0000	0.0000	0.0000	0.0000	0.0000	0.0001	0.0003
22	0.0000	0.0000	0.0000	0.0000	0.0000	0.0000	0.0000	0.0000	0.0001

APPENDIX B.6

TABLE OF RANDOM NUMBERS

```
02711  08182  75997  79866  58095  83319  80295  79741  74599  84379
94873  90935  31684  63952  09865  14491  99518  93394  34691  14985
54921  78680  06635  98689  17306  25170  65928  87709  30533  89736
77640  97636  37397  93379  56454  59818  45827  74164  71666  46977
61545  00835  93251  87203  36759  49197  85967  01704  19634  21898

17147  19519  22497  16857  42426  84822  92598  49186  88247  39967
13748  04742  92460  85801  53444  65626  58710  55406  17173  69776
87455  14813  50373  28037  91182  32786  65261  11173  34376  36408
08999  57409  91185  10200  61411  23392  47797  56377  71635  08601
78804  81333  53809  32471  46034  36306  22498  19239  85428  55721

82173  26921  28472  98958  07960  66124  89731  95069  18625  92405
97594  25168  89178  68190  05043  17407  48201  83917  11413  72920
73881  67176  93504  42636  38233  16154  96451  57925  29667  30859
46071  22912  90326  42453  88108  72064  58601  32357  90610  32921
44492  19686  12495  93135  95185  77799  52441  88272  22024  80631

31864  72170  37722  55794  14636  05148  54505  50113  21119  25228
51574  90692  43339  65689  76539  27909  05467  21727  51141  72949
35350  76132  92925  92124  92634  35681  43690  89136  35599  84138
46943  36502  01172  46045  46991  33804  80006  35542  61056  75666
22665  87226  33304  57975  03985  21566  65796  72915  81466  89205

39437  97957  11838  10433  21564  51570  73558  27495  34533  57808
77082  47784  40098  97962  89845  28392  78187  06112  08169  11261
24544  25649  43370  28007  06779  72402  62632  53956  24709  06978
27503  15558  37738  24849  70722  71859  83736  06016  94397  12529
24590  24545  06435  52758  45685  90151  46516  49644  92686  84870

48155  86226  40359  28723  15364  69125  12609  57171  86857  31702
20226  53752  90648  24362  83314  00014  19207  69413  97016  86290
70178  73444  38790  53626  93780  18629  68766  24371  74639  30782
10169  41465  51935  05711  09799  79077  88159  33437  68519  03040
81084  03701  28598  70013  63794  53169  97054  60303  23259  96196

69202  20777  21727  81511  51887  16175  53746  46516  70339  62727
80561  95787  89426  93325  86412  57479  54194  52153  19197  81877
08199  26703  95128  48599  09333  12584  24374  31232  61782  44032
98883  28220  39358  53720  80161  83371  15181  11131  12219  55920
84568  69286  76054  21615  80883  36797  82845  39139  90900  18172

04269  35173  95745  53893  86022  77722  52498  84193  22448  22571
10538  13124  36099  13140  37706  44562  57179  44693  67877  01549
77843  24955  25900  63843  95029  93859  93634  20205  66294  41218
12034  94636  49455  76362  83532  31062  69903  91186  65768  55949
10524  72829  47641  93315  80875  28090  97728  52560  34937  79548

68935  76632  46984  61772  92786  22651  07086  89754  44143  97687
89450  65665  29190  43709  11172  34481  95977  47535  25658  73898
90696  20451  24211  97310  60446  73530  62865  96574  13829  72226
49006  32047  93086  00112  20470  17136  28255  86328  07293  38809
74591  87025  52368  59416  34417  70557  86746  55809  53628  12000

06315  17012  77103  00968  07235  10728  42189  33292  51487  64443
62386  09184  62092  46617  99419  64230  95034  85481  07857  42510
86848  82122  04028  36959  87827  12813  08627  80699  13345  51695
65643  69480  46598  04501  40403  91408  32343  48130  49303  90689
11084  46534  78957  77353  39578  77868  22970  84349  09184  70603
```

APPENDIX B.7

WILCOXON *T* VALUES

N	2α .15 α .075	.10 .050	.05 .025	.04 .020	.03 .015	.02 .010	.01 .005
4	0						
5	1	0					
6	2	2	0	0			
7	4	3	2	1	0	0	
8	7	5	3	3	2	1	0
9	9	8	5	5	4	3	1
10	12	10	8	7	6	5	3
11	16	13	10	9	8	7	5
12	19	17	13	12	11	9	7
13	24	21	17	16	14	12	9
14	28	25	21	19	18	15	12
15	33	30	25	23	21	19	15
16	39	35	29	28	26	23	19
17	45	41	34	33	30	27	23
18	51	47	40	38	35	32	27
19	58	53	46	43	41	37	32
20	65	60	52	50	47	43	37
21	73	67	58	56	53	49	42
22	81	75	65	63	59	55	48
23	89	83	73	70	66	62	54
24	98	91	81	78	74	69	61
25	108	100	89	86	82	76	68
26	118	110	98	94	90	84	75
27	128	119	107	103	99	92	83
28	138	130	116	112	108	101	91
29	150	140	126	122	117	110	100
30	161	151	137	132	127	120	109
31	173	163	147	143	137	130	118
32	186	175	159	154	148	140	128
33	199	187	170	165	159	151	138
34	212	200	182	177	171	162	148
35	226	213	195	189	182	173	159
40	302	286	264	257	249	238	220
50	487	466	434	425	413	397	373
60	718	690	648	636	620	600	567
70	995	960	907	891	872	846	805
80	1,318	1,276	1,211	1,192	1,168	1,136	1,086
90	1,688	1,638	1,560	1,537	1,509	1,471	1,410
100	2,105	2,045	1,955	1,928	1,894	1,850	1,779

SOURCE: Abridged from Robert L. McCormack, "Extended Tables of the Wilcoxon Matched-Pair Signed Rank Statistic," *Journal of the American Statistical Association*, September 1965, pp. 866–67.

APPENDIX B.8

FACTORS FOR CONTROL CHARTS

Number of Items in Sample, n	Chart for Averages	Chart for Ranges		
	Factors for Control Limits	Factors for Central Line	Factors for Control Limits	
	A_2	d_2	D_3	D_4
2	1.880	1.128	0	3.267
3	1.023	1.693	0	2.575
4	.729	2.059	0	2.282
5	.577	2.326	0	2.115
6	.483	2.534	0	2.004
7	.419	2.704	.076	1.924
8	.373	2.847	.136	1.864
9	.337	2.970	.184	1.816
10	.308	3.078	.223	1.777
11	.285	3.173	.256	1.744
12	.266	3.258	.284	1.716
13	.249	3.336	.308	1.692
14	.235	3.407	.329	1.671
15	.223	3.472	.348	1.652

SOURCE: Adapted from American Society for Testing and Materials, *Manual on Quality Control of Materials,* 1951, Table B2, p. 115. For a more detailed table and explanation, see Acheson, J. Duncan, *Quality Control and Industrial Statistics,* 3d ed. (Homewood, Ill.: Richard D. Irwin, 1974), Table M, p. 927.

APPENDIX B.9

Binomial Probability Distribution

$n = 1$
PROBABILITY

r	0.05	0.10	0.20	0.30	0.40	0.50	0.60	0.70	0.80	0.90	0.95
0	0.950	0.900	0.800	0.700	0.600	0.500	0.400	0.300	0.200	0.100	0.050
1	0.050	0.100	0.200	0.300	0.400	0.500	0.600	0.700	0.800	0.900	0.950

$n = 2$
PROBABILITY

r	0.05	0.10	0.20	0.30	0.40	0.50	0.60	0.70	0.80	0.90	0.95
0	0.903	0.810	0.640	0.490	0.360	0.250	0.160	0.090	0.040	0.010	0.003
1	0.095	0.180	0.320	0.420	0.480	0.500	0.480	0.420	0.320	0.180	0.095
2	0.003	0.010	0.040	0.090	0.160	0.250	0.360	0.490	0.640	0.810	0.903

$n = 3$
PROBABILITY

r	0.05	0.10	0.20	0.30	0.40	0.50	0.60	0.70	0.80	0.90	0.95
0	0.857	0.729	0.512	0.343	0.216	0.125	0.064	0.027	0.008	0.001	0.000
1	0.135	0.243	0.384	0.441	0.432	0.375	0.288	0.189	0.096	0.027	0.007
2	0.007	0.027	0.096	0.189	0.288	0.375	0.432	0.441	0.384	0.243	0.135
3	0.000	0.001	0.008	0.027	0.064	0.125	0.216	0.343	0.512	0.729	0.857

$n = 4$
PROBABILITY

r	0.05	0.10	0.20	0.30	0.40	0.50	0.60	0.70	0.80	0.90	0.95
0	0.815	0.656	0.410	0.240	0.130	0.063	0.026	0.008	0.002	0.000	0.000
1	0.171	0.292	0.410	0.412	0.346	0.250	0.154	0.076	0.026	0.004	0.000
2	0.014	0.049	0.154	0.265	0.346	0.375	0.346	0.265	0.154	0.049	0.014
3	0.000	0.004	0.026	0.076	0.154	0.250	0.346	0.412	0.410	0.292	0.171
4	0.000	0.000	0.002	0.008	0.026	0.063	0.130	0.240	0.410	0.656	0.815

$n = 5$
PROBABILITY

r	0.05	0.10	0.20	0.30	0.40	0.50	0.60	0.70	0.80	0.90	0.95
0	0.774	0.590	0.328	0.168	0.078	0.031	0.010	0.002	0.000	0.000	0.000
1	0.204	0.328	0.410	0.360	0.259	0.156	0.077	0.028	0.006	0.000	0.000
2	0.021	0.073	0.205	0.309	0.346	0.313	0.230	0.132	0.051	0.008	0.001
3	0.001	0.008	0.051	0.132	0.230	0.313	0.346	0.309	0.205	0.073	0.021
4	0.000	0.000	0.006	0.028	0.077	0.156	0.259	0.360	0.410	0.328	0.204
5	0.000	0.000	0.000	0.002	0.010	0.031	0.078	0.168	0.328	0.590	0.774

$n = 6$
PROBABILITY

r	0.05	0.10	0.20	0.30	0.40	0.50	0.60	0.70	0.80	0.90	0.95
0	0.735	0.531	0.262	0.118	0.047	0.016	0.004	0.001	0.000	0.000	0.000
1	0.232	0.354	0.393	0.303	0.187	0.094	0.037	0.010	0.002	0.000	0.000
2	0.031	0.098	0.246	0.324	0.311	0.234	0.138	0.060	0.015	0.001	0.000
3	0.002	0.015	0.082	0.185	0.276	0.313	0.276	0.185	0.082	0.015	0.002
4	0.000	0.001	0.015	0.060	0.138	0.234	0.311	0.324	0.246	0.098	0.031
5	0.000	0.000	0.002	0.010	0.037	0.094	0.187	0.303	0.393	0.354	0.232
6	0.000	0.000	0.000	0.001	0.004	0.016	0.047	0.118	0.262	0.531	0.735

APPENDIX B.9

Binomial Probability Distribution (*continued*)

n = 7
PROBABILITY

r	0.05	0.10	0.20	0.30	0.40	0.50	0.60	0.70	0.80	0.90	0.95
0	0.698	0.478	0.210	0.082	0.028	0.008	0.002	0.000	0.000	0.000	0.000
1	0.257	0.372	0.367	0.247	0.131	0.055	0.017	0.004	0.000	0.000	0.000
2	0.041	0.124	0.275	0.318	0.261	0.164	0.077	0.025	0.004	0.000	0.000
3	0.004	0.023	0.115	0.227	0.290	0.273	0.194	0.097	0.029	0.003	0.000
4	0.000	0.003	0.029	0.097	0.194	0.273	0.290	0.227	0.115	0.023	0.004
5	0.000	0.000	0.004	0.025	0.077	0.164	0.261	0.318	0.275	0.124	0.041
6	0.000	0.000	0.000	0.004	0.017	0.055	0.131	0.247	0.367	0.372	0.257
7	0.000	0.000	0.000	0.000	0.002	0.008	0.028	0.082	0.210	0.478	0.698

n = 8
PROBABILITY

r	0.05	0.10	0.20	0.30	0.40	0.50	0.60	0.70	0.80	0.90	0.95
0	0.663	0.430	0.168	0.058	0.017	0.004	0.001	0.000	0.000	0.000	0.000
1	0.279	0.383	0.336	0.198	0.090	0.031	0.008	0.001	0.000	0.000	0.000
2	0.051	0.149	0.294	0.296	0.209	0.109	0.041	0.010	0.001	0.000	0.000
3	0.005	0.033	0.147	0.254	0.279	0.219	0.124	0.047	0.009	0.000	0.000
4	0.000	0.005	0.046	0.136	0.232	0.273	0.232	0.136	0.046	0.005	0.000
5	0.000	0.000	0.009	0.047	0.124	0.219	0.279	0.254	0.147	0.033	0.005
6	0.000	0.000	0.001	0.010	0.041	0.109	0.209	0.296	0.294	0.149	0.051
7	0.000	0.000	0.000	0.001	0.008	0.031	0.090	0.198	0.336	0.383	0.279
8	0.000	0.000	0.000	0.000	0.001	0.004	0.017	0.058	0.168	0.430	0.663

n = 9
PROBABILITY

r	0.05	0.10	0.20	0.30	0.40	0.50	0.60	0.70	0.80	0.90	0.95
0	0.630	0.387	0.134	0.040	0.010	0.002	0.000	0.000	0.000	0.000	0.000
1	0.299	0.387	0.302	0.156	0.060	0.018	0.004	0.000	0.000	0.000	0.000
2	0.063	0.172	0.302	0.267	0.161	0.070	0.021	0.004	0.000	0.000	0.000
3	0.008	0.045	0.176	0.267	0.251	0.164	0.074	0.021	0.003	0.000	0.000
4	0.001	0.007	0.066	0.172	0.251	0.246	0.167	0.074	0.017	0.001	0.000
5	0.000	0.001	0.017	0.074	0.167	0.246	0.251	0.172	0.066	0.007	0.001
6	0.000	0.000	0.003	0.021	0.074	0.164	0.251	0.267	0.176	0.045	0.008
7	0.000	0.000	0.000	0.004	0.021	0.070	0.161	0.267	0.302	0.172	0.063
8	0.000	0.000	0.000	0.000	0.004	0.018	0.060	0.156	0.302	0.387	0.299
9	0.000	0.000	0.000	0.000	0.000	0.002	0.010	0.040	0.134	0.387	0.630

APPENDIX B.9

BINOMIAL PROBABILITY DISTRIBUTION (*continued*)

$n = 10$
PROBABILITY

r	0.05	0.10	0.20	0.30	0.40	0.50	0.60	0.70	0.80	0.90	0.95
0	0.599	0.349	0.107	0.028	0.006	0.001	0.000	0.000	0.000	0.000	0.000
1	0.315	0.387	0.268	0.121	0.040	0.010	0.002	0.000	0.000	0.000	0.000
2	0.075	0.194	0.302	0.233	0.121	0.044	0.011	0.001	0.000	0.000	0.000
3	0.010	0.057	0.201	0.267	0.215	0.117	0.042	0.009	0.001	0.000	0.000
4	0.001	0.011	0.088	0.200	0.251	0.205	0.111	0.037	0.006	0.000	0.000
5	0.000	0.001	0.026	0.103	0.201	0.246	0.201	0.103	0.026	0.001	0.000
6	0.000	0.000	0.006	0.037	0.111	0.205	0.251	0.200	0.088	0.011	0.001
7	0.000	0.000	0.001	0.009	0.042	0.117	0.215	0.267	0.201	0.057	0.010
8	0.000	0.000	0.000	0.001	0.011	0.044	0.121	0.233	0.302	0.194	0.075
9	0.000	0.000	0.000	0.000	0.002	0.010	0.040	0.121	0.268	0.387	0.315
10	0.000	0.000	0.000	0.000	0.000	0.001	0.006	0.028	0.107	0.349	0.599

$n = 11$
PROBABILITY

r	0.05	0.10	0.20	0.30	0.40	0.50	0.60	0.70	0.80	0.90	0.95
0	0.569	0.314	0.086	0.020	0.004	0.000	0.000	0.000	0.000	0.000	0.000
1	0.329	0.384	0.236	0.093	0.027	0.005	0.001	0.000	0.000	0.000	0.000
2	0.087	0.213	0.295	0.200	0.089	0.027	0.005	0.001	0.000	0.000	0.000
3	0.014	0.071	0.221	0.257	0.177	0.081	0.023	0.004	0.000	0.000	0.000
4	0.001	0.016	0.111	0.220	0.236	0.161	0.070	0.017	0.002	0.000	0.000
5	0.000	0.002	0.039	0.132	0.221	0.226	0.147	0.057	0.010	0.000	0.000
6	0.000	0.000	0.010	0.057	0.147	0.226	0.221	0.132	0.039	0.002	0.000
7	0.000	0.000	0.002	0.017	0.070	0.161	0.236	0.220	0.111	0.016	0.001
8	0.000	0.000	0.000	0.004	0.023	0.081	0.177	0.257	0.221	0.071	0.014
9	0.000	0.000	0.000	0.001	0.005	0.027	0.089	0.200	0.295	0.213	0.087
10	0.000	0.000	0.000	0.000	0.001	0.005	0.027	0.093	0.236	0.384	0.329
11	0.000	0.000	0.000	0.000	0.000	0.000	0.004	0.020	0.086	0.314	0.569

$n = 12$
PROBABILITY

r	0.05	0.10	0.20	0.30	0.40	0.50	0.60	0.70	0.80	0.90	0.95
0	0.540	0.282	0.069	0.014	0.002	0.000	0.000	0.000	0.000	0.000	0.000
1	0.341	0.377	0.206	0.071	0.017	0.003	0.000	0.000	0.000	0.000	0.000
2	0.099	0.230	0.283	0.168	0.064	0.016	0.002	0.000	0.000	0.000	0.000
3	0.017	0.085	0.236	0.240	0.142	0.054	0.012	0.001	0.000	0.000	0.000
4	0.002	0.021	0.133	0.231	0.213	0.121	0.042	0.008	0.001	0.000	0.000
5	0.000	0.004	0.053	0.158	0.227	0.193	0.101	0.029	0.003	0.000	0.000
6	0.000	0.000	0.016	0.079	0.177	0.226	0.177	0.079	0.016	0.000	0.000
7	0.000	0.000	0.003	0.029	0.101	0.193	0.227	0.158	0.053	0.004	0.000
8	0.000	0.000	0.001	0.008	0.042	0.121	0.213	0.231	0.133	0.021	0.002
9	0.000	0.000	0.000	0.001	0.012	0.054	0.142	0.240	0.236	0.085	0.017
10	0.000	0.000	0.000	0.000	0.002	0.016	0.064	0.168	0.283	0.230	0.099
11	0.000	0.000	0.000	0.000	0.000	0.003	0.017	0.071	0.206	0.377	0.341
12	0.000	0.000	0.000	0.000	0.000	0.000	0.002	0.014	0.069	0.282	0.540

Appendix B.9
Binomial Probability Distribution

Binomial Probability Distribution (*continued*)

$n = 13$
PROBABILITY

r	0.05	0.10	0.20	0.30	0.40	0.50	0.60	0.70	0.80	0.90	0.95
0	0.513	0.254	0.055	0.010	0.001	0.000	0.000	0.000	0.000	0.000	0.000
1	0.351	0.367	0.179	0.054	0.011	0.002	0.000	0.000	0.000	0.000	0.000
2	0.111	0.245	0.268	0.139	0.045	0.010	0.001	0.000	0.000	0.000	0.000
3	0.021	0.100	0.246	0.218	0.111	0.035	0.006	0.001	0.000	0.000	0.000
4	0.003	0.028	0.154	0.234	0.184	0.087	0.024	0.003	0.000	0.000	0.000
5	0.000	0.006	0.069	0.180	0.221	0.157	0.066	0.014	0.001	0.000	0.000
6	0.000	0.001	0.023	0.103	0.197	0.209	0.131	0.044	0.006	0.000	0.000
7	0.000	0.000	0.006	0.044	0.131	0.209	0.197	0.103	0.023	0.001	0.000
8	0.000	0.000	0.001	0.014	0.066	0.157	0.221	0.180	0.069	0.006	0.000
9	0.000	0.000	0.000	0.003	0.024	0.087	0.184	0.234	0.154	0.028	0.003
10	0.000	0.000	0.000	0.001	0.006	0.035	0.111	0.218	0.246	0.100	0.021
11	0.000	0.000	0.000	0.000	0.001	0.010	0.045	0.139	0.268	0.245	0.111
12	0.000	0.000	0.000	0.000	0.000	0.002	0.011	0.054	0.179	0.367	0.351
13	0.000	0.000	0.000	0.000	0.000	0.000	0.001	0.010	0.055	0.254	0.513

$n = 14$
PROBABILITY

r	0.05	0.10	0.20	0.30	0.40	0.50	0.60	0.70	0.80	0.90	0.95
0	0.488	0.229	0.044	0.007	0.001	0.000	0.000	0.000	0.000	0.000	0.000
1	0.359	0.356	0.154	0.041	0.007	0.001	0.000	0.000	0.000	0.000	0.000
2	0.123	0.257	0.250	0.113	0.032	0.006	0.001	0.000	0.000	0.000	0.000
3	0.026	0.114	0.250	0.194	0.085	0.022	0.003	0.000	0.000	0.000	0.000
4	0.004	0.035	0.172	0.229	0.155	0.061	0.014	0.001	0.000	0.000	0.000
5	0.000	0.008	0.086	0.196	0.207	0.122	0.041	0.007	0.000	0.000	0.000
6	0.000	0.001	0.032	0.126	0.207	0.183	0.092	0.023	0.002	0.000	0.000
7	0.000	0.000	0.009	0.062	0.157	0.209	0.157	0.062	0.009	0.000	0.000
8	0.000	0.000	0.002	0.023	0.092	0.183	0.207	0.126	0.032	0.001	0.000
9	0.000	0.000	0.000	0.007	0.041	0.122	0.207	0.196	0.086	0.008	0.000
10	0.000	0.000	0.000	0.001	0.014	0.061	0.155	0.229	0.172	0.035	0.004
11	0.000	0.000	0.000	0.000	0.003	0.022	0.085	0.194	0.250	0.114	0.026
12	0.000	0.000	0.000	0.000	0.001	0.006	0.032	0.113	0.250	0.257	0.123
13	0.000	0.000	0.000	0.000	0.000	0.001	0.007	0.041	0.154	0.356	0.359
14	0.000	0.000	0.000	0.000	0.000	0.000	0.001	0.007	0.044	0.229	0.488

APPENDIX B.9

BINOMIAL PROBABILITY DISTRIBUTION (continued)

$n = 15$
PROBABILITY

r	0.05	0.10	0.20	0.30	0.40	0.50	0.60	0.70	0.80	0.90	0.95
0	0.463	0.206	0.035	0.005	0.000	0.000	0.000	0.000	0.000	0.000	0.000
1	0.366	0.343	0.132	0.031	0.005	0.000	0.000	0.000	0.000	0.000	0.000
2	0.135	0.267	0.231	0.092	0.022	0.003	0.000	0.000	0.000	0.000	0.000
3	0.031	0.129	0.250	0.170	0.063	0.014	0.002	0.000	0.000	0.000	0.000
4	0.005	0.043	0.188	0.219	0.127	0.042	0.007	0.001	0.000	0.000	0.000
5	0.001	0.010	0.103	0.206	0.186	0.092	0.024	0.003	0.000	0.000	0.000
6	0.000	0.002	0.043	0.147	0.207	0.153	0.061	0.012	0.001	0.000	0.000
7	0.000	0.000	0.014	0.081	0.177	0.196	0.118	0.035	0.003	0.000	0.000
8	0.000	0.000	0.003	0.035	0.118	0.196	0.177	0.081	0.014	0.000	0.000
9	0.000	0.000	0.001	0.012	0.061	0.153	0.207	0.147	0.043	0.002	0.000
10	0.000	0.000	0.000	0.003	0.024	0.092	0.186	0.206	0.103	0.010	0.001
11	0.000	0.000	0.000	0.001	0.007	0.042	0.127	0.219	0.188	0.043	0.005
12	0.000	0.000	0.000	0.000	0.002	0.014	0.063	0.170	0.250	0.129	0.031
13	0.000	0.000	0.000	0.000	0.000	0.003	0.022	0.092	0.231	0.267	0.135
14	0.000	0.000	0.000	0.000	0.000	0.000	0.005	0.031	0.132	0.343	0.366
15	0.000	0.000	0.000	0.000	0.000	0.000	0.000	0.005	0.035	0.206	0.463

$n = 16$
PROBABILITY

r	0.05	0.10	0.20	0.30	0.40	0.50	0.60	0.70	0.80	0.90	0.95
0	0.440	0.185	0.028	0.003	0.000	0.000	0.000	0.000	0.000	0.000	0.000
1	0.371	0.329	0.113	0.023	0.003	0.000	0.000	0.000	0.000	0.000	0.000
2	0.146	0.275	0.211	0.073	0.015	0.002	0.000	0.000	0.000	0.000	0.000
3	0.036	0.142	0.246	0.146	0.047	0.009	0.001	0.000	0.000	0.000	0.000
4	0.006	0.051	0.200	0.204	0.101	0.028	0.004	0.000	0.000	0.000	0.000
5	0.001	0.014	0.120	0.210	0.162	0.067	0.014	0.001	0.000	0.000	0.000
6	0.000	0.003	0.055	0.165	0.198	0.122	0.039	0.006	0.000	0.000	0.000
7	0.000	0.000	0.020	0.101	0.189	0.175	0.084	0.019	0.001	0.000	0.000
8	0.000	0.000	0.006	0.049	0.142	0.196	0.142	0.049	0.006	0.000	0.000
9	0.000	0.000	0.001	0.019	0.084	0.175	0.189	0.101	0.020	0.000	0.000
10	0.000	0.000	0.000	0.006	0.039	0.122	0.198	0.165	0.055	0.003	0.000
11	0.000	0.000	0.000	0.001	0.014	0.067	0.162	0.210	0.120	0.014	0.001
12	0.000	0.000	0.000	0.000	0.004	0.028	0.101	0.204	0.200	0.051	0.006
13	0.000	0.000	0.000	0.000	0.001	0.009	0.047	0.146	0.246	0.142	0.036
14	0.000	0.000	0.000	0.000	0.000	0.002	0.015	0.073	0.211	0.275	0.146
15	0.000	0.000	0.000	0.000	0.000	0.000	0.003	0.023	0.113	0.329	0.371
16	0.000	0.000	0.000	0.000	0.000	0.000	0.000	0.003	0.028	0.185	0.440